"LET THE WORD GO FORTH"

The Speeches, Statements, and Writings of John F. Kennedy, 1947–1963

"[Sorensen's] selections from more than 110 speeches and writings reflect the importance of historical insights in Kennedy's thoughts and actions."—*St. Louis Post-Dispatch*

"Certainly no president in this century, with the possible exception of Franklin D. Roosevelt, was more eloquent and strikingly at ease with the spoken word than John F. Kennedy, whose finely honed logic, measured cadence and sparkling wit mesmerized his listeners, friend and foe alike. The magic remains in his words."—*Houston Chronicle*

"Lovingly put together . . . Sorensen has seen fit to include the unusual as well as the expected."—*The Indianapolis Star*

"Likely to become a standard reference . . . even more important, it's a readable biography of the man who helped shape the dreams of a generation."—*Clarion Ledger–Jackson Daily News*

Books by Theodore C. Sorensen

"Let the Word Go Forth" (Editor)

A Widening Atlantic?
Domestic Change and Foreign Policy (Co-Author)

A Different Kind of Presidency:
A Proposal for Breaking the Political Deadlock

Watchmen in the Night:
Presidential Accountability After Watergate

The Kennedy Legacy

Kennedy

Decision-Making in the White House

In Berlin, 1963.
PHOTO BY ROBERT LACKENBACH/BLACK STAR.

"LET THE WORD GO FORTH"

The Speeches, Statements, and Writings of JOHN F. KENNEDY

1947–1963

Selected and with an Introduction by Theodore C. Sorensen

A LAUREL TRADE PAPERBACK
Published by
Dell Publishing
a division of
Bantam Doubleday Dell Publishing Group, Inc.
666 Fifth Avenue
New York, New York 10103

NOTE

Errors in typing or transcription have been corrected. Introductory, repetitive, transitional, and other paragraphs deemed less interesting or relevant by the editor, or too outdated or partisan for inclusion, have been deleted, as have various quotations, anecdotes, and certain other portions for reasons of space and flow. State of the Union messages have been divided by subject matter. Where appropriate, these deletions have been marked with ellipses. Those seeking complete texts should contact the John Fitzgerald Kennedy Library in Boston, whose cooperation is gratefully acknowledged.

ISBN: 0-440-50406-6

Reprinted by arrangement with Delacorte Press, New York, New York

Printed in the United States of America

Published simultaneously in Canada

November 1991

10 9 8 7 6 5 4 3 2 1

BVG

For GILLIAN

Who makes it all possible and worthwhile

Speaking in St. Paul, Minnesota, 1962.
PHOTO COURTESY CECIL W. STOUGHTON.

CONTENTS

"LET THE WORD GO FORTH"

The Inaugural Address, January 20, 1961.

INTRODUCTION

John F. Kennedy was so blessed with the gifts of reason, intellect, and vitality that eloquence came naturally to him. He believed in the power and glory of words—both written and spoken—to win votes, to set goals, to change minds, to move nations. He consistently took care to choose the right words in the right order that would send the right message. He did not regard old-fashioned eloquence as unsophisticated or unimportant, nor did he ever rise to speak in public indifferent or unprepared. In the dawn of the television era, his youthful good looks, cool confidence, and strong voice enhanced the inspirational appeal of his words; and this "style" was all-important to the continuing success of his political, legislative, diplomatic, and presidential efforts.

But he knew that words alone meant very little, that "saying so doesn't make it so." As he had planned to note in his undelivered speech in Dallas on November 22, 1963:

> Words alone are not enough. . . . Where our strength and determination are clear, our words need merely to convey conviction, not belligerence. If we are strong, our strength will speak for itself. If we are weak, words will be of no help.

Postwar Western Europe, he pointed out, had not been saved by George Marshall's speech at Harvard but by the economic recovery that the Marshall Plan sparked. His own words of warning to the Soviets over the Cuban missile crisis, he added, succeeded only because a strong and united West stood behind them.

Words and speeches, in short, were his medium, not the message. However exalted the rhetoric, he knew speeches were important only when the message was important. They were forceful only if the ideas they conveyed were forceful.

That is why accuracy, not modesty or loyalty, compels me to emphasize once again that John Kennedy was the true author of all of his speeches and writings. They set forth *his* ideas and ideals, *his* decisions and policies, *his* knowledge of history and politics. Every speech put *his* career on the line, reflecting choices for which he would be praised or blamed. Without claiming to have written every word of every draft—indeed, often generously acknowledging the assistance he received from others—he played a major role in every major speech, selecting subject matter and themes, arguments and conclusions, quotations and phrases. (The lesser talks—including some on the campaign trail, at formal dinners, or in the White House Rose Garden—were often delivered without notes or without glancing at those he had.) More importantly, he alone was responsible for the decision that lay at the heart of every major speech.

For great speeches reflect great decisions; and John F. Kennedy's greatest speeches all reflected turning points in American history for which he was responsible, including:

- his 1963 call at American University for a new look at U.S.–Soviet coexistence and a moratorium on nuclear testing in the atmosphere, the finest speech he ever gave;

- his 1963 televised address to the nation (his second most important speech, and by coincidence delivered less than thirty-three hours after his talk at American University) committing his Presidency to the abolition of all racial discrimination and segregation in this country;

- his 1961 Inaugural Address signaling the vigor and determination of our youngest elected President in history, the first to be born in this century, as he urged new national sacrifice and service;

• his 1960 campaign appeal to the Protestant clergy in Houston for an end to the unwritten rule that barred a Catholic from the White House;

• his 1962 televised declaration that the United States had spotted secret Soviet nuclear missile bases in Cuba and was determined upon their removal;

• his 1963 televised address hailing completion of the nuclear test-ban treaty, the first superpower step toward arms control; and

• his speech a few months earlier pledging this country's commitment to the freedom of millions of people gathered between the Wall and City Hall in West Berlin.

He drew strength and inspiration from his audience and surroundings in West Berlin, as he did on other historic occasions in other settings such as the U.S. Capitol, the United Nations, the Irish Parliament, Independence Hall, and the Paulskirche Assembly Hall in Frankfurt, West Germany.

Even his presidential campaign speeches offered memorable ideas—the revitalized Presidency, the Alliance for Progress, the Peace Corps, and the concept of the New Frontier itself—along with the usual partisan exhortations and platitudes.

Not surprisingly, JFK's worst major speech as President conveyed a nondecision—his televised address in August 1962 announcing that no tax cut was planned for that year.

That speech is not among those selected for this volume. Neither are others he later regretted, such as a youthful attack in the House of Representatives on President Truman's China policy, a futile presidential plea to news editors to exercise more restraint on national security stories, and a panic-inspiring emphasis on fallout shelters at the time of the Berlin crisis.

For this is not a collection, or even a representative sample, of every JFK speech or message. It is simply one man's selection of those bits and pieces in the public domain that show John F. Kennedy at his wisest, warmest, and wittiest—the most relevant for our times as well as the most eloquent, the most important in his time as well as the most inspirational, the best of his words as well as the most familiar. The objective is to gather that material in one handy volume for the first time for easy access by students of rhetoric and history, by speakers and speech writers, by those who want to remember John Kennedy better and those too young to remember him at all.

Reviewing all the words and works of Congressman, Senator, candidate, and President Kennedy was for me an exhilarating task. Reducing that vast mountain to a single volume was excruciating. Even after cutting the purely local, ephemeral, and political, even after dividing up and paring down his necessarily lengthy State of the Union addresses, a painful process of elimination remained. Space did not permit inclusion of most of the jokes, the biblical quotations, the invocations of Lincoln or Jefferson or FDR, and the references to history that made those speeches sparkle. Though he rarely spoke for more than twenty or twenty-five minutes, almost no speech could be included in full. Some important speeches and important topics could not be included at all.

Not all of the manifold subjects in which he was interested as congressman, senator, and President are of widespread interest today. It is unfortunate that long passages showing his mastery of detail and data could not be included, unfortunate that Senate speeches which produced proud legislative victories—on labor reform and the Electoral College, for example—could not be included. No doubt many readers will look in vain for a Kennedy speech that he or she particularly remembered or a Kennedy quotation especially cherished. All such errors of omission are mine.

But some of his best speeches, included here, are not particularly well remembered by Kennedy's fellow Americans. His Senate speeches on Algeria, India, and Indochina received only brief attention in this country but were widely hailed in the Third World. (It is interesting to note that JFK's best and most profound speech on Vietnam and Indochina was made while he was in the Senate, not in the White House, and that his best and most profound speech on civil rights was made in the White House, not in the Senate.) His speech to the Irish Parliament, little read here, is still revered in Dublin. His 1960 convention eve reply to former president Truman's attack on his youth and inexperience went unnoticed by many Fourth of July travelers. Two years later they also missed his 1962 Independence Day call for an Atlantic partnership that helped spur the movement toward integration in Western Europe.

Others on the list of Kennedy's best have simply been largely forgotten, including his "farewell" to the Massachusetts Legislature, his campaign-opening treatises on the Presidency, and his commencement addresses at Harvard, Yale, the University of Washington, and the University of California.

But not all are forgotten. Not since Winston Churchill (whose career and eloquence Kennedy admired equally) have any other public speaker's words and phrases become as large a part of our national memory. Those who are old enough remember how they reacted to his Cuban missile crisis TV address, how they cheered his first debate with Nixon, and how they scheduled their day around his televised press conferences. A "profile in courage" became part of our vocabulary. Humorists parody "Ich bin ein Berliner." Orators ask "not what your country can do for you . . ." Schoolchildren are assigned the Houston ministers speech. Even his quotations from John Winthrop ("a city upon a hill"), George Bernard Shaw ("Some men . . . ask why not"), and ancient Chinese proverbs ("defeat is an orphan" and "a journey of a thousand miles"), are mistakenly attributed to him.

During these last twenty-five years, no other previous president's words have been so frequently quoted, misquoted, or borrowed without attribution by politicians in both major parties.

To be sure, not everyone remembers Kennedy's speeches favorably. Some have written that his idealistic messages often set goals that could not realistically be reached in the lifetime of his audience. They are right. Others have asserted that JFK's speeches were less often interrupted by applause than were those of his successors. They are right. Critics on the right have charged that Kennedy often used Cold War rhetoric to advance liberal objectives. They also are right. Critics on the left have charged that Kennedy's tightfisted fiscal policies never matched his attacks on this country's social and economic ills. They also are right.

Still other faults can be found with the advantage of hindsight. Kennedy's Inaugural vow to "pay any price, bear any burden" reflected the Cold War atmosphere of the time (making all the more remarkable his urging the Soviets in that same speech to join in a range of peaceful pursuits). His repeated references to leadership in male terms only (e.g., "all free men are citizens of Berlin"), typical twenty-five years ago, would be unacceptable today. His speeches did not anticipate a thaw in our relations with the People's Republic of China and paid little attention to the repression in South Africa.

Moreover, much of what he did seek in these speeches and messages has never been achieved or, even worse, has been pushed further back by his successors—including his hopes for a stronger United Nations, a more cohesive Western Alliance, more foreign economic assistance, a greater emphasis on service instead of self-interest in Washington, a comprehensive ban on nuclear tests, and a free and democratic Central America.

Nevertheless, much of what he said and wrote remains valid and relevant today—on U.S.–Soviet relations and race relations, for example, expanding foreign trade and foreign aid, keeping budget deficits and price stability under control, strengthening the foreign service, and strengthening the Presidency itself.

It is not difficult to find in these speeches the beginnings of much that we take for granted today—equal rights for all Americans, the conquest of space, politics free from religious bias, federal help for higher education and the arts, the sale of American farm products to Moscow, public television, communications satellites, the Peace Corps, and much more. Perhaps his greatest legacy is the untold number of men and women, in this country and abroad, famous and obscure, who were induced to enter politics or public service by the exhortation or example of John F. Kennedy. In meeting government leaders the world around, I have frequently encountered those who have never forgotten attending one of President Kennedy's numerous sessions with foreign students gathered on the South Lawn of the White House.

Neither is it difficult to discern from these speeches what a different world we would inhabit today had John Kennedy not been cruelly cut down on November 22, 1963, at the peak of his power and prowess. Surely, as he remarked at a press conference, "life is unfair."

But John F. Kennedy was not an unhappy man. Concerned that his countrymen, unable "to see the enemy from the walls," might be unwilling to pay the price of greatness, convinced that the old ways of conventional politics and policy-making were not up to the challenge that his generation faced, his speeches often contained dire warnings and stern lectures. But they also reflected his zest for living, his love of humor and home, his pride in public service.

There is much more to a man than his speeches. As Lord Rosebery once wrote regarding the oratory of William Pitt: "It is not merely the thing that is said but the man who says it that counts, the character which breathes through the sentences." The republication here of John F. Kennedy's words cannot possibly convey in full the energy and vitality of the man, his courage as a leader, or his warmth as a friend. But they can convey his principles and his hopes; and those are worth remembering, now and for generations to come. Through his words, John F. Kennedy lives on.

The State of the Union Address, January 14, 1963.
PHOTO COURTESY CECIL W. STOUGHTON.

PART I

The Presidency

CHAPTER 1

The Inaugural Address

Aware that his words would be viewed skeptically by those in Congress and the country who thought him too inexperienced for the post, concerned by the speech only a short time earlier of Soviet Chairman Nikita Khrushchev that sounded like a call for a worldwide Communist revolution, John F. Kennedy wanted his first address as President of the United States to challenge his multiple audiences: to summon the American people to greatness, to remind free nations of their obligations, to offer the Soviet Union a choice between confrontation and cooperation, and to be his eloquent best.

We observe today not a victory of party but a celebration of freedom—symbolizing an end as well as a beginning—signifying renewal as well as change. For I have sworn before you and Almighty God the same solemn oath our forebears prescribed nearly a century and three quarters ago.

The world is very different now. For man holds in his mortal hands the power to abolish all forms of human poverty and all forms of human life. And yet the same revolutionary beliefs for which our forebears fought are still at issue around the globe—the belief that the rights of man come not from the generosity of the state but from the hand of God.

We dare not forget today that we are the heirs of that first revolution. Let the word go forth from this time and place, to friend and foe alike, that the torch has been passed to a new generation of Americans—born in this century, tempered by war, disciplined by a hard and bitter peace, proud of our ancient heritage—and unwilling to witness or permit the slow undoing of those human rights to which this nation has always been committed, and to which we are committed today at home and around the world.

Let every nation know, whether it wishes us well or ill, that we shall pay any price, bear any burden, meet any hardship, support any friend, oppose any foe, to assure the survival and the success of liberty.

This much we pledge—and more.

To those old allies whose cultural and spiritual origins we share, we pledge the loyalty of faithful friends. United, there is little we cannot do in a host of cooperative ventures. Divided, there is little we can do—for we dare not meet a powerful challenge at odds and split asunder.

To those new states whom we welcome to the ranks of the free, we pledge our word that one form of colonial control shall not have passed away merely to be replaced by a far more iron tyranny. We shall not always expect to find them supporting our view. But we shall always hope to find them strongly supporting their own freedom—and to remember that in the past, those who foolishly sought power by riding the back of the tiger ended up inside.

To those peoples in the huts and villages of half the globe struggling to break the bonds of mass misery, we pledge our best efforts to help them help themselves, for whatever period is required—not because the Communists may be doing it, not because we seek their votes, but because it is right. If a free society cannot help the many who are poor, it cannot save the few who are rich.

Let the word go forth from this time and place, to friend and foe alike, that the torch has been passed to a new generation of Americans.

To our sister republics south of our border, we offer a special pledge —to convert our good words into good deeds—in a new alliance for progress—to assist free men and free governments in casting off the chains of poverty. But this peaceful revolution of hope cannot become the prey of hostile powers. Let all our neighbors know that we shall join with them to oppose aggression or subversion anywhere in the Americas. And let every other power know that this hemisphere intends to remain the master of its own house.

To that world assembly of sovereign states, the United Nations, our last best hope in an age where the instruments of war have far outpaced the instruments of peace, we renew our pledge of support—to prevent it from becoming merely a forum for invective—to strengthen its shield of the new and the weak—and to enlarge the area in which its writ may run.

Finally, to those nations who would make themselves our adversary, we offer not a pledge but a request: that both sides begin anew the quest for peace, before the dark powers of destruction unleashed by science engulf all humanity in planned or accidental self-destruction.

We dare not tempt them with weakness. For only when our arms are sufficient beyond doubt can we be certain beyond doubt that they will never be employed.

But neither can two great and powerful groups of nations take comfort from our present course—both sides overburdened by the cost of modern weapons, both rightly alarmed by the steady spread of the deadly atom, yet both racing to alter that uncertain balance of terror that stays the hand of mankind's final war.

So let us begin anew—remembering on both sides that civility is not a sign of weakness, and sincerity is always subject to proof. Let us never negotiate out of fear. But let us never fear to negotiate.

Let both sides explore what problems unite us instead of belaboring those problems which divide us.

Let both sides, for the first time, formulate serious and precise proposals for the inspection and control of arms—and bring the absolute power to destroy other nations under the absolute control of all nations.

Let both sides seek to invoke the wonders of science instead of its terrors. Together let us explore the stars, conquer the deserts, eradicate disease, tap the ocean depths, and encourage the arts and commerce.

Let both sides unite to heed in all corners of the earth the command of Isaiah—to "undo the heavy burdens [and] let the oppressed go free."

And if a beachhead of cooperation may push back the jungle of suspicion, let both sides join in creating a new endeavor, not a new balance of power, but a new world of law, where the strong are just and the weak secure and the peace preserved.

All this will not be finished in the first one hundred days. Nor will it be finished in the first one thousand days, nor in the life of this administration, nor even perhaps in our lifetime on this planet. But let us begin.

In your hands, my fellow citizens, more than mine, will rest the final success or failure of our course. Since this country was founded, each generation of Americans has been summoned to give testimony to its national loyalty. The graves of young Americans who answered the call to service surround the globe.

Now the trumpet summons us again—not as a call to bear arms, though arms we need—not as a call to battle, though embattled we are—but as a call to bear the burden of a long twilight struggle, year in and year out, "rejoicing in hope, patient in tribulation"—a struggle against the common enemies of man: tyranny, poverty, disease, and war itself.

Can we forge against these enemies a grand and global alliance, North and South, East and West, that can assure a more fruitful life for all mankind? Will you join in that historic effort?

In the long history of the world, only a few generations have been granted the role of defending freedom in its hour of maximum danger. I do not shrink from this responsibility—I welcome it. I do not believe that any of us would exchange places with any other people or any other generation. The energy, the faith, the devotion which we bring to this endeavor will light our country and all who serve it—and the glow from that fire can truly light the world.

And so, my fellow Americans: ask not what your country can do for you—ask what you can do for your country.

My fellow citizens of the world: ask not what America will do for you, but what together we can do for the freedom of man.

And so, my fellow Americans: ask not what your country can do for you—ask what you can do for your country.

My fellow citizens of the world: ask not what America will do for you, but what together we can do for the freedom of man.

Finally, whether you are citizens of America or citizens of the world, ask of us here the same high standards of strength and sacrifice which we ask of you. With a good conscience our only sure reward, with history the final judge of our deeds, let us go forth to lead the land we love, asking His blessing and His help, but knowing that here on earth God's work must truly be our own.

The Inaugural Address
Washington, D.C.
January 20, 1961

At a Democratic fund-raising dinner one year later, Kennedy irreverently parodied his own Inaugural Address:

We observe tonight not a celebration of freedom but a victory of party. For we have sworn to pay off the same party debt our forebears ran up nearly a year and three months ago.

Our deficit will not be paid off in the next hundred days. Nor will it be paid off in the first one thousand days, nor in the life of this administration, perhaps even in our lifetime on this planet. But let us begin—remembering that generosity is not a sign of weakness and that ambassadors are always subject to Senate confirmation. For if the Democratic Party cannot be helped by the many who are poor, it cannot be saved by the few who are rich. So let us begin.

Washington, D.C.
January 20, 1962

CHAPTER 2

The Role of the President

Convinced that this country had been drifting uncertainly both at home and abroad, John Kennedy campaigned on the need to restore vigorous executive leadership in Washington. Once in the White House, he found the crises more intensive, the choices more difficult, and the criticism more inevitable than he had anticipated. By accepting both blame and brickbats with relative equanimity—particularly after the Cuban Bay of Pigs invasion fiasco early in his first year—he pleased and astonished Washington, learned from his mistakes, and built the kind of Presidency he had contemplated: dedicated, decisive, determined, and effective.

The Vital Center of Action

The modern presidential campaign covers every issue in and out of the platform from cranberries to creation. But the public is rarely alerted to a candidate's views about the central issue on which all the rest turn. That central issue . . . is not the farm problem or defense or India. It is the Presidency itself.

Of course, a candidate's views on specific policies are important, but Theodore Roosevelt and William Howard Taft shared policy views with entirely different results in the White House. Of course, it is important to elect a good man with good intentions, but Woodrow Wilson and Warren G. Harding were both good men of good intentions; so were Lincoln and Buchanan; but there is a Lincoln Room in the White House and no Buchanan Room.

The history of this nation—its brightest and its bleakest pages—has been written largely in terms of the different views our Presidents have had of the Presidency itself. This history ought to tell us that the American people in 1960 have an imperative right to know what any man bidding for the Presidency thinks about the place he is bidding for, whether he is aware of and willing to use the powerful resources of that office; whether his model will be Taft or Roosevelt, Wilson or Harding.

Not since the days of Woodrow Wilson has any candidate spoken on the Presidency itself before the votes have been irrevocably cast. Let us hope that the 1960 campaign, in addition to discussing the familiar issues where our positions too often blur, will also talk about the Presidency itself, as an instrument for dealing with these issues, as an office with varying roles, powers, and limitations.

During the past eight years, we have seen one concept of the Presidency at work. Our needs and hopes have been eloquently stated—but the initiative and follow-through have too often been left to others. And too often his own objectives have been lost by the President's failure to override objections from within his own party, in the Congress or even in his Cabinet.

The American people in 1952 and 1956 may have preferred this detached, limited concept of the Presidency after twenty years of fast-moving, creative presidential rule. Perhaps historians will regard this as necessarily one of those frequent periods of consolidation, a time to draw breath, recoup our national energy. To quote the State of the

Union message: "No Congress . . . on surveying the state of the nation, has met with a more pleasing prospect than that which appears at the present time."

Unfortunately this is not Mr. Eisenhower's last message to the Congress, but Calvin Coolidge's. He followed to the White House Mr. Harding, whose sponsor declared very frankly that the times did not demand a first-rate President. If true, the times and the man met.

But the question is what do the times—and the people—demand for the next four years in the White House?

They demand a vigorous proponent of the national interest—not a passive broker for conflicting private interests. They demand a man capable of acting as the commander in chief of the Grand Alliance, not merely a bookkeeper who feels that his work is done when the numbers on the balance sheet come out even. They demand that he be the head of the responsible party, not rise so far above politics as to be invisible—a man who will formulate and fight for legislative policies, not be a casual bystander to the legislative process.

Today a restricted concept of the Presidency is not enough. For beneath today's surface gloss of peace and prosperity are increasingly dangerous, unsolved, long postponed problems that will inevitably explode to the surface during the next four years of the next administration—the growing missile gap, the rise of Communist China, the despair of the underdeveloped nations, the explosive situations in Berlin and in the Formosa Straits, the deterioration of NATO, the lack of an arms control agreement, and all the domestic problems of our farms, cities, and schools.

This administration has not faced up to these and other problems. Much has been said—but I am reminded of the old Chinese proverb: "There is a great deal of noise on the stairs but nobody comes into the room."

The President's State of the Union message reminded me of the exhortation from *King Lear* that goes: "I will do such things—what they are I know not . . . but they shall be the wonders of the earth."

In the decade that lies ahead—in the challenging revolutionary sixties—the American Presidency will demand more than ringing manifestos issued from the rear of the battle. It will demand that the President place himself in the very thick of the fight, that he care passionately about the fate of the people he leads, that he be willing to serve them at the risk of incurring their momentary displeasure.

Whatever the political affiliation of our next President, whatever his views may be on all the issues and problems that rush in upon us, he must above all be the Chief Executive in every sense of the word. He must be prepared to exercise the fullest powers of his office—all that are specified and some that are not. He must master complex problems as well as receive one-page memoranda. He must originate action as well as study groups. He must reopen the channel of communication between the world of thought and the seat of power.

Ulysses Grant considered the President "a purely administrative officer." If he administered the government departments efficiently, delegated his functions smoothly, and performed his ceremonies of state with decorum and grace, no more was to be expected of him. But that is not the place the Presidency was meant to have in American life. The President is alone, at the top—the loneliest job there is, as Harry Truman has said.

If there is destructive dissension among the services, he alone can step in and straighten it out—instead of waiting for unanimity. If administrative agencies are not carrying out their mandate—if a brushfire threatens some part of the globe—he alone can act, without waiting for the Congress. If his farm program fails, he alone deserves the blame, not his secretary of agriculture.

"The President is at liberty, both in law and conscience, to be as big a man as he can." So wrote Professor Woodrow Wilson. But President Woodrow Wilson discovered that to be a big man in the White House inevitably brings cries of "dictatorship."

So did Lincoln and Jackson and the two Roosevelts. And so may the next occupant of that office, if he is the man the times demand. But how much better it would be, in the turbulent sixties, to have a Roosevelt or a Wilson than to have another James Buchanan, cringing in the White House, afraid to move.

For beneath today's surface gloss of peace and prosperity are increasingly dangerous, unsolved, long postponed problems that will inevitably explode to the surface.

Nor can we afford a Chief Executive who is praised primarily for what he did not do, the disasters he prevented, the bills he vetoed—a President wishing his subordinates would produce more missiles or build more schools. We will need instead what the Constitution envisioned: a Chief Executive who is the vital center of action in our whole scheme of government.

This includes the legislative process as well. The President cannot afford—for the sake of the office as well as the nation—to be another Warren G. Harding, described by one backer as a man who "would, when elected, sign whatever bill the Senate sent him—and not send bills for the Senate to pass." Rather he must know when to lead the Congress, when to consult it, and when he should act alone.

Having served fourteen years in the legislative branch, I would not look with favor upon its domination by the executive. Under our government of "power as the rival of power," to use Hamilton's phrase, Congress must not surrender its responsibilities. But neither should it dominate. However large its share in the formulation of domestic programs, it is the President alone who must make the major decisions of our foreign policy.

That is what the Constitution wisely commands. And, even domestically, the President must initiate policies and devise laws to meet the needs of the nation. And he must be prepared to use all the resources of his office to insure the enactment of that legislation—even when conflict is the result.

By the end of his term Theodore Roosevelt was not popular in the Congress—particularly when he criticized an amendment to the Treasury appropriation which forbade the use of Secret Service men to investigate congressmen.

And the feeling was mutual, Roosevelt saying: "I do not much admire the Senate, because it is such a helpless body when efficient work is to be done."

And Woodrow Wilson was even more bitter after his frustrating quarrels. Asked if he might run for the Senate in 1920, he replied: "Outside of the United States, the Senate does not amount to a damn. And inside the United States the Senate is mostly despised. They haven't had a thought down there in fifty years."

But, however bitter their farewells, the facts of the matter are that Roosevelt and Wilson did get things done—not only through their executive powers but through the Congress as well. Calvin Coolidge, on the other hand, departed from Washington with cheers of Congress still ringing in his ears. But when his World Court bill was under fire on Capitol Hill, he sent no messages, gave no encouragement to the bill's leaders, and paid little or no attention to the whole proceeding—and the cause of world justice was set back.

To be sure, Coolidge had held the usual White House breakfasts with congressional leaders—but they were aimed, as he himself said, at "good fellowship," not a discussion of "public business." And at his press conferences, according to press historians, where he preferred to talk about the local flower show and its exhibits, reporters who finally extracted from him a single sentence—"I'm against that bill"—would rush to file tongue-in-cheek dispatches, proclaiming that "President Coolidge, in a fighting mood, today served notice on Congress that he intended to combat, with all the resources at his command, the pending bill. . . ."

But in the coming years we will need a real fighting mood in the White House—a man who will not retreat in the face of pressure from his congressional leaders—who will not let down those supporting his views on the floor. Divided government over the past six years has only been further confused by this lack of legislative leadership. To restore it next year will help restore purpose to both the Presidency and the Congress.

The facts of the matter are that legislative leadership is not possible without party leadership, in the most political sense—and Mr. Eisenhower prefers to stay above politics (although a weekly newsmagazine last fall reported the startling news, and I quote, that "President Eisenhower is emerging as a major political figure"). When asked, early in his first term, how he liked the "game of politics," he replied with a frown that his questioner was using a derogatory phrase. "Being President," he said, "is a very great experience . . . but the word 'politics' . . . I have no great liking for that."

But no President, it seems to me, can escape politics. He has not only been chosen by the nation—he has been chosen by his party. And if he insists that he is "President of all the people" and should, therefore, offend none of them—if he blurs the issues and differences between the parties—if he neglects the party machinery and avoids his party's leadership—then he has not only weakened the political party as an instrument of the democratic process—he has dealt a blow to the democratic process itself.

I prefer the example of Abe Lincoln, who loved politics with the passion of a born practitioner. For example, he waited up all night in 1863 to get the crucial returns on the Ohio governorship. When the Unionist candidate was elected, Lincoln wired: "Glory to God in the highest. Ohio has saved the Nation."

But the White House is not only the center of political leadership. It must be the center of moral leadership—a "bully pulpit," as Theodore Roosevelt described it. For only the President represents the national interest. And upon him alone converge all the needs and aspirations of all parts of the country, all departments of government, all nations of the world.

It is not enough merely to represent prevailing sentiment—to follow McKinley's practice, as described by Joe Cannon, of "keeping his ear so close to the ground he got it full of grasshoppers." We will need in the sixties a President who is willing and able to summon his national constituency to its finest hour—to alert the people to our dangers and our opportunities—to demand of them the sacrifices that will be necessary. FDR's words in his first inaugural still ring true: "In every dark hour of our national life, a leadership of frankness and vigor has met with that understanding and support of the people themselves which is essential to victory."

Roosevelt fulfilled the role of moral leadership. So did Wilson and Lincoln, Truman and Jackson and Teddy Roosevelt. They led the people as well as the government—they fought for great ideals as well as bills. And the time has come to demand that kind of leadership again.

And so, as this vital campaign begins, let us discuss the issues the next President will face—but let us also discuss the powers and tools with which we must face them.

For we must endow that office with extraordinary strength and vision. We must act in the image of Abraham Lincoln summoning his wartime Cabinet to a meeting on the Emancipation Proclamation. That Cabinet had been carefully chosen to please and reflect many elements in the country. But "I have gathered you together," Lincoln said, "to hear what I have written down. I do not wish your advice about the main matter—that I have determined for myself."

And later, when he went to sign after several hours of exhausting handshaking that had left his arm weak, he said to those present: "If my name goes down in history, it will be for this act. My whole soul is in it. If my hand trembles when I sign this proclamation, all who examine the document hereafter will say: 'He hesitated.' "

But Lincoln's hand did not tremble. He did not hesitate. He did not equivocate. For he was the President of the United States.

It is in this spirit that we must go forth in the coming months and years.

National Press Club
Washington, D.C., January 14, 1960

The Leader of the Free World

I have premised my campaign on the central issue of the Presidency itself—its powers, their use and their decline. . . . For this is no mere popularity contest. We may enjoy the sideshows, the fanfare, and the headlines. But it is a President we are electing. And no Democrat can dodge the real issue of the Presidency's decline if he hopes to win in 1960. . . .

Perhaps we could afford a Coolidge following Harding. And perhaps we could afford a Pierce following Fillmore. But after Buchanan this nation needed a Lincoln—after Taft we needed a Wilson—after Hoover we needed Franklin Roosevelt. . . . And after eight years of Eisenhower, this nation needs a strong, creative Democrat in the White House.

And nowhere is this need more critical than in the conduct of our foreign affairs. For Pennsylvania Avenue is no longer a local thoroughfare. It runs through Paris and London, Ankara and Teheran, New Delhi and Tokyo. And if the soul of a journey is liberty, as Hazlitt has said, then the road from the White House that encircles the globe is freedom's way—the artery that makes all the Free World neighbors as well as allies.

And if Washington is the capital of the Free World, the President must be its leader. Our Constitution requires it—our history requires it—our very survival requires it. In foreign affairs, said the Supreme Court, "the

President alone has the power to speak or listen as the representative of this nation."

"The President alone . . ." And he is alone—at the top—in the loneliest job in the world. He cannot share this power, he cannot delegate it, he cannot adjourn. He alone is the Chief of State, not the National Security Council, Vice-President and all. He alone decides whether to recognize foreign governments, not his Senate minority leader. . . . He alone must decide what areas we defend—not the Congress or the military or the CIA, and certainly not some beleaguered generalissimo on an island domain.

If nuclear tests are to be halted—if disarmament is to become a reality—then he alone must lead the way, and not leave it to the warped judgment of the AEC [Atomic Energy Commission] and the Pentagon. And if India is to be saved—if the missile gap is to be closed—if we are to help Latin American democracies (instead of dictators)—the decision is his alone, and not that of the little men with little vision in the Bureau of the Budget.

In this 1960 campaign, four facts ought to be made clear about presidential responsibility in foreign affairs:

First, the President's responsibility cannot be delegated. For he is the one focal point of responsibility. His office is the single channel through which there flow the torrential pressures and needs of every state, every federal agency, every friend and foe.

He does not have to wait for unanimous agreement below, summed up in one-page memoranda that stifle dissent. He does not have to wait for crises to spur decisions that are long overdue. He must look ahead—and sometimes act alone—like Woodrow Wilson, locked in his study, typing his own notes to the Kaiser; or, in the words of his assistant, devouring a stack of state papers like "a starving man with a pile of flapjacks" (somewhat in contrast, I might add, to the veteran White House usher's description of Calvin Coolidge: "No other President in my time ever slept so much").

For Woodrow Wilson knew, in his own words, that in a nation's foreign affairs, the President must of necessity "be its guide—take every first step of action, utter every initial judgment . . . suggest and in large measure control its course." Thus most of the great landmarks of our foreign policy bear the name of the President who initiated them—Washington's Proclamation of Neutrality, Monroe's Doctrine, Wilson's Fourteen Points, Roosevelt's Four Freedoms, and Truman's Point Four Program.

Occasionally we remember secretaries of state as well—but usually when they overshadowed their chief: Seward for the Alaska purchase, not Andrew Johnson; Hay for the Open Door policy, not McKinley; Hughes for the Washington treaty, not Harding. . . . Certainly the President should use his secretary of state. But he should be the captain of the bridge, and not leave it to the helmsman to sail without direction. For in the words of Socrates: "If a man does not know to what port he is sailing, no wind is favorable."

Secondly, the President's responsibility cannot be abdicated to the Congress. Certainly Congress has a role in foreign affairs, constitutionally and practically. It can approve—it can appropriate. But it cannot exercise ultimate power—for it has no ultimate responsibility. It has no way of relating widely separated events, or assessing day-to-day dangers. It has no ambassadors or armies, no access to secret reports, no right to negotiate treaties or construct coalitions. We recognized this in our earliest days when we asked the king of Sweden to address no more letters "to the President and the Senate of the United States."

The President's responsibility cannot be delegated. For he is the one focal point of responsibility. His office is the single channel through which there flow the torrential pressures and needs of every state, every federal agency, every friend and foe.

For these burdens are essentially the President's—and he cannot shift his responsibility to the Congress, under the guise of bipartisanship, asking our support for an unknown policy on Quemoy and Matsu, asking our support for a Middle East doctrine that was more public relations than policy. For bipartisanship does not mean—and was never designed to mean—rubber-stamping every executive blunder without debate. . . .

No modern President of either party, of course, would deceive the Congress—like Secretary of State Webster, reportedly using his own secret map to convince the Senate that he had cheated the British in drawing the Canadian border, while at the same time Lord Ashburton was using his own secret map to convince Parliament that in reality he had cheated Webster. Nor will today's Congress and Executive actually meet in mortal combat—as Secretary of State Clay and Senator John Randolph did, when the Senate wasn't consulted on the Panama Conference, and the Senator denounced Clay's aged mother for bringing into the world "this being, so brilliant yet so corrupt, which, like a rotten mackerel by moonlight, shines and stinks."

But even today the President should be prepared to resist unwarranted congressional intrusions in foreign affairs. Above all, he must protect his Foreign Service against thoughtless congressional attacks and investigations. There are always some farm organizations looking out for their department—just as labor unions, veterans, business groups, and postal employees look out for theirs. But the Foreign Service has no pressure groups, no constituency—only the President. And the next President—a Democratic President—must champion and restore this vital agency.

Third, the President's responsibility is to all the people. He must strengthen them—and draw strength from them; educate them—and represent them; pledge his best—and inspire theirs. If he rejects "Operation Candor" as politically dangerous, if he constantly reassures an imperiled nation that all is well, if he answers all critics with an air of infallibility, or, worst of all, if he himself is not informed and therefore cannot inform the people—then the Presidency has failed the American people.

We cannot be reassured that we are building the best defense merely because we now have a general in the White House. For we have had generals in the White House before—and when Grant was asked in 1868 if he really wanted to be President, he was honest enough to reply: "No, I am a military man, not a statesman. I would just like to be Mayor of Galena long enough to build a sidewalk from my house to the station."

Our greatest foreign policy Presidents were not military men. They did not request unquestioning faith. They kept the people informed. They eloquently defined the aims and aspirations of the nation. Mr. Eisenhower's messages may be delivered in well-chosen words—but they sound more like the chairman of the board describing another profitable quarter.

There has been no willingness to say the harsh things that sometimes need to be said—to take the hard steps that may not be popular or convenient—like Thomas Jefferson, purchasing the Louisiana Territory despite outcries from the budget-cutters of his day that we could not afford $15 million for this "wilderness"—or like George Washington, standing by the Jay Treaty despite being abused, as he wrote, "in such exaggerated and indecent terms as could scarcely be applied to Nero, to a notorious defaulter or even to a common pickpocket."

Compare these Presidents to those who yielded to public pressure instead of educating it: Madison being dragged into a war he knew was unsound; McKinley being led into a war he knew was unnecessary; Harding blessing a disarmament conference he knew was unwise; Coolidge hailing a peace pact he knew was unworkable. We cannot afford in the turbulent sixties the persistent indecision of a James Buchanan, which caused Ohio's Senator Sherman to say: "The Constitution provides for every accidental contingency in the Executive—except a vacancy in the mind of the President."

In 1960 we must elect a President who will lead the people—who will risk, if he must, his popularity for his responsibility. . . .

Fourth and finally, the President's responsibility is to the Free World as well as the nation. Even before the Constitution was ratified, Jefferson predicted that "the election of a President some years hence will be much more interesting to certain nations of Europe than the election of a king of Poland ever was." And today, as the 1960 campaign begins, every nation of Europe—and the world—is in fact watching our politics and policies. As the British cartoonist David Low has said of every Free World citizen: "Fate has made us all Honorary Americans."

And thus the President of the United States—the leader of that Free World—must represent all its nations, in his every word and deed. And to them in turn his words—in his every press conference and message—represent the real "Voice of America." If they hear not one voice but many—from State, from Treasury, from Defense—they feel in doubt. And if they see him in doubt, they feel betrayed. . . .

But if the President is to be creative in foreign policy, his party must be creative. . . . Historically and inevitably the forces of inertia and reaction in the Republican Party oppose any powerful voice in the White House—Republican or Democrat—that seeks to speak for the nation as a whole. Theodore Roosevelt discovered that. Herbert Hoover discovered that and, even before he could run for President, Nelson Rockefeller discovered it. Even President Eisenhower considered forming a third party in 1954. No Republican President, no matter how dedicated, can escape the quicksand of his party's entrenched interests.

But the Democratic Party is a national party—it believes in strong leadership—and, with your help, we will give the nation that leadership in January 1961.

John Adams, our second Chief Executive, would not war with France, despite popular pressures from this young and reckless land. In this way he preserved the infant nation—he paved the way for the Louisiana Purchase—but he also insured his own bitter defeat for reelection. Yet later, as death drew near, he wrote to a trusted friend: "I desire no other inscription over my gravestone than this: 'Here lies John Adams, who took upon himself the responsibility of peace with France. . . .' "

In 1960, the next President of the United States must be prepared to take upon himself the responsibility of peace with all the world.

California Democratic Clubs Convention
Fresno, California, February 12, 1960

The Champion of Freedom

I run for the office of the Presidency not because I think it is an easy job. In many ways I think the next years are going to be the most difficult years in our history. I don't run for the office of the Presidency telling you that if you elect me life is going to be easy, because I don't think that life is going to be easy for Americans in the next decade. But I run for the Presidency because I do not want it said in the years when our generation held political power that those were the years when America began to slip, when America began to slide. I don't want historians writing in 1970 to say that the balance of power in the 1950s and the 1960s began to turn against the United States and against the cause of freedom. I don't want it said that when we held office and when we were citizens that the Russians and the Chinese Communists began to expand their power. The New Frontier is not what I promise I am going to do for you. The New Frontier is what I ask you to do for our country. Give me your help, your hand, your voice, and this country can move again.

Labor Day Campaign Kickoff
Detroit, Michigan, September 5, 1960

. . . When the Federalist Party was old and tired, Thomas Jefferson began the Democratic Party. His first action early as President was the Louisiana Purchase, against the wishes of all those who came from my own section of New England, who wanted the country to remain small, secluded, belonging to a few. Instead, he took a chance and spread the United States west, and even though when he became President the western boundary of America was Virginia, he sent Lewis and Clark all the way to the Pacific Ocean to open up the entire United States. That has been the spirit of the Democratic Party. It has been the spirit of Jackson and Roosevelt and Truman and all the rest, and that is the spirit we are going to recapture.

Campaign Remarks
Muskegon, Michigan, September 5, 1960

The Responsible Officer of Government

Q: Sir, since last Saturday a certain foreign policy situation [the failed Bay of Pigs invasion] has given rise to many conflicting stories. . . . In view of the fact we are taking a propaganda lambasting around the world, why is it not useful, sir, for us to explore with you the real facts behind this, or our motivations?

THE PRESIDENT: Well, I think, in answer to your question, that we have to make a judgment as to how much we can usefully say that would aid the interest of the United States. . . .

There's an old saying that victory has a hundred fathers and defeat is an orphan. . . .

But I will say to you, Mr. Vanocur, that I have said as much as I feel can be usefully said by me in regard to the events of the past few days. [Avoiding further] statements, detailed discussions, [is] not to conceal responsibility because I'm the responsible officer of the government—and that is quite obvious.

President's News Conference
Washington, D.C., April 21, 1961

Q: Mr. President, your brother, Ted, recently on television said that after seeing the cares of office on you, he wasn't sure he'd ever be interested in being the President. I wonder if you could tell us whether if you had it to do over again, you would work for the Presidency and whether you can recommend the job to others.

THE PRESIDENT: Well, the answer is . . . to the first is yes and the second is no. I don't recommend it to others—at least for a while.

President's News Conference
Washington, D.C., March 29, 1962

Q: Mr. President, perhaps . . . you would comment for us on the press in general, as you see it from the Presidency. Perhaps, its treatment of your administration, treatment of the issues of the day?

THE PRESIDENT: Well, I am reading more and enjoying it less . . . but I have not complained nor do I plan to make any general complaints. I read and talk to myself about it, but I don't plan to issue any general statement on the press. I think that they are doing their task, as a critical branch, the fourth estate. And I am attempting to do mine. And we are going to live together for a period, and then go our separate ways.

President's News Conference,
Washington, D.C., May 9, 1962

The Ultimate Decision Maker

WILLIAM H. LAWRENCE, AMERICAN BROADCASTING COMPANY: As you look back upon your first two years in office, sir, has your experience in the office matched your expectations? You had studied a good deal the power of the Presidency, the methods of its operations. How has this worked out as you saw it in advance?

THE PRESIDENT: . . . I would say that the problems are more difficult than I had imagined them to be. The responsibilities placed on the United States are greater than I imagined them to be, and there are greater limitations upon our ability to bring about a favorable result than I had imagined them to be. And I think that is probably true of anyone who becomes President, because there is such a difference between those who advise or speak or legislate, and between the man who must select from the various alternatives proposed and say that this shall be the policy of the United States. It is much easier to make the speeches than it is to finally make the judgments, because unfortunately your advisers are frequently divided. If you take the wrong course, and on occasion I have, the President bears the burden of the responsibility quite rightly. The advisers move on to new advice.

GEORGE E. HERMAN, COLUMBIA BROADCASTING SYSTEM: I would like to go back to the question of the consensus [on responding to Soviet missiles in Cuba] and your relationship to the consensus. You have said and the Constitution says that the decision can be made only by the President.

THE PRESIDENT: Well, you know that old story about Abraham Lincoln and the Cabinet. He says, "All in favor, say 'aye,'" and the whole Cabinet voted "aye," and then, "All opposed, 'no,'" and Lincoln voted "no," and he said, "The vote is no." So that naturally the Constitution places the responsibility on the President.

There was some disagreement with the course we finally adopted, but the course we finally adopted had the advantage of permitting other steps if this one was unsuccessful. In other words, we were starting in a sense at a minimum place. Then if that were unsuccessful, we could have gradually stepped it up until we had gone into a much more massive action, which might have become necessary if the first step had been unsuccessful. I would think that the majority finally came to accept that, though at the beginning there was a much sharper division. And after all, this was very valuable, because the people who were involved had particular responsibilities of their own; Mr. McNamara, Secretary of Defense, who therefore had to advise me on the military capacity of the United States in that area, the Secretary of State, who had to advise on the attitude of the OAS [Organization of American States] and NATO. So that in my opinion [the fact that] the majority came to accept the course we finally took . . . made it much easier. In the Cuban crisis of 1961 the advice of those who were brought in on the executive branch [side] was also unanimous, and the advice was wrong. And I was responsible. . . . No matter how many advisers you have, frequently they are divided, and the President must finally choose.

The other point is something that President Eisenhower said to me on January nineteenth [1961]. He said "There are no easy matters that will ever come to you as President. If they are easy, they will be settled at a lower level." So that the matters that come to you as President are always the difficult matters, and matters that carry with them large implications. So this contributes to some of the burdens of the office of the Presidency, which other Presidents have commented on.

It is much easier to make the speeches than it is to finally make the judgments, because unfortunately your advisers are frequently divided. If you take the wrong course, and on occasion I have, the President bears the burden of the responsibility quite rightly. The advisers move on to new advice.

SANDER VANOCUR, NATIONAL BROADCASTING COMPANY: . . . Is it true that during your first year, sir, you would get on the phone personally to the State Department and try to get a response to some inquiry that had been made?

THE PRESIDENT: Yes, I still do that when I can, because I think there is a great tendency in government to have papers stay on desks too long, and it seems to me that is really one function . . . after all, the President can't administer a department, but at least he can be a stimulant. . . .

MR. VANOCUR: You once said that you were reading more and enjoying it less. Are you still as avid a newspaper reader, magazine—I remember those of us who traveled with you on the campaign, a magazine wasn't safe around you.

THE PRESIDENT: Oh, yes. . . . It is never pleasant to be reading things that are not agreeable news, but I would say that it is an invaluable arm of the Presidency, as a check really on what is going on in the administration, and more things come to my attention that cause me concern or give me information. So I would think that Mr. Khrushchev, operating a totalitarian system—which has many "advantages" as far as being able to move in secret, and all the rest—there is a terrific disadvantage not having the abrasive quality of the press applied to you daily. . . . Even though we never like it, and even though we wish they didn't write it, and even though we disapprove, there isn't any doubt that we could not do the job at all in a free society without a very, very active press.

Now, on the other hand, the press has the responsibility not to distort things for political purposes, not to just [select] some news in order to prove a political point. It seems to me their obligation is to be as tough as they can on the administration but do it in a way which is directed toward getting as close to the truth as they can get and not merely because of some political motivation.

MR. VANOCUR: Mr. President, back before you were elected, your father used to have a favorite story he told reporters. He asked you once why do you want the job, and he cited the reasons why you shouldn't want it, and you apparently gave him an answer—I don't know whether it satisfied him, but apparently you satisfied yourself. Would you give him the same answer today after serving in this office for two years?

THE PRESIDENT: Oh, you mean "somebody is going to do it [be President]"?

MR. VANOCUR: Yes, sir.

THE PRESIDENT: Yes. I think that there are a lot of satisfactions to the Presidency, particularly, as I say, we are all concerned as citizens and as parents and all the rest, with all the problems we have been talking about tonight. They are all the problems which if I was not the President, I would be concerned about as a father or as a citizen. So at least you have an opportunity to do something about them. And if what you do is useful and successful, then of course that is a great satisfaction.

Television and Radio
Year-end Conversation with the President
Washington, D.C., December 17, 1962

The Party Leader

Our Founding Fathers did not realize that the basic fact which has made our system work was outside the Constitution. And that was the development of political parties in this country so that the American people would have the means of placing responsibility on one group, that group would have a chance to carry out its program, and the American people would have an opportunity to indicate their dissatisfaction by going to an alternative.

That system has served us well, and there is no greater responsibility in that sense that a President has, as President Truman has pointed out, than he has as a leader of a political party, and especially this political party, the oldest in the world, the oldest in our country's history.

When we stand here next to these pictures of Presidents Jefferson, Jackson, Cleveland, Wilson, Franklin Roosevelt, and Harry Truman, we are standing next to great Presidents. And we are also standing next to great party leaders who were able to use the party to carry out their programs. That is the purpose of all of our exercise. [Political power] is not an end in itself; it is a means of doing the things which this country needs in the sixties, and this country needs a lot at home and abroad.

Remarks to Members of National and State Democratic Committees at the White House Washington, D.C., January 18, 1963

The Happy President

Q: Mr. President: Just shortly after the Bay of Pigs I asked you how you liked being President, and as I remember you said you liked it better before the event. Now you have had a chance to appraise your job, and why do you like it and why do you want to stay in office four more years?

THE PRESIDENT: Well, I find the work rewarding. Whether I am going to stay and what my intentions are and all of the rest, it seems to me it is still a good many, many months away. But as far as the job of President goes, it is rewarding. And I have given before to this group the definition of happiness of the Greeks, and I will define it again: It is full use of your powers along lines of excellence. I find, therefore, the Presidency provides some happiness.

President's News Conference
Washington, D.C., October 31, 1963

CHAPTER 3

The Call to Public Service

John F. Kennedy believed there was no higher calling than politics and government. As a member of the Senate, he took special pride in recalling in his speeches and book, *Profiles in Courage,* the great senators of the past. As a candidate, he pledged a "ministry of talent" composed of the best men and women he could find, regardless of party. As President, he imbued in the career services—including a Foreign Service beleaguered by Senator Joe McCarthy and others—a new sense of pride and obligation, while simultaneously insisting upon higher ethical standards. One of his proudest achievements, the Peace Corps, exemplified his ideal of selfless, dedicated public service.

The Politician and the Intellectual

I can think of nothing more reassuring for all of us than to come again to this institution whose whole purpose is dedicated to the advancement of knowledge and the dissemination of truth.

I belong to a profession where the emphasis is somewhat different. Our political parties, our politicians, are interested, of necessity, in winning popular support—a majority; and only indirectly truth is the object of our controversy. From this polemic of contending factions, the general public is expected to make a discriminating judgment. As the problems have become more complex, as our role as a chief defender of Western civilization has become enlarged, the responsibility of the electorate as a court of last resort has become almost too great. The people desperately seek objectivity and a university such as this fulfills that function.

And the political profession needs to have its temperature lowered in the cooling waters of the scholastic pool. We need both the technical judgment and the disinterested viewpoint of the scholar, to prevent us from becoming imprisoned by our own slogans.

Therefore, it is regrettable that the gap between the intellectual and the politician seems to be growing. Instead of synthesis, clash and discord now characterize the relations between the two groups much of the time. Authors, scholars, and intellectuals can praise every aspect of American society but the political. My desk is flooded with books, articles, and pamphlets criticizing Congress. But rarely, if ever, have I seen any intellectual bestow praise on either the political profession or any political body for its accomplishments, its ability, or its integrity—much less for its intelligence. To many universities and scholars we reap nothing but censure, investigators and perpetrators of what has been called the swinish cult of anti-intellectualism.

James Russell Lowell's satiric attack more than one hundred years ago on Caleb Cushing, a celebrated attorney general and member of Congress, sets the tone: "Gineral C is a drefle smart man, he's ben on all sides that give places or pelf, but consistency still wiz a part of his plan—he's ben true to one party, that is himself."

But in fairness, the way of the intellectual is not altogether serene; in fact, so great has become popular suspicion that a recent survey of

American intellectuals by a national magazine elicited from one of our foremost literary figures the guarded response, "I ain't no intellectual."

Both sides in this battle, it seems to me, are motivated by largely unfounded feelings of distrust. The politician, whose authority rests upon the mandate of the popular will, is resentful of the scholar who can, with dexterity, slip from position to position without dragging the anchor of public opinion. It was this skill that caused Lord Melbourne to say of the youthful historian Macaulay that he wished he was as sure of anything as Macaulay was of everything.

The intellectual, on the other hand, finds it difficult to accept the differences between the laboratory and the legislature. In the former, the goal is truth, pure and simple, without regard to changing currents of public opinion; in the latter, compromises and majorities and procedural customs and rights affect the ultimate decision as to what is right or just or good. And even when they realize this difference, most intellectuals consider their chief functions that of the critic—and politicians are sensitive to critics (possibly because we have so many of them). "Many intellectuals," Sidney Hook has said, "would rather die than agree with the majority, even on the rare occasions when the majority is right."

It seems to me that the time has come for intellectuals and politicians alike to put aside those horrible weapons of modern internecine warfare, the barbed thrust, the acid pen, and, most sinister of all, the rhetorical blast. Let us not emphasize all on which we differ but all we have in common. Let us consider not what we fear separately but what we share together.

First, I would ask both groups to recall that the American politician of today and the American intellectual of today are descended from a common ancestry. Our nation's first great politicians were also among the nation's first great writers and scholars. The founders of the American Constitution were also the founders of American scholarship. The works of Jefferson, Madison, Hamilton, Franklin, Paine, and John Adams—to name but a few—influenced the literature of the world as well as its geography. Books were their tools, not their enemies. Locke, Milton, Sydney, Montesquieu, Coke, and Bolingbroke were among those widely read in political circles and frequently quoted in political pamphlets. Our political leaders traded in the free commerce of ideas with lasting results both here and abroad.

In those golden years, our political leaders moved from one field to another with amazing versatility and vitality. Jefferson and Franklin still throw long shadows over many fields of learning. A contemporary described Jefferson, "A gentleman of 32, who could calculate an eclipse, survey an estate, tie an artery, plan an edifice, try a cause, break a horse, dance a minuet, and play the violin."

Daniel Webster could throw thunderbolts at Hayne on the Senate floor and then stroll a few steps down the corridor and dominate the Supreme Court as the foremost lawyer of his time. John Quincy Adams, after being summarily dismissed from the Senate for a notable display of independence, could become Boylston Professor of Rhetoric and Oratory at Harvard and then become a great secretary of state. (Those were the happy days when Harvard professors had no difficulty getting Senate confirmation.)

I would urge that our political parties and our universities recognize the need for greater cooperation and understanding between politicians and intellectuals.

The versatility also existed on the frontier. An obituary of Missouri's first senator, Thomas Hart Benton, the man whose tavern brawl with Jackson in Tennessee caused him to flee the state, said, "With a readiness that was often surprising, he could quote from a Roman law or a Greek philosopher, from Virgil's Georgics, the Arabian Nights, Herodotus, or Sancho Panza, from the Sacred Carpets, the German reformers or Adam Smith; from Fenelon or Hudibras, from the financial reports of Necca or the doings of the Council of Trent, from the debates on the adoption of the Constitution or intrigues of the kitchen cabinet or from some forgotten speech of a deceased Member of Congress."

This link between the American scholar and the American politician remained for more than a century. Just one hundred years ago in the presidential campaign of 1856, the Republicans sent three brilliant orators around the campaign circuit: William Cullen Bryant, Henry Wadsworth Longfellow, and Ralph Waldo Emerson. Those were the carefree days when the eggheads were all Republicans.

I would hope that both groups, recalling their common heritage, might once again forge a link between the intellectual and political professions. I know that scholars may prefer the mysteries of pure scholarship or the delights of abstract discourse. But, "would you have counted him a friend of ancient Greece," as George William Curtis asked a century ago during the Kansas-Nebraska controversy, "who quietly discussed patriotism on the Greek summer day through whose hopeless and immortal hours Leonidas and his 300 stood at Thermopylae for liberty? Was John Milton to conjugate Greek verbs in his library or talk of the liberty of the ancient Shunamites when the liberty of Englishmen was imperiled?" No, the duty of the scholar, particularly in a republic such as ours, is to contribute his objective views and his sense of liberty to the affairs of his state and nation.

Secondly, I would remind both groups that the American politician and the American intellectual operate within a common framework—a framework we call liberty. Freedom of expression is not divisible into political expression and intellectual expression. The lock on the door of the legislature, the Parliament, or the assembly hall—by order of the king, the commissar, or the Führer—has historically been followed or preceded by a lock on the door of the university, the library, or the printshop. And if the first blow for freedom in any subjugated land is struck by a political leader, the second is struck by a book, a newspaper, or a pamphlet.

Unfortunately, in more recent times, politicians and intellectuals have quarreled bitterly, too bitterly in some cases, over how each group has met the modern challenge to freedom both at home and abroad. Politicians have questioned the discernment with which intellectuals have reacted to the siren call of the extreme left; and intellectuals have tended to accuse politicians of not always being aware, especially here at home, of the toxic effects of freedom restrained.

While differences in judgment where freedom is endangered are perhaps inevitable, there should, nevertheless, be more basic agreement on fundamentals. In this field we should be natural allies, working more closely for the common cause against the common enemy.

Third and finally, I would stress the great potential gain for both groups resulting from increased political cooperation.

The American intellectual and scholar today must decide, as Goethe put it, whether he is to be an anvil—or a hammer. Today, for many, the stage of the anvil, at least in its formal phases, is complete. The question he faces is whether he is to be a hammer—whether he is to give to the world in which he was reared and educated the broadest possible benefits of his learning. As one who is familiar with the political world, I can testify that we need it.

For example: The password for all legislation, promoted by either party, is "progress." But how do we tell what is progress and what is retreat? Those of us who may be too close to the issue, or too politically or emotionally involved in it, look for the objective word of the scholar. Indeed, the operation of our political life is such that we may not even be debating the real issues.

In foreign affairs, for example, the parties dispute over which is best fitted to implement the long-accepted policies of collective security and Soviet containment. But perhaps these policies are no longer adequate, perhaps these goals are no longer meaningful—the debate goes on nevertheless, for neither party is in a position to undertake the reappraisal necessary, particularly if the solutions presented are more complex to, and less popular with, the electorate.

Or take our agricultural program, for another example. Republicans and Democrats debate long over whether flexible or rigid price supports should be in effect. But this may not be the real issue at all—and in fact I am convinced that it is not, that neither program offers any long-range solution to our many real farm problems. The scholars and the universities might reexamine this whole area and come up with some real answers—the political parties and their conventions rarely will.

Other examples could be given indefinitely—where do we draw the line between free trade and protection; when does taxation become prohibitive; what is the most effective use we can make of our present nuclear potential? The intellectuals who can draw upon their rational disinterested approach and their fund of learning to help reshape our political life can make a tremendous contribution to their society while gaining new respect for their own group.

I do not say that our political and public life should be turned over to experts who ignore public opinion. Nor would I adopt from the Belgian constitution of 1893 the provision giving three votes instead of one to college graduates; or give Harvard a seat in the Congress as William and Mary was once represented in the Virginia House of Burgesses.

But, I would urge that our political parties and our universities recognize the need for greater cooperation and understanding between politicians and intellectuals. We do not need scholars or politicians like Lord John Russell, of whom Queen Victoria remarked, "he would be a better man if he knew a third subject—but he was interested in nothing but the constitution of 1688 and himself." What we need are men who can ride easily over broad fields of knowledge and recognize the mutual dependence of our two worlds.

"Don't teach my boy poetry," an English mother recently wrote the provost of Harrow. "Don't teach my boy poetry; he is going to stand for Parliament." Well, perhaps she was right—but if more politicians knew poetry, and more poets knew politics, I am convinced the world would be a little better place in which to live on this commencement day of 1956.

Harvard University Commencement
Cambridge, Massachusetts, June 14, 1956

The Senate's Distinguished Traditions

Mr. President, as chairman of the Special Senate Committee on the Senate Reception Room, established by Senate Resolution 145 of the 84th Congress, as amended, I wish to report to the Senate that our committee has completed its deliberations, and its surveys of scholarly and senatorial opinion as described in the committee report, and recommends that there be placed in the five unfilled spaces in the Senate reception room paintings portraying the following five outstanding senators of the past:

Senator Henry Clay, of Kentucky, who served in the Senate 1806–7, 1810–11, 1831–42, 1849–52. Resourceful expert in the art of the possible, his fertile mind, persuasive voice, skillful politics, and tireless energies were courageously devoted to the reconciliation of conflict between North and South, East and West, capitalism and agrarianism. A political leader who put the national good above party, a spokesman for the West whose love for the Union outweighed sectional pressures, he acquired more influence and more respect as responsible leader of the loyal but ardent opposition than many who occupied the White House. His adroit statesmanship and political finesse in times of national crisis demonstrated the values of intelligent compromise in a federal democracy, without impairing either his convictions or his courage to stand by them.

Senator Daniel Webster, of Massachusetts, who served in the Senate 1827–41, 1845–50. Eloquent and articulate champion of "Liberty and Union, now and forever, one and inseparable," he grasped in an age of divided loyalties the full meaning of the American Constitution and of the supremacy and indissolubility of the national government. Molding the symbols of the Union he cherished so strongly that neither secession nor war could break them, his steadfast courage and powerful leadership in two of the Senate's most historic and critical debates were brilliantly portrayed in orations attentively heard and eagerly read. Influential spokesman for industrial expansion, his dedication to Union above all personal and partisan considerations overshadowed the petty moral insensitivities which never compromised his national principles; and his splendid dignity and decorum elevated the status and prestige of the Senate.

Senator John C. Calhoun, of South Carolina, who served in the Senate 1832–43, 1845–50. Forceful logician of state sovereignty, masterful defender of the rights of a political minority against the dangers of an unchecked majority, his profoundly penetrating and original understanding of the social bases of government has significantly influenced American political theory and practice. Sincerely devoted to the public good as he saw it, the ultimate tragedy of his final cause neither detracts from the greatness of his leadership nor tarnishes his efforts to avert bloodshed. Outspoken yet respected, intellectual yet beloved, his leadership on every major issue in that critical era of transition significantly shaped the role of the Senate and the destiny of the nation.

Senator Robert M. La Follette, Sr., of Wisconsin, who served in the Senate 1906–25. Ceaseless battler for the underprivileged in an age of special privilege, courageous independent in an era of partisan conformity, he fought memorably against tremendous odds and stifling inertia for social and economic reforms which ultimately proved essential to American progress in the twentieth century. Determined to make law serve the rights of persons as well as property, to make government serve the interests of great social justice as well as great political parties, his constructive pioneering efforts to promote the general welfare aroused the slumbering conscience of the nation and made the Senate more responsive to it. The bitter antagonisms stirred by his unyielding opposition to international commitments and conflict were ultimately submerged by widespread admiration for his dedicated lifelong fight against political corruption and corporate greed.

Senator Robert A. Taft, of Ohio, who served in the Senate 1939–53. The conscience of the conservative movement, its ablest exponent and most constructive leader, his high integrity, analytical mind, and sheer industry quickly won him a select spot in the councils of his party and the hearts of all his colleagues. His Senate leadership transcended partisanship; his political courage and candor put principles above ambition. Dedicated to the Constitution and the American tradition of individual rights as his keen legal mind interpreted them, he demonstrated the importance of a balanced and responsible opposition in an age of powerful governments.

Speaking only for myself, I will say to the Senate that I had the most difficulty excluding from the list three other outstanding senators of the past:

George Norris, of Nebraska, one of the most courageous, dedicated men ever to sit in the Senate, and one whose influence on the public power, agricultural, labor, and political aspects of this nation will long endure.

Thomas Hart Benton, of Missouri, the great "Nestor of the Senate" from 1820 to 1850, who on more than one occasion took on the Great Triumvirate individually and collectively and bested them in the Senate itself; and Oliver Ellsworth, of Connecticut, the outstanding figure in the first Senate, who authorized the Federal Judiciary Act that will always remain a monument to his genius, and shepherded the Bill of Rights through the Senate.

Many others deserve recognition, [including]:

Alben W. Barkley, of Kentucky.
William Borah, of Idaho.
Stephen Douglas, of Illinois.
Carter Glass, of Virginia.
Justin Smith Morrill, of Vermont.
John Sherman, of Ohio.
Charles Sumner, of Massachusetts.
Lyman Trumbull, of Illinois.
Oscar Underwood, of Alabama.
Arthur Vandenberg, of Michigan.

Robert Wagner, of New York.
Thomas Walsh, of Montana.

. . . The committee has selected Senators Robert M. La Follette, Sr., of Wisconsin, and Robert A. Taft, of Ohio, as outstanding representatives of the progressive and conservative movements in the twentieth century. We realize, of course, that considerable controversy and sentiment still surround each of them; that it is impossible to prove that they deserve the honor more than Norris or Vandenberg, for example, or Borah, Carter Glass, Barkley, Wagner, Walsh, Underwood, or any among a dozen others who were seriously considered; and that whatever names are chosen from the twentieth century will appear to suffer in comparison with the Great Triumvirate.

Nevertheless, the committee believed La Follette and Taft to be the most appropriate choices under the terms of the resolution—particularly in view of the way in which they symbolized the progressive and conservative points of view on the great domestic issue that confronted the Senate during this century: the proper role of governmental activity in the economic and social life of this country.

Nevertheless, because of the controversy still surrounding the names of Taft and La Follette, it is important to recall that Clay, Calhoun, and Webster in their own times did not always enjoy the wide recognition of their talents that posterity has given them. Listen, for example, to these words spoken about Henry Clay: "He prefers the specious to the solid, and the plausible to the true. . . . He is a bad man, an impostor, a creator of wicked schemes."

Those words were spoken by John C. Calhoun, who ridiculed Clay's lack of education, moral conduct, and short temper. Daniel Webster said Clay was his "inferior in many respects"; and Andrew Jackson once characterized him as being as "reckless and as full of fury as a drunken man in a brothel." On the other hand, who was it that said that John C. Calhoun was a rigid, fanatic, ambitious, selfishly partisan, and sectional turncoat, with "too much genius and too little common sense," who would either die a traitor or a madman? Henry Clay, of course. When Calhoun boasted in debate that he had been Clay's political master, Clay retorted, "Sir, I would not own him as a slave." Both Clay and Calhoun from time to time fought with Webster; and from the other House the articulate John Quincy Adams viewed with alarm "the gigantic intellect, the envious temper, the ravenous ambition, and the rotten heart of Daniel Webster."

And yet our committee has selected Henry Clay, Daniel Webster, and John C. Calhoun—and felt it had no other choice. For over thirty years they dominated the Congress and the country, providing leadership and articulation on all the great issues of the growing nation—the tariff, fiscal policies, foreign relations, defense, internal improvements, agriculture, industrial development, westward expansion, states' rights, and slavery. From time to time they supported and opposed each other for the Presidency that each desired but never achieved. And despite whatever bitter words passed between them, their mutual respect for each other remained high. "I don't like Henry Clay," said John Calhoun, "I would not speak to him, but by God, I love him." Whatsoever Calhoun's aspirations, said Webster, "they were high, honorable, and noble. There was nothing groveling or low or nearly selfish that came near the head or the heart of Mr. Calhoun."

Henry Clay predicted that Calhoun's principles would "descend to posterity under the sanction of a great name." And whatever John Quincy Adams may have thought of Webster's "rotten heart," he considered his celebrated reply to Hayne to be the "most significant [act] since the founding of the Constitution."

This is not to say that objections cannot be raised to each of the three. Criticism of Henry Clay's moral conduct, scholarship, and political schemes may well be justified; and there are those who feel he carried the principle of compromise too far. It is true that Clay said, "It is a rule with me, when acting either in a public or a private character, to attempt nothing more than what there exists a prospect of accomplishment." And yet his spirit of compromise, in the words of Carl Schurz, "was illumined by a grand conception of the destinies of his country, a glowing national spirit, a lofty patriotism." His greatest anxiety was the preservation of the Union; and few did more to contribute toward its salvation. Abraham Lincoln called the Great Pacificator "my beau ideal of a statesman, the man for whom I fought all my humble life." An extraordinarily gifted figure, his brilliant oratorical talents, unusual vitality, and a unique gift of winning the hearts as well as the minds of his countrymen all enabled his three great compromise proposals in 1820, 1833, and 1850 to save the Union until it grew strong enough to save itself. "No other American politician," as Vernon Parrington has observed, "has been so loved by a hero-worshiping electorate—and so lovable."

Daniel Webster, it is true, portrayed, in the words of one of his intimate friends, an extraordinary "compound of strength and weakness, dust and divinity." It is true that he accepted a retainer from Nicholas Biddle of the Bank of the United States; that he accepted favors from the New England manufacturers; and that his decisions both as a senator and as a secretary of state appear to have been open to improper influence. Yet there is no serious evidence that his views on the bank, the tariff, and foreign policy would have been any different without these dubious connections—and, on the contrary, Professor Allan Nevins has written that he demonstrated more than any other colleague real insight into the problems of public finance, moderate protectionism, and international affairs. Whatever may have been petty about his financial affairs, there was nothing petty about his moral stature in times of national crisis or in his dedication to the Union.

The same answer, I believe, can be given to those objecting to the views entertained and defended by John C. Calhoun. "He was wrong," Pulitzer prize–winning historian Arthur Schlesinger, Jr., wrote us, "but he was a greater man and Senator than many people who have been right." In defending the views of his state and section on the practice of slavery, abhorrent to all of us today but a constitutionally recognized practice in his time, Calhoun was yielding to neither the pressures of expediency nor immorality—nor did his opponents at the time so regard it. Calhoun was not a proponent of disunion. Though he warned at the end of his career that secession might be the South's only means of achieving justice, he fought long and hard to keep the South in the Union.

Generally judged to be the most notable political thinker ever to sit in the Senate, whose doctrine of concurrent majorities has permanently influenced our political theory and practice, John Calhoun did more than any other senator in the nineteenth century, in the words of Professor Nevins, "to make men think clearly and carefully on fundamental political questions."

I conclude by stressing once again that I believe this project to have had for this body considerable value beyond the basic necessity for its creation. It is the committee's hope that the considerable interest evoked by this project will be of value at a time when the democratic way of life is under pressure from without and the problems and conflicting pressures involved in the political profession are frequently misunderstood within our own country. The committee has attempted in a small way to focus the nation's attention upon the Senate and its distinguished traditions, upon the high quality of men who have served in the Senate, and upon the significant role that the Senate has played in the history of our nation. The members of the special committee thus hope that an increasing awareness of national and senatorial history which should not be forgotten will be of benefit to the general public and to the Senate itself.

United States Senate
Washington, D.C., May 1, 1957

The Best People We Can Get

If we are to be successful in the days to come, if we are to implement a program for the 1960s, then we need a government that is honest, a government that is efficient, a government that is dedicated, a government that is committed solely to the public interest.

One cannot make such sweeping promises without recognizing that these promises have been made before. Every challenger for public office, especially for the Presidency, talks about a great crusade to end corruption; to obtain government clean as a hound's tooth. But experience has shown that promises are not enough. For ours is a government of men, not of promises, and some men yield to temptation. Other men lack discrimination, and other men see no wrong in pursuing their private interest in their public capacity.

The problem is not merely one of deep freezes and vicuna coats. Less flamboyant but at least equally flagrant are the cases of those who use their office to obtain contracts for firms in which they have a financial interest. Those who use their position to repay political or financial debts, those who extract [personal gain] from the information they receive, or the power they wield. These cases are not only tragic in the public sense, in terms of justice denied, of taxes wasted, of problems ignored. These tragedies have their private effects as well, for cheating in the government cannot help but affect cheating in the classroom, on the quiz show, in the expense account.

The appointment of good men, moreover, is not a matter of morality alone. It may not be unethical to appoint an ambassador who is not acquainted with the language or the problems of the countries involved, but it is harmful to the interest of our nation. It may not be immoral to appoint to key positions men drawn only from the area of private business who intend to return to that business as soon as possible. But the national interest cannot be maintained by men in our Defense Department with an average tenure of less than one year.

It may not be improper to confine presidential appointees to the members of one party, but the whole nation was the beneficiary of the service of Stimson, Knox, Forrestal, McCloy, and Lovett. Yet I cannot recall in the last eight years a single major member of my party who has been appointed to a high position in the national security field, in Defense or in State, with the exception of one man, the ambassador to Germany, Mr. David Bruce.

And if we are to open employment opportunities in this country for members of all races and creeds, then the federal government must set an example. There are twenty-six Negroes in the Foreign Service of the United States, and there are six thousand members of the Foreign Service. There is not a district judge, federal district judge, who is a Negro, in the United States, and there are more than two hundred. There are messengers, laborers, clerks, but very few heads of departments. . . . It is an interesting fact today that Africa has one fourth, or will shortly have, of all the votes of the General Assembly. And yet twenty-six Negroes, spread throughout the entire world, are speaking for us as a source of democracy in this country. I believe we can do better.

The President himself must set the key example. I am not going to promise a Cabinet post or any other post to any race or ethnic group. That is racism in reverse at its worst. So I do not promise to consider race or religion in my appointments if I am successful. I promise only that I will not consider them.

If we are going to keep the cost of living in line and protect the interest of the consumers, then those agencies which regulate the cost of the public services must be dedicated to that mission and not concern themselves with future employment or personalities. I am making no charges and mentioning no names, for history teaches us that no political party has a monopoly on honesty. Both parties attract their share of crooks and weaklings. But that does not mean that these problems are incapable of solution. That does not mean that a campaign promise is enough. A new administration must screen out those who regard government service as a door to power or wealth; those who cannot distinguish between private gain and the public interest, and those who believe that old-fashioned honesty with the public's money is both old and out of fashion. The next President himself must set the moral tone, and I refer not only to his language, but to his actions in office. For the Presidency, as Franklin Roosevelt himself has said, is preeminently a place of moral leadership. And I intend, if successful, to try to restore that leadership and atmosphere beginning in 1961.

Should I be elected President, it would be my intention to ask the ablest men in the country to make whatever sacrifice is required to bring to the government a ministry of the best talents available, men with a single-minded loyalty to the national interest, men who would regard public office as a public trust. For no government is better than the men who compose it, and I want the best, and we need the best, and we deserve the best.

It would further be my intention at the earliest possible opportunity to submit to the Congress a single comprehensive code on conflicts of interest, aimed at eliminating duplications, inadvertencies and gaps, drawing a clearer line between propriety and impropriety, and protecting the public against unethical behavior without making it impossible for the able and conscientious citizen to serve his government.

It would also be my intention, through executive orders, the appointing power and legislation, to reform and streamline our lagging administrative agencies. Of all the undiscussed problems of this campaign, one of the most important is the fact that it takes from one year to three years for a businessman, a labor union, an interest involved, to get a decision out of our national government, and justice delayed is justice denied. It would not have been necessary, perhaps, for us to have passed a labor-management reform bill a year ago if it did not require three years for the National Labor Relations Board to give the employer or the employee involved relief.

We have to do better than this if this great bureaucracy of ours, if this great government of ours, is going to function in the sixties. We have to prepare it for motion, we have to prepare it to move, we have to get the best people we can get, and then we have to organize our structure so that they can act. And that is not the situation today.

I therefore take this opportunity to give you the eight basic principles which I would use if elected President as a guide to the appointment and conduct of those who would serve in a new administration. It is not complete, but I think it does suggest at least the spirit with which we shall move.

First, no officer or employee of the executive branch shall use his official position for financial profit or personal gain, or reveal to others confidential information acquired through his position.

Second, no officer or employee shall engage in any business transactions with, or hold any financial interest in, or accept any gift, favor, or substantial hospitality for himself and his family from, any enterprise or person who is doing business or seeking to do business with that unit of the government which he serves, or is able to influence, or who is subject to regulation, investigation, or litigation under the jurisdiction of that unit. To be above criminality is not enough. Good judgment is also required.

The next President himself must set the moral tone, and I refer not only to his language, but to his actions in office. . . .

Third, all gifts which cannot appropriately be refused, such as gifts from public organizations or from foreign governments to the President of the United States, shall immediately be assigned to the Smithsonian Institution or other federal agencies for historic, scientific, or welfare use. The President must set the example. . . .

Fourth, no federal appointee to any public regulatory agency shall represent any view other than the public interest. . . . It has been unfortunate in both parties that . . . because public attention has passed away from these agencies, it is difficult to get the best talent to come to Washington and work. But we have to do it, because your future, the future of this country, is tied up with the quality of our leadership in all branches of our national service.

Fifth, no member of any such agency, and no person who assists in its decisions, shall entertain any ex parte communication from any person, including political pressure or requests originating within the executive or legislative branches. . . . And all communications from the executive branch or the legislative branch shall be made a part of the record, the public record, and every party in interest given an opportunity to reply. As Finley Peter Dunne's "Mr. Dooley" used to say, "Trust everyone, but cut the cards."

Sixth, all appointments, both high and low, will be made on the basis of ability, without regard to race, creed, national origin, sex, or occupation. Campaign contributions—and this may be bad news for us, at least for the next three weeks—campaign contributions will not be regarded as a substitute for training and experience for diplomatic positions. And appointees shall be drawn from all segments of the community, wherever the best talent can be found. This will not be a businessman's administration with "business in the saddle," as Secretary McKay [of the Interior] once described his mission. But neither will it be a labor administration or a farmers' administration. It will be an administration for and by the people.

Seventh, senior positions in the State Department, the Foreign Service, the Defense Department shall be filled by the best talent in both parties, and from the ranks of career diplomats and civil servants, and officials engaged primarily in the conduct of foreign and defense activities will not be permitted to participate actively in political campaigns. I do not want our politics colored by considerations of national security, and I do not want our national security colored by considerations of politics.

Eighth, and finally, preferences in appointments will be given to those willing to commit themselves to stay on the job long enough to learn what they must learn. The goal is a full-time effort for the full tenure of the presidential term, without regard to any prior affiliation or prospective employment. The prospects for the nation in the coming years are not easy. The tasks facing the President will not be easy, and no appointee should assume that his life will be any easier.

These eight guidelines are not a magic formula for achieving a government perfect in all its parts. All human weaknesses cannot be avoided. All errors of judgment cannot be predicted. A code of ethics by itself may be found to be either too general to be meaningful or too specific to be enforceable. But these guidelines can illustrate the atmosphere, a tone of government, an attitude which the new President must take. We emphasize this basic principle: The essence of any government that belongs to the people must lie in the biblical injunction, "No man can serve two masters, for either he will hate one and love the other, or else he will hold to one and despise the other." All America seeks a government in which no man holds to his own interest and despises the public interest, and where all men serve only the public and love that master well. . . .

I hope, in closing, that all of you who are students at this college will consider during your lifetime embarking on a career of public service. In the next ten years we are going to try to develop in this country a sense of the public interest comparable or superior to what the Soviet Union is able to develop in its country by power of the police state. How many young students at this college are willing to spend part of their lives in Africa or Latin America or Asia, are willing to spend part of their time in this college learning not merely French or Spanish or Italian, but learning some of the esoteric dialects of India or Africa, learning something about those countries, preparing themselves as doctors or teachers or engineers or scientists or nurses, or public health officials, or Foreign Service officers, to contribute part of your talents, part of the benefits of your education to society as a whole? This college was not founded and has not been maintained merely to give this school's graduates an economic advantage in the life struggle. There is a higher purpose. Professor Woodrow Wilson said that every man sent out from a college should be a man of his time as well as a man of his nation. I ask you to consider how you can best use the talents which society is now helping develop in you in order to maintain that free society. All of us are involved in the discipline of self-government. All of us in this country, in a sense, are officeholders. All of us make an important decision as to what this country must be and how it must move and what its function shall be, and what its image shall be, and whether it shall stand still, as I believe it is now doing, or whether it shall once again move forward.

Wittenberg College
Springfield, Ohio, October 17, 1960

. . . The President of the United States represents not only the Democrats of this country, he represents all of the people around the world who want to live in freedom, who look to us for hope and leadership.

I must say that if I am elected President of the United States, I am not going to attempt only to select men for positions of high leadership who happen to have the word "Democrat" after their name.

When Franklin Roosevelt became President in 1932 he selected three Republicans to be members of his first Cabinet. When President Truman was the President, he selected men like John McCloy, Robert Lovett. He kept on men like James Forrestal. He brought John Foster Dulles into the State Department to negotiate the Japanese treaty. He secured for the great positions of responsibility the best men and women he could get.

That is what we are going to do in the future. . . . In spite of all the debate between political parties, we have a common interest today to select the best people we can get, people who recognize the kind of state we live in, the kind of country we live in, the kind of world we live in; people who look to the future, who are ready to break into that future, who are ready to lead, and who want this country to move again.

Campaign Speech
Bangor, Maine, September 2, 1960

ty Upon a Hill

I have welcomed this opportunity to address this historic body and, through you, the people of Massachusetts to whom I am so deeply indebted for a lifetime of friendship and trust. For fourteen years I have placed my confidence in the citizens of Massachusetts—and they have generously responded by placing their confidence in me.

Now, on the Friday after next, I am to assume new and broader responsibilities. But I am not here to bid farewell to Massachusetts. For forty-three years—whether I was in London, or in Washington, or in the South Pacific, or elsewhere—this has been my home; and, God willing, wherever I serve, this shall remain my home.

It was here my grandparents were born—it is here I hope that my grandchildren will be born.

I speak neither from false provincial pride nor artful political flattery. For no man about to enter high office in this country can ever be unmindful of the contribution which this state has made to our national greatness. Its leaders have shaped our destiny since long before the great Republic was born.

Its principles have guided our footsteps in times of crisis as well as in times of calm. Its democratic institutions—including this historic body—have served as beacon lights for other nations as well as your sister states. For what Pericles said of the Athenians has long been true of this commonwealth:

"We do not imitate—for we are a model to others"

And so it is that I carry with me from this state to that high and lonely office to which I now succeed more than fond memories and firm friendships. The enduring qualities of Massachusetts—the common threads woven by the Pilgrim and the Puritan, the fisherman and the farmer, the Yankee and the immigrant—will not be and could not be forgotten in this nation's executive mansion. They are an indelible part of my life, my conviction, my view of the past, and my hopes for the future.

Allow me to illustrate: During the last sixty days I have been engaged in the task of constructing an administration. It has been a long and deliberate process. Some have counseled greater speed. Others have counseled more expedient tests.

For of those to whom much is given, much is required.

But I have been guided by the standard John Winthrop set before his shipmates on the flagship *Arabella* 331 years ago, as they, too, faced the task of building a new government on a new and perilous frontier.

"We must always consider," he said, "that we shall be as a city upon a hill—the eyes of all people are upon us."

Today, the eyes of all people are truly upon us—and our government, in every branch, at every level, national, state and local, must be as a city upon a hill—constructed and inhabited by men aware of their grave trust and their great responsibilities.

For we are setting out upon a voyage in 1961 no less hazardous than that undertaken by the *Arabella* in 1630. We are committing ourselves to tasks of statecraft no less awesome than that of governing the Massachusetts Bay Colony, beset as it then was by terror without and disorder within.

History will not judge our endeavors—and a government cannot be selected—merely on the basis of color or creed or even party affiliation. Neither will competence and loyalty and stature, while essential to the utmost, suffice in times such as these.

For of those to whom much is given, much is required. And when at some future date the high court of history sits in judgment on each one of us—recording whether in our brief span of service we fulfilled our responsibilities to the state—our success or failure, in whatever office we hold, will be measured by the answers to four questions:

First, were we truly men of courage—with the courage to stand up to one's enemies—and the courage to stand up, when necessary, to one's own associates—the courage to resist public pressure as well as private greed?

Secondly, were we truly men of judgment—with perceptive judgment of the future as well as the past—of our own mistakes as well as the mistakes of others—with enough wisdom to know what we did not know, and enough candor to admit it?

Third, were we truly men of integrity—men who never ran out on either the principles in which we believed or the people who believed in us—men whom neither financial gain nor political ambition could ever divert from the fulfillment of our sacred trust?

Finally, were we truly men of dedication—with an honor mortgaged to no single individual or group, and compromised by no private obligation or aim, but devoted solely to serving the public good and the national interest?

Courage—judgment—integrity—dedication—these are the historic qualities of the Bay Colony and the Bay State—the qualities which this state has consistently sent to this chamber here on Beacon Hill in Boston and to Capitol Hill back in Washington.

And these are the qualities which, with God's help, this son of Massachusetts hopes will characterize our government's conduct in the four stormy years that lie ahead.

Humbly I ask His help in this undertaking—but aware that on earth His will is worked by men, I ask for your help and your prayers, as I embark on this new and solemn journey.

Massachusetts State Legislature
Boston, Massachusetts, January 9, 1961

The Pride of a Public Career

. . . I would like to conclude with a few remarks about the state of the executive branch. We have found it full of honest and useful public servants—but their capacity to act decisively at the exact time action is needed has too often been muffled in the morass of committees, timidities, and fictitious theories which have created a growing gap between decision and execution, between planning and reality. In a time of rapidly deteriorating situations at home and abroad, this is bad for the public service and particularly bad for the country; and we mean to make a change.

I have pledged myself and my colleagues in the Cabinet to a continuous encouragement of initiative, responsibility, and energy in serving the public interest. Let every public servant know, whether his post is high or low, that a man's rank and reputation in this administration will be determined by the size of the job he does, and not by the size of his staff, his office, or his budget. Let it be clear that this administration recognizes the value of dissent and daring, that we greet healthy controversy as the hallmark of healthy change. Let the public service be a proud and lively career. And let every man and woman who works in any area of our national government, in any branch, at any level, be able to say with pride and with honor in future years: "I served the United States government in that hour of our nation's need."

State of the Union Address
The Capitol, Washington, D.C., January 30, 1961

The Peace Corps

I have today signed an executive order providing for the establishment of a Peace Corps on a temporary pilot basis. I am also sending to Congress a message proposing authorization of a permanent Peace Corps. This Corps will be a pool of trained American men and women sent overseas by the U.S. government or through private institutions and organizations to help foreign countries meet their urgent needs for skilled manpower.

It is our hope to have five hundred or more people in the field by the end of the year.

The initial reactions to the Peace Corps proposal are convincing proof that we have, in this country, an immense reservoir of such men and women—anxious to sacrifice their energies and time and toil to the cause of world peace and human progress.

In establishing our Peace Corps we intend to make full use of the resources and talents of private institutions and groups. Universities, voluntary agencies, labor unions, and industry will be asked to share in this effort—contributing diverse sources of energy and imagination—making it clear that the responsibility for peace is the responsibility of our entire society.

We will only send abroad Americans who are wanted by the host country—who have a real job to do—and who are qualified to do that job. Programs will be developed with care, and after full negotiation, in order to make sure that the Peace Corps is wanted and will contribute to the welfare of other people. Our Peace Corps is not designed as an instrument of diplomacy or propaganda or ideological conflict. It is designed to permit our people to exercise more fully their responsibilities in the great common cause of world development.

Life in the Peace Corps will not be easy. There will be no salary and allowances will be at a level sufficient only to maintain health and meet basic needs. Men and women will be expected to work and live alongside the nationals of the country in which they are stationed—doing the same work, eating the same food, talking the same language.

But if the life will not be easy, it will be rich and satisfying. For every young American who participates in the Peace Corps—who works in a foreign land—will know that he or she is sharing in the great common task of bringing to man that decent way of life which is the foundation of freedom and a condition of peace.

Statement Released to the Press
Washington, D.C., March 1, 1961

The New Ethical Standard

No responsibility of government is more fundamental than the responsibility of maintaining the highest standards of ethical behavior by those who conduct the public business. There can be no dissent from the principle that all officials must act with unwavering integrity, absolute impartiality, and complete devotion to the public interest. This principle must be followed not only in reality but in appearance. For the basis of effective government is public confidence, and that confidence is endangered when ethical standards falter or appear to falter.

I have firm confidence in the integrity and dedication of those who work for our government. Venal conduct by public officials in this country has been comparatively rare—and the few instances of official impropriety that have been uncovered have usually not suggested any widespread departure from high standards of ethics and moral conduct.

Nevertheless, in the past two decades, incidents have occurred to remind us that the laws and regulations governing ethics in government are not adequate to the changed role of the federal government, or to the changing conditions of our society. In addition, many of the ethical problems confronting our public servants have become so complex as to defy easy commonsense solutions on the part of men of goodwill seeking to observe the highest standards of conduct, and solutions have been hindered by lack of general regulatory guidelines. As a result many thoughtful observers have expressed concern about the moral tone of government, and about the need to restate basic principles in their application to contemporary facts.

Of course, public officials are not a group apart. They inevitably reflect the moral tone of the society in which they live. And if that moral tone is injured—by fixed athletic contests or television quiz shows; by widespread business conspiracies to fix prices; by the collusion of businessmen and unions with organized crime; by cheating on expense accounts, by the ignoring of traffic laws, or by petty tax evasion—then the conduct of our government must be affected. Inevitably, the moral standards of a society influence the conduct of all who live within it—the governed and those who govern.

The ultimate answer to ethical problems in government is honest people in a good ethical environment. No web of statute or regulation, however intricately conceived, can hope to deal with the myriad possible challenges to a man's integrity or his devotion to the public interest. Nevertheless, formal regulation is required—regulation which can lay down clear guidelines of policy, punish venality and double-dealing, and set a general ethical tone for the conduct of public business.

Such regulation—while setting the highest moral standards—must not impair the ability of the government to recruit personnel of the highest quality and capacity. Today's government needs men and women with a broad range of experience, knowledge, and ability. It needs increasing numbers of people with topflight executive talent. It needs hundreds of occasional and intermittent consultants and part-time experts to help deal with problems of increasing complexity and technical difficulty. In short, we need to draw upon America's entire reservoir of talent and skill to help conduct our generation's most important business—the public business.

Perhaps the gravest responsibility of all rests upon the office of President. No President can excuse or pardon the slightest deviation from irreproachable standards of behavior on the part of any member of the executive branch.

This need to tap America's human resources for public purposes has blurred the distinctions between public and private life. It has led to a constant flow of people in and out of business, academic life, and government. It has required us to contract with private institutions and call upon part-time consultants for important public work. It has resulted in a rapid rate of turnover among career government employees —as high as twenty percent a year. And, as a result, it has gravely multiplied the risk of conflicts of interest while seriously complicating the problem of maintaining ethical standards. . . .

To meet this need for statutory reform, I am transmitting to the Congress a proposed Executive Employees' Standards Act—a comprehensive revision of existing conflict-of-interest statutes. I believe that this bill maintains the highest possible standards of conduct, eliminates the technical deficiencies and anachronisms of existing laws, and makes it possible for the government to mobilize a wide range of talent and skill. . . .

Ultimately, high ethical standards can be maintained only if the leaders of government provide a personal example of dedication to the public service—and exercise their leadership to develop in all government employees an increasing sensitivity to the ethical and moral conditions imposed by public service. Their own conduct must be above reproach. And they must go beyond the imposition of general regulations to deal with individual problems as they arise—offering informal advice and personal consideration. It will often be difficult to assess the propriety of particular actions. In such subtle cases honest disclosure will often be the surest solution, for the public will understand good faith efforts to avoid improper use of public office when they are kept informed.

I realize, too, that perhaps the gravest responsibility of all rests upon the office of President. No President can excuse or pardon the slightest deviation from irreproachable standards of behavior on the part of any member of the executive branch. For his firmness and determination is the ultimate source of public confidence in the government of the United States. And there is no consideration that can justify the undermining of that confidence.

Special Message to Congress on Ethics in Government
Washington, D.C., April 27, 1961

The Obligations of Citizenship

Dear Mrs. Patterson:

Many thanks for your wire of May fourth. I appreciate your interest in our nation's needs and the spirit that motivates your telegram.

Apparently the demands of the "Cold War" are not as dramatic, and thus not as well-identified, as the demands of the traditional "shooting war"—such as rationing (which we do not need), a doubling of draft quotas (which would not help), or an increase in personal income taxes (which would only impede the recovery of our economic strength).

But that does not mean that nothing is being asked of our citizens. The facts of the matter are that all the programs I am seeking—to strengthen our economy, our defenses, our image abroad, our balance of payments position and our foreign policy tools—all make demands upon one or more groups of Americans, and most often upon all Americans jointly. All of them involve some effort, some inconvenience or some sacrifice—and, indeed, they are being opposed in some quarters on that basis.

For example: I have asked that we provide a leaner, more efficient defense establishment by terminating certain projects and closing a good many bases, although there are many protests from those who want economy practiced in someone else's community. I have asked that a major effort in foreign aid to other nations be maintained for many years to come, as burdensome as some regard it. I have asked young Americans to serve without pay or comfort in a Peace Corps for underdeveloped countries; I have asked many talented individuals to give up a higher income to serve their country in public office (and not all have been willing to do so); and I have asked all government officials to give up any incompatible financial interests.

I have asked that our excise and corporation tax rates not be permitted to fall as scheduled by law—that trucking companies and jet airline companies pay a higher tax for the highways and airways they use—that our business corporations pay a higher payroll tax for improved Social Security, unemployment compensation, and health insurance—and that certain taxpayers give up their privileges of expense account living, in yachts, hunting lodges, nightclubs, and all the rest. I have asked all Americans to help meet our deficit through higher postal rates. These requests for sacrifice are being strongly resisted by some unwilling to pay the price of national greatness.

I have asked other Americans to contribute to the strengthening of our economy by paying a decent minimum wage, to give up their right to purchase as many duty-free goods when they are traveling abroad—or, if they are farmers, to accept the limitations of our feed grain program. I have asked our businessmen and labor leaders, through my Advisory Committee, to adopt price and wage levels consistent with our economic goals and need to compete; and, more directly, I have asked them to take steps that will avoid harmful work stoppages in our missile and space effort.

I have asked the newspaper industry, without much success, to exercise more self-restraint in publishing intelligence data helpful to any enemy. My messages on education, urban affairs, and natural resources have all stressed the role the local community must assume if we are to make the most of our schools, our cities, and our water and other resources. We have made clear our very strong request to employers, labor unions, and indeed all citizens for an end to racial discrimination.

I have tried to make the whole tone and thrust of this office and this administration one that will demand a higher standard of excellence from every individual in his private life—in his education, his physical fitness, his attitudes toward foreign visitors, his obligations as a citizen, and all the rest.

And finally, each time we make any move or commitment in foreign affairs, I am in need of the support of the American people, their understanding, their patience, their willingness to endure setbacks and risks and hardships in order that this country can regain leadership and initiative.

So I have asked quite a lot of the American people—and I have been gratified at their response. There is much more to be done. But I do not wish to be misinterpreted. I think we have the will as well as the resources to prevail. And I think we will.

Sincerely,
John F. Kennedy

Letter to Mrs. Alicia Patterson, Editor and Publisher,* Newsday, *in response to her telegram questioning the sincerity of the President's Inaugural summons, May 16, 1961

The Front Line of Service

I know that many Foreign Service officers feel (like former Marines, who believe that the old days were the best days) that the days before World War II were the golden days of the Foreign Service, that since then the Foreign Service has fallen on hard times and that there is a good deal of uncertainty about what the future may bring.

I would like to differ with that view completely. In my opinion, today, as never before, is the golden period of the Foreign Service.

In the days before the war, we dealt with a few countries and a few leaders. I remember what Ambassador Dawes said, that the job was hard on the feet and easy on the brain. Theodore Roosevelt talked about those who resided in the Foreign Service rather than working in it. We were an isolationist country, by tradition and by policy and by statute. And therefore those of you who lived in the Foreign Service led a rather isolated life, dealing with comparatively few people, uninvolved in the affairs of this country or in many ways in the affairs of the country to which you may have been accredited.

That is all changed now. The power and influence of the United States are involved in the national life of dozens of countries that did not exist before 1945, many of which are so hard-pressed.

This is the great period of the Foreign Service, much greater than any period that has gone before. And it will be so through this decade, and perhaps even more in the years to come, if we are able to maintain ourselves with success.

But it places the heaviest burdens upon all of you. Instead of becoming merely experts in diplomatic history, or in current clippings from *The New York Times,* now you have to involve yourselves in every element of foreign life—labor, the class struggle, cultural affairs, and all the rest —attempting to predict in what direction the forces will move. The ambassador has to be the master of all these things, as well as knowing his own country. Now you have to know all about the United States, every facet of its life, all the great reforms of the thirties, the forties, and the fifties, if you are going to represent the United States powerfully and with strength and with vigor. When you represent the United States today, it is not a question of being accredited to a few people whose tenure is certain, but instead, of making predictions about what will be important events, what will be the elements of power or the elements of struggle, and which way we should move. And this calls for the finest judgment.

In the Foreign Service today you have a great chance and a great opportunity. And I hope that you recognize it, and realize that on your decisions hang the well-being and the future of this country.

There is a feeling, I think, in the Foreign Service, that the State Department and the Foreign Service are constantly under attack. Well, I would give two answers to that. In the first place, the questions with which you are dealing are so sophisticated and so technical that people who are not intimately involved week after week, month after month, reach judgments which are based upon emotion rather than knowledge of the real alternatives. They are bound to disagree and they are bound to focus their attacks upon the Department of State and upon the White House and upon the President of the United States. And in addition, party division in this country, where the parties are split almost evenly, and in spite of the long tradition of bipartisanship, accentuates the criticisms to which the Department of State and the White House are subjected.

If change were easy, everybody would change. But if you did not have change, you would have revolution. I think that change is what we need in a changing world, and therefore when we embark on new policies, we drag along all the anchors of old opinions and old views. You just have to put up with it. Those who cannot stand the heat should get out of the kitchen. Every member of Congress who subjects you to abuse is being subjected himself, every two years, to the possibility that his career also will come to an end. He doesn't live a charmed life. You have to remember that the hot breath is on him also, and it is on the Senate and it is on the President, and it is on everyone who deals with great matters.

This is not an easy career, to be a Foreign Service officer. It is not an easy life. The Foreign Service and the White House are bound to be in the center of every great controversy involving the security of the United States, and there is nothing you can do about it. You have to recognize that ultimately you will be subjected, as an institution, to the criticisms of the uninformed, and to attacks which are in many cases malicious and in many cases self-serving. But either you have to be able to put up with it, or you have to pick a more secluded spot.

Personally, I think the place to be is in the kitchen, and I am sure the Foreign Service officers of the United States feel the same way. . . . I regard the office of the Presidency and the White House, and the Secretary of State and the Department, as part of one chain, not separate but united, and committed to the maintenance of an effective foreign policy for the United States of America.

Therefore, in the final analysis, it depends on you.

That is why I believe this is the best period to be a Foreign Service officer. That is why I believe that the best talent that we have should come into the Foreign Service, because you today—even more than any other branch of government—are in the front line in every country of the world.

American Foreign Service Association
Washington, D.C., May 31, 1962

CHAPTER 4

The President and Congress

Because his party suffered a net loss of twenty-two seats in the House of Representatives in the 1960 election, Kennedy was warned upon entering the White House that conservative majorities in both houses would once again defeat the Democratic agenda that had long been stifled. But Kennedy wooed his congressional friends, both battled and bargained with his foes, and appealed, when necessary, to the American people. His first year as President saw passage of most of the measures previously stalled. His three years as President produced the most new legislation since the New Deal. He did not live to sign many of his principal proposals, including pioneer measures on civil rights, taxation, and education; but, undeterred by delay and defeat, he laid the groundwork for their ultimate enactment.

The Rules Committee Battle

Q: You said in the past, sir, that the President should be in the thick of the political battle, and I wondered, sir, if you could tell us what part you're playing in the effort to expand the Rules Committee and whether you feel your domestic program—whether the success of your domestic program in part depends on expanding the Rules Committee?

THE PRESIDENT: Well, the Constitution states that each house shall be the judge of its own rules, and therefore the Speaker of the House, Mr. Rayburn, has been extremely anxious that the House be permitted to settle this matter in its own way.

But it's no secret that I strongly believe that the members of the House should have an opportunity to vote themselves on the programs which we will present. . . . I'm hopeful that whatever judgment is made by the members of the House it will permit the members to vote on these bills. This is a very difficult time in the life of our country. Many controversial measures will be presented. . . . I hope a small group of men will not attempt to prevent the members from finally letting their judgments be known.

For example, we have the housing bill which is going to come before the Congress this year. We have an aid-to-education bill. We have legislation which will affect the income of farmers. Shouldn't the members of the House themselves and not merely the members of the Rules Committee have a chance to vote on those measures? But the responsibility rests with the members of the House, and I would not attempt in any way to infringe upon that responsibility. I merely give my view as an interested citizen.

President's News Conference
Washington, D.C., January 25, 1961

The Separate Responsibilities of Each Branch

It is a pleasure to return from whence I came. You are among my oldest friends in Washington—and this House is my oldest home. It was here, more than fourteen years ago, that I first took the oath of federal office. It was here, for fourteen years, that I gained both knowledge and inspiration from members of both parties in both houses—from your wise and generous leaders—and from the pronouncements which I can vividly recall sitting where you now sit—including the programs of two great Presidents, the undimmed eloquence of Churchill, the soaring idealism of Nehru, the steadfast words of General de Gaulle. To speak from this same historic rostrum is a sobering experience. To be back among so many friends is a happy one.

I am confident that that friendship will continue. Our Constitution wisely assigns both joint and separate roles to each branch of the government; and a President and Congress who hold each other in mutual respect will neither permit nor attempt any trespass. For my part, I shall withhold from neither the Congress nor the people any fact or report, past, present, or future, which is necessary for an informed judgment of our conduct and hazards. I shall neither shift the burden of executive decisions to the Congress, nor avoid responsibility for the outcome of those decisions.

State of the Union Address
The Capitol, Washington, D.C.
January 30, 1961

Members of the Congress, the Constitution makes us not rivals for power but partners for progress. We are all trustees for the American people, custodians of the American heritage. It is my task to report the State of the Union—to improve it is the task of us all.

In the past year, I have traveled not only across our own land but to other lands—to the North and the South, and across the seas. And I have found—as I am sure you have, in your travels—that people everywhere, in spite of occasional disappointments, look to us—not to our wealth or power, but to the splendor of our ideals. For our nation is commissioned by history to be either an observer of freedom's failure or the cause of its success.

State of the Union Address
The Capitol, Washington, D.C.
January 11, 1962

The Inevitable Accord and Discord

Q: Mr. President, I understand that an exchange of letters at the summit has settled the question of the B–70 or the RS–70. Can you tell us who won what and from whom?

THE PRESIDENT: Well, I think that if you took the powers of the executive and the powers of the Congress and pushed each to its logical, or at least its possible, conclusion—not its logical but its possible conclusion—you would have, in a government of divided powers, you would have a somewhat chaotic situation. If they refused to appropriate the salary of members of the government, if we took actions which failed to consider the responsibilities of the Congress—in a country where the Constitution gives divided responsibilities we have to attempt to adjust the strong feelings on both sides.

In my opinion, there was no winner and no loser except, I think, the relations between the Congress and I think the public interest [won].

President's News Conference
Washington, D.C., March 21, 1962

Q: Mr. President, according to Dr. Gallup's latest poll, there's been a sharp rise in pro-Republican sentiment in the Middle West and a parallel or opposite drop in your popularity stock of about ten points. Do you have any explanation of your own for this phenomenon, if it is one, and does it bother you with the administration facing now a midterm election?

THE PRESIDENT: Well, I think it said I dropped personally from seventy-nine percent to sixty-nine percent. I think that if I were still seventy-nine percent after a very intense congressional session I would feel that I had not met my responsibilities. The American people are rather evenly divided on a great many issues and as I make my views clearer on these issues, of course, some people increasingly are not going to approve of me. So I dropped to sixty-nine percent, and will probably drop some more. I don't think there is any doubt of that. President Eisenhower, I think, in the November election of 1954 was down to fifty-six percent. But he survived, and I suppose I will.

President's News Conference
Washington, D.C., July 23, 1962

MR. VANOCUR: . . . How do you use the Presidency, in Theodore Roosevelt's phrase "the bully pulpit," to move these men who really are kind of barons and sovereigns in their own right up there on the Hill? Have you any way to move them toward a course of action which you think is imperative?

THE PRESIDENT: Well, the Constitution and the development of the Congress all give advantage to delay. It is very easy to defeat a bill in the Congress. It is much more difficult to pass one. . . .

It is a tremendous change to go from being a senator to being a President. In the first months, it is very difficult. But I have no reason to believe that a President with the powers of this office and the responsibilities placed on it, if he has a judgment that some things need to be done, I think he can do it just as well the second time as the first, depending of course on the makeup of the Congress. The fact is I think the Congress looks more powerful sitting here than it did when I was there in the Congress. But that is because when you are in Congress you are one of a hundred in the Senate or one of four hundred and thirty-five in the House, so that the power is so divided. But from here I look at a Congress, and I look at the collective power of the Congress, particularly the bloc action, and it is a substantial power.

Television and Radio
Year-End Conversation with the President
Washington, D.C., December 17, 1962

Q: Mr. President, you have said that you are in favor of the two-term limit to the office of the Presidency. How do you feel about former president Eisenhower's suggestion that the terms of congressmen also be limited?

THE PRESIDENT: It's the sort of proposal which I may advance in a postpresidential period, but not right now.

President's News Conference
Washington, D.C., January 24, 1963

Q: Mr. President, back on the subject of Presidential advisers, Congressman Baring of Nevada, a Democrat, said you would do much better if you got rid of some of yours—and he named Bowles, Ball, Bell, Bunche, and Sylvester.

THE PRESIDENT: Yes, he has a fondness for alliteration and for "B's." And I would not add Congressman Baring to that list as I have a high regard for him and for the gentlemen that he named. But congressmen are always advising presidents to get rid of presidential advisers. That is one of the most constant threads that runs through American history and presidents ordinarily do not pay attention, nor do they in this case.

President's News Conference
Washington, D.C., May 8, 1963

On the campaign trail.

PHOTO BY HANK WALKER, LIFE MAGAZINE © TIME INC.

PART II

The Presidential Campaign

CHAPTER 5

The Road to the White House

Unlike many who attain high public office, John F. Kennedy continued to grow in mind and spirit throughout his service in Washington. His concern for his country, his compassion for others, his judgment, his skills as a speaker and leader, all expanded in each of his seventeen years in office. His political drive and instincts were heightened as well, and he became the first to conduct a four-year quest for the Presidency. Recognizing that his youth and religion would fatally handicap his chances for a nomination decided by power brokers in a convention "backroom," he outpaced, outorganized, and outsmarted his more powerful competitors for the nomination, winning a bare majority on the first ballot. By an equally exhaustive and exhausting effort that fall, in a campaign that even included some genuinely new and worthwhile proposals, he came from behind to nose out Richard Nixon for the Presidency.

The "Parochial" Young Congressman of 1952

MR. KENNEDY: Will the gentleman tell me why you allow in this bill $80 million for Oregon, around $37 million for California, and yet you reduce so drastically the money for the New England states? Five out of the six New England states will receive no money in this bill for any project.

MR. RABAUT: The gentleman from Massachusetts, since he has been on this floor today, has been strictly parochial in his arguments and viewpoint. I have not a dime in this bill for my district or for my state except some maintenance of some small harbors, so there is nothing in it for me. But all the gentleman has talked about since he has been here is New England.

MR. KENNEDY: Does the gentleman object to that?

MR. RABAUT: No; I do not object to it, but this is not a parochial bill; this is a bill for the benefit of the United States of America.

MR. KENNEDY: The point I want to make now is that New England is a part of the United States of America, and five out of the six New England states do not receive a penny of money from this nearly half-a-billion-dollar bill.

Colloquy, Floor of the U.S. House of Representatives,
Regarding Water Projects Appropriation Bill
Washington, D.C., April 1, 1952

The "National Interest" Senator of 1954

Mr. President, I am frank to admit that few issues during my service in the House of Representatives or the Senate have troubled me as much as the pending bill authorizing participation by the United States in the construction and operation of the St. Lawrence Seaway. As you may know, on six different occasions over a period of twenty years, no Massachusetts senator or representative has ever voted in favor of the seaway, and such opposition on the part of many of our citizens and officials continues to this day. . . .

The evidence appears to be conclusive that Canada will build the seaway.

Is it in the national interest of the United States that we participate in the construction, operation, and administration of the seaway as authorized by the Wiley bill? That question has been answered in the affirmative by every President, Secretary of Army and Defense, Secretary of Commerce, National Security Council, National Security Resources Board, and other administration officials for the past thirty years, including President Eisenhower and other representatives of his administration. The President stated in that part of his message on national defense:

> Both nations now need the St. Lawrence Seaway for security as well as for economic reasons. I urge the Congress promptly to approve our participation in its construction.

Mr. President, our ownership and control of a vital strategic international waterway along our own border would be lost without passage of this bill. If Canada builds the seaway alone, it may not only be a more expensive proposition, due to the difference in topography, requiring higher tolls over a longer period of time, but the seaway will still be paid for to a great extent by the American interests whose use thereof will be many times greater than the Canadians. Thus the economy of the United States will have paid for the greater part of the seaway at a higher cost, but the U.S. government will have no voice in the decisions regarding tolls, traffic, admission of foreign ships, defense and security measures, and priorities. Inasmuch as the United States is going to benefit both economically and militarily from the construction of the seaway, and inasmuch as the Wiley bill provides that the seaway will be self-liquidating, and require comparatively small appropriations over a five-year period, I believe that our participation is in the national interest, and, therefore, should not be defeated for sectional reasons. . . .

How will the St. Lawrence Seaway help Massachusetts? There have been a great many claims advanced along the lines that it would be of help to my state; but I have studied them with care and must say in all frankness that I think they are wholly speculative at best. I know of no direct economic benefit to the economy of Massachusetts or any segment thereof from the seaway, and I have been urged to oppose the seaway on these grounds, inasmuch as the initial investment, even though repaid, will come in part from Massachusetts tax revenues. . . .

But I am unable to accept such a narrow view of my function as U.S. Senator; and in speaking on the Senate floor on behalf of the New England economy I stressed my opposition to the idea that New England's interest is best served by opposing federal programs which contribute to the well-being of the country, particularly when those programs increase the purchasing power of New England's customers. Where federal action is necessary and appropriate, it is my firm belief that New England must fight for those national policies. . . .

Moreover, I have sought the support of senators from all sections of the country in my efforts on behalf of New England, pointing out to them not only the concern which they should have for an important region in our country, but also the fact that an increase in economic activity in New England would benefit the nation as a whole. For these reasons, I cannot oppose the seaway because the direct economic benefits will go largely to the Great Lakes and Middle Western areas. I could not conscientiously take such a position, and at the same time expect support from senators in the Middle West or any other part of the country for those programs and projects of aid to New England.

The seaway is going to be built; the only question is the part we shall play in opening our fourth coastline. To those in my state and elsewhere who oppose our participation in the construction of this project for national security merely because the economic benefits go elsewhere, I would say that it has been this arbitrary refusal of many New Englanders to recognize the legitimate needs and aspirations of other sections which has contributed to the neglect of, and even opposition to, the needs of our own region by the representatives of other areas. We cannot continue so narrow and destructive a position. As was so well stated by a famous Massachusetts senator over one hundred years ago, our aim should not be "States dissevered, discordant [or] belligerent"; but "one country, one constitution, one destiny."

United States Senate
Debate on St. Lawrence Seaway
Washington, D.C., January 14, 1954

The National Convention Speaker of 1956

We have come here today not merely to nominate a Democratic candidate, but to nominate a President of the United States.

Sometimes in the heat of a political convention, we forget the grave responsibilities which we as delegates possess. For we here today are selecting a man who must be something more than a good candidate, something more than a good speaker, more than a good politician, a good liberal, or a good conservative. We are selecting the head of the most powerful nation on earth, the man who literally will hold in his hands the powers of survival or destruction, of freedom or slavery, of success or failure for us all. We are selecting here today the man who for the next four years will be guiding, for good or evil, for better or worse, the destinies of our nation and, to a large extent, the destiny of the free world.

I ask you, therefore, to think beyond the balloting of tonight and tomorrow—to think beyond even the election in November and to think instead of those four years that lie ahead, and of the crises that will come with them.

Of overwhelming importance are the ever-mounting threats to our survival that confront us abroad, threats that require a prompt return to firm, decisive leadership. Each Republican year of indecision and hesitation has brought new Communist advances—in Indochina, in the Middle East, in North Africa, in all the tense and troubled areas of the world. The Grand Alliance of the West—that chain for freedom forged by Truman and Marshall and the rest—is cracking, its unity deteriorating, its strength dissipating. We are hesitant on Suez, silent on colonialism, uncertain on disarmament, and contradictory on the other major issues of the day. . . . Once we are able to cut through the slogans and the press releases and the vague reassurances, we realize to our shock and dismay that the next four years of this hydrogen age represent the most dangerous and the most difficult period in the history of our nation.

In such a period, one man, and one man only, can bear the full and final burden of responsibility and leadership—not his Cabinet, not his assistants, not his Vice-President—only the President of the United States himself. It is for these reasons that I ask this convention in its deliberations on the Presidency to consider those four troubled years that lie ahead, and the necessity of selecting a President with the courage and the vigor and the vision equal to the task.

And consider, too, the four years that face us as a nation at home. For here, too, the absence of new ideas, the lack of new leadership, the failure to keep pace with new developments, have all contributed to the growth of gigantic economic and social problems—problems that can perhaps be postponed or explained away or ignored now, but problems that during the next four years will burst forth with continuing velocity. The problem of the nation's distressed farmers, the problem of our declining small business, the problem of our maldistribution of economic gains, the problem of our hopelessly inadequate schools, the problem of our nation's health—and many more. . . . Conferences are held, to be sure—commissions are convened—but no new steps are taken and no bold programs are effected.

Ladies and gentlemen of the convention: it is now my privilege to present to this convention, as a candidate for President of the United States . . . the man from Libertyville—the next Democratic nominee and the next President of the United States—Adlai E. Stevenson.

These are problems that cry out for solution—they cry out for leadership—they cry out for a man equal to the times. And the Democratic Party can say to the nation today—we have such a man!

We can offer to the nation today a man uniquely qualified by inheritance, by training, and by conviction, to lead us out of this crisis of complacency, and into a new era of life and fulfillment. During the past four years his wise and perceptive analyses of the world crisis have pierced through the vacillations and the contradictions of official Washington to give understanding and hope to people at home and abroad. And his eloquent, courageous, and experienced outlook on our problems here at home have stood in shining contrast to the collection of broken promises, neglected problems, and dangerous blunders that pave the road from Gettysburg to the White House.

Of course, in a democracy, it is not enough to have the right man—for first he must be elected, he must show the nation that he is the right man, he must be a winner. And I say we have a winner—in the man who became governor of this state in 1948 with the largest majority in the history of Illinois—in the man who in 1956 has shown in primary after primary that he, and only he, is the top vote-getter in the Democratic Party today.

And let us be frank about the campaign that lies ahead. Our party will be up against two of the toughest, most skillful campaigners in its history—one who takes the high road, and one who takes the low. If we are to overcome that combination in November, this convention must nominate the candidate who can best carry our case to the American people—the one who is by all odds and by all counts our most eloquent, our most forceful, our most appealing figure.

The American people saw and heard and admired this man for the first time four years ago, when, out of the usual sea of campaign promises and dreary oratory and catchy slogans, there came something new and different, something great and good—a campaign and a candidate dedicated to telling the truth. Sometimes the truth hurt—sometimes it wasn't believed, sometimes it wasn't popular—but it was always the truth, the same truth, North, South, East and West. It was a campaign that brought home to the American people two great qualities of the candidate—his natural talent for government, which had previously been demonstrated in his able, efficient, and economical administration of the state of Illinois—and, secondly, his natural talent for campaigning, for meeting people of all kinds, under all circumstances, with a zest for hard work and a will to win.

These are, as I have said, critical times—times that demand the best we have, times that demand the best America has. We have, therefore, an obligation to pick the man best qualified, not only to lead our party, but to lead our country. The nation is entitled to expect that of us. For what we do here today affects more than a nomination, more than an election—it affects the life and the way of life of all of our fellow Americans.

The time is ripe. The hour has struck. The man is here; and he is ready. Let the word go forth that we have fulfilled our responsibility to the nation.

Ladies and gentlemen of the convention: it is now my privilege to present to this convention, as a candidate for President of the United States, the name of the man uniquely qualified—by virtue of his compassion, his conscience, and his courage—to follow in the great traditions of Jefferson, Jackson, Wilson, Roosevelt, and the man from Independence. Fellow Delegates, I give you the man from Libertyville—the next Democratic nominee and the next President of the United States—Adlai E. Stevenson.

Nomination of Adlai E. Stevenson for
President of the United States
Democratic National Convention
Chicago, Illinois, August 16, 1956

The Defeated Vice-Presidential Contender of 1956

I want to take this opportunity first to express my appreciation to Democrats from all parts of the country, North and South, East and West, who have been so generous and kind to me this afternoon. I think that it proves as nothing else can prove how strong and united the Democratic Party is.

Secondly, I think what has happened today bears out the good judgment of our Governor Stevenson in deciding that this issue should be taken to the floor of the convention.

I believe that the Democratic Party will go from this convention far stronger for what we have done here today. And therefore, ladies and gentlemen, recognizing that this convention has selected a man who has campaigned in all parts of the country, who has worked untiringly for the party, who will serve as an admirable running mate to Governor Stevenson, I hope that this convention will make Estes Kefauver's nomination unanimous.

Concession of Vice-Presidential Nomination
Democratic National Convention
Chicago, Illinois, August 17, 1956

The Presidential Prospect of 1958

I have just received the following wire from my generous daddy: "Dear Jack: Don't buy a single vote more than is necessary—I'll be damned if I'm going to pay for a landslide."

I am grateful to my father for his support—but I am even more grateful to "Mr. Sam" Rayburn. At the last Democratic convention, if he had not recognized the Tennessee and Oklahoma delegations when he did, I might have won that race with Senator Kefauver—and my political career would now be over.

I have been told tonight that if I will only not reveal the truth about the members of the Gridiron Club in front of their bosses, they in turn can insure me the Democratic Presidential nomination. I am not the first politician to be thus tempted by the newspaper fraternity. When Speaker Joe Cannon half a century ago was told by the ANPA [American Newspaper Publishers Association] that, in exchange for his opposition to the newsprint tariff, the publishers would deliver him the Presidency, Speaker Cannon removed his cigar and replied: "You know, two thousand years ago or so, another fellow was tempted like this. And the tempter led him up on the highest mountaintop; and showed him all the kingdoms of the world, and all the valleys of milk and honey—and he said, 'If you will fall down and worship me, all of this will I give you.' But the truth of the matter is," Speaker Cannon went on, "he didn't own one damn inch of it." I am not sure that the members of the Gridiron Club do either. . . .

I dreamed about 1960 the other night, and I told Stuart Symington and Lyndon Johnson about it in the Cloakroom yesterday. I told them how the Lord came into my bedroom, anointed my head, and said: "John Kennedy, I hereby anoint you President of the United States." Stu Symington said: "That's strange, Jack, because I, too, had a similar dream last night, in which the Lord anointed me and declared me, Stuart Symington, President of the United States *and* outer space." And Lyndon Johnson said: "That's very interesting, gentlemen; because I, too, had a similar dream last night—and I don't remember anointing either one of you!"

We do have lots of candidates. A recent AP survey asked each senator about his preference for the Presidency—and ninety-six senators each received one vote.

The Gridiron Club
Washington, D.C., March 15, 1958

The Declaration of Candidacy in 1960

I am announcing today my candidacy for the Presidency of the United States.

The Presidency is the most powerful office in the Free World. Through its leadership can come a more vital life for our people. In it are centered the hopes of the globe around us for freedom and a more secure life. For it is in the executive branch that the most crucial decisions of this century must be made in the next four years—how to end or alter the burdensome arms race, where Soviet gains already threaten our very existence; how to maintain freedom and order in the newly emerging nations; how to rebuild the stature of American science and education; how to prevent the collapse of our farm economy and the decay of our cities; how to achieve, without further inflation or unemployment, expanded economic growth benefiting all Americans; and how to give direction to our traditional moral purpose, awakening every American to the dangers and opportunities that confront us.

I am announcing today my candidacy for the Presidency of the United States.

These are among the real issues of 1960. And it is on the basis of these issues that the American people must make their fateful choice for the future.

In the past forty months, I have toured every state in the Union and I have talked to Democrats in all walks of life. My candidacy is therefore based on the conviction that I can win both the nomination and the election.

I believe that any Democratic aspirant to this important nomination should be willing to submit to the voters his views, record, and competence in a series of primary contests. I am therefore now announcing my intention of filing in the New Hampshire primary and I shall announce my plans with respect to the other primaries as their filing dates approach.

I believe that the Democratic Party has a historic function to perform in the winning of the 1960 election, comparable to its role in 1932. I intend to do my utmost to see that that victory is won.

For eighteen years, I have been in the service of the United States, first as a naval officer in the Pacific during World War II and for the past fourteen years as a member of the Congress. In the last twenty years, I have traveled in nearly every continent and country—from Leningrad to Saigon, from Bucharest to Lima. From all of this, I have developed an image of America as fulfilling a noble and historic role as the defender of freedom in a time of maximum peril—and of the American people as confident, courageous, and persevering.

It is with this image that I begin this campaign.

Statement of Declaration for the Presidency
Washington, D.C., January 2, 1960

The Question of Age

Last Saturday one of our most dedicated and courageous Presidents gave the nation his views on the forthcoming Democratic convention. Inasmuch as Mr. Truman's remarks were directed at me, I am taking this opportunity to respond to his statement.

First, Mr. Truman suggested that I step aside as a candidate in 1960.

In response, let me say I do not intend to step aside at anyone's request.

I was the only candidate to risk my chances in all the primaries; the only one to visit every state. I have encountered and survived every kind of hazard and opposition, and I do not intend to withdraw my name now on the eve of the convention.

Secondly, Mr. Truman asserted that the convention would be controlled or prearranged.

In response, let me say to the extent that I have anything to do with it, it will be an open convention, as every convention of our broadly based party is open, even though our candidate has been selected on the first ballot in every single convention but one since 1932, including the 1948 convention, which nominated Mr. Truman.

To me, an open convention means one reflecting the free will of delegates, freely elected in contested primaries and in state conventions.

But based on my observations of him in 1952 and in 1956, and last Saturday, Mr. Truman regards an open convention as one which studies all the candidates, reviews their records, and then takes his advice.

Nevertheless, I share his hope that our convention will consider all prospective nominees, including all those he named, and some he did not name. And I hope that Mr. Truman will attend the convention, and should I be the nominee, I hope he will support me in the fall.

Third, Mr. Truman accused my supporters of using improper pressure on the delegates. Not one concrete example has ever been named. I do not want any votes that have been pressured. And the facts of the matter are that my votes come from the primaries—and I entered all that were open—and from rank-and-file Democrats who voted for me in state conventions.

The prospective candidates Mr. Truman named could have entered those primaries. Some of them were traveling widely all year, and supporting my primary opponents. But not one of them entered a primary on his own.

The other candidates also had the same opportunity as I to present their record and views to the individual delegates and state conventions. Many of them have already been properly sized up, to use Mr. Truman's words, and they have their own backers who are not, I am told, without influence and the opportunity to pressure delegates.

The heart of Mr. Truman's objection . . . is his question as to whether I am ready for the country or the country is ready for me in terms of maturity and experience.

Fourth and finally, the heart of Mr. Truman's objection, it seems, is his question as to whether I am ready for the country or the country is ready for me in terms of maturity and experience.

Let me say this as objectively as I can. I did not undertake lightly to seek the Presidency. It is not a prize or a normal object of ambition. It is the greatest office in the world . . .

My writings, addresses, and activities in foreign and domestic affairs speak for themselves, and I am willing to let our party and nation be the judge of my experience and ability.

But this much ought to be understood: If we are to establish a test for the Presidency whereby fourteen years in major elective office is insufficient experience, then all but three of the ten possibilities mentioned by Mr. Truman last Saturday must be ruled out, and every President elevated to that office in the twentieth century should have been ruled out, including the three great Democratic Presidents, Woodrow Wilson, Franklin Roosevelt, and Harry Truman himself.

And if we are to establish a so-called maturity test which finds men forty-three years of age or younger unfit for leadership, a test, by the way, not met by all those listed by Mr. Truman, and not in keeping with the constitutional test of thirty-five, which is prescribed in the Constitution, then history has repeatedly violated this principle—in the lives of President Theodore Roosevelt, Prime Minister William Pitt, and a whole host of other leaders stretching back through Napoleon to Alexander the Great.

To exclude from positions of trust and command all those below the age of forty-four would have kept Jefferson from writing the Declaration of Independence, Washington from commanding the Continental Army, Madison from fathering the Constitution, Hamilton from serving as Secretary of the Treasury, Clay from being elected Speaker of the House, and even Christopher Columbus from discovering America.

But I do not believe the American people are willing to impose any such test, for this is still a young country, founded by young men 184 years ago today and it is still young in heart, youthful in spirit, and blessed with new young leaders in both parties, in both houses of Congress, and in governor's chairs throughout the country.

The balance of power is shifting. There are new and more terrible weapons, new and uncertain nations, new pressures of population and automation that were never considered before.

The strength and health and vigor of these young men is equally needed in the White House. For during my lifetime alone four out of our seven Presidents have suffered major health setbacks that impaired at least temporarily their exercise of executive leadership. Older men may always be appointed to the Cabinet. Their wise counsel of experience will be invaluable, but then if ill health cuts short their work others may replace them. But a President is selected for four—or possibly eight—years and the voters deserve to know that his strength and vigor will remain at the helm.

So, if in the coming weeks both parties in their respective conventions should nominate candidates still in their forties, and Mr. Nixon and I, as a matter of fact, entered the Congress together fourteen years ago, the country will, I am confident, be ready for that choice.

We have had six previous Presidents in their forties and many presidential candidates, some in fact in their thirties.

It is true, of course, that almost all of the major world leaders today on both sides of the Iron Curtain are men past the age of sixty-five. It is true that the world today is largely in the hands of men whose education was completed before the whole course of international events was altered by two world wars.

But who is to say how successful they have been in improving the fate of the world? And who is to replace these men as the passage of time removes from the scene those born in the nineteenth century?

The world is changing, the old ways will not do.

The balance of power is shifting. There are new and more terrible weapons, new and uncertain nations, new pressures of population and automation that were never considered before. And in many of these new countries I have noticed, in both Africa and Asia, they are electing young men to leadership—men who are not bound by the traditions of the past, men who are not blinded by the old fears and rivalries, men who can cast off the old slogans and illusions, and suspicions.

It is time for a new generation of leadership to cope with new problems and new opportunities. For there is a new world to be won, a world of peace and goodwill, a world of hope and abundance, and I want America to lead the way to that new world.

Mr. Truman asked me if I think I am ready. I am reminded that one hundred years ago Abraham Lincoln, not yet President and under fire from veteran politicians, wrote these words: "I see the storm coming and I know His hand is in it. If He has a place and work for me, I believe that I am ready."

Today I say to you, with full knowledge of the responsibilities of that high office, if the people of the nation select me to be their President, I believe that I am ready.

Televised News Conference
New York, New York, July 4, 1960

The Final Appeal

The preconvention campaign is over. For the candidates, the hour of unity is at hand. We have all been friends for a long time. I know we always will. We have always supported our party's nominee. I know we all will in 1960.

For we are all Democrats—not northern or southern Democrats, not liberal or conservative Democrats—but Democrats by birth, conviction, and choice. We know it is neither the party of war nor the party of appeasement—our only war is against injustice, hunger, and disease—and in that war there can be no appeasement.

And we know that there is only one legitimate issue of health in this campaign—and that is the anemic health of the American economy today.

There is only one legitimate issue of age in this campaign—and that is the tragic failure of this administration to meet the needs of our older citizens, and particularly their need for medical care.

There is only one legitimate issue of creed in this campaign, and that is our devotion to the public good ahead of private interests—a creed the Republicans call creeping socialism—but FDR called it "A New Deal."

This fall will see the classic, age-old struggle—between the party of hope and the party of memory—the party of the future versus the party of the past—the party that breaks precedents versus the party that breaks promises. And every candidate here tonight joins me in one final campaign promise—we are going to win that struggle in November.

For those of you who are delegates, your hour of decision is also at hand. In the pomp and pageantry of convention politics, it is easy to forget the context of your decision: the Free World that anxiously awaits a leader—the dark clouds gathering ominously on the world horizon—the cries for help that come from around the country, from abandoned farms and mines, from overcrowded slums and schools, from the unemployed and the underpaid and the unprotected—a hundred, a thousand voices crying, here and around the world—cries that have not been heard—cries that must now be heard.

One hundred and seventy-three years ago, in another dark and uncertain hour, an earlier national convention was called—its delegates undertook to draft a new constitution. May your work as delegates here this week stand the test of time as well as theirs. May your decisions—like theirs—have meaning for future generations to come, and ignite a beacon light for all the world to see.

In the words of the poet Longfellow:

Humanity with all its fears,
With all its hopes of future years
Is hanging breathless on thy fate.

Democratic National Committee Dinner
Los Angeles, California, July 10, 1960

The Opening of the New Frontier

With a deep sense of duty and high resolve, I accept your nomination.

I accept it with a full and grateful heart—without reservation—and with only one obligation—the obligation to devote every effort of body, mind, and spirit to lead our party back to victory and our nation back to greatness.

I am grateful, too, that you have provided me with such an eloquent statement of our party's platform. Pledges which are made so eloquently are made to be kept. "The Rights of Man"—the civil and economic rights essential to the human dignity of all men—are indeed our goal and our first principles. This is a platform on which I can run with enthusiasm and conviction.

And I am grateful, finally, that I can rely in the coming months on so many others—on a distinguished running mate who brings unity to our ticket and strength to our platform, Lyndon Johnson; on one of the most articulate statesmen of our time, Adlai Stevenson; on a great spokesman for our needs as a nation and a people, Stuart Symington; and on that fighting campaigner whose support I welcome, President Harry S Truman.

I feel a lot safer now that they are on my side again. And I am proud of the contrast with our Republican competitors. For their ranks are apparently so thin that not one challenger has come forth with both the competence and the courage to make theirs an open convention.

I am telling you now what you are entitled to know: that my decisions on every public policy will be my own—as an American, a Democrat, and a free man.

I am fully aware of the fact that the Democratic Party, by nominating someone of my faith, has taken on what many regard as a new and hazardous risk—new, at least, since 1928. But I look at it this way: the Democratic Party has once again placed its confidence in the American people, and in their ability to render a free, fair judgment. And you have, at the same time, placed your confidence in me, and in my ability to render a free, fair judgment—to uphold the Constitution and my oath of office—and to reject any kind of religious pressure or obligation that might directly or indirectly interfere with my conduct of the Presidency in the national interest. My record of fourteen years supporting public education—supporting complete separation of church and state—and resisting pressure from any source on any issue should be clear by now to everyone.

I hope that no American, considering the really critical issues facing this country, will waste his franchise by voting either for me or against me solely on account of my religious affiliation. It is not relevant, I want to stress, what some other political or religious leader may have said on this subject. It is not relevant what abuses may have existed in other countries or in other times. It is not relevant what pressures, if any, might conceivably be brought to bear on me. I am telling you now what you are entitled to know: that my decisions on every public policy will be my own—as an American, a Democrat, and a free man.

Under any circumstances, however, the victory we seek in November will not be easy. We all know that in our hearts. We recognize the power of the forces that will be aligned against us. We know they will invoke the name of Abraham Lincoln on behalf of their candidate—despite the fact that the political career of their candidate has often seemed to show charity toward none and malice for all.

We know that it will not be easy to campaign against a man who has spoken or voted on every known side of every known issue. Mr. Nixon may feel it is his turn now, after the New Deal and the Fair Deal—but before he deals, someone had better cut the cards.

That "someone" may be the millions of Americans who voted for President Eisenhower but balk at his would-be, self-appointed successor. For just as historians tell us that Richard I was not fit to fill the shoes of bold Henry II—and that Richard Cromwell was not fit to wear the mantle of his uncle [sic]—they might add in future years that Richard Nixon did not measure to the footsteps of Dwight D. Eisenhower.

Perhaps he could carry on the party policies—the policies of Nixon, Benson, Dirksen, and Goldwater. But this nation cannot afford such a luxury. Perhaps we could afford a Coolidge following Harding. And perhaps we could afford a Pierce following Fillmore. But after Buchanan this nation needed a Lincoln—after Taft we needed a Wilson—after Hoover we needed Franklin Roosevelt. . . . And after eight years of drugged and fitful sleep, this nation needs strong, creative Democratic leadership in the White House.

But we are not merely running against Mr. Nixon. Our task is not merely one of itemizing Republican failures. Nor is that wholly necessary. For the families forced from the farm will know how to vote without our telling them. The unemployed miners and textile workers will know how to vote. The old people without medical care, the families without a decent home, the parents of children without adequate food or schools, they all know that it's time for a change.

But I think the American people expect more from us than cries of indignation and attack. The times are too grave, the challenge too urgent, and the stakes too high to permit the customary passions of political debate. We are not here to curse the darkness, but to light the candle that can guide us through that darkness to a safe and sane future. As Winston Churchill said on taking office some twenty years ago: If we open a quarrel between the present and the past, we shall be in danger of losing the future.

Today our concern must be with that future. For the world is changing. The old era is ending. The old ways will not do.

Abroad, the balance of power is shifting. There are new and more terrible weapons, new and uncertain nations, new pressures of population and deprivation. One third of the world, it has been said, may be free—but one third is the victim of cruel repression, and the other one third is rocked by the pangs of poverty, hunger, and envy. More energy is released by the awakening of these new nations than by the fission of the atom itself.

Meanwhile, Communist influence has penetrated farther into Asia, stood astride the Middle East, and now festers some ninety miles off the coast of Florida. Friends have slipped into neutrality—and neutrals into hostility. As our keynoter reminded us, the President who began his career by going to Korea ends it by staying away from Japan.

The world has been close to war before—but now man, who has survived all previous threats to his existence, has taken into his mortal hands the power to exterminate the entire species some seven times over.

Here at home, the changing face of the future is equally revolutionary. The New Deal and the Fair Deal were bold measures for their generations—but this is a new generation.

A technological revolution on the farm has led to an output explosion—but we have not yet learned to harness that explosion usefully, while protecting our farmers' right to full parity income.

An urban population revolution has overcrowded our schools, cluttered up our suburbs, and increased the squalor of our slums.

A peaceful revolution for human rights—demanding an end to racial discrimination in all parts of our community life—has strained at the leashes imposed by timid executive leadership.

A medical revolution has extended the life of our elder citizens without providing the dignity and security those later years deserve. And a revolution of automation finds machines replacing men in the mines and mills of America, without replacing their incomes or their training or their need to pay the family doctor, grocer, and landlord.

There has also been a change—a slippage—in our intellectual and moral strength. Seven lean years of drought and famine have withered a field of ideas. Blight has descended on our regulatory agencies, and a dry rot, beginning in Washington, is seeping into every corner of America—in the payola mentality, the expense account way of life, the confusion between what is legal and what is right. Too many Americans have lost their way, their will and their sense of historic purpose.

It is a time, in short, for a new generation of leadership—new men to cope with new problems and new opportunities.

All over the world, particularly in the newer nations, young men are coming to power—men who are not bound by the traditions of the past—men who are not blinded by the old fears and hates and rivalries—young men who can cast off the old slogans and delusions and suspicions.

The Republican nominee-to-be, of course, is also a young man. But his approach is as old as McKinley. His party is the party of the past. His speeches are generalities from *Poor Richard's Almanack.* Their platform, made up of leftover Democratic planks, has the courage of our old convictions. Their pledge is a pledge to the status quo—and today there can be no status quo.

Mr. Nixon may feel it is his turn now, after the New Deal and the Fair Deal—but before he deals, someone had better cut the cards.

For I stand tonight facing west on what was once the last frontier. From the lands that stretch three thousand miles behind me, the pioneers of old gave up their safety, their comfort, and sometimes their lives to build a new world here in the West. They were not the captives of their own doubts, the prisoners of their own price tags. Their motto was not "every man for himself"—but "all for the common cause." They were determined to make that new world strong and free, to overcome its hazards and its hardships, to conquer the enemies that threatened from without and within.

Today some would say that those struggles are all over—that all the horizons have been explored, that all the battles have been won, that there is no longer an American frontier.

But I trust that no one in this vast assemblage will agree with those sentiments. For the problems are not all solved and the battles are not all won—and we stand today on the edge of a New Frontier—the frontier of the 1960s—a frontier of unknown opportunities and perils—a frontier of unfulfilled hopes and threats.

Woodrow Wilson's New Freedom promised our nation a new political and economic framework. Franklin Roosevelt's New Deal promised security and succor to those in need. But the New Frontier of which I speak is not a set of promises—it is a set of challenges. It sums up not what I intend to offer the American people, but what I intend to ask of them. It appeals to their pride, not to their pocketbook—it holds out the promise of more sacrifice instead of more security.

But I tell you the New Frontier is here, whether we seek it or not. Beyond that frontier are the uncharted areas of science and space, unsolved problems of peace and war, unconquered pockets of ignorance and prejudice, unanswered questions of poverty and surplus. It would be easier to shrink back from that frontier, to look to the safe mediocrity of the past, to be lulled by good intentions and high rhetoric—and those who prefer that course should not cast their votes for me, regardless of party.

But I believe the times demand invention, innovation, imagination, decision. I am asking each of you to be new pioneers on that New Frontier. My call is to the young in heart, regardless of age—to the stout in spirit, regardless of party—to all who respond to the scriptural call: "Be strong and of a good courage; be not afraid, neither be thou dismayed."

For courage, not complacency, is our need today—leadership, not salesmanship. And the only valid test of leadership is the ability to lead, and lead vigorously. A tired nation, said David Lloyd George, is a Tory nation—and the United States today cannot afford to be either tired or Tory.

There may be those who wish to hear more—more promises to this group or that, more harsh rhetoric about the men in the Kremlin, more assurances of a golden future, where taxes are always low and subsidies ever high. But my promises are in the platform you have adopted; our ends will not be won by rhetoric; and we can have faith in the future only if we have faith in ourselves.

For the harsh facts of the matter are that we stand on this frontier at a turning point in history. We must prove all over again whether this nation—or any nation so conceived—can long endure; whether our society—with its freedom of choice, its breadth of opportunity, its range of alternatives—can compete with the single-minded advance of the Communist system.

Can a nation organized and governed such as ours endure? That is the real question. Have we the nerve and the will? Can we carry through in an age where we will witness not only new breakthroughs in weapons of destruction but also a race for mastery of the sky and the rain, the ocean and the tides, the far side of space and the inside of men's minds?

Are we up to the task—are we equal to the challenge? Are we willing to match the Russian sacrifice of the present for the future—or must we sacrifice our future in order to enjoy the present?

That is the question of the New Frontier. That is the choice our nation must make—a choice that lies not merely between two men or two parties, but between the public interest and private comfort—between national greatness and national decline—between the fresh air of progress and the stale, dank atmosphere of "normalcy"—between determined dedication and creeping mediocrity.

All mankind waits upon our decision. A whole world looks to see what we will do. We cannot fail their trust, we cannot fail to try.

It has been a long road from that first snowy day in New Hampshire to this crowded convention city. Now begins another long journey, taking me into your cities and homes all over America. Give me your help, your hand, your voice, your vote. Recall with me the words of Isaiah: "They that wait upon the Lord shall renew their strength; they shall mount up with wings as eagles; they shall run, and not be weary."

As we face the coming challenge, we, too, shall wait upon the Lord, and ask that He renew our strength. Then shall we be equal to the test. Then we shall not be weary. And then we shall prevail.

Acceptance of Presidential Nomination
Democratic National Convention
Los Angeles, California, July 15, 1960

The First Debate

In the election of 1860, Abraham Lincoln said the question was whether this nation could exist half slave or half free.

In the election of 1960, and in the world around us, the question is whether the world will exist half slave or half free, whether it will move in the direction of freedom, in the direction of the road that we are taking or whether it will move in the direction of slavery.

I think it will depend in great measure upon what we do here in the United States, on the kind of society that we build, on the kind of strength that we maintain.

We discuss tonight domestic issues, but I would not want any implication to be given that this does not involve directly our struggle with Mr. Khrushchev for survival.

Mr. Khrushchev is in New York and he maintains the Communist offensive throughout the world because of the productive power of the Soviet Union itself.

The Chinese Communists have always had a large population but they are important and dangerous now because they are mounting a major effort within their own country. The kind of country we have here, the kind of society we have, the kind of strength we build in the United States, will be the defense of freedom.

If we do well here, if we meet our obligations, if we are moving ahead, then I think freedom will be secure around the world. If we fail, then freedom fails.

Therefore, I think the question before the American people is: Are we doing as much as we can do? Are we as strong as we should be? Are we as strong as we must be if we are going to maintain our independence, and if we're going to maintain and hold out the hand of friendship to those who look to us for assistance, to those who look to us for survival? I should make it very clear that I do not think we're doing enough, that I am not satisfied as an American with the progress that we are making.

This is a great country, but I think it could be a greater country, and this is a powerful country but I think it could be a more powerful country.

I'm not satisfied to have fifty percent of our steel mill capacity unused.

I'm not satisfied when the United States had last year the lowest rate of economic growth of any major industrialized society in the world—

because economic growth means strength and vitality. It means we're able to sustain our defenses. It means we're able to meet our commitments abroad.

I'm not satisfied when we have over $9 billion worth of food, some of it rotting even though there is a hungry world and even though four million Americans wait every month for a food package from the government which averages five cents a day per individual.

I saw cases in West Virginia, here in the United States, where children took home part of their school lunch in order to feed their families. I don't think we are meeting our obligations toward these Americans.

I'm not satisfied when the Soviet Union is turning out twice as many scientists and engineers as we are.

I'm not satisfied when many of our teachers are inadequately paid or when our children go to school on part-time shifts. I think we should have an educational system second to none.

I'm not satisfied when I see men like Jimmy Hoffa, in charge of the largest union in the United States, still free.

I'm not satisfied when we are failing to develop the natural resources of the United States to the fullest. Here in the United States, which developed the Tennessee Valley and which built the Grand Coulee and the other dams in the northwest United States, at the present rate of hydropower production—and that is a hallmark of an industrialized society—the Soviet Union by 1975 will be producing more power than we are. . . .

I'm not satisfied until every American enjoys his full constitutional rights. If a Negro baby is born, and this is true also of Puerto Ricans and Mexicans in some of our cities, he has about one half as much chance to get through high school as a white baby. He has one third as much chance to get through college as a white student. He has about a third as much chance to be a professional man, and about half as much chance to own a house. He has about four times as much chance that he'll be out of work in his life as the white baby. I think we can do better. I don't want the talents of any American to go to waste.

I know that there are those who say that we want to turn everything over to the government. I don't at all. I want the individuals to meet their responsibilities and I want the states to meet their responsibilities. But I think there is also a national responsibility.

That argument has been used against every piece of social legislation in the last twenty-five years. The people of the United States individually could not have developed the Tennessee Valley. Collectively, they could have.

A cotton farmer in Georgia or a peanut farmer, or a dairy farmer in Wisconsin or Minnesota—cannot protect himself against the forces of supply and demand in the marketplace; but, working together in effective governmental programs, they can do so.

Seventeen million Americans over sixty-five who live on an average Social Security check of about seventy-eight dollars a month—they're not able to sustain themselves individually, but they can sustain themselves through the Social Security system.

I don't believe in big government, but I believe in effective governmental action, and I think that's the only way that the United States is going to maintain its freedom; it's the only way that we're going to move ahead. I think we can do a better job. I think we're going to have to do a better job if we are going to meet the responsibilities which time and events have placed upon us.

We cannot turn the job over to anyone else. If the United States fails, then the whole cause of freedom fails, and I think it depends in great measure on what we do here in this country.

The reason Franklin Roosevelt was a good neighbor in Latin America was because he was a good neighbor in the United States, because they felt that the American society was moving again. I want us to recapture that image. I want people in Latin America and Africa and Asia to start to look to America to see how we're doing things, to wonder what the President of the United States is doing, and not to look at Khrushchev or look at the Chinese Communists. That is the obligation upon our generation.

In 1933 Franklin Roosevelt said in his inaugural that this generation of Americans has a "rendezvous with destiny." I think our generation of Americans has the same "rendezvous." The question now is: Can freedom be maintained under the most severe attack it has ever known? I think it can be, and I think in the final analysis it depends upon what we do here. I think it's time America started moving again.

Opening Statement, First Televised Presidential Candidates Debate Chicago, Illinois, September 26, 1960

The Definition of Liberal

What do our opponents mean when they apply to us the label "Liberal"? If by "Liberal" they mean, as they want people to believe, someone who is soft in his policies abroad, who is against local government, and who is unconcerned with the taxpayer's dollar, then the record of this party and its members demonstrate that we are not that kind of "Liberal." But if by a "Liberal" they mean someone who looks ahead and not behind, someone who welcomes new ideas without rigid reactions, someone who cares about the welfare of the people—their health, their housing, their schools, their jobs, their civil rights, and their civil liberties—someone who believes that we can break through the stalemate and suspicions that grip us in our policies abroad, if that is what they mean by a "Liberal," then I'm proud to say that I'm a "Liberal."

But first, I would like to say what I understand the word "Liberal" to mean and explain in the process why I consider myself to be a "Liberal," and what it means in the presidential election of 1960.

In short, having set forth my view—I hope for all time—two nights ago in Houston, on the proper relationship between church and state, I want to take this opportunity to set forth my views on the proper relationship between the state and the citizen. This is my political credo:

I believe in human dignity as the source of national purpose, in human liberty as the source of national action, in the human heart as the source of national compassion, and in the human mind as the source of our invention and our ideas. It is, I believe, this faith in our fellow citizens as individuals and as people that lies at the heart of the liberal faith. For liberalism is not so much a party creed or a set of fixed platform promises as it is an attitude of mind and heart, a faith in man's ability through the experiences of his reason and judgment to increase for himself and his fellow men the amount of justice and freedom and brotherhood which all human life deserves.

I believe also in the United States of America, in the promise that it contains and has contained throughout our history of producing a society so abundant and creative and so free and responsible that it cannot only fulfill the aspirations of its citizens, but serve equally well as a beacon for all mankind. I do not believe in a superstate. I see no magic to tax dollars which are sent to Washington and then returned. I abhor the waste and incompetence of large-scale federal bureaucracies in this administration as well as in others. I do not favor state compulsion when voluntary individual effort can do the job and do it well. But I believe in a government which acts, which exercises its full powers and its full responsibilities. Government is an art and a precious obligation; and when it has a job to do, I believe it should do it. And this requires not only great ends but that we propose concrete means of achieving them.

Our responsibility is not discharged by announcement of virtuous ends. Our responsibility is to achieve these objectives with social invention, with political skill, and executive vigor. I believe for these reasons that liberalism is our best and our only hope in the world today. For the liberal society is a free society, and it is at the same time and for that reason a strong society. Its strength is drawn from the will of free people committed to great ends and peacefully striving to meet them. Only liberalism, in short, can repair our national power, restore our national purpose, and liberate our national energies. And the only basic issue in the 1960 presidential campaign is whether our government will fall in a conservative rut and die there, or whether we will move ahead in the liberal spirit of daring, of breaking new ground, of doing in our generation what Woodrow Wilson and Franklin Roosevelt and Harry Truman and Adlai Stevenson did in their time of influence and responsibility.

Our liberalism has its roots in our diverse origins. Most of us are descended from that segment of the American population which was once called an immigrant minority. Today, along with our children and grandchildren, we do not feel minor. We feel proud of our origins and we are not second to any group in our sense of national purpose. For many years New York represented the new frontier to all those who came from the ends of the earth to find new opportunity and new freedom, generations of men and women who fled from the despotism of the czars, the horrors of the Nazis, the tyranny of hunger, who came here to the new frontier in the state of New York. These men and women, a living cross section of American history, indeed, a cross section of the entire world's history of pain and hope, made of this city not only a new world of opportunity, but a new world of the spirit as well.

Tonight we salute Governor and Senator Herbert Lehman as a symbol of that spirit, and as a reminder that the fight for full constitutional rights for all Americans is a fight that must be carried on in 1961.

Many of these same immigrant families produced the pioneers and builders of the American labor movement. They are the men who sweated in our shops, who struggled to create a union, who were driven by longing for education for their children and for their children's development. They went to night schools; they built their own future, their union's future, and their country's future, brick by brick, block by block, neighborhood by neighborhood, and now in their children's time, suburb by suburb.

Tonight we salute George Meany as a symbol of that struggle and as a reminder that the fight to eliminate poverty and human exploitation is a fight that goes on in our own day. But in 1960 the cause of liberalism cannot content itself with carrying on the fight for human justice and economic liberalism here at home. For here and around the world the fear of war hangs over us every morning and every night. It lies, expressed or silent, in the minds of every American. We cannot banish it by repeating that we are economically first or that we are militarily first, for saying so doesn't make it so. More will be needed than goodwill missions or talking back to Soviet politicians or increasing the tempo of the arms race. More will be needed than good intentions, for we know where that paving leads.

In Winston Churchill's words, "We cannot escape our dangers by recoiling from them. We dare not pretend such dangers do not exist."

And tonight we salute Adlai Stevenson as an eloquent spokesman for the effort to achieve an intelligent foreign policy. Our opponents would like the people to believe that in a time of danger it would be hazardous to change the administration that has brought us to this time of danger. I think it would be hazardous not to change. I think it would be hazardous to continue four more years of stagnation and indifference at home and abroad, of starving the underpinnings of our national power, including not only our defense but our image abroad as a friend.

This is an important election. This is an important election—in many ways as important as any in this century—and I think that the Democratic Party and the Liberal Party here in New York, and those who believe in progress all over the United States, should be associated with us in this great effort.

The reason that Woodrow Wilson and Franklin Roosevelt and Harry Truman and Adlai Stevenson had influence abroad, and the United States in their time had it, was because they moved this country here at home, because they stood for something here in the United States, for expanding the benefits of our society to our own people, and the people around the world looked to us as a symbol of hope.

I think it is our task to re-create that same atmosphere in our own time. Our national elections have often proved to be the turning point in the course of our country. I am proposing that 1960 be another turning point in the history of the great Republic.

Some pundits are saying that it's 1928 all over again. I say it's 1932 all over again. I say this is the great opportunity that we will have in our time to move our people and this country and the people of the free world beyond the new frontiers of the 1960s.

Acceptance of New York Liberal Party Nomination
New York City, September 14, 1960

The Issue of Latin America

Twenty years ago this month President Franklin Roosevelt in a radio broadcast to the Western Hemisphere called upon the people of Latin America to join hands with the United States in a common struggle to keep the forces of tyranny from the shores of the Americas. "So bound together," he said, "we are able to withstand any attack from the East or the West. Together we are able to ward off any infiltration of alien political and economic ideas that would destroy our freedom and our democracy."

The nations of South America responded to Franklin Roosevelt's call. Foreign efforts to capture control of the governments of Latin America were halted. American independence was maintained. And the nations of the Western Hemisphere combined in a common effort which ultimately brought about the collapse of Nazi despotism throughout the world.

Today, once again, the independence of the Western Hemisphere is menaced from abroad. Today, once again, the combined efforts of all the American states are vital to the preservation of that independence. Today, once again, only the leadership of the United States can summon all the resources of the hemisphere to the defense of freedom. But today, unlike 1940, we have failed to exercise that leadership. Today, unlike 1940, the nations of Latin America are distrustful of our guidance, suspicious of our intentions, disillusioned by our actions. And today, unlike 1940, the forces of alien tyranny have already found their way into the Western Hemisphere—to within ninety miles of your coast—to the island of Cuba.

And this change has come about in the past eight years.

In 1953 the Republicans inherited an inter-American system in good working order. They inherited a good-neighbor policy which was more than an empty slogan. They inherited a Latin America composed of nations friendly to the United States.

But in eight short years that bright heritage, the heritage of twenty Democratic years, has been largely dissipated and destroyed, and much of the goodwill, which it took two decades to build, has been lost.

In Cuba the Communists have gained a satellite and established a base for the attempted infiltration and subversion of all Latin America. In Venezuela angry mobs have assaulted the Vice-President of the United States. In Mexico City rioting crowds have protested American policy and castigated America itself. In Panama anti-American demonstrations have imperiled the security of the Panama Canal. In Brazil, the newly elected President felt it necessary to appeal to rising anti-American sentiment in order to win the election. And every report, every broadcast, every newspaper dispatch from the south brings fresh news of unrest, of tension, of misunderstanding.

Today, time is running out for the United States in Latin America. . . .

It is time now to renew our understanding and begin to act. For although the Cold War will not be won in Latin America, it may very well be lost there.

Our first failure in Latin America has been the failure to identify ourselves with the rising tide of freedom.

Victor Hugo once wrote that no army can withstand the force of an idea whose time has come. For most of Latin America the time of freedom has come. In 1954 there were thirteen military strongmen in Latin America; today there are only five. And, if we live up to our responsibilities, in the coming months and years we may expect the elimination of all despotism in Latin America—until the American hemisphere is a free hemisphere—not partly free, not almost free, but completely free from Cape Horn to the Arctic Circle.

But the United States, the home of freedom, has been viewed far too often not as the friend of this rising tide of freedom, but as the supporter of toppling and brutal dictatorships.

In 1953 the dictator of Peru was given a medal by the United States.

In 1954 the dictator of Venezuela was awarded the Legion of Merit by our ambassador.

In 1955 our Secretary of the Navy went to Argentina and made an eloquent address comparing dictator Perón to Lincoln—to Perón's advantage.

In 1956 the dictator of Paraguay received his medal from America.

We have warmly embraced Trujillo, the brutal despot of the Dominican Republic, and recently one of our ambassadors was photographed embracing Trujillo's envoy as he was being thrown out of Nicaragua because the OAS had virtually outlawed his government.

We have dumped more than $500 million worth of arms and ammunition into Latin America over the past eight years, much of which has been used to strengthen the hand of dictatorships. And even now, despite the hard lessons of the past, our air force is planning to invite the co-dictator of Nicaragua to Washington as a guest of honor.

Although the Cold War will not be won in Latin America, it may very well be lost there.

The result of these blunders has been disaster. The people of Latin America have begun to feel that we are more interested in stable regimes than in free governments; more interested in fighting against communism than in fighting for freedom; more interested in the possible loss of our investments than in the actual loss of the lives of the thousands of young Latins who have died fighting dictators; and thus when the dictatorships fell, our actions of support were remembered, and we have been distrusted because of them.

Our second major failure in Latin America has been our failure to help the people of Latin America to achieve their economic aspirations.

Latin America is the fastest-growing area in the world. By the end of the century it will have 512 million people—more than twice as many as all of North America. And this enormous population explosion is taking place in countries where millions of people are already condemned to a life of poverty and hunger and disease; where the average family income is less than $300 a year and where population growth is outdistancing economic growth, driving this meager standard of living still lower.

Poverty is not new to Latin America. But what is new is the determination to emerge from poverty, to wipe out hunger and want, to create a modern growing economy in a small fraction of the time it took to build a modern United States or Europe.

The people of Latin America want better homes, better schools, and better living standards; they want land reform, and tax reform, and an end to the corruption which drains off a nation's resources. In short, they want a new deal for South America. And that is why in every Latin American capital there is a street or park named after Franklin Roosevelt—but I do not know of one that is named after Hoover or Coolidge or Harding or Richard M. Nixon.

The people of South America have looked to the United States—their good neighbor—the richest land on earth—for help in this great effort to develop their economy. But in the past eight years we have sent less than five percent of our economic aid to all of Latin America. We refused to enter into discussions to stabilize the commodity prices on which the Latin American economy depends, prices whose rapid fluctuation has caused the loss of more foreign exchange than all that has been gained from our total foreign-aid program. We fought the establishment of an Inter-American Bank until events forced it upon us. We ignored the President of Brazil's imaginative proposal for a large-scale "Operation Pan-America" to develop the economy of Latin America. And we had our Secretary of State leave the Inter-American Conference in 1954, after securing a resolution against Guatemala, but before the Latin American nations had been given a chance to discuss the economic problems which were the purpose of the meeting. . . .

Our third major failure in Latin America has been our failure to demonstrate America's continuing concern with the problems of the people to the south, to establish the contact between nations and people which was the essence of the good-neighbor policy.

Although Latin America is desperately in need of educated and trained men to run a modern, developing economy, in the past eight years we have brought [fewer] than four hundred students a year from all of South America to study here in the United States.

Although misunderstanding of America has been on the increase, we suspended all regular Voice of America Spanish-language broadcasts to South America between 1953 and 1959, with the exception of the six months of the Hungarian crisis. And even today, we only broadcast one hour a day. And we have also cut the number and size of all our other information programs in Latin America. Although our relations with the restless volatile nations of Latin America require the most skilled and constant attention, our diplomatic posts there have too often been viewed merely as a reward for contributions to the Republican campaign treasury, with the result that our representatives have committed blunders which have lost us respect. They have embraced doomed dictators; and they have failed to understand the rising tide of popular discontent which the Communists have so tirelessly worked to exploit.

And while we have ignored the needs of Latin America, during these last eight years of failure and defeat, the Communists have been hard at work in South America. The Soviet Union is offering programs of technical assistance, encouraging young Latins to study behind the Iron Curtain, putting more than $100 million a year into the support of local Communist parties, and offering tempting trade agreements.

When the United States refused to give Argentina credits for petroleum development, the Russians offered $100 million worth of such credits. Brazil and the Soviet Union have signed a $208 million trade agreement, and Russia has become a major importer of Uruguayan wool. Already the Soviet Union has captured one country in Latin America and is using that country as a base from which to export propaganda and revolution throughout the continent. . . .

We must end our open and warm backing of dictators. Our honors must be reserved for democratic leaders, not despots.

There is much to encourage hope in Latin America; the forces of liberal democracy are still strong and are working to create the framework of economic advance, the steady elimination of poverty and want, on which the preservation of freedom will ultimately depend. But our help and our understanding are needed; and needed now, for the time of decision in Latin America has come. And the survival of freedom in the Western Hemisphere will depend on the boldness of our programs in the years to come.

First, we need a new attitude and new approach to the nations of Latin America. Franklin Roosevelt's good-neighbor policy was a success because it demonstrated a continuing concern with hemispheric problems. But in the past eight years we have not demonstrated such concern. We have reacted to a crisis in Guatemala or a crisis in Panama or a crisis in Cuba, and then, when the crisis was over, we continued to ignore the long-range problems and needs which were at the root of all the trouble. The good-neighbor policy is no longer enough. The good-partner policy has been discredited. Our new policy can best be summed up in the Spanish words *alianza para el progreso,* an alliance for progress—an alliance of nations with a common interest in freedom and economic advance in a great common effort to develop the resources of the entire hemisphere, strengthen the forces of democracy, and widen the vocational and educational opportunities of every person in all the Americas. This policy also means constant consultation with Latin American nations on hemispheric problems, as well as on issues of worldwide significance. And it is an alliance, not merely directed against communism, but aimed at helping our sister republics for their own sake.

Secondly, we must give constant and unequivocal support to democracy in Latin America. We must end our open and warm backing of dictators. Our honors must be reserved for democratic leaders, not despots. Our ambassadors must be spokesmen for democracy, not supporters of tyrants. And we must constantly press for free elections in any country where such elections are not held. We must also strongly support the Commission on Human Rights of the OAS, a commission which can serve as a forum before which the crimes and repressions of dictators like Castro and Trujillo can be brought to the attention of all the people of Latin America.

Third, we must help provide the funds, the long-term development loans, essential to a growing economy, an economy which can raise standards of living and keep up with the population explosion, and which will also provide an increasingly important market for American goods.

Until the recent authorization of $500 million for development, nearly all our economic aid had been in the form of loans to buy American exports. As a result basic ends were ignored and a crushing burden of interest payments was imposed on Latin America. For example, Latin America will pay more in interest this year to the Export-Import Bank than the entire $500 million recently authorized by the Congress.

Future programs must emphasize the development of the basic resources on which a modern economy depends, resources like roads and power and schools, resources which private investment cannot provide; but resources which are the fundamental precondition of rising living standards. We must plan our aid in full cooperation with the Latin American states, carefully mapping the often widely varying needs of each nation, and financing a development program through the revenues of the affected nation as well as long-term loans from the United States.

In this effort we should seek the help of those of our Western allies who have historic ties with Latin America, as well as the help of the Latin American nations themselves. For there is a great deal of difference between the economic problems of Argentina, with a GNP of $500 per person, and Bolivia, with a GNP of $100 per person. And perhaps the wealthier nations of South America will be able to offer help, at least in the form of technical assistance, to the poorer countries.

Fourth, we must act to stabilize the prices of the principal commodity exports of Latin America. Almost every country in Latin America depends on one or two basic commodities for nearly all its exports, and basic commodities account for ninety percent of all South American exports. The prices of these commodities are subject to violent change. And a sudden fall can cause a decline which will sharply reduce the national income, upset the budget, and wreck the foreign-exchange position. It is plain that no program of economic development can be effected unless something is done to stabilize commodity prices. . . .

Fifth, we must encourage and assist programs of land reform. In some South American nations archaic systems of absentee ownership still keep land in the grip of a few wealthy landowners, while the mass of the people struggle for a subsistence living as tenants. This concentration of land ownership was one of the principal grievances which underlay the Cuban revolution, and which is behind most of the revolutions in modern South America.

Of course, any decision to reform the system of land ownership can only be made by the country involved. But we should always stand ready to assist them in carrying out this decision by providing technical assistance and loans, as well as helping the new landowners to set up their farms on a productive basis.

Sixth, we must act to stimulate private investment in Latin America, through improved consular services, through the basic development programs which will provide the resources which private industry needs, and by working out international agreements designed to safeguard our investments abroad. . . .

Seventh, we must expand our programs of technical assistance. We need to send an increased flow of engineers, technicians, factory managers, and others to train the Latin Americans in the techniques of modern industry and modern agriculture.

At the same time we must train more South Americans in these same skills. . . .

Eighth, we must step up our own student-exchange program, to provide education for future Latin leaders, perhaps establishing an inter-American university in Puerto Rico to which young men and women from all over the hemisphere could attend.

At the same time we must increase our sadly lagging Voice of America broadcasts, both in Spanish and in Portuguese, and all our other information programs, in order to carry the message of America to the people of Latin America.

Ninth, we must send skilled and trained men to man our diplomatic posts in Latin America, men who will be appointed not for the size of their campaign contributions, but for their interest in and knowledge of the problems of the country in which they represent the United States.

Tenth, we must make every effort to bring about some type of arms control agreement in South America, an agreement which is fully compatible with the national security needs of every nation in the hemisphere. Such an agreement would end the wasteful arms race, which now absorbs sixty percent of the budget of some Latin American nations, dissipates resources which might be used for economic development, and increases tension throughout the hemisphere. . . .

[A] program like this . . . is the ultimate answer to Castro and the Communists. For if Latin America is moving forward, if it is progressing under democratic government, then eventually the people of Cuba too will demand freedom for themselves, and Communist rule in Latin America will perish where it began—in the streets of Havana.

I believe in a Western Hemisphere where we in the United States do not speak patronizingly of "our backyard" or our "little brothers," and where the people of South America do not speak with hostility of the "colossus of the north" or shout "Yankee go home." I believe in a hemisphere of independent and free nations, sharing common traditions and goals, living in peace and mutual respect. In short, I believe in a Western Hemisphere where all people—the Americans of the South and the Americans of the North—the United States and the nations of Latin America—are joined together in an alliance for progress—*alianza para el progreso.*

Campaign Speech
Tampa, Florida, October 18, 1960

The Issue of Peace

I come here tonight and ask your support in picking this country up and moving it forward. One week from tonight the next President of the United States will be turning to the arduous task that lies ahead, the preparation of a legislative program, the selection of men and women to serve our country, and a preparation for the fight for peace abroad. But whoever our next President may be, his efforts for a successful policy abroad will depend on the men and women whom he selects to conduct that policy.

Speaking in this state a month ago, Mr. Nixon showed an incapacity to grasp the essential fact. He set up new machinery intended to win the struggle for peace and freedom. But it turned out to be nothing more than a series of conferences, committees, and goodwill tours. This should come as no surprise. For the last eight years we have faced problem after problem, and the solution to each of them has been to appoint a committee. I think it is time for action. I think it is time we met our problems.

It takes more than words, hard or soft, more than tours, more than parades, more than conferences. It takes a stronger America, militarily, economically, scientifically, and educationally. We need a stronger free world, a stronger attack on world poverty, a stronger United Nations, a stronger United States foreign policy speaking for a stronger America, and that is what we are going to get.

We can push a button to start the next war but there is no push-button magic to winning a lasting and enduring peace. To be peace loving is not enough, for the Sermon on the Mount saved its blessings for the peacemakers. The generation which I speak for has seen enough of warmongers. Let our great role in history be that of peacemakers. But in the two areas where peace can be won, in the field of disarmament and in our representations abroad, this country has been ill served.

Disarmament planning is the most glaring omission in the field of national security and world peace of the last eight years. This administration has [fewer] than one hundred people working full-time on the subject in the entire national government. This is one fifth as many government employees as take care of the cemeteries and memorials for the U.S. Battle Commission. One hundred people working for peace. As a result we have gone to every conference unprepared. Our chief negotiator admitted at the 1958 conference on preventing surprise attacks that we, and I quote him, "hadn't up to this time really given the intense study of the kind of measure which would make this . . . possible." [They] had not given intense study to the very program that they were then putting forward.

A year ago when we went to the disarmament conference, we appointed an attorney from Massachusetts to set up an ad hoc committee. That committee met for three months. It was then dismissed. Four months before the conference began we drafted an attorney from New York to head our mission.

The result was we had no program and we accepted that of the British. How could we be so indifferent to one of our great chances for peace? We are going to have to do better. If we are successful on Tuesday, we are going to set up in the national government a national peace agency, an arms research institute, to prepare the studies which are necessary, to conduct the scientific research which is essential if we are going to speak with vigor and precision in this vital area of opportunity.

Secondly, we are going to have to be better represented. We are going to have to have the best Americans we can get to speak for our country abroad. All of us have admired what Dr. Tom Dooley has done in Laos. And others have been discouraged by the examples that we read of the ugly American. And I think that the United States is going to have to do much better in this area if we are going to defend freedom and peace in the 1960s. For the fact of the matter is that out of Moscow and Peiping and Czechoslovakia and Eastern Germany are hundreds of men and women, scientists, physicists, teachers, engineers, doctors, nurses, studying in those institutes, prepared to spend their lives abroad in the service of world communism. A friend of mine visiting the Soviet Union last summer met a young Russian couple studying Swahili and African customs at the Moscow Institute of Languages. They were not language teachers. He was a sanitation engineer and she was a nurse, and they were being prepared to live their lives in Africa as missionaries for world communism.

This can only be countered by the skill and dedication of Americans who are willing to spend their lives serving the cause of freedom. The key arm of our Foreign Service abroad are the ambassadors and members of our missions. Too many ambassadors have been chosen who are ill equipped and ill briefed. Campaign contributions have been regarded as a substitute for experience. Men who lack compassion for the needy here in the United States were sent abroad to represent us in countries which were marked by disease and poverty and illiteracy and ignorance, and they did not identify us with those causes and the fight against them. They did not demonstrate compassion there. Men who do not even know how to pronounce the name of the head of the country to which they are accredited, as we saw two years ago in the case of our ambassador to Ceylon, have been sent to important countries, essential countries, in the struggle between East and West. How can they compete with Communist emissaries long trained and dedicated and committed to the cause of extending communism in those countries?

In 1958, it was reported that our ambassador to Moscow was the only American ambassador who could speak the [local] language accredited behind the Iron Curtain, only one. Only two of our nine ambassadors to the Arabic-speaking countries spoke Arabic. In eight of the twelve non-English-speaking countries of Western Europe, our ambassadors lack a workable knowledge of the language of the country to which they were accredited.

Our ambassador to Paris could not even discuss negotiations with General de Gaulle, because he lacked that skill in French. This country is going to have to do much better.

It was reported last month that seventy percent of all new Foreign Service officers had no language skill at all. Only three of forty-four

Americans in our embassy in Belgrade could speak Yugoslavian. In Athens only six of seventy-nine Americans spoke modern Greek. In New Delhi, not a single American could speak an Indian dialect fluently. We cannot understand what is in the minds of other people if we cannot even speak to them. That is why we are given tongues. Yet do you think it is possible for us, in the most deadly struggle in which freedom has ever been engaged, to win if we approach it as casually as these statistics indicate that we are?

After the key African state of Guinea, now voting with the Soviet Union in Communist foreign policy, gained its independence, a Russian ambassador showed up the next day. Our ambassador did not show up for nine months. Today, we do not have a single American diplomat in residence in six new countries of Africa which are now members of the United Nations, not a single American diplomat in residence in any of the six. Of the sixteen new African countries which were admitted to the United Nations, do you know how many voted with us on the admission of Red China? None. There are only twenty-six Negroes in the six thousand of our Foreign Service officers, and yet Africa today contains one quarter of all the votes in the General Assembly. I think we can do better.

In the two areas where peace can be won, in the field of disarmament and in our representations abroad, this country has been ill served.

I therefore propose that our inadequate efforts in this area be supplemented by a peace corps of talented young men and women, willing and able to serve their country in this fashion for three years as an alternative or as a supplement to peacetime selective service, well qualified through rigorous standards, well trained in the languages, skills, and customs they will need to know, and directed and paid by the ICA Point Four [foreign aid] agencies.

We cannot discontinue training our young men as soldiers of war, but we also want them to be ambassadors of peace. . . . General Gavin, who jumped with his division in northern France, said that no young man today could serve his country with more distinction than in this struggle for peace around the world.

This would be a volunteer corps, and volunteers would be sought among not only talented young men and women, but all Americans, of whatever age, who wished to serve the great Republic and serve the cause of freedom. Men and women who have taught, or engineers or doctors or nurses, who have reached the age of retirement, or who in the midst of their work wished to serve their country and freedom, should be given an opportunity and an agency in which their talents could serve our country around the globe.

I am convinced that the pool of people in this country of ours anxious to respond to the public service is greater than it has ever been in our history. I am convinced that our men and women, dedicated to freedom, are able to be missionaries, not only for freedom and peace, but to join in a worldwide struggle against poverty and disease and ignorance, diseases in Latin America, for example, which prevented any child in two villages in Brazil in the last twelve months from reaching one year of age.

I think this country in the 1960s can start to move forward again. We can demonstrate what a free society, freely moving and working, can do.

Archimedes said, "Give me a fulcrum and I will move the world." We in the sixties are going to move the world again in the direction of freedom and I ask your help in doing so.

Campaign Speech
San Francisco, California, November 2, 1960

The End of the Campaign

. . . I come here in the last forty-eight hours of this campaign to the greatest rally that we have had in this entire campaign, right here in this city. (It is now a quarter to three [a.m.]—Dick Nixon has been in bed for four hours. . . .)

I run as a candidate for the Presidency with a view that this is a great country, but it must be greater. I want to see us build here in this country a strong and vital and progressive society that will serve as an inspiration to all those people who desire to follow the road that we have followed. . . . We defend freedom. If we succeed here, if we can build a strong and vital society, then the cause of freedom is strengthened. If we fail here, if we drift, if we lie at anchor, if we don't provide an example of what freedom can do in the 1960s, then we have betrayed not only ourselves and our destiny, but all those who desire to be free and are not free. That is why I think this election is important. That is why this is an important campaign.

Street Rally
Waterbury, Connecticut, November 6, 1960

The margin is narrow, but the responsibility is clear . . . a margin of only one vote would still be a mandate.

Press Conference
Hyannis Port, Massachusetts, November 9, 1960

I campaigned downstate with the . . . Lieutenant Governor. Politics is a rather humbling experience. I introduced Sam Shapiro all over Illinois and I figured that I was really going to help him along, and he told me tonight that he won by 250 thousand [votes]—I grabbed Sam Shapiro's coattail and he dragged me in.

Democratic Dinner
Chicago, Illinois, April 28, 1961

I have not always considered the membership of the NAM as among my strongest supporters. . . . I recognize that in the last campaign, most of the members of this luncheon group today supported my opponent, except for a very few—who were under the impression that I was my father's son.

National Association of Manufacturers
New York, New York, December 6, 1961

There is no city in the United States in which I get a warmer welcome and less votes than Columbus, Ohio!

Democratic Dinner
Columbus, Ohio, January 6, 1962

. . . Whatever other qualifications I may have had when I became President, one of them at least was that I knew Wisconsin better than any other President of the United States. That is an unchallengeable statement. My foot-tracks are in every house in this state. . . . I suppose that there is no training ground for the Presidency, but I don't think it's a bad idea for a President to have stood outside of Maier's meat factory in Madison, Wisconsin . . . at five-thirty in the morning, with the temperature ten above.

Wisconsin Democratic Dinner
Milwaukee, Wisconsin, May 12, 1962

CHAPTER 6

The Religious Issue

No obstacle to the Presidency handicapped or antagonized John F. Kennedy more than the widespread charge that a Catholic in the White House could not uphold this country's traditional and constitutional separation of church and state and could not place the national interest ahead of the dictates of his church hierarchy. Many who recalled Al Smith's defeat in the 1928 presidential election opposed Kennedy's nomination in the belief that he was unelectable. His primary victory in West Virginia, an overwhelmingly Protestant state, silenced many of the skeptics but not the bigots, whose charges Kennedy answered in historic fashion in his September 1960 address to the Houston Ministers Association. Even then, according to the University of Michigan post-election survey, Kennedy lost at least 4.5 million Protestant Democrats. Barring a presidential candidate on religious grounds was actually ended not by Kennedy's accession to the White House office but by his conduct of that office in strict adherence to his Houston pledge.

The Responsibility of the Press

I have decided to speak with you today about what has widely been called "the religious issue" in American politics. The phrase covers a multitude of meanings. It is inaccurate to state that my "candidacy created the issue"—that, because I am replying to the bigots, I am now "running on the religious issue in West Virginia" or that my statements in response to interrogation are "fanning the controversy." I am not "trying to be the first Catholic President," as some have written. I happen to believe I can serve my nation as President—and I also happen to have been born a Catholic.

Nor am I appealing, as is too often claimed, to a so-called Catholic vote. Even if such a vote exists—which I doubt—I want no votes solely on account of my religion. Any voter, Catholic or otherwise, who feels another candidate would be a superior president should support that candidate.

Neither do I want anyone to support my candidacy merely to prove that this nation is not bigoted—and that a Catholic can be elected President. I have never suggested that those opposed to me are thereby anti-Catholic. There are ample legitimate grounds for supporting other candidates (although I will not, of course, detail them here). Nor have I ever suggested that the Democratic Party is required to nominate me or face a Catholic revolt in November.

For my religion is hardly, in this critical year of 1960, the dominant issue of our time. It is hardly the most important criterion—or even a relevant criterion—on which the American people should make their choice for Chief Executive.

The members of the press should report the facts as they find them. They should describe the issues as they see them. But they should beware, it seems to me, of either magnifying this issue or oversimplifying it.

One article, for example, supposedly summing the Wisconsin primary up in advance, mentioned the word "Catholic" twenty times in fifteen paragraphs—not mentioning even once dairy farms, disarmament, labor legislation, or any other issue. And on the Sunday before the primary, the *Milwaukee Journal* featured a map of the state, listing county by county the relative strength of three types of voters—Democrats, Republicans, and Catholics.

In West Virginia, it is the same story. As reported in yesterday's *Washington Post,* the great bulk of West Virginians paid very little attention to my religion—until they read repeatedly in the nation's press that this was the decisive issue in West Virginia. There are many serious problems in that state—problems big enough to dominate any campaign—but religion is not one of them.

For the past months and years, I have answered almost daily inquiries from the press about the religious issue. I want to take this opportunity to turn the tables—and to raise some questions for your thoughtful consideration.

First: Is the religious issue a legitimate issue in this campaign? There is only one legitimate question underlying all the rest: Would you, as President of the United States, be responsive in any way to ecclesiastical pressures or obligations of any kind that might in any fashion influence or interfere with your conduct of that office in the national interest? I have answered that question many times. My answer was—and is—*no.*

First: Is the religious issue a legitimate issue in this campaign? . . . Secondly: Can we justify analyzing voters as well as candidates strictly in terms of their religion?

Once that question is answered, there is no legitimate issue of my religion. But there are, I think, legitimate questions of public policy of concern to religious groups which no one should feel bigoted about raising, and to which I do not object to answering. But I do object to being the only candidate required to answer those questions.

Federal assistance to parochial schools, for example, is a very legitimate issue actually before the Congress. I am opposed to it. I believe it is clearly unconstitutional. I voted against it on the Senate floor this year, when offered by Senator Morse. But, interestingly enough, I was the only announced candidate in the Senate who did so. (Nevertheless I have not yet charged my opponents with taking orders from Rome.)

An ambassador to the Vatican could conceivably become a real issue again. I am opposed to it, and said so long ago. But even though it was last proposed by a Baptist President, I know of no other candidate who has been even asked about this matter.

The prospects of any President ever receiving for his signature a bill providing foreign aid funds for birth control are very remote indeed. It is hardly the major issue some have suggested. Nevertheless I have made it clear that I would neither veto nor sign such a bill on any basis except what I considered to be the public interest, without regard to my private religious views. I have said the same about bills dealing with censorship, divorce, our relations with Spain, or any other subject.

These are legitimate inquiries about real questions which the next President may conceivably have to face. But these inquiries ought to be directed equally to all candidates. I have made it clear that I strongly support—out of conviction as well as constitutional obligation—the guarantees of religious equality provided by the First Amendment; and I ask only that these same guarantees be extended to me.

Secondly: Can we justify analyzing voters as well as candidates strictly in terms of their religion? I think the voters of Wisconsin objected to being categorized simply as either Catholics or Protestants in analyzing their political choices. I think they objected to being accosted by reporters outside of political meetings and asked one question only—their religion—not their occupation or education or philosophy or income, only their religion.

Only this week, I received a very careful analysis of the Wisconsin results. It conclusively shows two significant patterns of bloc voting: I ran strongest in those areas where the average temperature in January was twenty degrees or higher, and poorest in those areas where it was fourteen degrees or lower—and I ran well in the beech tree and basswood counties and not so well among the hemlock and pine.

This analysis stands up statistically much better than all the so-called analyses of the religious vote. And so do analyses of each county based on their distance from the Minnesota border, the length of their Democratic tradition, and their inclusion in my campaign itinerary. I carried some areas with large proportions of voters who are Catholics—and I lost some. I carried some areas where Protestants predominate—and I lost some.

For voters are more than Catholics, Protestants, or Jews. They make up their minds for many diverse reasons, good and bad. To submit the candidates to a religious test is unfair enough—to apply it to the voters themselves is divisive, degrading, and wholly unwarranted.

Third and finally: Is there any justification for applying special religious tests to one office only: the Presidency? Little or no attention was paid to my religion when I took the oath as Senator in 1953—as a Congressman in 1947—or as a naval officer in 1941. Members of my faith abound in public office at every level except the White House. What is there about the Presidency that justifies this constant emphasis upon a candidate's religion and that of his supporters?

The Presidency is not, after all, the British Crown, serving a dual capacity in both church and state. The President is not elected to be protector of the faith or guardian of the public morals. His attendance at church on Sunday should be his business alone, not a showcase for the nation.

On the other hand, the President, however intent he may be on subverting our institutions, cannot ignore the Congress—or the voters—or the courts. And our highest court, incidentally, has a long history of Catholic justices, none of whom, as far as I know, was ever challenged on the fairness of his rulings on sensitive church-state issues.

Some may say we treat the Presidency differently because we have had only one previous Catholic candidate for President. But I am growing weary of that term. I am not the Catholic candidate for President. I do not speak for the Catholic Church on issues of public policy—and no one in that Church speaks for me. My record on aid to education, aid to Tito, the Conant nomination, and other issues has displeased some prominent Catholic clergymen and organizations; and it has been approved by others. The fact is that the Catholic Church is not a monolith—it is committed in this country to the principles of individual liberty—and it has no claim over my conduct as a public officer sworn to do the public interest.

So I hope we can see the beginning of the end of references to me as "the Catholic candidate" for President. Do not expect me to explain or defend every act or statement of every pope or priest, in this country or some other, in this century or the last.

I have tried to examine with you today the press's responsibility in meeting this religious issue. The question remains: What is *my* responsibility? I am a candidate. The issue is here. Two alternatives have been suggested:

1. The first suggestion is that I withdraw to avoid a "dangerous religious controversy," and accept the Vice-Presidential nomination in order to placate the so-called Catholic vote.

I find that suggestion highly distasteful. It assumes the worst about a country which prides itself on being more tolerant and better educated than it was in 1928. It assumes that Catholics are a pawn on the political chessboard, moved hither and yon, and somehow "bought off" by the party putting in the second spot a Catholic whom the party barred from the top. And it forgets, finally, that such a performance would have an effect on our image abroad as well as our self-respect here at home.

Are we going to admit to the world that a Jew can be elected mayor of Dublin, a Protestant can be chosen foreign minister of France, a Moslem can serve in the Israeli Parliament—but a Catholic cannot be President of the United States? Are we to tell Chancellor Adenauer, for example, that we want him risking his all on our front lines; but that if he were an American, we would never entrust him with our Presidency—nor would we accept our distinguished guest, General de Gaulle? Are we to admit to the world—worse still, are we to admit to ourselves—that one third of our population is forever barred from the White House?

So I am not impressed by those pleas that I settle for the Vice-Presidency in order to avert a religious spectacle. Surely those who believe it dangerous to elect a Catholic as President will not want him to serve as Vice-President, a heartbeat away from the office.

2. The alternative is to proceed with the primaries, the convention, and the election. If there is bigotry in the country, then so be it—there is bigotry. If that bigotry is too great to permit the fair consideration of a Catholic who has made clear his complete independence and his complete dedication to separation of church and state, then we ought to know it.

But I do not believe that this is the case. I believe the American people are more concerned with a man's views and abilities than with the church to which he belongs. I believe that the Founding Fathers meant it when they provided in Article VI of the Constitution that there should be no religious test for public office—a provision that brought not one dissenting vote, only the comment of Roger Sherman that it was surely unnecessary.

I am confident that the press and other media of this country will recognize their responsibilities in this area—to refute falsehood, to inform the ignorant, and to concentrate on the issues, the *real* issues, in this hour of the nation's peril.

American Society of Newspaper Editors
Washington, D.C., April 21, 1960

I sat next to Cardinal Spellman at dinner the other evening, and asked him what I should say when voters question me about the doctrine of the pope's infallibility. "I don't know, Senator," the Cardinal told me. "All I know is he keeps calling me Spillman."

Bronx Democratic Dinner
New York, New York, April 1960

The Refutation of Bigotry

I am grateful for your generous invitation to speak my views.

While the so-called religious issue is necessarily and properly the chief topic here tonight, I want to emphasize from the outset that we have far more critical issues to face in the 1960 election; the spread of Communist influence, until it now festers ninety miles off the coast of Florida; the humiliating treatment of our President and Vice-President by those who no longer respect our power; the hungry children I saw in West Virginia, the old people who cannot pay their doctor bills, the families forced to give up their farms; an America with too many slums, with too few schools, and too late to the moon and outer space.

These are the real issues which should decide this campaign. And they are not religious issues—for war and hunger and ignorance and despair know no religious barriers.

But because I am a Catholic, and no Catholic has ever been elected President, the real issues in this campaign have been obscured—perhaps deliberately, in some quarters less responsible than this. So it is apparently necessary for me to state once again—not what kind of church I believe in, for that should be important only to me—but what kind of America I believe in.

I believe in an America where the separation of church and state is absolute—where no Catholic prelate would tell the President (should he be Catholic) how to act, and no Protestant minister would tell his parishioners for whom to vote—where no church or church school is granted any public funds or political preference—and where no man is denied public office merely because his religion differs from the President who might appoint him or the people who might elect him.

I believe in an America that is officially neither Catholic, Protestant, nor Jewish—where no public official either requests or accepts instructions on public policy from the pope, the National Council of Churches, or any other ecclesiastical source—where no religious body seeks to impose its will directly or indirectly upon the general populace or the public acts of its officials—and where religious liberty is so indivisible that an act against one church is treated as an act against all.

For while this year it may be a Catholic against whom the finger of suspicion is pointed, in other years it has been, and may someday be again, a Jew—or a Quaker—or a Unitarian—or a Baptist. It was Virginia's harassment of Baptist preachers, for example, that helped lead to Jefferson's Statute of Religious Freedom. Today I may be the victim—but tomorrow it may be you—until the whole fabric of our harmonious society is ripped at a time of great national peril.

Finally, I believe in an America where religious intolerance will someday end—where all men and all churches are treated as equal—where every man has the same right to attend or not attend the church of his choice—where there is no Catholic vote, no anti-Catholic vote, no bloc voting of any kind—and where Catholics, Protestants, and Jews, at both the lay and pastoral level, will refrain from those attitudes of disdain and division which have so often marred their works in the past, and promote instead the American ideal of brotherhood.

That is the kind of America in which I believe. And it represents the kind of Presidency in which I believe—a great office that must neither be humbled by making it the instrument of any one religious group nor tarnished by arbitrarily withholding its occupancy from the members of any one religious group. I believe in a President whose religious views are his own private affair, neither imposed by him upon the nation or imposed by the nation upon him as a condition to holding that office.

I would not look with favor upon a President working to subvert the First Amendment's guarantees of religious liberty. Nor would our system of checks and balances permit him to do so—and neither do I look with favor upon those who would work to subvert Article VI of the Constitution by requiring a religious test—even by indirection—for public office. If they disagree with that safeguard, they should be out openly working to repeal it.

I want a Chief Executive whose public acts are responsible to all groups and obligated to none—who can attend any ceremony, service, or dinner his office may appropriately require of him—and whose fulfillment of his presidential oath is not limited or conditioned by any religious oath, ritual, or obligation.

This is the kind of America I believe in—and this is the kind I fought for in the South Pacific, and the kind my brother died for in Europe. No one suggested then that we might have a "divided loyalty," that we did "not believe in liberty," or that we belonged to a disloyal group that threatened the "freedoms for which our forefathers died."

And in fact this is the kind of America for which our forefathers died—when they fled here to escape religious test oaths that denied office to members of less favored churches—when they fought for the Constitution, the Bill of Rights, and the Virginia Statute of Religious Freedom—and when they fought at the shrine I visited today, the Alamo. For side by side with Bowie and Crockett died McCafferty and Bailey and Carey—but no one knows whether they were Catholics or not. For there was no religious test at the Alamo.

I believe in an America where the separation of church and state is absolute. . . . I believe in a President whose religious views are his own private affair.

I ask you tonight to follow in that tradition—to judge me on the basis of my record of fourteen years in Congress—on my declared stands against an ambassador to the Vatican, against unconstitutional aid to parochial schools, and against any boycott of the public schools (which I have attended myself)—instead of judging me on the basis of these pamphlets and publications we all have seen that carefully select quotations out of context from the statements of Catholic leaders, usually in other countries, frequently in other centuries, and always omitting, of course, the statement of the American bishops in 1948 which strongly endorsed church-state separation, and which more nearly reflects the views of almost every American Catholic.

I do not consider these other quotations binding upon my public acts—why should you? But let me say, with respect to other countries, that I am wholly opposed to the state being used by any religious group, Catholic or Protestant, to compel, prohibit, or persecute the free exercise of any other religion. And I hope that you and I condemn with equal fervor those nations which deny their Presidency to Protestants and those which deny it to Catholics. And rather than cite the misdeeds of those who differ, I would cite the record of the Catholic Church in such nations as Ireland and France—and the independence of such statesmen as Adenauer and de Gaulle.

But let me stress again that these are my views—for, contrary to common newspaper usages I am not the Catholic candidate for President. I am the Democratic Party's candidate for President who happens also to be a Catholic. I do not speak for my church on public matters—and the Church does not speak for me.

Whatever issue may come before me as President—on birth control, divorce, censorship, gambling, or any other subject—I will make my decision in accordance with these views, in accordance with what my conscience tells me to be the national interest, and without regard to outside religious pressures or dictates. And no power or threat of punishment could cause me to decide otherwise.

But if the time should ever come—and I do not concede any conflict to be even remotely possible—when my office would require me to either violate my conscience or violate the national interest, then I would resign the office; and I hope any conscientious public servant would do the same.

But I do not intend to apologize for these views to my critics of either Catholic or Protestant faith—nor do I intend to disavow either my views or my church in order to win this election.

If I should lose on the real issues, I shall return to my seat in the Senate, satisfied that I had tried my best and was fairly judged. But if this election is decided on the basis that forty million Americans lost their chance of being President on the day they were baptized, then it is the whole nation that will be the loser, in the eyes of Catholics and non-Catholics around the world, in the eyes of history, and in the eyes of our own people.

But if, on the other hand, I should win the election, then I shall devote every effort of mind and spirit to fulfilling the oath of the Presidency—practically identical, I might add, to the oath I have taken for fourteen years in the Congress. For, without reservation, I can "solemnly swear that I will faithfully execute the office of President of the United States, and will to the best of my ability preserve, protect, and defend the Constitution . . . so help me God."

Q: If this meeting tonight were held in the sanctuary of my church, it is the policy of my city that has many fine Catholics in it, it is the policy of the Catholic leadership to forbid them to attend a Protestant service. If we tonight were in the sanctuary of my church, as we are, could you and would you attend, as you have here?

SENATOR KENNEDY: Yes; I could. As I said in my statement I would attend any service that has any connection with my public office, or, in the case of a private ceremony, weddings, funerals and so on, of course I would participate and have participated. I think the only question would be whether I could participate as a participant, a believer in your faith, and maintain my membership in my church. That, it seems to me, comes within the private beliefs that a Catholic might have. But as far as whether I could attend this sort of a function in your church, whether I as Senator or President could attend a function in your service connected with my position of office, then I could attend and would attend. . . .

Q: If you are elected President, will you use your influence to get the Roman Catholic countries of South America and Spain to stop persecuting Protestant missionaries and enable them to propagate their faith as the United States gives to the Roman Catholics or any other group?

SENATOR KENNEDY: I would use my influence as President of the United States to permit, to encourage the development of freedom all over the world. One of the rights which I consider to be important is the right of free speech, the right of assembly, the right of free religious practice, and I would hope that the United States and the President would stand for those rights all around the globe without regard to geography or religion.

Q: Senator Kennedy, I have received today a copy of a resolution passed by the Baptist Pastors Conference of St. Louis, and they are going to confront you with this tomorrow night. I would like you to answer to the Houston crowd before you get to St. Louis. This is the resolution:

> With deep sincerity and in Christian grace, we plead with Senator John F. Kennedy as the person presently concerned in this matter to appeal to Cardinal Cushing, Mr. Kennedy's own hierarchical superior in Boston, to present to the Vatican Senator Kennedy's statement relative to the separation of church and state in the United States and religious freedom as separated in the Constitution of the United States, in order that the Vatican may officially authorize such a belief for all Roman Catholics in the United States.

SENATOR KENNEDY: May I just say that, as I do not accept the right of any ecclesiastical official to tell me what I shall do in the sphere of my public responsibility as an elected official, I do not propose to ask Cardinal Cushing to ask the Vatican to take some action. I do not propose to interfere with their free right to do exactly what they want. There is no doubt in my mind that the viewpoint that I have expressed tonight publicly represents the opinion of the overwhelming majority of American Catholics, and I think that my view is known to Catholics around the world.

Q: We appreciate your forthright statement. May I say we have great admiration for you. But until we know this is the position of your church, because there will be many Catholics who will be appointed if you are elected President, we would like to know that they, too, are free to make such statements as you have been so courageous to make.

SENATOR KENNEDY: Let me say that anyone that I would appoint to office as a Senator or as a President, would, I hope, hold the same view, of necessity, of living up to not only the letter of the Constitution but the spirit. I believe I am stating the viewpoint that Catholics in this country hold on the happy relationship which exists between church and state.

Q: Do you state it with the approval of the Vatican?

SENATOR KENNEDY: I don't have to have approval in that sense. I have not submitted my statement before I read it to the Vatican. I did not submit it to Cardinal Cushing. But my judgment is that Cardinal Cushing, who is the Cardinal of the diocese of which I am a member, would approve of this statement, [but] I am the one that is running for the office of the Presidency and not Cardinal Cushing and not anyone else. . . .

I guess our time is coming to an end, but let me say finally that I am delighted to come here today. I don't want anyone to think, because they interrogate me on this very important question, that I regard that as unfair questioning or unreasonable, or that somebody who is concerned about the matter is prejudiced or bigoted. I think this fight for religious freedom is basic in the establishment of the American system, and therefore any candidate for the office should submit himself to the questions of any reasonable man.

My only objection would be—my only limit to that would be—if somebody said: "regardless of Senator Kennedy's position, regardless of how much evidence he has given that what he says he means, I still would not vote for him because he is a member of that church." I would consider that unreasonable. What I would consider to be reasonable, in an exercise of free will and free choice, is to ask the candidate to state his views as broadly as possible, to investigate his record to see whether what he states he believes, and then to make an independent, rational judgment as to whether he could be entrusted with this highly important position.

I want you to know that I am grateful to you for inviting me tonight. I am sure I have made no converts to my church. But I do hope that at least my view, which I believe to be the view of my fellow Catholics who hold office, may be of some value in assisting you to make a careful judgment. Thank you.

Greater Houston Ministerial Association
Houston, Texas, September 12, 1960

The Differences From 1928

I am glad to be here at this notable dinner once again, and I am glad that Mr. Nixon is here also. Now that Cardinal Spellman has demonstrated the proper spirit, I assume that shortly I will be invited to a Quaker dinner honoring Herbert Hoover.

Cardinal Spellman is the only man so widely respected in American politics that he could bring together, amicably, at the same banquet table, for the first time in this campaign, two political leaders who are increasingly apprehensive about the November election, who have long eyed each other suspiciously, and who have disagreed so strongly, both publicly and privately, Vice-President Nixon and Governor Rockefeller.

Mr. Nixon, like the rest of us, has had his troubles in this campaign. At one point even *The Wall Street Journal* was criticizing his tactics. That is like the *Osservatore Romano* criticizing the pope. . . .

One of the inspiring notes that was struck in the last debate was struck by the Vice-President in his very moving warning to the children of the nation and the candidates against the use of profanity by Presidents and ex-Presidents when they are on the stump. (And I know after fourteen years in the Congress with the Vice-President that he was very sincere in his views about the use of profanity.) But I am told that a prominent Republican said to him yesterday in Jacksonville, Florida, "Mr. Vice-President, that was a damn fine speech." And the Vice-President said, "I appreciate the compliment but not the language." And the Republican went on, "Yes, sir, I liked it so much that I contributed a thousand dollars to your campaign." And Mr. Nixon replied, "The hell you say."

However, I would not want to give the impression that I am taking former president Truman's use of language lightly. I have sent him the following wire:

> Dear Mr. President: I have noted with interest your suggestion as to where those who vote for my opponent should go. While I understand and sympathize with your deep motivation, I think it is important that our side try to refrain from raising the religious issue.

One of the subjects that interests candidates and those who write about candidates is whether 1960 will be another 1928. I have had some interest in that question myself. Looking at the speeches of Governor

Smith in the 1928 campaign, I am struck by the continuity of the themes. The 1928 and 1960 campaigns, with all of the obvious differences, have much in common. In 1928, as in 1960, the Yankees won the pennant, the Postmaster General was promising efficient mail delivery at last, and farm purchasing power was down some twenty percent compared to eight years earlier. Three million people had left the farms in that period, just as they have in the last eight years. The stock market was unstable and two thirds of all corporate profits went to one fourth of one percent of the corporations.

In 1960, the citizens of this country face not only the great question of whether freedom will prevail, but also whether it will even endure.

In September 1928, the Republican candidate for the Presidency declared: "Real wages have improved more during the past seven and a half years than in any similar period in the history of our country." He spoke of the country's unparalleled progress. He stressed that American comfort, hope, and confidence for the future were immeasurably higher than they were seven and a half years ago.

The Democratic candidate in 1928 questioned how stable our prosperity was. He pointed to the pockets of industrial unemployment. He warned of a farm depression. He criticized administration farm vetoes. He stressed, and I quote him, "the necessity for the restoration of cordial relations with Latin America" and he called for more effective action on disarmament.

The Democratic nominee in 1928 spoke . . . about building a stronger America, strengthening not only our economy but our sense of moral purpose and our public duty. In all of these and other ways, 1960 and 1928 may be sisters under the skin.

Some say that this will also be true when the ballots are counted, that the religious convictions of the candidates will influence the outcome more than their convictions on the issues. But this is where I believe that

1928 and 1960 are very different. Regardless of the outcome, and regardless of these similarities, I do not believe the American voter in 1960 is the same as the American voter of 1928. For we live in a different world.

There are a billion more people crowding our globe, and every American can hear the rumbling of a distant drum. The next President will have a budget twenty-five times as large as that of the candidates in Al Smith's time—and he will face problems unprecedented in that time or in any time in our long history, automation and unemployment, farm surpluses and food shortages, a high cost of living in the midst of an economic slump, new nations, new leaders. The world is different across the street and on the other side of the moon. The white race is in the minority, the free-enterprise system is in the minority and the majority are looking at us harder and longer than they ever looked before.

The people who live in the tenements of Africa and Asia and Latin America want to fight their way out of the slums. The Lower East Side of the world is looking for help, and unlike 1928 the Lower East Side of the world has a voice and a vote.

"The world is large," John Boyle O'Reilly wrote, "the world is large when its weary league two loving hearts divide, but the world is small when your enemy is loose on the other side."

In 1960, as never before, our enemy is loose on the other side. In 1928 the voters perhaps could be excused for not seeing the storm coming, the Depression, the Japanese conquest of Manchuria, Hitler's rise, and all the rest. But in 1960, the citizens of this country face not only the great question of whether freedom will prevail, but also whether it will even endure. Thus, 1960 and 1928 are very different. It will be with this view of America that we shall accept the fortunes of November 8, 1960, be they favorable or unfavorable, good or bad.

The American people in 1960 see the storm coming. They see the perils ahead. 1960 is not 1928. I am confident that, whatever their verdict, Republican or Democratic, myself or Mr. Nixon, their judgment will be based not on any extraneous issue, but on the real issues of our time, on what is best for our country, on the hard facts that face us, on the convictions of the candidates and their parties, and on their ability to interpret them.

When this happens, then the bitter memory of 1928 will begin to fade, and all that will remain will be the figure of Al Smith, large against the horizon, true, courageous, and honest, who, in the words of the Cardinal, served his country well, and having served his country well, nobly served his God.

Annual Al Smith Memorial Dinner
New York, New York, October 19, 1960

The Responsibility of Parents

Q: Mr. President, in the furor over the Supreme Court's decision on prayer in the schools, some members of Congress have been introducing legislation for constitutional amendments specifically to sanction prayer or religious exercise in the schools. Can you give us your opinion of the decision itself and of these moves of the Congress to circumvent it?

THE PRESIDENT: I haven't seen the measures in the Congress and . . . would have to make a determination of what the language was and what effect it would have on the First Amendment. The Supreme Court has made its judgment, and a good many people obviously will disagree with it. . . . But I think it is important, if we are going to maintain our constitutional principle, [to]support the Supreme Court decisions even when we may not agree with them.

In addition, we have in this case a very easy remedy and that is to pray ourselves. I would think that it would be a welcome reminder to every American family that we can pray a good deal more at home, we can attend our churches with a good deal more fidelity, and we can make the true meaning of prayer much more important in the lives of all of our children. . . . I would hope that as a result of this decision that all American parents will intensify their efforts at home—and the rest of us will support the Constitution and the responsibility of the Supreme Court in interpreting it—which is theirs, and given to them by the Constitution.

President's News Conference
Washington, D.C., June 27, 1962

On the stump, 1962.
PHOTO COURTESY CECIL W. STOUGHTON.

PART III

The New Frontier

CHAPTER 7

The Restoration of Economic Growth

In 1960, America was crippled by a spreading recession, and John Kennedy campaigned on a vow "to get this country moving again." Once elected, he set out to do just that, moved by the same sense of economic justice that had sparked his plea for veterans' housing in one of his earliest speeches in Congress. Though he felt more expert regarding foreign affairs, the long hours that he invested in new or revamped economic, social, budgetary, and anti-inflationary policies helped produce this century's longest and strongest period of American economic growth.

The Angry Young Congressman

Mr. Speaker, this Congress will adjourn Saturday. It will have considered action on many matters of varying importance, but it will not have taken any action to meet the most pressing problem with which this country is now confronted—the severe ever-growing shortage of housing which faces our veterans and others of moderate income. . . .

The Bureau of the Census, in a recent survey, stated that there were 160,000 veterans of World War II in the Boston area in July of 1946. Forty-two percent of the veterans who were married among this group were living in rented rooms or doubled up. Their need is drastic. . . .

The inflated costs of building have priced new homes right out of the price level that veterans can afford to pay. This is the situation facing every veteran in this country today. It is the most important problem they face.

The majority party of this House has done nothing to help these men meet this great problem. They have spent $35 billion. They have subsidized industries. They have late this afternoon called for an investigation of the housing shortage. Since before the war ended we have been making investigations. The facts are known. This gesture by the Republican Party is a fraud—in order to draw attention away from their crass ignorance of this problem during the seven months they have been in control. They have always been receptive to the best interests of the real estate and building associations, but when it came to spending money to secure homes for the people of this country, they just were not interested.

I was sent to this Congress by the people of my district to help solve the most pressing problem facing the country—the housing crisis.

I am going to have to go back to my district Saturday, a district that sent probably more boys per family into this last war than any in the country, and when they ask me if I was able to get them any homes, I will have to answer, "not a one—not a single one."

U.S. House of Representatives
Washington, D.C., July 24, 1947

The Determined New President

The present state of our economy is disturbing. We take office in the wake of seven months of recession, three and one half years of slack, seven years of diminished economic growth, and nine years of falling farm income.

Business bankruptcies have reached their highest level since the Great Depression. Since 1951 farm income has been squeezed down by twenty-five percent. Save for a brief period in 1958, insured unemployment is at the highest peak in our history. Of some five and one-half million Americans who are without jobs, more than one million have been searching for work for more than four months. And during each month some 150,000 workers are exhausting their already meager jobless benefit rights.

Nearly one eighth of those who are without jobs live almost without hope in nearly one hundred especially depressed and troubled areas. The rest include new school graduates unable to use their talents, farmers forced to give up their part-time jobs which helped balance their family budgets, skilled and unskilled workers laid off in such important industries as metals, machinery, automobiles, and apparel.

Our recovery from the 1958 recession, moreover, was anemic and incomplete. Our gross national product never regained its full potential. Unemployment never returned to normal levels. Maximum use of our national industrial capacity was never restored.

In short, the American economy is in trouble. The most resourceful industrialized country on earth ranks among the last in the rate of economic growth. Since last spring our economic growth rate has actually receded. Business investment is in a decline. Profits have fallen below predicted levels. Construction is off. A million unsold automobiles are in inventory. Fewer people are working and the average work week has shrunk well below forty hours. Yet prices have continued to rise—so that now too many Americans have less to spend for items that cost more to buy.

Economic prophecy is at best an uncertain art—as demonstrated by the prediction one year ago from this same podium that 1960 would be, and I quote, "the most prosperous year in our history." Nevertheless, forecasts of continued slack and only slightly reduced unemployment through 1961 and 1962 have been made with alarming unanimity—and this administration does not intend to stand helplessly by.

We cannot afford to waste idle hours and empty plants while awaiting the end of the recession. We must show the world what a free economy can do—to reduce unemployment, to put unused capacity to work, to spur new productivity, and to foster higher economic growth within a range of sound fiscal policies and relative price stability.

I will propose to the Congress within the next fourteen days measures to improve unemployment compensation through temporary increases in duration on a self-supporting basis—to provide more food for the families of the unemployed, and to aid their needy children; to redevelop our areas of chronic labor surplus; to expand the services of the U.S. employment offices; to stimulate housing and construction; to secure more purchasing power for our lowest-paid workers by raising and expanding the minimum wage; to offer tax incentives for sound plant investment; to increase the development of our natural resources; to encourage price stability; and to take other steps aimed at insuring a prompt recovery and paving the way for increased long-range growth. This is not a partisan program concentrating on our weaknesses—it is, I hope, a national program to realize our national strength. . . .

We must show the world what a free economy can do.

Our national household is cluttered with unfinished and neglected tasks. Our cities are being engulfed in squalor. Twelve long years after Congress declared our goal to be "a decent home and a suitable environment for every American family," we still have 25 million Americans living in substandard homes. A new housing program under a new Housing and Urban Affairs Department will be needed this year.

Our classrooms contain 2 million more children than they can properly have room for, taught by 90,000 teachers not properly qualified to teach. One third of our most promising high school graduates are financially unable to continue the development of their talents. The war babies of the 1940s, who overcrowded our schools in the 1950s, are now descending in 1960 upon our colleges—with two college students for every one, ten years from now—and our colleges are ill prepared. We lack the scientists, the engineers, and the teachers our world obligations require. We have neglected oceanography, saline-water conversion, and the basic research that lies at the root of all progress. Federal grants for both higher and public school education can no longer be delayed.

Medical research has achieved new wonders—but these wonders are too often beyond the reach of too many people, owing to a lack of income (particularly among the aged), a lack of hospital beds, a lack of nursing homes, and a lack of doctors and dentists. Measures to provide health care for the aged under Social Security, and to increase the supply of both facilities and personnel, must be undertaken this year.

Our supply of clean water is dwindling. Organized and juvenile crimes cost the taxpayers millions of dollars each year, making it essential that we have improved enforcement and new legislative safeguards. The denial of constitutional rights to some of our fellow Americans on account of race—at the ballot box and elsewhere—disturbs the national conscience, and subjects us to the charge of world opinion that our democracy is not equal to the high promise of our heritage. Morality in private business has not been sufficiently spurred by morality in public business. A host of problems and projects in all fifty states, though not possible to include in this message, deserves—and will receive—the attention of both the Congress and the executive branch. On most of these matters, messages will be sent to the Congress within the next two weeks.

State of the Union Address
The Capitol, Washington, D.C.
January 30, 1961

The Road to Recovery

Today, I would briefly mention three areas of common concern . . . economic growth, plant modernization, and price stability.

I

First: Economic growth has come to resemble the Washington weather —everyone talks about it, no one says precisely what to do about it, and our only satisfaction is that it can't get any worse.

The economic program which I have set before the Congress is essentially a program for recovery—and I do not equate recovery with growth. But it is an essential first step. Only by putting millions of people back to work can we expand purchasing power and markets. Only by higher income and profits can we provide the incentive and the means for increased investment. And only when we are using our plants at near capacity can we expect any solid expansion.

Capacity operation is the key. No matter what other arguments or stimulants are used, the incentives for investing new capital to expand manufacturing plants and equipment are weak as long as manufacturers are operating at less than eighty percent of their capacity. From 1950 to 1958, we put only one sixth of our total output into capital formation, while Japan, Germany, Italy, the Netherlands, Canada, and Sweden were all investing one fifth or more of their total output in capital goods. So it is not surprising that each of these and other nations over the past several years have all surpassed us in average annual rate of economic growth.

I think we can do better. Working together, business and government must do better—putting people back to work, using plants to capacity, and spurring savings and investments with at least a large part of our economic gains—beginning not when our economy is back at the top, but beginning now.

II

Secondly: New plant investment not only means expansion of capacity—it means modernization as well. Gleaming new factories and headlines about automation have diverted our attention from an aging industrial plant. Obsolescence is slowing down our growth, handicapping our productivity, and worsening our competitive position abroad.

Nothing can reverse our balance of payments deficit if American machinery and equipment cannot produce the newest products of the highest quality in the most efficient manner. The available evidence on the age of our industrial plant is unofficial and fragmentary; but the trend is unmistakable—we are falling behind.

The average age of equipment in American factories today is about nine years. In a dynamic economy, that average should be falling, as new equipment is put into place. Instead, the available evidence suggests that it has been slowly rising.

Private surveys of machine tools used by manufacturers of general industrial equipment found less than half of these tools over ten years old in 1949 but two thirds over that age in 1958. Nineteen percent of our machine tools were found to be over twenty years old.

But modernization and productivity depend upon more than investment in physical resources . . . there is a direct connection between increased emphasis on education in this country and also upon increased productivity and technological change.

Meanwhile, other countries have been lowering the average age of their fixed capital. The German example is the most spectacular—their proportion of capital equipment and plants under five years of age grew from one sixth of the total in 1948 to two fifths in 1957.

All of these facts point in one direction: We must start now to provide additional stimulus to the modernization of American industrial plants. Within the next few weeks, I shall propose to the Congress a new tax incentive for businesses to expand their normal investment in plants and equipment.

But modernization and productivity depend upon more than investment in physical resources. . . . Equally essential is investment in human resources. And I think that this is obvious to those of us who have considered the problems of unemployment and depressed areas. There is no doubt that the maximum impact of a reducing economy falls upon those who are at the bottom of the educational ladder. The first people unemployed are those with the least education, the last people to be hired back are those with the least education. So there is a direct connection between increased emphasis on education in this country and also upon increased productivity and technological change.

Without strengthened programs for health, education, and science and research, the new modern plant would only be a hollow shell. Many of these programs are within the province of state and local governments. Full recovery will increase the tax revenues that they so sorely need. But the federal government will have to pay its fair share of developing these human resources.

III

Finally, government and business must turn their attention to the problem of price stability. Concern over the resumption of inflationary pressures hangs over all our efforts to restore the economy, to stimulate its growth, and to maintain our competitive status abroad. In recent days, complaints have been voiced in some quarters that this administration was not meeting its responsibilities in this area. But the facts are that, whatever one may regard our responsibilities to be, we are almost totally without direct and enforceable powers over the central problem. A free government in a free society has only a limited influence—provided that they are above the minimum—over prices and wages freely set and bargained for by free individuals and free enterprises. And this is as it should be if our economy is to remain free.

Nevertheless, the public interest in major wage and price determinations is substantial. Ways must be found to bring that public interest before the parties concerned in a fair and orderly manner.

For this reason, I have announced my determination to establish a Presidential Advisory Committee on Labor-Management Policy, with members drawn from labor, management, and the public. I want this committee to play a major role in helping promote sound wage and price policies, productivity increases, and a betterment of America's competitive position in world markets. I will look to this committee to make an important contribution to labor-management relations, and to a wider understanding of their impact on price stability and our economic health. And in this undertaking, I ask and urge the constructive cooperation of this organization and its members.

Economic growth, plant modernization, price stability—these are all intangible and elusive goals. But they are all essential to your success, and to the success of our country. Initiative, innovation, hard work, and cooperation will be required, on your part, and on ours.

But I have confidence in our nation, confidence in our economy, and confidence in your ability to meet your obligations fully. I hope that my associates and I can merit your confidence as well. For I can assure you that we love our country, not for what it was, though it has always been great—not for what it is, though of this we are deeply proud—but for what it someday can and, through the efforts of us all, someday will be.

National Industrial Conference Board
Washington, D.C., February 13, 1961

The Prudent Steward

This administration intends to adhere during the course of its term of office to the following basic principles:

1. Federal revenue and expenditure levels must be adequate to meet effectively and efficiently those essential needs of the nation which require public support as well as, or in place of, private effort. We can afford to do what must be done, publicly and privately, up to the limit of our economic capacity—a limit we have not even approached for several years.

2. Federal revenues and expenditures—the federal budget—should, apart from any threat to national security, be in balance over the years of the business cycle, running a deficit in years of recession when revenues decline and the economy needs the stimulus of additional expenditures, and running a surplus in years of prosperity, thus curbing inflation, reducing the public debt, and freeing funds for private investment.

3. Federal expenditure and revenue programs should contribute to economic growth and maximum employment within a setting of reasonable price stability. Because of the limits which our balance of payments deficit currently places upon the use of monetary policy, especially the lowering of short-term interest rates, as a means of stimulating economic growth and employment, fiscal policy—our budget and tax policies—must assume a heavier share of the responsibility.

4. Each expenditure proposed will be evaluated in terms of our national needs and priorities, consistent with the limitations and objectives described above and compared with the urgency of other budgetary requirements. We will not waste our resources on inefficient or undesirable expenditure simply because the economy is slack—nor, in order to run a surplus, will we deny our people essential services or security simply because the economy is prosperous.

5. As the nation, its needs, and their complexity continue to grow, federal nondefense expenditures may also be expected to increase, as predicted by a 1960 Bureau of the Budget study, and as indicated by the nearly forty-five percent increase from fiscal 1953 to fiscal 1961 in expenditures other than national security. But we must not allow expenditures to rise of their own momentum, without regard to value received, prospective revenues, economic conditions, the possibilities

of closing out old activities when initiating new ones, and the weight of current taxes on the individual citizen and the economy. It is my determined purpose to be a prudent steward of the public funds—to obtain a dollar's worth of results for every dollar we spend.

Special Message to Congress on Budget and Fiscal Policy
Washington, D.C., March 24, 1961

The Expansion of Opportunity

When the youngest child alive today has grown to the cares of manhood, our position in the world will be determined first of all by what provisions we make today—for his education, his health, and his opportunities for a good home and a good job and a good life.

At home, we began the year in the valley of recession—we completed it on the high road of recovery and growth. . . . At year's end the economy which Mr. Khrushchev once called a "stumbling horse" was racing to new records in consumer spending, labor income, and industrial production.

We are gratified—but we are not satisfied. Too many unemployed are still looking for the blessings of prosperity. As those who leave our schools and farms demand new jobs, automation takes old jobs away. To expand our growth and job opportunities, I urge on the Congress measures [for] Manpower Training and Development . . . Youth Employment Opportunities . . . and tax credits for investment in machinery and equipment.

Moreover—pleasant as it may be to bask in the warmth of recovery—let us not forget that we have suffered three recessions in the last seven years. The time to repair the roof is when the sun is shining—by filling . . . basic gaps in our antirecession protection. . . .

If we enact this . . . program, we can show the whole world that a free economy need not be an unstable economy—that a free system need not leave men unemployed—and that a free society is not only the most productive but the most stable form of organization yet fashioned by man.

But recession is only one enemy of a free economy—inflation is another. Last year, 1961, despite rising production and demand, consumer prices held almost steady—and wholesale prices declined. This is the best record of overall price stability of any comparable period of recovery since the end of World War II.

Inflation too often follows in the shadow of growth—while price stability is made easy by stagnation or controls. But we mean to maintain both stability and growth in a climate of freedom.

Our first line of defense against inflation is the good sense and public spirit of business and labor—keeping their total increases in wages and profits in step with productivity. There is no single statistical test to guide each company and each union. But I strongly urge them—for their country's interest, and for their own—to apply the test of the public interest to these transactions.

I am submitting for fiscal 1963 a balanced federal budget.

I am submitting for fiscal 1963 a balanced federal budget.

But a stronger nation and economy require more than a balanced budget. They require progress in those programs that spur our growth and fortify our strength. . . . a new Department of Urban Affairs and Housing . . . a new comprehensive farm program . . . a new long-range conservation and recreation program—expansion of our superb national parks and forests; preservation of our authentic wilderness areas; new starts on water and power projects as our population steadily increases; and expanded REA [Rural Electrification Administration] generation and transmission loans.

Finally, a strong America cannot neglect the aspirations of its citizens—the welfare of the needy, the health care of the elderly, the education of the young. For we are not developing the nation's wealth for its own sake. Wealth is the means—and people are the ends. All our material riches will avail us little if we do not use them to expand the opportunities of our people. . . .

To help those least fortunate of all, I am recommending a new public welfare program, stressing services instead of support, rehabilitation instead of relief, and training for useful work instead of prolonged dependency.

I am proposing a mass immunization program . . . improvements in the Food and Drug laws . . . the enactment . . . of health insurance for the aged . . . a massive attack to end adult illiteracy . . . bills to improve educational quality, to stimulate the arts . . . federally financed scholarships . . . federal aid to public school construction.

To relieve the critical shortage of doctors and dentists—and this is a matter which should concern us all—and expand research, I urge action to aid medical and dental colleges and scholarships and to establish new national institutes of health.

To take advantage of modern vaccination achievements, I am proposing a mass immunization program, aimed at the virtual elimination of such ancient enemies of our children as polio, diphtheria, whooping cough, and tetanus.

To protect our consumers from the careless and the unscrupulous, I shall recommend improvements in the Food and Drug laws—strengthening inspection and standards, halting unsafe and worthless products, preventing misleading labels, and cracking down on the illicit sale of habit-forming drugs.

But in matters of health, no piece of unfinished business is more important or more urgent than the enactment under the Social Security system of health insurance for the aged. . . . I shall recommend plans for a massive attack to end adult illiteracy . . . bills to improve educational quality, to stimulate the arts, and, at the college level, to provide federal loans for the construction of academic facilities and federally financed scholarships . . . federal aid to public school construction and teachers' salaries.

These are not unrelated measures addressed to specific gaps or grievances in our national life. They are the pattern of our intentions and the foundation of our hopes. "I believe in democracy," said Woodrow Wilson, "because it releases the energy of every human being." The dynamic of democracy is the power and the purpose of the individual, and the policy of this administration is to give to the individual the opportunity to realize his own highest possibilities.

Our program is to open to all the opportunity for steady and productive employment, to remove from all the handicap of arbitrary or irrational exclusion, to offer to all the facilities for education and health and welfare, to make society the servant of the individual and the individual the source of progress, and thus to realize for all the full promise of American life.

State of the Union Address
The Capitol, Washington, D.C.
January 11, 1962

The Preservation of Price Stability

I have several announcements to make.

Simultaneous and identical actions of United States Steel and other leading steel corporations increasing steel prices by some six dollars a ton constitute a wholly unjustifiable and irresponsible defiance of the public interest. In this serious hour in our nation's history, when we are confronted with grave crises in Berlin and Southeast Asia, when we are devoting our energies to economic recovery and stability, when we are asking reservists to leave their homes and families for months on end and servicemen to risk their lives—and four were killed in the last two days in Vietnam—and asking union members to hold down their wage requests, at a time when restraint and sacrifice are being asked of every citizen, the American people will find it hard, as I do, to accept a situation in which a tiny handful of steel executives, whose pursuit of private power and profit exceeds their sense of public responsibility, can show such utter contempt for the interests of 185 million Americans.

If this rise in the cost of steel is imitated by the rest of the industry, instead of rescinded, it would increase the cost of homes, autos, appliances, and most other items for every American family. It would increase the cost of machinery and tools to every American businessman and farmer. It would seriously handicap our efforts to prevent an inflationary spiral from eating up the pensions of our older citizens, and our new gains in purchasing power.

It would add, Secretary McNamara informed me this morning, an estimated $1 billion to the cost of our defenses, at a time when every dollar is needed for national security and other purposes. It would make it more difficult for American goods to compete in foreign markets, more difficult to withstand competition from foreign imports, and thus more difficult to improve our balance of payments position and stem the flow of gold. And it is necessary to stem it for our national security, if we're going to pay for our security commitments abroad. And it would surely handicap our efforts to induce other industries and unions to adopt responsible price and wage policies.

The facts of the matter are that there is no justification for an increase in steel prices. The recent settlement between the industry and the union, which does not even take place until July first, was widely acknowledged to be noninflationary, and the whole purpose and effect of this administration's role, which both parties understood, was to achieve an agreement which would make unnecessary any increase in prices. Steel output per man is rising so fast that labor costs per ton of steel can actually be expected to decline in the next twelve months. And in fact, the acting commissioner of the Bureau of Labor Statistics informed me this morning that, and I quote, "employment costs per unit of steel output in 1961 were essentially the same as they were in 1958."

The American people have a right to expect . . . a higher sense of business responsibility for the welfare of their country.

The cost of the major raw materials, steel scrap and coal, has also been declining, and for an industry which has been generally operating at less than two thirds of capacity, its profit rate has been normal and can be expected to rise sharply this year in view of the reduction in idle capacity. Their lot has been easier than that of one hundred thousand steelworkers thrown out of work in the last three years. The industry's cash dividends have exceeded $600 million in each of the last five years, and earnings in the first quarter of this year were estimated in the February twenty-eighth *Wall Street Journal* to be among the highest in history.

In short, at a time when they could be exploring how more efficiency and better prices could be obtained, reducing prices in this industry in recognition of lower costs, their unusually good labor contract, their foreign competition and their increase in production and profits which are coming this year, a few gigantic corporations have decided to increase prices in ruthless disregard of their public responsibilities.

The Steelworkers Union can be proud that it abided by its responsibilities in this agreement, and this government also has responsibilities which we intend to meet. The Department of Justice and the Federal Trade Commission are examining the significance of this action in a free, competitive economy. The Department of Defense and other agencies are reviewing its impact on their policies of procurement. And I am informed that steps are under way by those members of the Congress who plan appropriate inquiries into how these price decisions are so quickly made and reached and what legislative safeguards may be needed to protect the public interest.

Price and wage decisions in this country, except for a very limited restriction in the case of monopolies and national emergency strikes, are and ought to be freely and privately made. But the American people have a right to expect, in return for that freedom, a higher sense of business responsibility for the welfare of their country than has been shown in the last two days.

Some time ago I asked each American to consider what he would do for his country and I asked the steel companies. In the last twenty-four hours we had their answer. . . .

Q: Mr. President, the unusually strong language which you used in discussing the steel situation would indicate that you might be considering some pretty strong action. Are you thinking in terms of requesting or reviving the need for wage-price controls?

THE PRESIDENT: I think that my statement states what the situation is today. This is a free country. In all the conversations which were held by members of this administration and myself with the leaders of the steel union and the companies, it was always very obvious that they could proceed with freedom to do what they thought was best within the limitations of law. But I did very clearly emphasize on every occasion that my only interest was in trying to secure an agreement which would not provide an increase in prices, because I thought that price stability in steel would have the most far-reaching consequences for industrial and economic stability and for our position abroad, and price instability would have the most far-reaching consequences in making our lot much more difficult.

When the agreement was signed, and the agreement was a moderate one and within the range of productivity increases, as I've said, actually, there will be reduction in cost per unit during the next year—I thought, I was hopeful, we'd achieved our goal. Now the actions that will be taken will be—are being now considered by the administration. The Department of Justice is particularly anxious, in view of the very speedy action of the companies who have entirely different economic problems facing them than did United States Steel . . . to require an examination of our present laws, and whether they're being obeyed. . . . I'm very interested in the respective investigations that will be conducted in the House and Senate, and whether we shall need additional legislation, which I would come to very reluctantly. But I must say the last twenty-four hours indicate that those with great power are not always concerned about the national interest.

Q: In your conversation with Mr. Blough yesterday, did you make a direct request that this price increase be either deferred or rescinded?

THE PRESIDENT: I was informed about the price increase after the announcement had gone out to the papers. I told Mr. Blough of my very keen disappointment and what I thought would be the most unfortunate effects of it. And of course we were hopeful [about] other companies who, as I've said, have a different situation in regard to profits and all of the rest than U.S. Steel. . . .

I was hopeful particularly, in view of the statement in the paper by the president of Bethlehem in which he stated—though now he says he's misquoted—that there should be no price increase, and we are investigating that statement. I was hopeful that the others would not follow the example, that therefore the pressures of the competitive marketplace would bring United States Steel back to their original prices. But the parade began. But it came to me after the decision was made. There was no prior consultation or information given to the administration. . . .

Q: Mr. President, if I could get back to steel for a minute, you mentioned an investigation into the suddenness of the decision to increase prices. Did you—is the position of the administration that it believed it had the assurance of the steel industry at the time of the recent labor agreement that it would not increase prices?

THE PRESIDENT: We did not ask either side to give us any assurance, because there is a very proper limitation to the power of the government in this free economy. All we did in our meetings was to emphasize how important it was that there be price stability, and we stressed that our whole purpose in attempting to persuade the union to begin to bargain early and to make an agreement which would not affect prices, of course, was for the purpose of maintaining price stability. That was the thread that ran through every discussion which I had or Secretary Goldberg had. We never at any time asked for a commitment in regard to the terms, precise terms, of the agreement from either Mr. McDonald or Mr. Blough, representing the steel company, because in our opinion that would be passing over the line of propriety. But I don't think that there was any question that our great interest in attempting to secure the kind of settlement that was finally secured was to maintain price stability, which we regard as very essential at this particular time. That agreement provided for price stability—up to yesterday. . . .

Q: Mr. President, to carry a previous question just one step further, as a result of the emphasis that you placed on holding the price line, did any word or impression come to you from the negotiations that there would be no price increase under the type of agreement that was signed?

THE PRESIDENT: I will say that in our conversations we asked no commitments in regard to the details of the agreement or in regard to any policies [of] the union or the company—our central thrust was that price stability was necessary and that the way to do it was to have a responsible agreement, which we got.

Now, at no time did anyone suggest that if such an agreement was gained it would still be necessary to put up prices. That word did not come until last night.

President's News Conference
Washington, D.C., April 11, 1962

When a mistake has been retracted and the public interest preserved, nothing is to be gained from further public recriminations. . . . Our chief concern last week was to prevent an inflationary spiral. . . . What we attempted to do was project before the steel companies the public interest. And it was a combination of the public interest, placed upon the table in front of them, and competition which I think brought the price down. . . . Several companies refused to increase prices, and therefore competition worked its will.

President's News Conference
Washington, D.C., April 18, 1962

Later that month, at a press dinner, Kennedy parodied his own attack on big steel:

I have a few opening announcements: First, the sudden and arbitrary action of the officers of this organization in increasing the price of dinner tickets by $2.50 over last year constitutes a wholly unjustifiable defiance of the public interest. If this increase is

The Myths of Economic Debate

Let me begin by expressing my appreciation for the very deep honor that you have conferred upon me. As General de Gaulle occasionally acknowledges America to be the daughter of Europe, so I am pleased to come to Yale, the daughter of Harvard. It might be said now that I have the best of both worlds, a Harvard education and a Yale degree.

I am particularly glad to become a Yale man because, as I think about my troubles, I find that a lot of them have come from other Yale men. Among businessmen, I have had a minor disagreement with Roger Blough, of the law school class of 1931, and I have had some complaints, too, from my friend Henry Ford, of the class of 1940. In journalism I seem to have a difference with John Hay Whitney, of the class of 1926—and sometimes I also displease Henry Luce of the class of 1920, not to mention also William F. Buckley, Jr., of the class of 1950.

I even have some trouble with my Yale advisers. I get along with them, but I am not always sure how they get along with each other. I have the warmest feelings for Chester Bowles of the class of 1924, and for Dean Acheson of the class of 1915, and my assistant, McGeorge Bundy, of the class of 1940. But I am not one hundred percent sure that these three wise and experienced Yale men wholly agree with each other on every issue. So this administration, which aims at peaceful cooperation among all Americans, has been the victim of a certain natural pugnacity developed in this city among Yale men. Now that I, too, am a Yale man, it is time for peace. Last week at West Point, in the historic tradition of that academy, I availed myself of the powers of Commander-in-Chief to remit all sentences of offending cadets. In that same spirit, and in the

---

not rescinded but is imitated by the Gridiron, radio, TV, and other dinners, it will have a serious impact on the entire economy of this city.

In this serious hour in our nation's history, when newsmen are awakened in the middle of the night to be given a front-page story, when expense accounts are being scrutinized by the Congress, when correspondents are required to leave their families for long and lonely weekends at Palm Beach, the American people will find it hard to accept this ruthless decision made by a tiny handful of executives whose only interest is in the pursuit of pleasure. I am hopeful that the Women's Press Club will not join this price rise and will thereby force a rescission.

White House Correspondents and News Photographers Associations Dinner
Washington, D.C., April 27, 1962

historic tradition of Yale, let me now offer to smoke the clay pipe of friendship with all of my brother Elis, and I hope that they may be friends not only with me but even with each other. . . .

The great enemy of the truth is very often not the deliberate, contrived, and dishonest—but the myth—persistent, persuasive, and unrealistic. Too often we hold fast to the clichés of our forebears. We subject all facts to a prefabricated set of interpretations. We enjoy the comfort of opinion without the discomfort of thought.

Mythology distracts us everywhere—in government as in business, in politics as in economics, in foreign affairs as in domestic affairs. But today I want to particularly consider the myth and reality in our national economy. In recent months many have come to feel, as I do, that the dialogue between the parties—between business and government, between the government and the public—is clogged by illusion and platitude and fails to reflect the true realities of contemporary American society.

There are three great areas of our domestic affairs in which, today, there is a danger that illusion may prevent effective action. They are, first, the question of the size and the shape of government's responsibilities; second, the question of public fiscal policy; and third, the matter of confidence, business confidence or public confidence, or simply confidence in America. I want to talk about all three.

. . . Let us take first the question of the size and shape of government. The myth here is that government is big, and bad—and steadily getting bigger and worse. Obviously this myth has some excuse for existence. It is true that in recent history each new administration has spent much more money than its predecessor. Thus President Roosevelt outspent President Hoover, and with allowances for the special case of the Second World War, President Truman outspent President Roosevelt. Just to prove that this was not a partisan matter, President Eisenhower then outspent President Truman by the handsome figure of $182 billion. It is even possible, some think, that this trend may continue.

But does it follow from this that big government is growing relatively bigger? It does not—for the fact is for the last fifteen years, the federal government—and also the federal debt—and also the federal bureaucracy—have grown less rapidly than the economy as a whole. If we leave defense and space expenditures aside, the federal government since the Second World War has expanded less than any other major sector of our national life—less than industry, less than commerce, less than agriculture, less than higher education, and very much less than the noise about big government. The truth about big government is the truth about any other great activity—it is complex. Certainly it is true that size brings dangers—but it is also true that size can bring benefits. Here at Yale, which has contributed so much to our national progress in science and medicine, it may be proper for me to mention one great and little noticed expansion of government which has brought strength to our whole society—the new role of our federal government as the major patron of research in science and in medicine. Few people realize that in 1961, in support of all university research in science and medicine, three dollars out of every four came from the federal government. I need hardly point out that this has taken place without undue enlargement of government control—that American scientists remain second to none in their independence and in their individualism. . . .

I am not suggesting that federal expenditures cannot bring some measure of control. The whole thrust of federal expenditures in agriculture has been related by purpose and design to control, as a means of dealing with the problems created by our farmers and our growing productivity. Each sector, my point is, of activity must be approached on its own merits and in terms of specific national needs. Generalities in regard to federal expenditures, therefore, can be misleading—each case, science, urban renewal, education, agriculture, natural resources, each case must be determined on its merits if we are to profit from our unrivaled ability to combine the strength of public and private purpose.

Few people realize that in 1961, in support of all university research in science and medicine, three dollars out of every four came from the federal government.

Next, let us turn to the problem of our fiscal policy. Here the myths are legion and the truth hard to find. But let me take as a prime example the problem of the federal budget. We persist in measuring our federal fiscal integrity today by the conventional or administrative budget—with results which would be regarded as absurd in any business firm, in any country of Europe, or in any careful assessment of the reality of our national finances. The administrative budget has sound administrative uses. But for wider purposes it is less helpful. It omits our special trust funds and the effect that they have on our economy; it neglects changes in assets or inventories. It cannot tell a loan from a straight expenditure —and worst of all it cannot distinguish between operating expenditures and long-term investments.

This budget, in relation to the great problems of federal fiscal policy which are basic to our economy in 1962, is not simply irrelevant; it can be actively misleading. And yet there is a mythology that measures all of our national soundness or unsoundness on the single simple basis of this same annual administrative budget. If our federal budget is to serve not the debate but the country, we must and will find ways of clarifying this area of discourse.

Still in the area of fiscal policy, let me say a word about deficits. The myth persists that federal deficits create inflation and budget surpluses prevent it. Yet sizable budget surpluses after the war did not prevent inflation, and persistent deficits for the last several years have not upset our basic price stability. Obviously deficits are sometimes dangerous— and so are surpluses. But honest assessment plainly requires a more sophisticated view than the old and automatic cliché that deficits automatically bring inflation.

There are myths also about our public debt. It is widely supposed that this debt is growing at a dangerously rapid rate. In fact, both the debt per person and the debt as a proportion of our gross national product have declined sharply since the Second World War. In absolute terms the national debt since the end of World War II has increased only 8 percent, while private debt was increasing 305 percent, and the debts of state and local governments—on whom people frequently suggest we should place additional burdens—the debts of state and local governments have increased 378 percent. Moreover, debts, public and private, are neither good nor bad, in and of themselves. Borrowing can lead to overextension and collapse—but it can also lead to expansion and strength. There is no single, simple slogan in this field that we can trust.

Finally, I come to the problem of confidence. Confidence is a matter of myth and also a matter of truth—and this time let me take the truth of the matter first.

It is true—and of high importance—that the prosperity of this country depends on the assurance that all major elements within it will live up to their responsibilities. If business were to neglect its obligations to the public, if labor were blind to all public responsibility, above all, if government were to abandon its obvious—and statutory—duty of watchful concern for our economic health—if any of these things should happen, then confidence might well be weakened and the danger of stagnation would increase. This is the true issue of confidence.

But there is also the false issue—and its simplest form is the assertion that any and all unfavorable turns of the speculative wheel—however temporary and however plainly speculative in character—are the result of, and I quote, "a lack of confidence in the national administration." This I must tell you, while comforting, is not wholly true. . . . The solid ground of mutual confidence is the necessary partnership of government with all of the sectors of our society in the steady quest for economic progress.

Corporate plans are based not on a political confidence in party leaders but on an economic confidence in the nation's ability to invest and produce and consume. Business had full confidence in the administrations in power in 1929, 1954, 1958, and 1960—but this was not enough to prevent recession when business lacked full confidence in the economy. What matters is the capacity of the nation as a whole to deal with its economic problems and its opportunities. . . .

What is at stake in our economic decisions today is not some grand warfare of rival ideologies which will sweep the country with passion but the practical management of a modern economy. What we need is not labels and clichés but more basic discussion of the sophisticated and technical questions involved in keeping a great economic machinery moving ahead.

The national interest lies in high employment and steady expansion of output, in stable prices and a strong dollar. The declaration of such objectives is easy; their attainment in an intricate and interdependent economy and world is a little more difficult. To attain them, we require not some automatic response but hard thought. . . .

As we work in consonance to meet the authentic problems of our times, we will generate a vision and an energy which will demonstrate anew to the world the superior vitality and the strength of the free society.

Commencement Address, Yale University
New Haven, Connecticut, June 11, 1962

The Politics of Confidence

Q: Mr. President, a lot of people seem to feel that the idea of a Democratic administration trying to win the confidence of business is something like the Republicans trying to win the confidence of labor unions. Do you feel, sir, you are making headway in your efforts? Have you seen anything to indicate that business is coming around to your point of view on the economy and that the confidence you asked for is being restored to the marketplace?

THE PRESIDENT: Well, as I said, what is [important] is not really whether some businessmen may be Republicans—most businessmen are Republicans, have been traditionally, have voted Republican in every presidential election. But that is not the important point—whether there is political agreement.

The important point is that they recognize and the government recognizes, and every group recognizes, the necessity of attempting to work out economic policies which will maintain our economy at an adequate rate of growth. That is the great problem. . . . They feel that they would be happier if there were a Republican in the White House, but there was a Republican in the White House in 1958 and we had a recession and [again] in 1960. . . . I could be away from the scene, which might make them happy, and they might have a Republican in the White House, but the economic problems would still be there. . . .

Q: Mr. President, there is a feeling in some quarters that big business is using the stock market slump as a means of forcing you to come to terms with business. One reputable columnist, after talking to businessmen, obviously, reported this week their attitude is now, we have you where we want you. Have you seen any reflection of this attitude?

THE PRESIDENT. I can't believe I'm where business—big business—wants me.

President's News Conference
Washington, D.C., June 14, 1962

The Foundation for Freedom's Success

America has enjoyed twenty-two months of uninterrupted economic recovery. But recovery is not enough. If we are to prevail in the long run, we must expand the long-run strength of our economy. We must move along the path to a higher rate of growth and full employment. . . .

To achieve these greater gains, one step, above all, is essential—the enactment this year of a substantial reduction and revision in federal income taxes. . . .

I do not say that a measure for tax reduction and reform is the only way to achieve these goals.

No doubt a massive increase in federal spending could also create jobs and growth—but, in today's setting, private consumers, employers, and investors should be given a full opportunity first.

No doubt a temporary tax cut could provide a spur to our economy—but a long-run problem compels a long-run solution.

No doubt a reduction in either individual or corporation taxes alone would be of great help—but corporations need customers and job seekers need jobs.

No doubt tax reduction without reform would sound simpler and more attractive to many—but our growth is also hampered by a host of tax inequities and special preferences which have distorted the flow of investment.

And, finally, there are no doubt some who would prefer to put off a tax cut in the hope that ultimately an end to the Cold War would make possible an equivalent cut in expenditures—but that end is not in view and to wait for it would be costly and self-defeating. . . .

Tax reduction, alone, however, is not enough to strengthen our society, to provide opportunities for the four million Americans who are born each year, to improve the lives of thirty-two million Americans who live on the outskirts of poverty.

The quality of American life must keep pace with the quantity of American goods.

This country cannot afford to be materially rich and spiritually poor. . . .

First, we need to strengthen our nation by investing in our youth:

The future of any country which is dependent upon the will and wisdom of its citizens is damaged, and irreparably damaged, whenever any of its children is not educated to the full extent of his talent, from grade school through graduate school. Today, an estimated four out of every ten students in the fifth grade will not even finish high school—and that is a waste we cannot afford.

In addition, there is no reason why one million young Americans, out of school and out of work, should all remain unwanted and often untrained on our city streets when their energies can be put to good use. . . .

Second, we need to strengthen our nation by safeguarding its health . . . I believe that the abandonment of the mentally ill and the mentally retarded to the grim mercy of custodial institutions too often inflicts on them and on their families a needless cruelty which this nation should not endure. The incidence of mental retardation in this country is three times as high as that of Sweden, for example—and that figure can and must be reduced. . . .

We shall be judged more by what we do at home than by what we preach abroad. Nothing we could do to help the developing countries would help them half as much as a booming U.S. economy. And nothing our opponents could do to encourage their own ambitions would encourage them half as much as a chronic lagging U.S. economy. These domestic tasks do not divert energy from our security—they provide the very foundation for freedom's survival and success.

State of the Union Address
The Capitol, Washington, D.C.
January 14, 1963

CHAPTER 8

The Exploration of Space

Warned that outer space could be militarily dominated by a hostile power, concerned that the early Soviet lead in space exploration would be viewed by emerging nations as evidence of communism's success and democracy's decline, President Kennedy ascertained early in 1961 that this country would probably be unable to overtake the U.S.S.R. in any stage of the "space race" before a manned lunar landing a decade away. He thereupon proclaimed that dramatic goal as a means of focusing and mobilizing our lagging space efforts, establishing a stronger American scientific profile, and obtaining some bargaining chips for U.S.–Soviet negotiation on the exploration and governance of space.

The Adventure of Space

Since early in my term, our efforts in space have been under review. . . . We have examined where we are strong and where we are not, where we may succeed and where we may not. Now it is time to take longer strides—time for a great new American enterprise—time for this nation to take a clearly leading role in space achievement, which in many ways may hold the key to our future on earth.

I believe we possess all the resources and talents necessary. But the facts of the matter are that we have never made the national decisions or marshaled the national resources required for such leadership. We have never specified long-range goals on an urgent time schedule, or managed our resources and our time so as to insure their fulfillment.

We go into space because whatever mankind must undertake, free men must fully share. . . . I believe we should go to the moon.

Recognizing the head start obtained by the Soviets with their large rocket engines, which gives them many months of lead time, and recognizing the likelihood that they will exploit this lead for some time to come in still more impressive successes, we nevertheless are required to make new efforts on our own. For while we cannot guarantee that we shall one day be first, we can guarantee that any failure to make this effort will make us last. . . . But this is not merely a race. Space is open to us now; and our eagerness to share its meaning is not governed by the efforts of others. We go into space because whatever mankind must undertake, free men must fully share.

I therefore ask the Congress, above and beyond the increases I have earlier requested for space activities, to provide the funds which are needed to meet the following national goals:

First, I believe that this nation should commit itself to achieving the goal, before this decade is out, of landing a man on the moon and returning him safely to the earth. No single space project in this period will be more impressive to mankind, or more important for the long-range exploration of space; and none will be so difficult or expensive to accomplish. . . . But in a very real sense, it will not be one man going to the moon—if we make this judgment affirmatively, it will be an entire nation. For all of us must work to put him there. . . .

I believe we should go to the moon. But I think every citizen of this country as well as the members of the Congress should consider the matter carefully in making their judgment, to which we have given attention over many weeks and months, because it is a heavy burden, and there is no sense in agreeing or desiring that the United States take an affirmative position in outer space, unless we are prepared to do the work and bear the burdens to make it successful. If we are not, we should decide today and this year.

This decision demands a major national commitment of scientific and technical manpower, material, and facilities, and the possibility of their diversion from other important activities where they are already thinly spread. It means a degree of dedication, organization, and discipline which have not always characterized our research and development efforts. It means we cannot afford undue work stoppages, inflated costs of material or talent, wasteful interagency rivalries, or a high turnover of key personnel.

New objectives and new money cannot solve these problems. They could, in fact, aggravate them further—unless every scientist, every engineer, every serviceman, every technician, contractor, and civil servant gives his personal pledge that this nation will move forward, with the full speed of freedom, in the exciting adventure of space.

Special Address to Congress on Urgent National Needs
The Capitol, Washington, D.C. May 25, 1961

The chimpanzee who is flying in space took off at 10:08. He reports that everything is perfect and working well.

President's News Conference
Washington, D.C., November 29, 1961

The Universal Language of Space

This has been a week of momentous events around the world. The long and painful struggle in Algeria has come to an end. Both nuclear powers and neutrals labored at Geneva for a solution to the problem of a spiraling arms race, and also to the problems that so vex our relations with the Soviet Union. The Congress opened hearings on a trade bill, which is far more than a trade bill, but an opportunity to build a stronger and closer Atlantic Community. And my wife had her first and last ride on an elephant!

But history may well remember this as a week for an act of lesser immediate impact, and that is the decision by the United States and the Soviet Union to seek concrete agreements on the joint exploration of space. Experience has taught us that an agreement to negotiate does not always mean a negotiated agreement. But should such a joint effort be realized, its significance could well be tremendous for us all. In terms of space science, our combined knowledge and efforts can benefit the people of all nations: joint weather satellites to provide more ample warnings against destructive storms—joint communications systems to draw the world more closely together—and cooperation on space medicine research and space tracking operations to speed the day when man will go to the moon and beyond.

But the scientific gains from such a joint effort would offer, I believe, less realized return than the gains for world peace. For a cooperative Soviet-American effort in space science and exploration would emphasize the interests that must unite us, rather than those that always divide us. It offers us an area in which the stale and sterile dogmas of the Cold War could be literally left a quarter of a million miles behind. And it would remind us on both sides that knowledge, not hate, is the passkey to the future—that knowledge transcends national antagonisms—that it speaks a universal language—that it is the possession, not of a single class, or of a single nation or a single ideology, but of all mankind.

Address to the University of California
Berkeley, California, March 23, 1962

The New Ocean of Space

We meet at a college noted for knowledge, in a city noted for progress, in a state noted for strength, and we stand in need of all three. For we meet in an hour of change and challenge, in a decade of hope and fear, in an age of both knowledge and ignorance. The greater our knowledge increases, the greater our ignorance unfolds.

Despite the striking fact that most of the scientists that the world has ever known are alive and working today, despite the fact that this nation's own scientific manpower is doubling every twelve years in a rate of growth more than three times that of our population as a whole, despite all that, the vast stretches of the unknown and the unanswered and the unfinished still far outstrip our collective comprehension.

No man can fully grasp how far and how fast we have come, but condense, if you will, the fifty thousand years of man's recorded history in a time span of but a half century. Stated in these terms, we know very little about the first forty years, except at the end of them advanced man had learned to use the skins of animals to cover himself. Then about ten years ago, under this standard, man emerged from his caves to construct other kinds of shelter. Only five years ago man learned to write and use a cart with wheels. Christianity began less than two years ago. The printing press came this year, and then less than two months ago, during this whole fifty-year span of human history, the steam engine provided a new source of power and Newton explored the meaning of gravity. Last month electric lights and telephones and automobiles and airplanes became available. Only last week did we develop penicillin and television and nuclear power. And now if America's new spacecraft succeeds in reaching Venus, we will have literally reached the stars before midnight tonight.

This is a breathtaking pace, and such a pace cannot help but create new ills as it dispels old, new ignorance, new problems, new dangers. Surely the opening vistas of space promise high costs and hardships, as well as high reward.

So it is not surprising that some would have us stay where we are a little longer to rest, to wait. But this city of Houston, this state of Texas, this country of the United States, were not built by those who waited and rested and wished to look behind them. This country was conquered by those who moved forward—and so will space [be conquered].

If this capsule history of our progress teaches us anything, it is that man, in his quest for knowledge and progress, is determined and cannot be deterred. The exploration of space will go ahead, whether we join in it or not. It is one of the great adventures of all time, and no nation which expects to be the leader of other nations can expect to stay behind in this race for space.

We have vowed that we shall see space filled not with weapons of mass destruction, but with instruments of knowledge and understanding.

Those who came before us made certain that this country rode the first waves of the industrial revolution, the first waves of modern invention, and the first wave of nuclear power; and this generation does not intend to founder in the backwash of the coming age of space. We mean to be a part of it—we mean to lead it. For the eyes of the world now look into space, to the moon, and to the planets beyond, and we have vowed that we shall see space governed not by a hostile flag of conquest, but by a banner of freedom and peace. We have vowed that we shall see space filled not with weapons of mass destruction, but with instruments of knowledge and understanding.

Yet the vows of this nation can only be fulfilled if we in this nation are first, and, therefore, we intend to be first. In short, our leadership in science and in industry, our hopes for peace and security, our obligations to ourselves as well as others, all require us to make this effort, to solve these mysteries, to solve them for the good of all men, and to become the world's leading space-faring nation.

We set sail on this new sea because there is new knowledge to be gained, and new rights to be won, and they must be won and used for the progress of all people. For space science, like nuclear science and all technology, has no conscience of its own. Whether it will become a force for good or ill depends on man, and only if the United States occupies a position of preeminence can we help decide whether this new ocean will be a sea of peace or a new terrifying theater of war. I do not say that we should or will go unprotected against the hostile misuse of space any more than we go unprotected against the hostile use of land or sea, but I do say that space can be explored and mastered without feeding the fires of war, without repeating the mistakes that man has made in extending his writ around this globe of ours.

There is no strife, no prejudice, no national conflict in outer space as yet. Its hazards are hostile to us all. Its conquest deserves the best of all mankind, and its opportunity for peaceful cooperation may never come again. But why, some say, the moon? Why choose this as our goal? And they may well ask why climb the highest mountain. Why, thirty-five years ago, fly the Atlantic? Why does Rice play Texas?

We choose to go to the moon. We choose to go to the moon in this decade and do the other things, not because they are easy, but because they are hard, because that goal will serve to organize and measure the best of our energies and skills, because that challenge is one that we are willing to accept, one we are unwilling to postpone, and one which we intend to win. . . .

It is for these reasons that I regard the decision last year to shift our efforts in space from low to high gear as among the most important decisions that will be made during my incumbency in the office of the Presidency.

In the last twenty-four hours we have seen facilities now being created for the greatest and most complex exploration in man's history. We have felt the ground shake and the air shattered by the testing of a Saturn C-1 booster rocket, many times as powerful as the Atlas which launched John Glenn, generating power equivalent to ten thousand automobiles with their accelerators on the floor. We have seen the site where five F-1 rocket engines, each one as powerful as all eight engines of the Saturn combined, will be clustered together to make the advanced Saturn missile, assembled in a new building to be built at Cape Canaveral as tall as a forty-eight-story structure, as wide as a city block, and as long as two lengths of this field.

Within these last nineteen months at least forty-five satellites have circled the earth. Some forty of them were "made in the United States of America" and they were far more sophisticated and supplied far more knowledge to the people of the world than those of the Soviet Union.

The Mariner spacecraft now on its way to Venus is the most intricate instrument in the history of space science. The accuracy of that shot is comparable to firing a missile from Cape Canaveral and dropping it in this stadium between the forty-yard lines.

Transit satellites are helping our ships at sea to steer a safer course. Tiros satellites have given us unprecedented warnings of hurricanes and storms, and will do the same for forest fires and icebergs.

We have had our failures, but so have others, even if they do not admit them. And they may be less public.

To be sure, we are behind, and will be behind for some time in manned flight. But we do not intend to stay behind, and in this decade we shall make up and move ahead.

The growth of our science and education will be enriched by new knowledge of our universe and environment, by new techniques of learning and mapping and observation, by new tools and computers for industry, medicine, the home as well as the school. . . .

I regard the decision last year to shift our efforts in space from low to high gear as among the most important decisions that will be made during my incumbency in the office of the Presidency.

To be sure, all this costs us all a good deal of money. This year's space budget is three times what it was in January 1961, and it is greater than the space budget of the previous eight years combined. That budget now stands at $5,400 million a year—a staggering sum, though somewhat less than we pay for cigarettes and cigars every year. Space expenditures will soon rise some more, from ten cents per person per week to more than fifty cents a week for every man, woman, and child in the United States, for we have given this program a high national priority—even though I realize that this is in some measure an act of faith and vision, for we do not now know what benefits await us. But if I were to say, my fellow citizens, that we shall send to the moon, 240,000 miles away from the control station in Houston, a giant rocket more than three hundred feet tall, the length of this football field, made of new metal alloys, some of which have not yet been invented, capable of standing heat and stresses several times more than have ever been experienced, fitted together with a precision better than the finest watch, carrying all the equipment needed for propulsion, guidance, control, communications, food, and survival, on an untried mission, to an unknown celestial body, and then return it safely to earth, reentering the atmosphere at speeds of over 25,000 miles per hour, causing heat about half that of the temperature of the sun—almost as hot as it is here today—and do all this, and do it right, and do it first before this decade is out, then we must be bold. . . .

I think we're going to do it, and I think that we must pay what needs to be paid. I don't think we ought to waste any money, but I think we ought to do the job. And this will be done in the decade of the sixties. It may be done while some of you are still here at school at this college and university. It will be done during the terms of office of some of the people who sit here on this platform. But it will be done. And it will be done before the end of this decade. . . .

Many years ago the great British explorer George Mallory, who was to die on Mount Everest, was asked why did he want to climb it. He said, "Because it is there."

Well, space is there, and we're going to climb it, and the moon and the planets are there, and new hopes for knowledge and peace are there. And, therefore, as we set sail, we ask God's blessing on the most hazardous and dangerous and the greatest adventure on which man has ever embarked.

Rice University
Houston, Texas, September 12, 1962

The High Wall of Space

We have a long way to go. Many weeks and months and years of long, tedious work lie ahead. There will be setbacks and frustrations and disappointments. There will be, as there always are, pressures in this country to do less in this area as in so many others, and temptations to do something else that is perhaps easier. But this research here must go on. This space effort must go on. The conquest of space must and will go ahead. That much we know. That much we can say with confidence and conviction.

Frank O'Connor, the Irish writer, tells in one of his books how, as a boy, he and his friends would make their way across the countryside, and when they came to an orchard wall that seemed too high and too doubtful to try and too difficult to permit their voyage to continue, they took off their hats and tossed them over the wall—and then they had no choice but to follow them.

This nation has tossed its cap over the wall of space, and we have no choice but to follow it. Whatever the difficulties, they will be overcome. Whatever the hazards, they must be guarded against. With the vital help of this Aerospace Medical Center, with the help of all those who labor in the space endeavor, with the help and support of all Americans, we will climb this wall with safety and with speed—and we shall then explore the wonders on the other side.

Remarks at Dedication of Aerospace Medical Health Center
San Antonio, Texas, November 21, 1963

CHAPTER 9

The Fight for Civil Rights

Initially wary of civil rights as a political issue, John Kennedy came to recognize that the battle for equal rights and opportunity for all races was the great moral issue of our time. He forthrightly placed the Presidency at the front of that battle in a way that no twentieth-century president had done before. Shocked by the brutality endured by civil rights protesters across the nation and determined to enforce judicial orders admitting blacks to state institutions of higher learning, the President launched in mid-1963 an unprecedented and comprehensive legislative, regulatory, and educational drive to fundamentally change this country's course in black-white relations.

The American Vision

We meet on the eve of a great national convention. There our choice is more than the choice of candidates—it is the choice of party roles and responsibilities. Will we face up to the issues that face America—or will we, as Randolph said of Van Buren, "row to [our] object with muffled oars?" Will we appeal to the lowest common denominator—or will we offer leadership where leadership has so long been lacking? Will we inquire as to whether a policy is good for the North, South, East, or West—or will we know that a policy, if really good, is good for all people everywhere? And finally, will we confine our campaign to abuse of the party in power—or will we realize, to paraphrase a noted statesman, that a great "nay" is not enough—we need a mighty "yes" as well?

I hope my own views are clear. I want our party to speak out with courage and candor on every issue—and that includes civil rights. I want no compromise of basic principles—no evasion of basic controversies—and no second-class citizenship for any American anywhere in this country. I have not made nor will I make any commitments inconsistent with these objectives.

While we point with pride to the strides we have made in fulfilling our forefathers' dream of the equality of man, let us not overlook how far we still have to go. While we point with concern to denials of civil rights in one part of the country, let us not overlook the more subtle but equally vicious forms of discrimination that are found in the clubs and churches and neighborhoods of the rest of the country.

Our job is to turn the American vision of a society in which no man has to suffer discrimination based on race into a living reality everywhere in our land. And that means we must secure to every American equal access to all parts of our public life—to the voting booth, to the schoolroom, to jobs, to housing, to all public facilities including lunch counters.

Let us trust no one who offers slick and easy answers—for the only final answer will come from the work of thousands of individual answers, large and small, in the Congress, the courts, and the White House, in states and cities all over America, in the actions of brave and wise public servants, and in the reactions of determined private citizens such as yourselves.

What we are seeking, after all, is really very simple. It's merely a recognition that this is one nation and we are all one great people. Our origins may be different but our destiny is the same, our aspirations are identical. There can be no artificial distinctions, no arbitrary barriers, in securing these rights:

The right of every man to work as he wants to work, to be educated as every human being deserves to be educated, and to receive for his labor or his crops or his goods a just compensation, which he can spend as he pleases, in the nation's finest luxury store or the most modest five-and-ten.

The right of every family to live in a decent home in a decent neighborhood of his own free choice.

The right of every individual to obtain security in sickness as well as health, in retirement as well as youth.

The right of every American to think, to vote, to speak, to read, and to worship as he pleases—to stand up for his rights and, when necessary, to sit down for them.

And finally, the right of all people to be free from the tensions and terrors and burdens of war, its preparation and its consequences.

These are not minority rights or even merely civil rights—they are the goals desired and required for every American. There is nothing complicated about these goals, however difficult their achievement. There is nothing unreasonable or unusual about these goals, however much some may resist them. But they will not be achieved without leadership—moral, political, legislative, and, above all, executive leadership.

Our job is to turn the American vision of a society in which no man has to suffer discrimination based on race into a living reality everywhere in our land.

The next President of the United States cannot stand above the battle engaging in vague little sermons on brotherhood. The immense moral authority of the White House must be used to offer leadership and inspiration to those of every race and section who recognize their responsibilities. And the immense legal authority of the White House must be used to direct implementation of all constitutional rights, protection of the right to vote, fulfillment of the requirement of school desegregation, and an end to discrimination in the government's own midst—in public contracts, in employment and in all federal housing programs.

Finally, if that President is to truly be President of all the people, then he must act to bring them together to accomplish these objectives. How, without communication, can we ever proceed in democracy? There can be no progress without communication. There can be no reconciliation without meeting and talking with each other.

To be sure, there will be protest and disagreement—but if the end result is to be permanent progress instead of frustration, there must be more meetings of men and minds. And the place to begin is the White House itself, where the Chief Executive, with his prestige and influence, should exert firm and positive leadership.

Let us bear in mind that this is not merely a regional problem—it is not merely a national problem—it is international in scope and effect. For the average American of Caucasian descent does not realize that it is *he* who is a member of a minority race—and a minority religion—and a minority political system—and that he is regarded with some suspicion, if not hostility, by most of that restless, envious, surging majority. The tide of human dignity is worldwide—and the eyes of that world are upon us.

It is not enough to restate our claim to the Declaration of Independence. It is not enough to deplore violence in other lands. It is up to us to prove that our way—the way of peaceful change and democratic processes—can fulfill those goals better than any other system under the sun. It is up to us to rebuild our image abroad by rebuilding our image here at home.

The time is short—but the agenda is long. Much is to be done—but many are willing.

Francis Bacon once wrote: "There is hope enough and to spare—not only to make a bold man try—but also to make a sober-minded man believe."

My friends—if you are sober-minded enough to believe, then—to the extent that these tasks require the support, the guidance, and the leadership of the American Presidency—I am bold enough to try.

NAACP Rally
Los Angeles, California, July 10, 1960

The Standard of John C. Calhoun

For eight years . . . I have occupied the seat once held by a distinguished senator from Massachusetts, Senator Daniel Webster. He served in the time before 1850, when the Senate was at its height, and included within its ranks Cass, Clay, Douglas, Benton, and all the rest. But none of these were considered by Daniel Webster to match the talents and the character of the senator from South Carolina, John C. Calhoun. They were both born in the same year; Calhoun was a native of Abingdon, South Carolina. They both went to college in New England, one to Yale and the other to Dartmouth. They both entered Congress as young men, and they both stayed in Congress for forty years until they died, in 1850 John Calhoun, and in 1852 Daniel Webster. They worked together on foreign relations, the development of the United States, fiscal improvements. Each served in the House as well as in the Senate. Each was Secretary of State. And yet through most of their lives, they also differed on great questions. But to his dying day, Senator Daniel Webster said of John C. Calhoun, "He was much the ablest man I ever knew. He could have demolished Newton, Calvin, or Locke as a logician." He admired above all his powerful mind and his courage.

Sitting as I do in the U.S. Senate, succeeding Senator Webster, I have also admired John C. Calhoun. When I was chairman of a committee to pick five outstanding senators in the history of this country, John C. Calhoun's name led all the rest, and his portrait is now in the Senate reception room. And when I wrote a book about courageous senators, I mentioned John C. Calhoun. I am not here in South Carolina to make glittering promises or glowing predictions, but to express the hope that in 1960, South Carolina and the nation will be guided by the spirit of Calhoun and his courage. "I never know what South Carolina thinks of a measure," he once said. "I act to the best of my judgment and according to my conscience. If she approves, well and good. If she does not, and wishes anyone to take my place, I am ready to vacate. We are even."

"Are we bound in all cases to do what is popular?"

He demonstrated this in 1816 when he voted to raise the pay of congressmen from $6 a day to the munificent sum of $1,500 a year. Congressman after congressman was defeated. And yet John C. Calhoun, speaking in the House, spoke words that I invoke today. "This House is at liberty to decide on this question according to the dictates of its best judgment. Are we bound in all cases to do what is popular? Have the people of this country snatched the power of deliberation from this body? If we act in opposition to conscience and reason, are political errors, once prevalent, never to be corrected?"

That is the spirit of the Democratic Party, that is the spirit of Thomas Jefferson and Woodrow Wilson and Franklin Roosevelt and Harry Truman. Are we bound in all cases to do what is popular? In 1960, the people of the United States have a very clear choice to make between Mr. Nixon and myself. We see America in different terms, and we see the future in entirely different terms. He runs on a slogan of "You have never had it so good." I run on the slogan, "This is a great country that must be greater." I think we can do better. . . .

The test of popularity, rather than Calhoun's test of conscience, has been applied by my opponent in the sensitive area of civil rights. He makes a great show of discussing this subject when he comes south, but it is hardly the same speech he delivered in New York City last week. Up north he talks about legislation. Down here he emphasizes that laws alone are not enough. Up there he stresses how quickly he will act in all these areas. Down here he says, "I know this is a difficult problem." Up there he criticizes the Democratic Party for having nominated a southerner on the ticket. Down here he omits the civil rights plank in his own platform.

I don't think Mr. Nixon is fooling anyone, north or south. I think it is clear that, if we are to have progress in this area, and we must have progress to be true to our ideals and responsibilities, then presidential leadership is necessary so that every American can enjoy his full constitutional rights. Some of you may disagree with that view, but at least I have not changed that view in an election year, or according to where I am standing. . . .

I ask you to join us in building a stronger America, an America which will serve as an example to a watching world as we sit on a most conspicuous stage. We will give leadership if we are successful, and I can promise you this country will start to move again.

Campaign Speech
Columbia, South Carolina, October 10, 1960

The Enforcement of Court Orders

The orders of the court in the case of Meredith versus Fair are beginning to be carried out. Mr. James Meredith is now in residence on the campus of the University of Mississippi. . . .

All students, members of the faculty, and public officials in both Mississippi and the nation will be able, it is hoped, to return to their normal activities with full confidence in the integrity of American law.

This is as it should be. For our nation is founded on the principle that observance of the law is the eternal safeguard of liberty and defiance of the law is the surest road to tyranny. The law which we obey includes the final rulings of the courts, as well as the enactments of our legislative bodies. Even among law-abiding men few laws are universally loved, but they are uniformly respected and not resisted.

Americans are free, in short, to disagree with the law but not to disobey it. For in a government of laws and not of men, no man, however prominent or powerful, and no mob, however unruly or boisterous, is entitled to defy a court of law. If this country should ever reach the point where any man or group of men by force or threat of force could long defy the commands of our Court and our Constitution, then no law would stand free from doubt, no judge would be sure of his writ, and no citizen would be safe from his neighbors.

In this case in which the United States government was not until recently involved, Mr. Meredith brought a private suit in federal court against those who were excluding him from the university. A series of federal courts all the way to the Supreme Court repeatedly ordered Mr. Meredith's admission to the university. When those orders were defied, and those who sought to implement them threatened with arrest and violence, the United States Court of Appeals consisting of Chief Judge Tuttle of Georgia, Judge Hutcheson of Texas, Judge Rives of Alabama, Judge Jones of Florida, Judge Brown of Texas, Judge Wisdom of Louisiana, Judge Girwin of Alabama, and Judge Bell of Georgia, made clear the fact that the enforcement of its order had become an obligation of the United States government. Even though this government had not originally been a party to the case, my responsibility as President was therefore inescapable. I accept it. My obligation under the Constitution and the statutes of the United States was and is to implement the orders of the court with whatever means are necessary, and with as little force and civil disorder as the circumstances permit.

It was for this reason that I federalized the Mississippi National Guard as the most appropriate instrument, should any be needed, to preserve law and order while United States marshals carried out the orders of the court, and prepared to back them up with whatever other civil or military enforcement might have been required.

I deeply regret the fact that any action by the executive branch was necessary in this case, but all other avenues and alternatives, including persuasion and conciliation, had been tried and exhausted. Had the police powers of Mississippi been used to support the orders of the court, instead of deliberately and unlawfully blocking them, had the University of Mississippi fulfilled its standard of excellence by quietly admitting this applicant in conformity with what so many other southern state universities have done for so many years, a peaceable and sensible solution would have been possible without any federal intervention.

This nation is proud of the many instances in which governors, educators, and everyday citizens from the South have shown to the world the gains that can be made by persuasion and goodwill in a society ruled by law. Specifically, I would like to take this occasion to express the thanks of this nation to those southerners who have contributed to the progress of our democratic development in the entrance of students regardless of race to such great institutions as the state-supported universities of Virginia, North Carolina, Georgia, Florida, Texas, Louisiana, Tennessee, Arkansas, and Kentucky.

I recognize that the present period of transition and adjustment in our nation's southland is a hard one for many people. Neither Mississippi nor any other southern state deserves to be charged with all the accumulated wrongs of the last hundred years of race relations. To the extent that there has been failure, the responsibility for that failure must be shared by us all, by every state, by every citizen.

Mississippi and her university, moreover, are noted for their courage, for their contribution of talent and thought to the affairs of this nation. This is the state of Lucius Lamar and many others who have placed the national good ahead of sectional interest. This is the state which had four Medal of Honor winners in the Korean War alone. In fact, the Guard unit federalized this morning, early, is part of the 155th Infantry, one of the ten oldest regiments in the Union and one of the most decorated for sacrifice and bravery in six wars.

In 1945 a Mississippi sergeant, Jake Lindsey, was honored by an unusual joint session of the Congress. I close therefore with this appeal to the students of the university, the people who are most concerned.

You have a great tradition to uphold, a tradition of honor and courage won on the field of battle and on the gridiron as well as the university campus. You have a new opportunity to show that you are men of patriotism and integrity. For the most effective means of upholding the law is not the state policeman or the marshals or the National Guard. It is you. It lies in your courage to accept those laws with which you disagree as well as those with which you agree. The eyes of the nation and of all the world are upon you and upon all of us, and the honor of your university and state are in the balance. I am certain that the great majority of the students will uphold that honor.

There is, in short, no reason why the books on this case cannot now be quickly and quietly closed in the manner directed by the court. Let us preserve both the law and the peace, and then, healing those wounds that are within we can turn to the greater crises that are without and stand united as one people in our pledge to man's freedom.

Televised Address
Washington, D.C., September 30, 1962

The Right to Vote

. . . The most precious and powerful right in the world, the right to vote in a free American election, must not be denied to any citizen on grounds of his race or color. I wish that all qualified Americans permitted to vote were willing to vote, but surely in this centennial year of Emancipation all those who are willing to vote should always be permitted.

State of the Union Address
The Capitol, Washington, D.C.
January 14, 1963

The Peaceful Revolution

This afternoon, following a series of threats and defiant statements, the presence of Alabama National Guardsmen was required on the University of Alabama to carry out the final and unequivocal order of the United States District Court of the Northern District of Alabama. That order called for the admission of two clearly qualified young Alabama residents who happened to have been born Negro.

That they were admitted peacefully on the campus is due in good measure to the conduct of the students of the University of Alabama, who met their responsibilities in a constructive way.

I hope that every American, regardless of where he lives, will stop and examine his conscience about this and other related incidents. This nation was founded by men of many nations and backgrounds. It was founded on the principle that all men are created equal, and that the rights of every man are diminished when the rights of one man are threatened.

Today we are committed to a worldwide struggle to promote and protect the rights of all who wish to be free. When Americans are sent to Vietnam or West Berlin, we do not ask for whites only. It ought to be possible, therefore, for American students of any color to attend any public institution they select without having to be backed up by troops.

It ought to be possible for American consumers of any color to receive equal service in places of public accommodation, such as hotels and restaurants and theaters and retail stores, without being forced to resort to demonstrations in the street. It ought to be possible for American citizens of any color to register and to vote in a free election without interference or fear of reprisal.

It ought to be possible, in short, for every American to enjoy the privileges of being American without regard to his race or his color. In short, every American ought to have the right to be treated as he would wish to be treated, as one would wish his children to be treated. But this is not the case today.

The rights of every man are diminished when the rights of one man are threatened.

The Negro baby born in America today, regardless of the section of the nation in which he is born, has about one half as much chance of completing high school as a white baby born in the same place on the same day, one third as much chance of completing college, one third as much chance of becoming a professional man, twice as much chance of becoming unemployed, about one seventh as much chance of earning $10,000 a year or more, a life expectancy which is seven years shorter, and the prospects of earning only half as much.

This is not a sectional issue. Difficulties over segregation and discrimination exist in every city, in every state of the Union, producing in many cities a rising tide of discontent that threatens the public safety. Nor is this a partisan issue. In a time of domestic crisis men of goodwill and generosity should be able to unite regardless of party or politics. This is not even a legal or legislative issue alone. It is better to settle these matters in the courts than on the streets, and new laws are needed at every level, but law alone cannot make men see right.

We are confronted primarily with a moral issue. It is as old as the Scriptures and is as clear as the American Constitution.

The heart of the question is whether all Americans are to be afforded equal rights and equal opportunities, whether we are going to treat our fellow Americans as we want to be treated. If an American, because his skin is dark, cannot eat lunch in a restaurant open to the public, if he cannot send his children to the best public school available, if he cannot vote for the public officials who represent him, if, in short, he cannot enjoy the full and free life which all of us want, then who among us would be content to have the color of his skin changed and stand in his place? Who among us would then be content with the counsels of patience and delay?

One hundred years of delay have passed since President Lincoln freed the slaves, yet their heirs, their grandsons, are not fully free. They are not yet freed from the bonds of injustice. They are not yet freed from social and economic oppression. And this nation, for all its hopes and all its boasts, will not be fully free until all its citizens are free.

We preach freedom around the world, and we mean it, and we cherish our freedom here at home; but are we to say to the world, and, much more importantly, to each other, that this is a land of the free except for the Negroes; that we have no second-class citizens except Negroes; that we have no class or caste system, no ghettos, no master race, except with respect to Negroes?

Now the time has come for this nation to fulfill its promise. The events in Birmingham and elsewhere have so increased the cries for equality that no city or state or legislative body can prudently choose to ignore them.

The fires of frustration and discord are burning in every city, North and South, where legal remedies are not at hand. Redress is sought in the streets, in demonstrations, parades, and protests which create tensions and threaten violence and threaten lives.

We face, therefore, a moral crisis as a country and as a people. It cannot be met by repressive police action. It cannot be left to increased demonstrations in the streets. It cannot be quieted by token moves or talk. It is a time to act in the Congress, in your state and local legislative bodies and, above all, in all of our daily lives.

It is not enough to pin the blame on others, to say this is a problem of one section of the country or another, or deplore the facts that we face. A great change is at hand, and our task, our obligation, is to make that revolution, that change, peaceful and constructive for all.

Those who do nothing are inviting shame as well as violence. Those who act boldly are recognizing right as well as reality.

Next week I shall ask the Congress of the United States to act, to make a commitment it has not fully made in this century to the proposition that race has no place in American life or law. The federal judiciary has upheld that proposition in a series of forthright cases. The executive branch has adopted that proposition in the conduct of its affairs, including the employment of federal personnel, the use of federal facilities, and the sale of federally financed housing.

But there are other necessary measures which only the Congress can provide, and they must be provided at this session. The old code of equity law under which we live commands for every wrong a remedy, but in too many communities, in too many parts of the country, wrongs are inflicted on Negro citizens and there are no remedies at law. Unless the Congress acts, their only remedy is in the street.

I am, therefore, asking the Congress to enact legislation giving all Americans the right to be served in facilities which are open to the public—hotels, restaurants, theaters, retail stores, and similar establishments.

This seems to me to be an elementary right. Its denial is an arbitrary indignity that no American in 1963 should have to endure. But many do.

Next week I shall ask the Congress of the United States to act, to make a commitment it has not fully made in this century to the proposition that race has no place in American life or law.

I have recently met with scores of business leaders urging them to take voluntary action to end this discrimination, and I have been encouraged by their response. In the last two weeks over seventy-five cities have seen progress made in desegregating these kinds of facilities. But many are unwilling to act alone, and for this reason, nationwide legislation is needed if we are to move this problem from the streets to the courts.

I am also asking Congress to authorize the federal government to participate more fully in lawsuits designed to end segregation in public education. We have succeeded in persuading many districts to desegregate voluntarily. Dozens have admitted Negroes without violence. Today a Negro is attending a state-supported institution in every one of our fifty states. But the pace is very slow.

Too many Negro children entering segregated grade schools at the time of the Supreme Court's decision nine years ago will enter segregated high schools this fall, having suffered a loss which can never be restored. The lack of an adequate education denies the Negro a chance to get a decent job.

The orderly implementation of the Supreme Court decision, therefore, cannot be left solely to those who may not have the economic resources to carry the legal action or who may be subject to harassment.

Other features will also be requested, including greater protection for the right to vote. But legislation, I repeat, cannot solve this problem alone. It must be solved in the homes of every American in every community across our country.

In this respect, I want to pay tribute to those citizens, North and South, who have been working in their communities to make life better for all. They are acting not out of a sense of legal duty but out of a sense of human decency. Like our soldiers and sailors in all parts of the world, they are meeting freedom's challenge on the firing line, and I salute them for their honor and their courage.

My fellow Americans, this is a problem which faces us all—in every city of the North as well as the South. Today there are Negroes, unemployed—two or three times as many compared to whites—with inadequate education, moving into the large cities, unable to find work, young people particularly out of work and without hope, denied equal rights, denied the opportunity to eat at a restaurant or lunch counter or go to a movie theater, denied the right to a decent education. . . . It seems to me that these are matters which concern us all, not merely Presidents or congressmen or governors, but every citizen of the United States.

This is one country. It has become one country because all the people who came here had an equal chance to develop their talents.

We cannot say to ten percent of the population that you can't have that right; that your children can't have the chance to develop whatever talents they have; that the only way that they are going to get their rights is to go into the streets and demonstrate. I think we owe them and we owe ourselves a better country than that.

Therefore, I am asking for your help in making it easier for us to move ahead and to provide the kind of equality of treatment which we would want ourselves; to give a chance for every child to be educated to the limit of his talents.

As I have said before, not every child has an equal talent or an equal ability or an equal motivation, but they should have the equal right to develop their talent and their ability and their motivation, to make something of themselves.

We have a right to expect that the Negro community will be responsible and will uphold the law; but they have a right to expect that the law will be fair, that the Constitution will be color blind, as Justice Harlan said at the turn of the century.

This is what we are talking about. This is a matter which concerns this country and what it stands for, and in meeting it I ask the support of all our citizens.

Televised Address
Washington, D.C., June 11, 1963

The Role of the Military

Dear Mr. Secretary:

. . . We have come a long way in the fifteen years since President Truman ordered the desegregation of the Armed Forces. The military services lead almost every other segment of our society in establishing equality of opportunity for all Americans. Yet a great deal remains to be done. . . .

A serious morale problem is created for Negro military personnel when various forms of segregation and discrimination exist in communities neighboring military bases. Discriminatory practices are morally wrong wherever they occur—they are especially inequitable and iniquitous when they inconvenience and embarrass those serving in the Armed Services and their families. Responsible citizens of all races in these communities should work together to open up public accommodations and housing for Negro military personnel and their dependents. This effort is required by the interests of our national defense, national policy and basic considerations of human decency. . . .

I realize that I am asking the military community to take a leadership role, but I believe that this is proper. The Armed Services will, I am confident, be equal to the task. In this area, as in so many others, the U.S. Infantry motto "Follow Me" is an appropriate guide for action.

Sincerely,
John F. Kennedy

Letter to the Secretary of Defense
Washington, D.C., June 22, 1963

The Civil Rights Act of 1963

In short, the time has come for the Congress of the United States to join with the executive and judicial branches in making it clear to all that race has no place in American life or law. . . .

For these reasons, I am proposing that the Congress stay in session this year until it has enacted—preferably as a single omnibus bill—the most responsible, reasonable, and urgently needed solutions to this problem, solutions which should be acceptable to all fair-minded men. This bill would be known as the "Civil Rights Act of 1963," and would include—in addition to the aforementioned provisions on voting rights and the Civil Rights Commission—additional titles on public accommodations, employment, federally assisted programs, a Community Relations Service, and education, with the latter including my previous recommendation on this subject. In addition, I am requesting certain legislative and budget amendments designed to improve the training, skills, and economic opportunities of the economically distressed and discontented, white and Negro alike. Certain executive actions are also reviewed here; but legislative action is imperative. . . .

Events of recent weeks have again underlined how deeply our Negro citizens resent the injustice of being arbitrarily denied equal access to those facilities and accommodations which are otherwise open to the general public. That is a daily insult which has no place in a country proud of its heritage—the heritage of the melting pot, of equal rights, of one nation and one people. No one has been barred on account of his race from fighting or dying for America—there are no "white" or "colored" signs on the foxholes or graveyards of battle. Surely, in 1963, one hundred years after Emancipation, it should not be necessary for any American citizen to demonstrate in the streets for the opportunity to stop at a hotel, or to eat at a lunch counter in the very department store in which he is shopping, or to enter a motion picture house, on the same terms as any other customer. . . .

For these reasons, I am today proposing, as part of the Civil Rights Act of 1963, a provision to guarantee all citizens equal access to the services and facilities of hotels, restaurants, places of amusement, and retail establishments. . . .

This provision will open doors in every part of the country which never should have been closed. Its enactment will hasten the end to practices which have no place in a free and united nation, and thus help move this potentially dangerous problem from the streets to the courts. . . .

In order to achieve a more orderly and consistent compliance with the Supreme Court's school and college desegregation decisions, therefore, I recommend that the Congress asserts its specific constitutional authority to implement the Fourteenth Amendment by including in the Civil Rights Act of 1963 a new title. . . .

Racial discrimination in employment must be eliminated. Denial of the right to work is unfair, regardless of its victim. It is doubly unfair to throw its burden on an individual because of his race or color. Men who served side by side with each other on the field of battle should have no difficulty working side by side on an assembly line or construction project. . . .

This problem of unequal job opportunity must not be allowed to grow, as the result of either recession or discrimination. I enlist every employer, every labor union, and every agency of government—whether affected directly by these measures or not—in the task of seeing to it that no false lines are drawn in assuring equality of the right and opportunity to make a decent living. . . .

I am today proposing, as part of the Civil Rights Act of 1963, a provision to guarantee all citizens equal access to the services and facilities of hotels, restaurants, places of amusement, and retail establishments.

Many problems remain that cannot be ignored. The enactment of the legislation I have recommended will not solve all our problems of race relations. This bill must be supplemented by action in every branch of government at the federal, state, and local level. It must be supplemented as well by enlightened private citizens, private businesses, and private labor and civic organizations, by responsible educators and editors, and certainly by religious leaders who recognize the conflict between racial bigotry and the Holy Word. . . .

We will not solve these problems by blaming any group or section for the legacy which has been handed down by past generations. But neither will these problems be solved by clinging to the patterns of the past. Nor, finally, can they be solved in the streets, by lawless acts on either side, or by the physical actions or presence of any private group or public official, however appealing such melodramatic devices may seem to some. . . .

The legal remedies I have proposed are the embodiment of this nation's basic posture of common sense and common justice. They involve every American's right to vote, to go to school, to get a job, and to be served in a public place without arbitrary discrimination—rights which most Americans take for granted. . . .

I therefore ask every member of Congress to set aside sectional and political ties, and to look at this issue from the viewpoint of the nation. I ask you to look into your hearts—not in search of charity, for the Negro neither wants nor needs condescension—but for the one plain, proud, and priceless quality that unites us all as Americans: a sense of justice. In this year of the Emancipation Centennial, justice requires us to insure the blessings of liberty for all Americans and their posterity—not merely for reasons of economic efficiency, world diplomacy, and domestic tranquillity—but, above all, because it is right.

Special Message to the Congress
on Civil Rights and Job Opportunities
Washington, D.C., June 19, 1963

The March on Washington

We have witnessed today in Washington tens of thousands of Americans—both Negro and white—exercising their right to assemble peaceably and direct the widest possible attention to a great national issue . . . to secure equal treatment and equal opportunity for all without regard to race, color, creed, or nationality. . . .

Although this summer has seen remarkable progress in translating civil rights from principles into practices, we have a very long way yet to travel. One cannot help but be impressed with the deep fervor and the quiet dignity that characterize the thousands who have gathered in the nation's capital from across the country to demonstrate their faith and confidence in our democratic form of government. History has seen many demonstrations—of widely varying character and for a whole host of reasons. As our thoughts travel to other demonstrations that have occurred in different parts of the world, this nation can properly be proud of the demonstration that has occurred here today. The leaders of the organizations sponsoring the march and all who have participated in it deserve our appreciation for the detailed preparations that made it possible and for the orderly manner in which it has been conducted.

The executive branch of the federal government will continue its efforts to obtain increased employment and to eliminate discrimination in employment practices, two of the prime goals of the march. In addition, our efforts to secure enactment of the legislative proposals made to the Congress will be maintained. . . .

The cause of twenty million Negroes has been advanced by the program conducted so appropriately before the nation's shrine to the Great Emancipator, but even more significant is the contribution to all mankind.

Statement on March on Washington for Jobs and Freedom
Washington, D.C., August 28, 1963

The Long View

Q: Mr. President, this is a related question. It is about the Gallup poll. It has to do with a racial question. Agents of Dr. Gallup asked people this question: Do you think the Kennedy administration is pushing integration too fast or not fast enough? Fifty percent replied that they thought you were pushing too fast. Would you comment?

THE PRESIDENT: No, I think probably he is accurate. The fact of the matter is, this is not a matter on which you can take the temperature every week or two weeks or three weeks, depending on what the newspaper headlines might be. I think you must make a judgment about the movement of a great historical event which is taking place in this country after a period of time. You judged 1863 after a good many years—its full effect. I think we will stand, after a period of time has gone by. The fact is, that same poll showed forty percent or so thought it was more or less right. I thought that was rather impressive, because it is change; change always disturbs, and therefore I was surprised that there wasn't greater opposition. I think we are going at about the right tempo.

President's News Conference
Washington, D.C., September 12, 1963

The Final Word

. . . I pledged in 1960 that a new administration would strive to secure for every American his full constitutional rights. That pledge has been and is being fulfilled. We have not yet secured the objectives desired or the legislation required. But we have, in the last three years . . . opened more new doors to members of minority groups—doors to transportation, voting, education, employment, and places of public accommodation—than had been opened in any three-year or thirty-year period in this century. There is no uncontroversial way to fulfill our constitutional pledge to establish justice and promote domestic tranquillity, but we intend to fulfill those obligations because they are right.

Remarks intended for delivery to
Texas Democratic Dinner
Austin, Texas, November 22, 1963

CHAPTER 10

The Promotion of the Arts

President and Mrs. Kennedy sparked a revival of national interest in matters cultural and intellectual. Nobel prize winners, authors, and scholars dined in the Executive Mansion, and great American concert performers were regularly heard there. From the re-creation of the historic White House through the redesign of a fading Pennsylvania Avenue to the recognition given America's finest poets and artists, the Kennedys more by example and exhortation than by public expenditure, honored what they truly believed to be an enduring source of national pride and greatness. John Kennedy's knowledge and talent in music and painting never matched his skills as writer and orator; but in his encouragement of the arts (as in so many other areas impossible to include in this single volume), he set a standard of excellence to which all who follow might aspire.

The Liberation of the Human Mind

In 1664, Louis the Fourteenth, in his own efforts to encourage the arts, donned brilliant tights and played in a drama called *Furious Roland* before a happy court. Moreover, he drafted the highest officers of his administration for the play so that, according to an account, all clad in brilliant tights themselves, they passed before the queen and the court.

This was suggested tonight but for some reason or other the committee turned it down. But we are glad to be here in any case. . . . And we are very much indebted to all the artists who have so willingly taken part in this work tonight. For when Thomas Jefferson wrote that the one thing, which from the heart he envied certain other nations, was their art, he spoke from a deep understanding of the enduring sources of national greatness and national achievement.

But our culture and art do not speak to America alone. To the extent that artists struggle to express beauty in form and color and sound, to the extent that they write about man's struggle with nature or society or himself, to that extent they strike a responsive chord in all humanity. Today, Sophocles speaks to us from more than two thousand years. And in our own time, even when political communications have been strained, the Russian people have bought more than twenty thousand copies of the works of Jack London, more than ten million books of Mark Twain, and hundreds and thousands of copies of Hemingway, Steinbeck, Whitman, and Poe; and our own people, through the works of Tolstoy and Dostoevski and Pasternak, have gained an insight into the shared problems of the human heart. Thus today, as always, art knows no national boundaries.

Genius can speak at any time, and the entire world will hear it and listen. Behind the storm of daily conflict and crisis, the dramatic confrontations, the tumult of political struggle, the poet, the artist, the musician, continues the quiet work of centuries, building bridges of experience between peoples, reminding man of the universality of his feelings and desires and despairs, and reminding him that the forces that unite are deeper than those that divide.

Thus, art and the encouragement of art are political in the most profound sense, not as a weapon in the struggle, but as an instrument of understanding of the futility of struggle between those who share man's faith. Aeschylus and Plato are remembered today long after the triumphs of imperial Athens are gone. Dante outlived the ambitions of thirteenth-century Florence. Goethe stands serenely above the politics of Germany. And I am certain that, after the dust of centuries has passed over our cities, we, too, will be remembered not for victories or defeats in battle or in politics, but for our contribution to the human spirit.

It was Pericles' proudest boast that politically Athens was the school of Hellas. If we can make our country one of the great schools of civilization, then on that achievement will surely rest our claim to the ultimate gratitude of mankind.

Moreover, as a great democratic society, we have a special responsibility to the arts. For art is the great democrat, calling forth creative genius from every sector of society, disregarding race or religion or wealth or color. The mere accumulation of wealth and power is available to the dictator and the democrat alike. What freedom alone can bring is the liberation of the human mind and spirit which finds its greatest flowering in the free society.

Thus, in our fulfillment of these responsibilities toward the arts lies our unique achievement as a free society.

National Cultural Center Dinner
Washington, D.C., November 29, 1962

The Central Purpose of Civilization

. . . This painting is the second lady that the people of France have sent to the United States, and though she will not stay with us as long as the Statue of Liberty, our appreciation is equally great. Indeed, this loan is the last in a long series of events which have bound together two nations separated by a wide ocean, but linked in their past to the modern world. Our two nations have fought on the same side in four wars during a span of the last 185 years. Each has been delivered from the foreign rule of another by the other's friendship and courage. Our two revolutions helped define the meaning of democracy and freedom which are so much contested in the world today. Today, here in this Gallery, in front of this great painting, we are renewing our commitment to those ideals which have proved such a strong link through so many hazards.

At the same time that the creator of this painting was opening up such a wide new world to Western civilization, his fellow countryman from Italy, Columbus, was opening up a new world to a new civilization. The life of this painting here before us tonight spans the entire life of that new world. We citizens of nations unborn at the time of its creation are among the inheritors and protectors of the ideals which gave it birth. For this painting is not only one of the towering achievements of the skill and vision of art, but its creator embodied the central purpose of our civilization.

Leonardo da Vinci was not only an artist and a sculptor, an architect and a scientist, he was also a military engineer, an occupation which he pursued, he tells us, in order to preserve the chief gift of nature, which is liberty. In this belief he expresses the most profound premises of our own two nations.

National Gallery of Art
Opening of **Mona Lisa** *Exhibition*
Washington, D.C., January 8, 1963

The Fiber of Our National Life

Robert Frost was one of the granite figures of our time in America. He was supremely two things: an artist and an American. A nation reveals itself not only by the men it produces but also by the men it honors, the men it remembers.

In America, our heroes have customarily run to men of large accomplishments. But today this college and country honor a man whose contribution was not to our size but to our spirit, not to our political beliefs but to our insight, not to our self-esteem, but to our self-comprehension. In honoring Robert Frost, we therefore can pay honor to the deepest sources of our national strength. That strength takes many forms, and the most obvious are not always the most significant. The men who create power make an indispensable contribution to the nation's greatness, but the men who question power make a contribution just as indispensable, especially when that questioning is disinterested, for they determine whether we use power or power uses us.

Our national strength matters, but the spirit which informs and controls our strength matters just as much. This was the special significance of Robert Frost. He brought an unsparing instinct for reality to bear on the platitudes and pieties of society. His sense of the human tragedy fortified him against self-deception and easy consolation. "I have been," he wrote, "one acquainted with the night." And because he knew the midnight as well as the high noon, because he understood the ordeal as well as the triumph of the human spirit, he gave his age strength with which to overcome despair. At bottom, he held a deep faith in the spirit of man, and it is hardly an accident that Robert Frost coupled poetry and power, for he saw poetry as the means of saving power from itself. When power leads man toward arrogance, poetry reminds him of his limitations. When power narrows the areas of man's concern, poetry reminds him of the richness and diversity of his existence. When power corrupts, poetry cleanses. For art establishes the basic human truth which must serve as the touchstone of our judgment.

The artist, however faithful to his personal vision of reality, becomes the last champion of the individual mind and sensibility against an intrusive society and an officious state. The great artist is thus a solitary figure. He has, as Frost said, a lover's quarrel with the world. In pursuing his perceptions of reality, he must often sail against the currents of his time. This is not a popular role. If Robert Frost was much honored during his lifetime, it was because a good many preferred to ignore his darker truths. Yet in retrospect, we see how the artist's fidelity has strengthened the fiber of our national life.

If sometimes our great artists have been the most critical of our society, it is because their sensitivity and their concern for justice, which must motivate any true artist, makes him aware that our nation falls short of its highest potential. I see little of more importance to the future of our country and our civilization than full recognition of the place of the artist.

I see little of more importance to the future of our country and our civilization than full recognition of the place of the artist.

If art is to nourish the roots of our culture, society must set the artist free to follow his vision wherever it takes him. We must never forget that art is not a form of propaganda; it is a form of truth. And as Mr. MacLeish once remarked of poets, there is nothing worse for our trade than to be in style. In free society art is not a weapon and it does not belong to the sphere of polemics and ideology. Artists are not engineers of the soul. It may be different elsewhere. But in a democratic society the highest duty of the writer, the composer, the artist is to remain true to himself and to let the chips fall where they may. In serving his vision of the truth, the artist best serves his nation. And the nation which disdains the mission of art invites the fate of Robert Frost's hired man, the fate of having "nothing to look backward to with pride, and nothing to look forward to with hope."

I look forward to a great future for America, a future in which our country will match its military strength with our moral restraint, its wealth with our wisdom, its power with our purpose. I look forward to an America which will not be afraid of grace and beauty, which will protect the beauty of our natural environment, which will preserve the great old American houses and squares and parks of our national past, and which will build handsome and balanced cities for our future.

I look forward to an America which will reward achievement in the arts as we reward achievement in business or statecraft. I look forward to an America which will steadily raise the standards of artistic accomplishment and which will steadily enlarge cultural opportunities for all of our citizens. I look forward to an America which commands respect throughout the world not only for its strength but for its civilization as well. And I look forward to a world which will be safe not only for democracy and diversity but also for personal distinction.

Robert Frost was often skeptical about projects for human improvement, yet I do not think he would disdain this hope. As he wrote during the uncertain days of the Second [World] War:

Take human nature altogether since time began . . .
And it must be a little more in favor of man,
Say a fraction of one percent at the very least . . .
Our hold on the planet wouldn't have so increased.

Because of Mr. Frost's life and work, because of the life and work of this college, our hold on this planet has increased.

Amherst College
Amherst, Massachusetts, October 26, 1963

Signing the Cuban missile crisis quarantine proclamation halting the delivery of offensive weapons to Cuba, October 23, 1962.

PHOTO BY ABBIE ROWE, REPRINTED COURTESY THE JOHN FITZGERALD KENNEDY LIBRARY.

PART IV

The Pursuit of Peace and Security

CHAPTER 11

The Tide Is Turned

John F. Kennedy, as senator, candidate, and President, felt strongly that time was running out on America's necessary role as leader and defender of world freedom. In 1960, the Cold War was at a peak. The Soviet Union was flexing its military, scientific, economic, and diplomatic muscle. All prospects seemed dim for controlling the arms race, solidifying the Alliance, and preventing in the developing world the economic despair and chaos on which violence and despotism fed. In Berlin, Cuba, the Congo, Laos, Vietnam, the United Nations, the Formosa Straits, and a dozen or so other places, the new President faced mounting challenge and crisis. His speeches were designed to stir the country's conscience and awaken it to the dangers and opportunities it faced.

The Urgent Agenda

May 17, 1960, marked the end of an era—an era of illusion, the illusion that personal goodwill is a substitute for hard, carefully prepared bargaining on concrete issues, the illusion that good intentions and pious principles are a substitute for strong, creative leadership.

For on May 17, 1960, the long-awaited, highly publicized summit conference collapsed. That collapse was the direct result of Soviet determination to destroy the talks. The insults and distortions of Mr. Khrushchev and the violence of his attacks shocked all Americans, and united the country in admiration for the dignity and self-control of President Eisenhower. Regardless of party, all of us deeply shared a common disappointment at the failure of the conference. Nevertheless, it is imperative that we, as a nation, rise above our resentment and frustration to a critical reexamination of the events at Paris and their meaning for America.

For the harsh facts of the matter are that the effort to eliminate world tensions and end the Cold War through a summit meeting—necessary as such an effort was to demonstrate America's willingness to seek peaceful solutions—was doomed to failure long before the U-2 ever fell on Soviet soil. This effort was doomed to failure because we have failed for the past eight years to build the positions of long-term strength essential to successful negotiation. It was doomed because we were unprepared with new policies or new programs for the settlement of outstanding substantive issues.

Trunkloads of papers, I am told, were sent to Paris, but no new plans or positions were included. Our unwillingness to go to the summit had changed, but the steady decrease in our relative strength had not changed. Our allies and our own people had been misled into believing that there was some point to holding a summit conference, that we were prepared to say more than what changes in the status quo we would not accept, that by a miracle of personal charm and public relations the Russians could be cajoled into yielding some of their hard-won positions of strength, that we had some conception of alternative settlements that were both acceptable to us and possibly acceptable to the Soviets.

But the truth of the matter is that we were not prepared for any such negotiations and that there was no real success which the summit could have achieved, for words and discussions are not a substitute for strength—they are an instrument for the translation of strength into survival and peace.

This is the real issue of American foreign policy today, not the ill-considered timing of the U-2 or the inconsistent statements of our government. The real issue—and the real lesson of Paris—is the lack of long-range preparation, the lack of policy planning, the lack of a coherent and purposeful national strategy backed by strength.

This is an issue worthy of a great debate, a debate by the American people through the media of their political parties—and that debate must not be stifled or degraded by empty appeals to national unity, false cries of appeasement, or deceptive slogans about "standing up to Khrushchev." For the issue is not who can best "stand up to Khrushchev" or who can best swap threats and insults. The real issue is who can stand up and summon America's vast resources to the defense of freedom against the most dangerous enemy it has ever faced.

If the 1960 campaign should degenerate into a contest of who can talk toughest to Khrushchev, or which party is the "party of war" or the "party of appeasement," or which candidate can tell the American voters what they want to hear, rather than what they need to hear, or who is soft on communism, or who can be hardest on foreign aid, then, in my opinion, it makes very little difference who the winners are in July and in November, for the American people and the whole free world will be the losers.

For the next President of the United States, whoever he may be, will find he has considerably more to do than "stand up to Khrushchev," balance the budget, and mouth popular slogans, if he is to restore our nation's relative strength and leadership. For he will find himself with far-flung commitments without the strength to meet them or to back them up. He will inherit policies formed largely as reactions to Soviet action, their limits set by budgeteers without regard to world conditions or America's needs, their effectiveness often undercut by overlapping or competing agencies. He will inherit membership in alliances of uncertain stability and in international organizations of obsolete structure. He will inherit programs which have been frequently administered by shortsighted, unsympathetic men opposed to the very programs they are administering, awaiting their own return to private industry, and so lacking in compassion for our domestic needs as to be incapable of compassion for the desperate needs of the world's peoples. He will face a world of revolution and turmoil armed with policies which seek only to freeze the status quo and turn back the inevitable tides of change.

Words and discussions are not a substitute for strength—they are an instrument for the translation of strength into survival and peace.

To be sure, we have, in 1960, most of the formal tools of foreign policy: We have a defense establishment, a foreign-aid program, a Western alliance, a Disarmament Committee, an information service, an intelligence operation, and a National Security Council. But . . . we have failed to adapt these tools to the formulation of a long-range, coordinated strategy to meet the determined Soviet program for world domination—a program which skillfully blends the weapons of military might, political subversion, economic penetration, and ideological conquest. We are forced to rely upon piecemeal programs, obsolete policies, and meaningless slogans. . . . We have as our grand strategy only the arms race and the Cold War. . . .

As a substitute for policy, President Eisenhower has tried smiling at the Russians; our State Department has tried frowning at them; and Mr. Nixon has tried both. None have succeeded. For we cannot conceal or overcome our lack of purpose, and our failure of planning, by talking tough; nor can we compensate for our weaknesses by talking smoothly and by assuming that the righteousness of our principles will insure their victory. For just as we know that might never makes right, we must also remember that right, unfortunately, never makes might.

Our task is to devise a national strategy—based not on eleventh-hour responses to Soviet-created crises—but a comprehensive set of carefully prepared, long-term policies designed to increase the strength of the non-Communist world.

The hour is late, but the agenda is long.

First. We must make invulnerable a nuclear retaliatory power second to none. . . .

Second. We must regain the ability to intervene effectively and swiftly in any limited war anywhere in the world. . . .

Third. We must rebuild NATO into a viable and consolidated military force capable of deterring any kind of attack, unified in weaponry and responsibility . . . aiming beyond a narrow military alliance united only by mutual fears. . . .

Fourth. We must . . . greatly increase the flow of capital to the underdeveloped areas of Asia, Africa, the Middle East, and Latin America . . . enabling emerging nations to achieve economic as well as political independence. . . .

Fifth. We must reconstruct our relations with the Latin American democracies. . . .

Sixth. We must formulate . . . a new approach to the Middle East. . . .

Seventh. We must greatly increase our efforts to encourage the newly emerging nations of the vast continent of Africa. . . .

Eighth. We must plan a long-range solution to the problems of Berlin. . . .

Ninth. We must prepare and hold in readiness more flexible and realistic tools for use in Eastern Europe. . . .

Tenth. We must reassess a China policy which has failed dismally [and] work to improve at least our communications with mainland China. . . .

Eleventh. We must begin to develop new, workable programs for peace and the control of arms . . . to strengthen the United Nations and to increase its role in resolving international conflicts. . . .

Twelfth, and finally, we must work to build the stronger America on which our ultimate ability to defend ourselves and the free world depends . . . our own scientific effort . . . educational system . . . economy . . . equal opportunity and economic justice. . . .

I realize . . . that the length of this agenda is in sharp contrast with the rosy reassurances of the administration. "America is today," the Vice-President told his national committee Saturday, summarizing our position in the world, "the strongest country militarily, the strongest country economically, with the best educational system and the finest scientists in the world, overall." To feed that kind of diet to the American people during the coming months—to confine our national posture to one of talking louder and louder while carrying a smaller and smaller stick—is to trade the long-range needs of the nation and the free world for the short-term appearance of security.

For all America—its President, and its people—the coming years will be a time of decision. We must decide whether we have reached our limit—whether our greatness is past—whether we can go no further—or whether, in the words of Thomas Wolfe, "the true discovery of America is before us—the true fulfillment of our mighty and immortal land is yet to come."

United States Senate
Washington, D.C., June 14, 1960

The Response to Multiple Crises

I speak today in an hour of national peril and national opportunity. Before my term has ended, we shall have to test anew whether a nation organized and governed such as ours can endure. The outcome is by no means certain. The answers are by no means clear. All of us together—this administration, this Congress, this nation—must forge those answers.

To state the facts frankly is not to despair the future nor indict the past. The prudent heir takes careful inventory of his legacies, and gives a faithful accounting to those whom he owes an obligation of trust. And, while the occasion does not call for another recital of our blessings and assets, we do have no greater asset than the willingness of a free and determined people, through its elected officials, to face all problems frankly and meet all dangers free from panic or fear. . . .

No man entering upon this office, regardless of his party, regardless of his previous service in Washington, could fail to be staggered upon learning—even in this brief ten-day period—the harsh enormity of the trials through which we must pass in the next four years. Each day the crises multiply. Each day their solution grows more difficult. Each day we draw nearer the hour of maximum danger, as weapons spread and hostile forces grow stronger. I feel I must inform the Congress that our analyses over the last ten days make it clear that—in each of the principal areas of crisis—the tide of events has been running out and time has not been our friend.

In Asia, the relentless pressures of the Chinese Communists menace the security of the entire area—from the borders of India and South Vietnam to the jungles of Laos, struggling to protect its newly won independence. We seek in Laos what we seek in all Asia, and, indeed, in all of the world—freedom for the people and independence for the government. And this nation shall persevere in our pursuit of these objectives.

In Africa, the Congo has been brutally torn by civil strife, political unrest, and public disorder. We shall continue to support the heroic efforts of the United Nations to restore peace and order—efforts which are now endangered by mounting tensions, unsolved problems, and decreasing support from many member states.

In Latin America, Communist agents seeking to exploit that region's peaceful revolution of hope have established a base on Cuba, only ninety miles from our shores. Our objection with Cuba is not over the people's drive for a better life. Our objection is to their domination by foreign and domestic tyrannies. Cuban social and economic reform should be encouraged. Questions of economic and trade policy can always be negotiated. But Communist domination in this hemisphere can never be negotiated.

We are pledged to work with our sister republics to free the Americas of all such foreign domination and all tyranny, working toward the goal of a free hemisphere of free governments, extending from Cape Horn to the Arctic Circle.

In Europe, our alliances are unfulfilled and in some disarray. The unity of NATO has been weakened by economic rivalry and partially eroded by national interest. It has not yet fully mobilized its resources nor fully achieved a common outlook. Yet no Atlantic power can meet on its own the mutual problems now facing us in defense, foreign aid, monetary reserves, and a host of other areas; and our close ties with those whose hopes and interests we share are among this nation's most powerful assets.

Our greatest challenge is still the world that lies beyond the Cold War—but the first great obstacle is still our relations with the Soviet Union and Communist China. We must never be lulled into believing that either power has yielded its ambitions for world domination—ambitions which they forcefully restated only a short time ago. On the contrary, our task is to convince them that aggression and subversion will not be profitable routes to pursue these ends. Open and peaceful competition—for prestige, for markets, for scientific achievement, even for men's minds—is something else again. For if freedom and communism were to compete for man's allegiance in a world at peace, I would look to the future with ever increasing confidence.

No man entering upon this office, regardless of his party, regardless of his previous service in Washington, could fail to be staggered upon learning—even in this brief ten-day period—the harsh enormity of the trials through which we must pass in the next four years.

To meet this array of challenges—to fulfill the role we cannot avoid on the world scene—we must reexamine and revise our whole arsenal of tools: military, economic, and political.

One must not overshadow the other. On the presidential coat of arms, the American eagle holds in his right talon the olive branch, while in his left he holds a bundle of arrows. We intend to give equal attention to both.

First, we must strengthen our military tools. We are moving into a period of uncertain risk and great commitment in which both the military and diplomatic possibilities require a Free World force so powerful as to make any aggression clearly futile. Yet in the past, lack of a consistent, coherent military strategy, the absence of basic assumptions about our national requirements, and the faulty estimates and duplication arising from interservice rivalries have all made it difficult to assess accurately how adequate—or inadequate—our defenses really are.

I have, therefore, instructed the Secretary of Defense to reappraise our entire defense strategy—our ability to fulfill our commitments—the effectiveness, vulnerability, and dispersal of our strategic bases, forces, and warning systems—the efficiency and economy of our operation and organization—the elimination of obsolete bases and installations—and the adequacy, modernization, and mobility of our present conventional and nuclear forces and weapons systems in the light of present and future dangers. I have asked for preliminary conclusions by the end of February—and I then shall recommend whatever legislative, budgetary, or executive action is needed in the light of these conclusions.

In the meantime, I have asked the Defense Secretary to initiate immediately three new steps most clearly needed now:

(a) I have directed prompt attention to increase our airlift capacity . . .

(b) I have directed prompt action to step up our Polaris submarine program . . .

(c) I have directed prompt action to accelerate our entire missile program . . .

Secondly, we must improve our economic tools. Our role is essential and unavoidable in the construction of a sound and expanding economy for the entire non-Communist world, helping other nations build the strength to meet their own problems, to satisfy their own aspirations—to surmount their own dangers. The problems in achieving this goal are towering and unprecedented—the response must be towering and unprecedented as well, much as Lend-Lease and the Marshall Plan were in earlier years, which brought such fruitful results.

I intend to ask the Congress for authority to establish a new and more effective program for assisting the economic, educational, and social development of other countries and continents. That program must stimulate and take more effectively into account the contributions of our allies, and provide central policy direction for all our own programs that now so often overlap, conflict, or diffuse our energies and resources. Such a program, compared to past programs, will require

—more flexibility for short-run emergencies

—more commitment to long-term development

—new attention to education at all levels

—greater emphasis on the recipient nations' role, their effort, their purpose, with greater social justice for their people, broader distribution and participation by their people, and more efficient public administration and more efficient tax systems of their own; and

—orderly planning for national and regional development instead of a piecemeal approach. . . .

To our sister republics to the south, we have pledged a new alliance for progress—*alianza para el progreso.* Our goal is a free and prosperous

Latin America, realizing for all its states and all its citizens a degree of economic and social progress that matches their historic contributions of culture, intellect, and liberty.

This administration is expanding its Food for Peace program in every possible way. The product of our abundance must be used more effectively to relieve hunger and help economic growth in all corners of the globe.

An even more valuable national asset is our reservoir of dedicated men and women—not only on our college campuses but in every age group—who have indicated their desire to contribute their skills, their efforts, and a part of their lives to the fight for world order. We can mobilize this talent through the formation of a National Peace Corps, enlisting the services of all those with the desire and capacity to help foreign lands meet their urgent needs for trained personnel.

Finally, while our attention is centered on the development of the non-Communist world, we must never forget our hopes for the ultimate freedom and welfare of the Eastern European peoples. In order to be prepared to help reestablish historic ties of friendship, I am asking the Congress for increased discretion to use economic tools in this area whenever this is found to be clearly in the national interest.

Third, we must sharpen our political and diplomatic tools—the means of cooperation and agreement on which an enforceable world order must ultimately rest.

I have already taken steps to coordinate and expand our disarmament effort—to increase our programs of research and study—and to make arms control a central goal of our national policy under my direction. The deadly arms race, and the huge resources it absorbs, have too long overshadowed all else we must do. We must prevent that arms race from spreading to new nations, to new nuclear powers, and to the reaches of outer space. We must make certain that our negotiators are better informed and better prepared—to formulate workable proposals of our own and to make sound judgments about the proposals of others.

Our problems are critical. The tide is unfavorable. The news will be worse before it is better. And while hoping and working for the best, we should prepare ourselves now for the worst.

We cannot escape our dangers—neither must we let them drive us into panic or narrow isolation. In many areas of the world where the balance of power already rests with our adversaries, the forces of freedom are sharply divided. It is one of the ironies of our time that the techniques of a harsh and repressive system should be able to instill discipline and ardor in its servants—while the blessings of liberty have too often stood for privilege, materialism, and a life of ease.

But I have a different view of liberty.

Life in 1961 will not be easy. Wishing it, predicting it, even asking for it, will not make it so. There will be further setbacks before the tide is turned. But turn it we must. The hopes of all mankind rest upon us—not simply upon those of us in this chamber, but upon the peasant in Laos, the fisherman in Nigeria, the exile from Cuba, the spirit that moves every man and nation who shares our hopes for freedom and the future. And in the final analysis, they rest most of all upon the pride and perseverance of our fellow citizens of the great Republic.

In the words of a great President, whose birthday we honor today, closing his final State of the Union message sixteen years ago, "We pray that we may be worthy of the unlimited opportunities that God has given us."

State of the Union Address
The Capitol, Washington, D.C.
January 30, 1961

The Freedom Doctrine

The Constitution imposes upon me the obligation to "from time to time give to the Congress information of the State of the Union." While this has traditionally been interpreted as an annual affair, this tradition has been broken in extraordinary times.

These are extraordinary times. And we face an extraordinary challenge. Our strength as well as our convictions have imposed upon this nation the role of leader in freedom's cause.

No role in history could be more difficult or more important. We stand for freedom. That is our conviction for ourselves—that is our only commitment to others. No friend, no neutral, and no adversary should think otherwise. We are not against any man—or any nation—or any system—except as it is hostile to freedom. Nor am I here to present a new military doctrine, bearing any one name or aimed at any one area. I am here to promote the freedom doctrine.

I

The great battleground for the defense and expansion of freedom today is the whole southern half of the globe—Asia, Latin America, Africa, and the Middle East—the lands of the rising peoples. Their revolution is the greatest in human history. They seek an end to injustice, tyranny, and exploitation. More than an end, they seek a beginning.

Theirs is a revolution which we would support regardless of the Cold War, and regardless of which political or economic route they should choose to freedom.

For the adversaries of freedom did not create the revolution; nor did they create the conditions which compel it. But they are seeking to ride the crest of its wave—to capture it for themselves.

Yet their aggression is more often concealed than open. They have fired no missiles; and their troops are seldom seen. They send arms, agitators, aid, technicians, and propaganda to every troubled area. But where fighting is required, it is usually done by others—by guerrillas striking at night, by assassins striking alone—assassins who have taken the lives of four thousand civil officers in the last twelve months in

Vietnam alone—by subversives and saboteurs and insurrectionists, who in some cases control whole areas inside of independent nations.

With these formidable weapons, the adversaries of freedom plan to consolidate their territory—to exploit, to control, and finally to destroy the hopes of the world's newest nations; and they have ambition to do it before the end of this decade. It is a contest of will and purpose as well as force and violence—a battle for minds and souls as well as lives and territory. And in that contest, we cannot stand aside.

We stand, as we have always stood from our earliest beginnings, for the independence and equality of all nations. This nation was born of revolution and raised in freedom. And we do not intend to leave an open road for despotism.

Our patience at the bargaining table is nearly inexhaustible, though our credulity is limited . . . our hopes for peace are unfailing, while our determination to protect our security is resolute.

There is no single simple policy which meets this challenge. Experience has taught us that no one nation has the power or the wisdom to solve all the problems of the world or manage its revolutionary tides—that extending our commitments does not always increase our security—that any initiative carries with it the risk of a temporary defeat—that nuclear weapons cannot prevent subversion—that no free people can be kept free without will and energy of their own and that no two nations or situations are exactly alike.

Yet there is much we can do—and must do. . . .

In conclusion, let me emphasize one point: that we are determined, as a nation in 1961, that freedom shall survive and succeed—and whatever the peril and setbacks, we have some very large advantages.

The first is the simple fact that we are on the side of liberty—and since the beginning of history, and particularly since the end of the Second World War, liberty has been winning out all over the globe.

A second great asset is that we are not alone. We have friends and allies all over the world who share our devotion to freedom. May I cite as a symbol of traditional and effective friendship the great ally I am about to visit—France. I look forward to my visit to France, and to my discussion with a great captain of the Western world, President de Gaulle, as a meeting of particular significance, permitting the kind of close and ranging consultation that will strengthen both our countries and serve the common purposes of worldwide peace and liberty. Such serious conversations do not require a pale unanimity—they are rather the instruments of trust and understanding over a long road.

A third asset is our desire for peace. It is sincere, and I believe the world knows it. We are proving it in our patience at the test-ban table, and we are proving it in the UN, where our efforts have been directed to maintaining that organization's usefulness as a protector of the independence of small nations. In these and other instances, the response of our opponents has not been encouraging.

Yet it is important to know that our patience at the bargaining table is nearly inexhaustible, though our credulity is limited—that our hopes for peace are unfailing, while our determination to protect our security is resolute. For these reasons I have long thought it wise to meet with the Soviet Premier for a personal exchange of views. A meeting in Vienna turned out to be convenient for us both; and the Austrian government has kindly made us welcome. No formal agenda is planned and no negotiations will be undertaken; but we will make clear America's enduring concern is for both peace and freedom—that we are anxious to live in harmony with the Russian people—that we seek no conquests, no satellites, no riches—that we seek only the day when "nation shall not lift up sword against nation, neither shall they learn war any more."

Finally, our greatest asset in this struggle is the American people—their willingness to pay the price for these programs—to understand and accept a long struggle—to share their resources with other less fortunate people—to meet the tax levels and close the tax loopholes I have requested—to exercise self-restraint, instead of pushing up wages or prices, or over-producing certain crops, or spreading military secrets, or urging unessential expenditures or improper monopolies or harmful work stoppages—to serve in the Peace Corps or the Armed Services or the federal Civil Service or the Congress—to strive for excellence in their schools, in their cities, and in their physical fitness and that of their children—to take part in Civil Defense—to pay higher postal rates, and higher payroll taxes, and higher teachers' salaries, in order to strengthen our society—to show friendship to students and visitors from other lands who visit us and go back in many cases to be the future leaders, with an image of America—and I want that image, and I know you do, to be affirmative and positive—and, finally, to practice democracy at home, in all states, with all races, to respect each other and to protect the constitutional rights of all citizens.

I have not asked for a single program which did not cause one or all Americans some inconvenience, or some hardship, or some sacrifice. But they have responded and you in the Congress have responded to your duty—and I feel confident in asking today for a similar response to these new and larger demands. It is heartening to know, as I journey abroad, that our country is united in its commitment to freedom—and is ready to do its duty.

Special Address to Congress on Urgent National Needs
The Capitol, Washington, D.C.
May 25, 1961

The Great Defender of Freedom

Since the close of the Second World War, a global civil war has divided and tormented mankind. But it is not our military might, or our higher standard of living, that has most distinguished us from our adversaries. It is our belief that the state is the servant of the citizen and not his master.

This basic clash of ideas and wills is but one of the forces reshaping our globe—swept as it is by the tides of hope and fear, by crises in the headlines today that become mere footnotes tomorrow. Both the successes and the setbacks of the past year remain on our agenda of unfinished business. For every apparent blessing contains the seeds of danger—every area of trouble gives out a ray of hope—and the one unchangeable certainty is that nothing is certain or unchangeable. . . .

Yet our basic goals remain the same: a peaceful world community of free and independent states—free to choose their own future and their own system, so long as it does not threaten the freedom of others.

Some may choose forms and ways that we would not choose for ourselves—but it is not for us that they are choosing. We can welcome diversity—the Communists cannot. For we offer a world of choice—they offer the world of coercion. And the way of the past shows clearly that freedom, not coercion, is the wave of the future. At times our goal has been obscured by crisis or endangered by conflict—but it draws sustenance from five basic sources of strength:

- the moral and physical strength of the United States;
- the united strength of the Atlantic Community;
- the regional strength of our hemispheric relations;
- the creative strength of our efforts in the new and developing nations; and
- the peacekeeping strength of the United Nations.

Our moral and physical strength begins at home as already discussed. But it includes our military strength as well. So long as fanaticism and fear brood over the affairs of men, we must arm to deter others from aggression.

This nation belongs among the first to explore [space], and among the first—if not the first—we shall be. We are offering our know-how and our cooperation to the United Nations. . . . But peace in space will help us naught once peace on earth is gone. World order will be secured only when the whole world has laid down these weapons which seem to offer us present security but threaten the future survival of the human race. That armistice day seems very far away. The vast resources of this planet are being devoted more and more to the means of destroying, instead of enriching, human life.

But the world was not meant to be a prison in which man awaits his execution. Nor has mankind survived the tests and trials of thousands of years to surrender everything—including its existence—now. This nation has the will and the faith to make a supreme effort to break the log jam on disarmament and nuclear tests—and we will persist until we prevail, until the rule of law has replaced the ever dangerous use of force.

These various elements in our foreign policy lead . . . to a single goal—the goal of a peaceful world of free and independent states. This is our guide for the present and our vision for the future—a free community of nations, independent but interdependent, uniting North and South, East and West, in one great family of man, outgrowing and transcending the hates and fears that rend our age.

It is the fate of this generation . . . to live with a struggle we did not start, in a world we did not make.

We will not reach that goal today, or tomorrow. We may not reach it in our own lifetime. But the quest is the greatest adventure of our century. We sometimes chafe at the burden of our obligations, the complexity of our decisions, the agony of our choices. But there is no comfort or security for us in evasion, no solution in abdication, no relief in irresponsibility.

A year ago, in assuming the tasks of the Presidency, I said that few generations, in all history, had been granted the role of being the great defender of freedom in its hour of maximum danger. This is our good fortune; and I welcome it now as I did a year ago. For it is the fate of this generation—of you in the Congress and of me as President—to live with a struggle we did not start, in a world we did not make. But the pressures of life are not always distributed by choice. And while no nation has ever faced such a challenge, no nation has ever been so ready to seize the burden and the glory of freedom. And in this high endeavor, may God watch over the United States of America.

State of the Union Address
The Capitol, Washington, D.C.
January 11, 1962

The Tides of Human Freedom

Little more than a hundred weeks ago I assumed the office of President of the United States. In seeking the help of the Congress and our countrymen, I pledged no easy answers. I pledged—and asked—only toil and dedication. These the Congress and the people have given in good measure. And today, having witnessed in recent months a heightened respect for our national purpose and power—having seen the courageous calm of a united people in a perilous hour—and having observed a steady improvement in the opportunities and well-being of our citizens—I can report to you that the state of this old but youthful Union, in the one hundred and seventy-fifth year of its life, is good.

In the world beyond our borders, steady progress has been made in building a world of order. The people of West Berlin remain both free and secure. A settlement, though still precarious, has been reached in Laos. The spearpoint of aggression has been blunted in Vietnam. The end of agony may be in sight in the Congo. The doctrine of troika is dead. And, while danger continues, a deadly threat has been removed in Cuba.

At home, the recession is behind us. . . . In short, both at home and abroad, there may now be a temptation to relax. For the road has been long, the burden heavy, and the pace consistently urgent.

But we cannot be satisfied to rest here. This is the side of the hill, not the top. The mere absence of war is not peace. The mere absence of recession is not growth. We have made a beginning—but we have only begun.

Now the time has come to make the most of our gains—to translate the renewal of our national strength into the achievement of our national purpose.

Turning to the world outside, it was only a few years ago in Southeast Asia, Africa, Eastern Europe, Latin America, even outer space—that communism sought to convey the image of a unified, confident, and expanding empire, closing in on a sluggish America and a free world in disarray. But few people would hold to that picture today.

In these past months we have reaffirmed the scientific and military superiority of freedom. We have doubled our efforts in space, to assure us of being first in the future. We have undertaken the most far-reaching defense improvements in the peacetime history of this country. And we have maintained the frontiers of freedom from Vietnam to West Berlin.

But complacency or self-congratulation can imperil our security as much as the weapons of tyranny. A moment of pause is not a promise of peace. . . .

In short, let our adversaries choose. If they choose peaceful competition, they shall have it. If they come to realize that their ambitions cannot succeed—if they see their "wars of liberation" and subversion will ultimately fail—if they recognize that there is more security in accepting inspection than in permitting new nations to master the black arts of nuclear war—and if they are willing to turn their energies, as we are, to the great unfinished tasks of our own peoples—then, surely, the areas of agreement can be very wide indeed; a clear understanding about Berlin, stability in Southeast Asia, an end to nuclear testing, new checks on surprise or accidental attack, and, ultimately, general and complete disarmament.

For we seek not the worldwide victory of one nation or system but a worldwide victory of man. The modern globe is too small, its weapons are too destructive, and its disorders are too contagious to permit any other kind of victory.

To achieve this end, the United States will continue to spend a greater portion of its national production than any other people in the free world. For fifteen years no other free nation has demanded so much of itself. Through hot wars and cold, through recession and prosperity, through the ages of the atom and outer space, the American people have never faltered and their faith has never lagged. If at times our actions seem to make life difficult for others, it is only because history has made life difficult for us all.

But difficult days need not be dark. I think these are proud and memorable days in the cause of peace and freedom. We are proud, for example, of Major Rudolf Anderson, who gave his life over the island of Cuba. We salute Specialist James Allen Johnson, who died on the border of South Korea. We pay honor to Sergeant Gerald Pendell, who was killed in Vietnam. They are among the many who in this century, far from home, have died for our country. Our task now, and the task of all Americans is to live up to their commitment.

My friends: I close on a note of hope. We are not lulled by the momentary calm of the sea or the somewhat clearer skies above. We know the turbulence that lies below, and the storms that are beyond the horizon this year. But now the winds of change appear to be blowing more strongly than ever, in the world of communism as well as our own. For 175 years we have sailed with those winds at our back, and with the tides of human freedom in our favor. We steer our ship with hope, as Thomas Jefferson said, "leaving Fear astern."

Today we still welcome those winds of change—and we have every reason to believe that our tide is running strong. With thanks to Almighty God for seeing us through a perilous passage, we ask His help anew in guiding the "good ship *Union.*"

State of the Union Address
The Capitol, Washington, D.C.
January 14, 1963

CHAPTER 12

The National Defense

Improved photographic reconnaissance and intelligence estimates in 1961 informed President Kennedy that the most serious shortcoming in our capacity to deter a hostile assault was not a "missile gap," as his 1959 and 1960 campaign speeches had charged, but insufficient conventional forces to meet a serious challenge in Berlin and elsewhere. Maintaining strong civilian leadership and budget controls, he began a long, steady buildup of our Armed Forces. Commending their service and sacrifice, he addressed the graduating classes of all three military academies, toured U.S. installations across the country and globe, and met regularly with his principal military advisers.

The Cautious Commander-in-Chief

In my role as Commander-in-Chief of the American Armed Forces, and with my concern over the security of this nation now and in the future, no single question of policy has concerned me more since entering upon these responsibilities than the adequacy of our present and planned military forces to accomplish our major national security objectives. . . .

1. The primary purpose of our arms is peace, not war—to make certain that they will never have to be used—to deter all wars, general or limited, nuclear or conventional, large or small—to convince all potential aggressors that any attack would be futile—to provide backing for diplomatic settlement of disputes—to insure the adequacy of our bargaining power for an end to the arms race. The basic problems facing the world today are not susceptible to a military solution. Neither our strategy nor our psychology as a nation—and certainly not our economy—must become dependent upon the permanent maintenance of a large military establishment. Our military posture must be sufficiently flexible and under control to be consistent with our efforts to explore all possibilities and to take every step to lessen tensions, to obtain peaceful solutions, and to secure arms limitations. Diplomacy and defense are no longer distinct alternatives, one to be used where the other fails—both must complement each other.

The basic problems facing the world today are not susceptible to a military solution.

Disarmament, so difficult and so urgent, has been much discussed since 1945, but progress has not been made. Recrimination in such matters is seldom useful, and we for our part are determined to try again. In so doing, we note that, in the public position of both sides in recent years, the determination to be strong has been coupled with announced willingness to negotiate. For our part, we know there can be dialectical truth in such a position, and we shall do all we can to prove it in action. This budget is wholly consistent with our earnest desire for serious conversation with the other side on disarmament. If genuine progress is made, then as tension is reduced, so will be our arms.

2. Our arms will never be used to strike the first blow in any attack. This is not a confession of weakness but a statement of strength. It is our national tradition. We must offset whatever advantage this may appear to hand an aggressor by so increasing the capability of our forces to respond swiftly and effectively to any aggressive move as to convince any would-be aggressor that such a movement would be too futile and costly to undertake. In the area of general war, this doctrine means that such capability must rest with that portion of our forces which would survive the initial attack. We are not creating forces for a first strike against any other nation. We shall never threaten, provoke, or initiate aggression—but if aggression should come, our response will be swift and effective.

3. Our arms must be adequate to meet our commitments and insure our security, without being bound by arbitrary budget ceilings. This nation can afford to be strong—it cannot afford to be weak. We shall do what is needed to make and to keep us strong. We must, of course, take advantage of every opportunity to reduce military outlays as a result of scientific or managerial progress, new strategy concepts, a more efficient, manageable, and thus more effective defense establishment, or international agreements for the control and limitation of arms. But we must not shrink from additional costs where they are necessary. The additional . . . expenditures for fiscal 1962 which I am recommending today, while relatively small, are too urgent to be governed by a budget largely decided before our defense review had been completed. Indeed, in the long run the net effect of all the changes I am recommending will be to provide a more economical budget. But I cannot promise that in later years we need not be prepared to spend still more for what is indispensable. Much depends on the course followed by other nations. As a proportion of gross national product, as a share of our total budget, and in comparison with our national effort in earlier times of war, this increase in defense expenditures is still substantially below what our citizens have been willing and are now able to support as insurance on their security—insurance we hope is never needed—but insurance we must nevertheless purchase.

4. Our arms must be subject to ultimate civilian control and command at all times, in war as well as peace. The basic decisions on our participation in any conflict and our response to any threat—including all decisions relating to the use of nuclear weapons, or the escalation of a small war into a large one—will be made by the regularly constituted civilian authorities. This requires effective and protected organization, procedures, facilities, and communication in the event of attack directed toward this objective, as well as defensive measures designed to insure thoughtful and selective decisions by the civilian authorities. This message and budget also reflect that basic principle. The Secretary of Defense and I have had the earnest counsel of our senior military advisers and many others and in fact they support the great majority of the decisions reflected in this budget. But I have not delegated to anyone else the responsibilities for decisions which are imposed upon me by the Constitution.

Decisions on our participation in any conflict and our response to any threat . . . will be made by the regularly constituted civilian authorities. . . . I have not delegated to anyone else the responsibilities for decisions which are imposed upon me by the Constitution.

5. Our strategic arms and defenses must be adequate to deter any deliberate nuclear attack on the United States or our allies—by making clear to any potential aggressor that sufficient retaliatory forces will be able to survive a first strike and penetrate his defenses in order to inflict unacceptable losses upon him. As I indicated in an address to the Senate some thirty-one months ago, this deterrence does not depend upon a simple comparison of missiles on hand before an attack. It has been publicly acknowledged for several years that this nation has not led the world in missile strength. Moreover, we will not strike first in any

conflict. But what we have and must continue to have is the ability to survive a first blow and respond with devastating power. This deterrent power depends not only on the number of our missiles and bombers, but on their state of readiness, their ability to survive attack, and the flexibility and sureness with which we can control them to achieve our national purpose and strategic objectives.

6. The strength and deployment of our forces in combination with those of our allies should be sufficiently powerful and mobile to prevent the steady erosion of the Free World through limited wars; and it is this role that should constitute the primary mission of our overseas forces. Non-nuclear wars, and sub-limited or guerrilla warfare, have since 1945 constituted the most active and constant threat to Free World security. Those units of our forces which are stationed overseas, or designed to fight overseas, can be most usefully oriented toward deterring or confining those conflicts which do not justify and must not lead to a general nuclear attack. In the event of a major aggression that could not be repulsed by conventional forces, we must be prepared to take whatever action with whatever weapons are appropriate. But our objective now is to increase our ability to confine our response to non-nuclear weapons, and to lessen the incentive for any limited aggression by making clear what our response will accomplish. In most areas of the world, the main burden of local defense against overt attack, subversion, and guerrilla warfare must rest on local populations and forces. But given the great likelihood and seriousness of this threat, we must be prepared to make a substantial contribution in the form of strong, highly mobile forces trained in this type of warfare, some of which must be deployed in forward areas, with a substantial airlift and sealift capacity and prestocked overseas bases.

7. Our defense posture must be both flexible and determined. Any potential aggressor contemplating an attack on any part of the Free World with any kind of weapons, conventional or nuclear, must know that our response will be suitable, selective, swift, and effective. While he may be uncertain of its exact nature and location, there must be no uncertainty about our determination and capacity to take whatever steps are necessary to meet our obligations. We must be able to make deliberate choices in weapons and strategy, shift the tempo of our production, and alter the direction of our forces to meet rapidly changing conditions or objectives at very short notice and under any circumstances. Our weapons systems must be usable in a manner permitting deliberation and discrimination as to timing, scope, and targets in re-

sponse to civilian authority; and our defenses must be secure against prolonged re-attack as well as a surprise first strike. To purchase productive capacity and to initiate development programs that may never need to be used—as this budget proposes—adopts an insurance policy of buying alternative future options.

8. Our defense posture must be designed to reduce the danger of irrational or unpremeditated general war—the danger of an unnecessary escalation of a small war into a large one, or of miscalculation or misinterpretation of an incident or enemy intention. Our diplomatic efforts to reach agreements on the prevention of surprise attack, an end to the spread of nuclear weapons—indeed, all our efforts to end the arms race—are aimed at this objective. We shall strive for improved communication among all nations, to make clear our own intentions and resolution, and to prevent any nation from underestimating the response of any other, as has too often happened in the past. In addition our own military activities must be safeguarded against the possibility of inadvertent triggering incidents. But even more importantly, we must make certain that our retaliatory power does not rest on decisions made in ambiguous circumstances, or permit a catastrophic mistake. . . .

As a power which will never strike first, our hopes for anything close to an absolute deterrent must rest on weapons which come from hidden, moving, or invulnerable bases which will not be wiped out by a surprise attack. A retaliatory capacity based on adequate numbers of these weapons would deter any aggressor from launching or even threatening an attack—an attack he knew could not find or destroy enough of our force to prevent his own destruction. . . .

The Free World's security can be endangered not only by a nuclear attack, but also by being slowly nibbled away at the periphery, regardless of our strategic power, by forces of subversion, infiltration, intimidation, indirect or non-overt aggression, internal revolution, diplomatic blackmail, guerrilla warfare, or a series of limited wars.

In this area of local wars, we must inevitably count on the cooperative efforts of other peoples and nations who share our concern. Indeed, their interests are more often directly engaged in such conflicts. The self-reliant are also those whom it is easiest to help—and for these reasons we must continue and reshape the Military Assistance Program which I have discussed earlier in my special message on foreign aid.

The elimination of waste, duplication, and outmoded or unjustifiable expenditure items from the defense budget is a long and arduous undertaking, resisted by special arguments and interests from economic, military, technical, and other special groups. There are hundreds of ways, most of them with some merit, for spending billions of dollars on defense; and it is understandable that every critic of this budget will have a strong preference for economy on some expenditures other than those that affect his branch of the service, or his plant, or his community.

But hard decisions must be made. Unneeded facilities or projects must be phased out. The defense establishment must be lean and fit, efficient and effective, always adjusting to new opportunities and advances, and planning for the future. The national interest must be weighed against special or local interests; and it is the national interest that calls upon us to cut our losses and cut back those programs in which a very dim promise no longer justifies a very large cost. . . .

It is not pleasant to request additional funds at this time for national security. Our interest, as I have emphasized, lies in peaceful solutions, in reducing tension, in settling disputes at the conference table and not on the battlefield. I am hopeful that these policies will help secure these ends.

Special Message to Congress on Defense Policies and Principles
Washington, D.C., March 28, 1961

The Modern Military Officer

Nearly a half century ago, President Woodrow Wilson came here to Annapolis on a similar mission, and addressed the Class of 1914. That day, the graduating class numbered 154 men. There has been, since that time, a revolution in the size of our military establishment, and that revolution has been reflected in the revolution in the world around us.

When Wilson addressed the class in 1914, the Victorian structure of power was still intact, the world was dominated by Europe, and Europe itself was the scene of an uneasy balance of power between dominant figures. America was a spectator on a remote sideline.

The autumn after Wilson came to Annapolis, the Victorian world began to fall to pieces, and our world one half a century later is vastly different. Today we are witnesses to the most extraordinary revolution, nearly, in the history of the world, as the emergent nations of Latin America, Africa, and Asia awaken from long centuries of torpor and impatience.

Today the Victorian certitudes which were taken to be so much a part of man's natural existence are under siege by a faith committed to the destruction of liberal civilization, and today the United States is no longer the spectator, but the leader.

This half century, therefore, has not only revolutionized the size of our military establishment, it has also brought about a more striking revolution in the things that the nation expects from the men in our service.

Fifty years ago the graduates of the Naval Academy were expected to be seamen and leaders of men. They were reminded of the saying of John Paul Jones, "Give me a fair ship so that I might go into harm's way."

When Captain Mahan began to write in the nineties on the general issues of war and peace and naval strategy, the Navy quickly shipped him to sea duty. Today we expect all of you . . . to be prepared not only to handle a ship in a storm or a landing party on a beach, but to make great determinations which affect the survival of this country.

The revolution in the technology of war makes it necessary—in order that you, when you hold positions of command, may make an educated judgment between various techniques—that you also be a scientist and an engineer and a physicist, and your responsibilities go far beyond the classic problems of tactics and strategy.

You must know something about strategy and tactics and logistics, but also economics and politics and diplomacy and history. You must know everything you can know about military power, and you must also understand the limits of military power.

In the years to come, some of you will serve, as your Commandant did last year, as an adviser to foreign governments; some will negotiate, as Admiral Burke did in Korea, with other governments on behalf of the United States; some will go to the far reaches of space and some will go to the bottom of the ocean. Many of you, from one time or another, in positions of command or as members of staff, will participate in great decisions which go far beyond the narrow reaches of professional competence.

You gentlemen, therefore, have a most important responsibility, to recognize that your education is just beginning, and to be prepared, in the most difficult period in the life of our country, to play the role that the country hopes and needs and expects from you. You must understand not only this country but other countries. You must know something about strategy and tactics and logistics, but also economics and politics and diplomacy and history. You must know everything you can know about military power, and you must also understand the limits of military power.

You must understand that few of the important problems of our time have, in the final analysis, been finally solved by military power alone. . . . You must be more than the servants of national policy. You must be prepared to play a constructive role in the development of national policy, a policy which protects our interests and our security and the peace of the world.

Woodrow Wilson reminded your predecessors that you were not serving a government or an administration, but a people. In serving the American people, you represent the American people and the best of the ideals of this free society. Your posture and your performance will provide many people far beyond our shores, who know very little of our country, the only evidence they will ever see as to whether America is truly dedicated to the cause of justice and freedom.

In my Inaugural Address, I said that each citizen should be concerned not with what his country can do for him, but what he can do for his country. What you have chosen to do for your country, by devoting your life to the service of our country, is the greatest contribution that any man could make. It is easy for you, in a moment of exhilaration today, to say that you freely and gladly dedicate your life to the United States. But the life of service is a constant test of your will.

It will be hard at times to face the personal sacrifice and family inconvenience, to maintain this high resolve, to place the needs of your country above all else. When there is a visible enemy to fight, the tide of patriotism in this country runs strong. But when there is a long, slow struggle, with no immediate visible foe, when you watch your contemporaries indulging the urge for material gain and comfort and personal advancement, your choice will seem hard, and you will recall, I am sure, the lines found in an old sentry box at Gibraltar, "God and the soldier all men adore in time of trouble and no more, for when war is over, and all things righted, God is neglected and the old soldier slighted."

Never forget, however, that the battle for freedom takes many forms. . . . The answer to those who challenge us so severely in so many parts of the globe lies in our willingness to freely commit ourselves to the maintenance of our country and the things for which it stands.

This ceremony today represents the kind of commitment which you are willing to make. For that reason, I am proud to be here. This nation salutes you . . . and I congratulate you and thank you.

U.S. Naval Academy Commencement
Annapolis, Maryland, June 7, 1961

The Inequities of Service

Q: Mr. President, at some of our military camps there have been demonstrations by mobilized reservists, including in one case an attempted hunger strike. I wonder if you couldn't comment on these demonstrations, and couldn't you give the reservists some notion of when they might be released?

THE PRESIDENT: Well, I understand the feeling of any reservist, particularly those who may have fulfilled their duty and then they are called back. And they see others going along in normal life, and therefore they feel: how long are we going to be kept?

We will release them on the first possible date consistent with our national security. They were called up because of the crisis in Berlin, and because of the threats in Southeast Asia. And I do not think that anyone can possibly read the papers and come to the conclusion that these threats do not continue. There is no evidence that we are going to quickly reach a settlement in either one of these areas.

Life is unfair.

These reservists are doing a very important job. In my judgment, the fact they were called up and the fact they responded has strengthened the foreign policy of the United States measurably since last July and August.

Now, secondly, there is always inequity in life. Some men are killed in a war and some men are wounded, and some men never leave the country, and some men are stationed in the Antarctic and some are stationed in San Francisco. It's very hard in military or in personal life to assure complete equality. Life is unfair. . . . Some people are sick and others are well—but I do hope that these people recognize that they are fulfilling a valuable function, and that, however humdrum it is, and however much their life is disturbed and years yanked out of it, they will have the satisfaction afterwards of feeling that they contributed importantly to the security of their families and their country at a significant time.

President's News Conference
Washington, D.C., March 21, 1962

The Best Defense in the World

. . . What can we do to move from the present pause toward enduring peace? Again I would counsel caution. I foresee no spectacular reversal in Communist methods or goals. But if all these trends and developments can persuade the Soviet Union to walk the path of peace, then let her know that all free nations will journey with her. But until that choice is made, and until the world can develop a reliable system of international security, the free peoples have no choice but to keep their arms nearby.

This country, therefore, continues to require the best defense in the world—a defense which is suited to the sixties. This means, unfortunately, a rising defense budget—for there is no substitute for adequate defense, and no "bargain basement" way of achieving it. It means the expenditure of more than $15 billion this year on nuclear weapons systems alone, a sum which is about equal to the combined defense budgets of our European Allies.

But it also means improved air and missile defenses, improved civil defense, a strengthened antiguerrilla capacity and, of prime importance, more powerful and flexible non-nuclear forces. For threats of massive retaliation may not deter piecemeal aggression—and a line of destroyers in a quarantine, or a division of well-equipped men on a border, may be more useful to our real security than the multiplication of awesome weapons beyond all rational need.

State of the Union Address
The Capitol, Washington, D.C.
January 14, 1963

CHAPTER 13

The U.S.–Soviet Competition

This longest chapter in this book reflects the most important chapter in the Kennedy Presidency. That chapter began badly with an ill-conceived call to arms at Cuba's Bay of Pigs. It ended grandly with a heartfelt call for peace at the United Nations and a breakthrough sale of American wheat for Soviet consumers. In between, the world's first potential nuclear confrontation over Soviet missiles in Cuba required a steel nerve, a cool hand, and a President willing to balance deterrence with dialogue. By resolving the Cuban missile crisis with Khrushchev without firing a shot, Kennedy enormously increased his worldwide stature and confidence. As the Cold War began to recede and nuclear war no longer seemed ultimately inevitable, the first concrete measures were taken to halt not only the endless arms race but endless U.S.–U.S.S.R. belligerence.

The Real Revolution

I believe, Mr. Chairman, that you should recognize that free people in all parts of the world do not accept the claims of historical inevitability for the Communist revolution. What your government believes is its own business; what it does in the world is the world's business. The great revolution in the history of man, past, present, and future, is the revolution of those determined to be free.

Public Message to Soviet Chairman Khrushchev
after the Bay of Pigs
Washington, D.C., April 18, 1961

The Summit Encounter

I went to Vienna to meet the leader of the Soviet Union, Mr. Khrushchev. For two days we met in sober, intensive conversation, and I believe it is my obligation to the people, to the Congress, and to our allies to report on those conversations candidly and publicly.

Mr. Khrushchev and I had a very full and frank exchange of views on the major issues that now divide our two countries. I will tell you now that it was a very sober two days. There was no discourtesy, no loss of temper, no threats or ultimatums by either side; no advantage or concession was either gained or given; no major decision was either planned or taken; no spectacular progress was either achieved or pretended.

This kind of informal exchange may not be as exciting as a full-fledged summit meeting with a fixed agenda and a large corps of advisers, where negotiations are attempted and new agreements sought, but this was not intended to be and was not such a meeting, nor did we plan any future summit meetings at Vienna.

But I found this meeting with Chairman Khrushchev, as somber as it was, to be immensely useful. I had read his speeches and of his policies. I had been advised on his views. I had been told by other leaders of the West, General de Gaulle, Chancellor Adenauer, Prime Minister Macmillan, what manner of man he was.

But I bear the responsibility of the Presidency of the United States, and it is my duty to make decisions that no adviser and no ally can make for me. It is my obligation and responsibility to see that these decisions are as informed as possible, that they are based on as much direct, firsthand knowledge as possible.

I therefore thought it was of immense importance that I know Mr. Khrushchev, that I gain as much insight and understanding as I could on his present and future policies. At the same time, I wanted to make certain Mr. Khrushchev knew this country and its policies, that he understood our strength and our determination, and that he knew that we desired peace with all nations of every kind.

I wanted to present our views to him directly, precisely, realistically, and with an opportunity for discussion and clarification. This was done. No new aims were stated in private that have not been stated in public on either side. The gap between us was not, in such a short period, materially reduced, but at least the channels of communication were opened more fully, at least the chances of a dangerous misjudgment on either side should now be less, and at least the men on whose decisions the peace in part depends have agreed to remain in contact.

This is important, for neither of us tried merely to please the other, to agree merely to be agreeable, to say what the other wanted to hear. And just as our judicial system relies on witnesses appearing in court and on cross-examination, instead of hearsay testimony or affidavits on paper, so, too, was this direct give-and-take of immeasurable value in making clear and precise what we considered to be vital.

For the facts of the matter are that the Soviets and ourselves give wholly different meanings to the same words—war, peace, democracy, and popular will. We have wholly different views of right and wrong, of what is an internal affair and what is aggression. Above all, we have wholly different concepts of where the world is and where it is going.

Only by such a discussion was it possible for me to be sure that Mr. Khrushchev knew how differently we view the present and the future. Our views contrasted sharply but at least we knew better at the end where we both stood. Neither of us was there to dictate a settlement or to convert the other to a cause or to concede our basic interests. But both of us were there, I think, because we realized that each nation has the power to inflict enormous damage upon the other, that such a war could and should be avoided if at all possible, since it would settle no dispute and prove no doctrine, and that care should thus be taken to prevent our conflicting interests from so directly confronting each other that war necessarily ensued.

We believe in a system of national freedom and independence. He believes in an expanding and dynamic concept of world communism; and the question is whether these two systems can ever hope to live in peace without permitting any loss of security or any denial of the freedom of our friends. However difficult it may seem to answer this question in the affirmative as we approach so many harsh tests, I think we owe it to all mankind to make every possible effort.

That is why I considered the Vienna talks to be useful. The somber mood that they conveyed was not cause for elation or relaxation, nor was it cause for undue pessimism or fear. It simply demonstrated how much work we in the Free World have to do and how long and hard a struggle must be our fate as Americans in this generation as the chief defenders of the cause of liberty.

The one area which afforded some immediate prospect of accord was Laos. Both sides recognized the need to reduce the dangers in that situation. Both sides endorsed the concept of a neutral and independent Laos, much in the manner of Burma or Cambodia. Of critical importance to the current conference on Laos in Geneva, both sides recognized the importance of an effective cease-fire. It is urgent that this be translated into new attitudes at Geneva, enabling the International Control Commission to do its duty, to make certain that a cease-fire is enforced and maintained. I am hopeful that progress can be made on this matter in the coming days at Geneva for that would greatly improve the international atmosphere.

No such hope emerged, however, with respect to the other deadlocked Geneva conference, seeking a treaty to ban nuclear tests. Mr. Khrushchev made it clear that there could not be a neutral administrator—in his opinion—because no one was truly neutral; that a Soviet veto would have to apply to acts of enforcement; that inspection was only a subterfuge for espionage, in the absence of total disarmament; and that the present test-ban negotiations appeared futile. In short, our hopes for an end to nuclear tests, for an end to the spread of nuclear weapons, and for some slowing down of the arms race have been struck a serious blow. Nevertheless, the stakes are too important for us to abandon the draft treaty we have offered at Geneva.

The Soviets and ourselves give wholly different meanings to the same words—war, peace, democracy, and popular will. We have wholly different views of right and wrong, of what is an internal affair and what is aggression.

But our most somber talks were on the subject of Germany and Berlin. I made it clear to Mr. Khrushchev that the security of Western Europe and therefore our own security are deeply involved in our presence and our access rights to West Berlin, that those rights are based on law and not on sufferance, and that we are determined to maintain those rights at any risk, and thus meet our obligation to the people of West Berlin and their right to choose their own future.

Mr. Khrushchev, in turn, presented his views in detail, and his presentation will be the subject of further communications. But we are not seeking to change the present situation. A binding German peace treaty is a matter for all who were at war with Germany, and we and our allies cannot abandon our obligations to the people of West Berlin.

Generally, Mr. Khrushchev did not talk in terms of war. He believes the world will move his way without resort to force. He spoke of his nation's achievements in space. He stressed his intention to outdo us in industrial production, to out-trade us, to prove to the world the superiority of his system over ours. Most of all, he predicted the triumph of communism in the new and less-developed countries.

He was certain that the tide there was moving his way, that the revolution of rising peoples would eventually be a Communist revolution, and that the so-called wars of liberation, supported by the Kremlin, would replace the old methods of direct aggression and invasion.

In the 1940s and early fifties, the great danger was from Communist armies marching across free borders, which we saw in Korea. Our nuclear monopoly helped to prevent this in other areas. Now we face a new and different threat. We no longer have a nuclear monopoly. Their missiles, they believe, will hold off our missiles, and their troops can match our troops should we intervene in these so-called wars of liberation. Thus, the local conflict they support can turn in their favor through guerrillas or insurgents or subversion. A small group of disciplined Communists could exploit discontent and misery in a country where the average income may be sixty or seventy dollars a year, and seize control of an entire country without Communist troops ever crossing any international frontier. This is the Communist theory.

But I believe just as strongly that time will prove it wrong, that liberty and independence and self-determination—not communism—are the future of man, and that free men have the will and the resources to win the struggle for freedom. But it is clear that this struggle in this area of the new and poorer nations will be a continuing crisis of this decade.

Mr. Khrushchev made one point which I wish to pass on. He said there are many disorders throughout the world, and he should not be blamed for them all. He is quite right. It is easy to dismiss as Communist-inspired every anti-government or anti-American riot, every overthrow of a corrupt regime, or every mass protest against misery and despair. These are not all Communist-inspired. The Communists move in to exploit them, to infiltrate their leadership, to ride their crest to victory. But the Communists did not create the conditions which caused them.

In short, the hopes for freedom in these areas which see so much poverty and illiteracy, so many children who are sick, so many children who die in the first year, so many families without homes, so many families without hope—the future for freedom in these areas rests with the local peoples and their governments.

If they have the will to determine their own future, if their governments have the support of their own people, if their honest and progressive measures—helping their people—have inspired confidence and zeal, then no guerrilla or insurgent action can succeed. But where those conditions do not exist, a military guarantee against external attack from across a border offers little protection against internal decay.

Yet all this does not mean that our nation and the West and the Free World can only sit by. On the contrary, we have an historic opportunity to help these countries build their societies until they are so strong and broadly based that only an outside invasion could topple them, and that threat, we know, can be stopped. . . .

May I conclude by saying simply that I am glad to be home. We have on this trip admired splendid places and seen stirring sights, but we are glad to be home. No demonstration of support abroad could mean so much as the support which you, the American people, have so generously given to our country. With that support I am not fearful of the future. We must be patient. We must be determined. We must be courageous. We must accept both risks and burdens, but with the will and the work freedom will prevail.

Televised Address
Washington, D.C., June 6, 1961

The Running Tiger

Chairman Khrushchev has compared the United States to a worn-out runner living on its past performance and stated that the Soviet Union would outproduce the United States by 1970.

Without wishing to trade hyperbole with the Chairman, I do suggest that he reminds me of the tiger hunter who has picked a place on the wall to hang the tiger's skin long before he has caught the tiger. This tiger has other ideas.

I believe that we can maintain our productive development and also our system of freedom. We invite the U.S.S.R. to engage in this competition which is peaceful and which could only result in a better living standard for both of our people.

In short, the United States is not such an aged runner and, to paraphrase Mr. Coolidge, "We do choose to run."

President's News Conference
Washington, D.C., June 28, 1961

The Berlin Crisis

In consultation and full agreement with its British and French allies, and with the benefit of the views of the Federal Republic of Germany, and after consultation with the other member governments of the North Atlantic Treaty Organization, the United States on Monday delivered through its Embassy in Moscow its reply to the aide-mémoire on Germany and Berlin received from the Soviet government on June fourth. Our reply speaks for itself and advances what I believe to be an irrefutable legal, moral, and political position. In this statement I should like to convey to the American people and the people of the world the basic issues which underlie the somewhat more formal language of diplomacy.

The Soviet aide-mémoire is a document which speaks of peace but threatens to disturb it. It speaks of ending the abnormal situation in Germany but insists on making permanent its abnormal division. It refers to the four-power alliance of World War II but seeks the unilateral abrogation of the rights of the other three powers. It calls for new international agreements while preparing to violate existing ones. It offers certain assurances while making it plain that its previous assurances are not to be relied upon. It professes concern for the rights of the citizens of West Berlin while seeking to expose them to the immediate or eventual domination of a regime which permits no self-determination.

Three simple facts are clear:

1. Today there is peace in Berlin, in Germany, and in Europe. If that peace is destroyed by the unilateral actions of the Soviet Union, its leaders will bear a heavy responsibility before world opinion and history.

2. Today the people of West Berlin are free. In that sense it is already a "free city"—free to determine its own leaders and free to enjoy the fundamental human rights reaffirmed in the United Nations Charter.

3. Today the continued presence in West Berlin of the United States, the United Kingdom, and France is by clear legal right, arising from war, acknowledged in many agreements signed by the Soviet Union, and strongly supported by the overwhelming majority of the people of that city. Their freedom is dependent upon our exercise of these rights —an exercise which is thus a political and moral obligation as well as a

legal right. Inasmuch as these rights, including the right of access to Berlin, are not held from the Soviet government, they cannot be ended by any unilateral action of the Soviet Union. They cannot be affected by a so-called peace treaty, covering only a part of Germany, with a regime of the Soviet Union's own creation—a regime which is not freely representative of all or any part of Germany, and does not enjoy the confidence of the 17 million East Germans. The steady stream of German refugees from East to West is eloquent testimony to that fact.

The world knows that there is no reason for a crisis over Berlin today—and that, if one develops, it will be caused by the Soviet government's attempt to invade the rights of others.

The United States has been prepared since the close of the war, and is prepared today, to achieve, in agreement with its World War II allies, a freely negotiated peace treaty covering all of Germany and based on the freely expressed will of all of the German people. We have never suggested that, in violation of international law and earlier four-power agreements, we might legally negotiate a settlement with only a part of Germany, or without the participation of the other principal World War II allies. We know of no sound reason why the Soviet government should now believe that the rights of the Western powers, derived from Nazi Germany's surrender, could be invalidated by such an action on the part of the Soviet Union.

The United States has consistently sought the goal of a just and comprehensive peace treaty for all of Germany since first suggesting in 1946 that a special commission be appointed for this purpose. We still recognize the desirability of change—but it should be a change in the direction of greater, not less, freedom of choice for the people of Germany and Berlin. The Western peace plan and the all-Berlin solution proposed by the Western allies at Geneva in 1959 were constructive, practical offers to obtain this kind of fair settlement in Central

Europe. Our objective is not to perpetuate our presence in either Germany or Berlin—our objective is the perpetuation of the peace and freedom of their citizens.

But the Soviet Union has blocked all progress toward the conclusion of a just treaty based on the self-determination of the German people, and has instead repeatedly heightened world tensions over this issue. The Soviet blockade of Berlin in 1948, the Soviet note of November 27, 1958, and this most recent Soviet aide-mémoire of June 4, 1961, have greatly disturbed the tranquillity of this area.

The real intent of the June 4 aide-mémoire is that East Berlin, a part of a city under four-power status, would be formally absorbed into the so-called German Democratic Republic while West Berlin, even though called a "free city," would lose the protection presently provided by the Western powers and become subject to the will of a totalitarian regime. Its leader, Herr Ulbricht, has made clear his intention, once this so-called peace treaty is signed, to curb West Berlin's communications with the Free World and to suffocate the freedom it now enjoys.

The area thus newly subjected to Soviet threats of heightened tension poses no danger whatsoever to the peace of the world or to the security of any nation. The world knows that there is no reason for a crisis over Berlin today—and that, if one develops, it will be caused by the Soviet government's attempt to invade the rights of others and manufacture tensions. It is, moreover, misusing the words "freedom" and "peace." For, as our reply states, "freedom" and "peace" are not merely words—nor can they be achieved by words or promises alone. They are representative of a state of affairs.

A city does not become free merely by calling it a "free city." For a city or a people to be free requires that they be given the opportunity, without economic, political, or police pressure, to make their own choice and to live their own lives. The people of West Berlin today have that freedom. It is the objective of our policy that they shall continue to have it.

Peace does not come automatically from a "peace treaty." There is peace in Germany today even though the situation is "abnormal." A "peace treaty" that adversely affects the lives and rights of millions will not bring peace with it. A "peace treaty" that attempts to affect adversely the solemn commitments of three great powers will not bring peace with it. We again urge the Soviet government to reconsider its course, to return to the path of constructive cooperation it so frequently states it desires, and to work with its World War II allies in concluding a just and enduring settlement of issues remaining from that conflict.

Statement on Berlin Crisis
Washington, D.C., July 19, 1961

Seven weeks ago tonight I returned from Europe to report on my meeting with Premier Khrushchev and the others. His grim warnings about the future of the world, his aide-mémoire on Berlin, his subsequent speeches and threats which he and his agents have launched, and the increase in the Soviet military budget that he has announced, have all prompted a series of decisions by the administration and a series of consultations with the members of the NATO organization. In Berlin, as you recall, he intends to bring to an end, through a stroke of the pen, first our legal rights to be in West Berlin—and secondly our ability to make good on our commitment to the two million free people of that city. That we cannot permit.

We are clear about what must be done—and we intend to do it. I want to talk frankly with you tonight about the first steps that we shall take. These actions will require sacrifice on the part of many of our citizens. More will be required in the future. They will require, from all of us, courage and perseverance in the years to come. But if we and our allies act out of strength and unity of purpose—with calm determination and steady nerves—using restraint in our words as well as our weapons—I am hopeful that both peace and freedom will be sustained.

The immediate threat to free men is in West Berlin. But that isolated outpost is not an isolated problem. The threat is worldwide. Our effort must be equally wide and strong, and not be obsessed by any single manufactured crisis. We face a challenge in Berlin, but there is also a challenge in Southeast Asia, where the borders are less guarded, the enemy harder to find, and the dangers of communism less apparent to those who have so little. We face a challenge in our own hemisphere, and indeed wherever else the freedom of human beings is at stake.

Let me remind you that the fortunes of war and diplomacy left the free people of West Berlin, in 1945, 110 miles behind the Iron Curtain.

We are there as a result of our victory over Nazi Germany—and our basic rights to be there, deriving from that victory, include both our presence in West Berlin and the enjoyment of access across East Germany. These rights have been repeatedly confirmed and recognized in special agreements with the Soviet Union. Berlin is not a part of East Germany, but a separate territory under the control of the allied powers. Thus our rights there are clear and deep-rooted. But in addition to those rights is our commitment to sustain—and defend, if need be—the opportunity for more than two million people to determine their own future and choose their own way of life.

Thus, our presence in West Berlin, and our access thereto, cannot be ended by any act of the Soviet government. The NATO shield was long ago extended to cover West Berlin—and we have given our word that an attack upon that city will be regarded as an attack upon us all.

For West Berlin—lying exposed 110 miles inside East Germany, surrounded by Soviet troops and close to Soviet supply lines, has many roles. It is more than a showcase of liberty, a symbol, an island of freedom in a Communist sea. It is even more than a link with the Free World, a beacon of hope behind the Iron Curtain, an escape hatch for refugees.

West Berlin is all of that. But above all it has now become—as never before—the great testing place of Western courage and will, a focal point where our solemn commitments, stretching back over the years since 1945, and Soviet ambitions now meet in basic confrontation.

It would be a mistake for others to look upon Berlin, because of its location, as a tempting target. The United States is there; the United Kingdom and France are there; the pledge of NATO is there—and the people of Berlin are there. It is as secure, in that sense, as the rest of us—for we cannot separate its safety from our own.

I hear it said that West Berlin is militarily untenable. And so was Bastogne. And so, in fact, was Stalingrad. Any dangerous spot is tenable if men—brave men—will make it so.

We do not want to fight—but we have fought before. And others in earlier times have made the same dangerous mistake of assuming that the West was too selfish and too soft and too divided to resist invasions of freedom in other lands. Those who threaten to unleash the forces of war on a dispute over West Berlin should recall the words of the ancient philosopher: "A man who causes fear cannot be free from fear."

We cannot and will not permit the Communists to drive us out of Berlin, either gradually or by force. For the fulfillment of our pledge to that city is essential to the morale and security of Western Germany, to the unity of Western Europe, and to the faith of the entire Free World.

Soviet strategy has long been aimed, not merely at Berlin, but at dividing and neutralizing all of Europe, forcing us back on our own shores. We must meet our oft-stated pledge to the free peoples of West Berlin—and maintain our rights and their safety, even in the face of force—in order to maintain the confidence of other free peoples in our word and our resolve. The strength of the alliance on which our security depends is dependent in turn on our willingness to meet our commitments to them.

So long as the Communists insist that they are preparing to end by themselves unilaterally our rights in West Berlin and our commitments to its people, we must be prepared to defend those rights and those commitments. We will at all times be ready to talk, if talk will help. But we must also be ready to resist with force, if force is used upon us. Either alone would fail. Together, they can serve the cause of freedom and peace.

The new preparations that we shall make to defend the peace are part of the long-term buildup in our strength which has been under way since January. They are based on our needs to meet a worldwide threat, on a basis which stretches far beyond the present Berlin crisis. Our primary purpose is neither propaganda nor provocation—but preparation.

A first need is to hasten progress toward the military goals which the North Atlantic allies have set for themselves. In Europe today nothing less will suffice. We will put even greater resources into fulfilling those goals, and we look to our allies to do the same. . . .

In the days and months ahead, I shall not hesitate to ask the Congress for additional measures, or exercise any of the executive powers that I possess to meet this threat to peace. Everything essential to the security of freedom must be done; and if that should require more men, or more taxes, or more controls, or other new powers, I shall not hesitate to ask them. The measures proposed today will be constantly studied, and altered as necessary. But while we will not let panic shape our policy, neither will we permit timidity to direct our program. . . .

I am well aware of the fact that many American families will bear the burden of these requests. Studies or careers will be interrupted; husbands and sons will be called away; incomes in some cases will be reduced. But these are burdens which must be borne if freedom is to be defended—Americans have willingly borne them before—and they will not flinch from the task now.

But I must emphasize again that the choice is not merely between resistance and retreat, between atomic holocaust and surrender. Our peacetime military posture is traditionally defensive; but our diplomatic posture need not be. Our response to the Berlin crisis will not be merely military or negative. It will be more than merely standing firm. For we do not intend to leave it to others to choose and monopolize the forum and the framework of discussion. We do not intend to abandon our duty to mankind to seek a peaceful solution.

We cannot and will not permit the Communists to drive us out of Berlin, either gradually or by force.

As signers of the UN Charter, we shall always be prepared to discuss international problems with any and all nations that are willing to talk—and listen—with reason. If they have proposals—not demands—we shall hear them. If they seek genuine understanding—not concessions of our rights—we shall meet with them. We have previously indicated our readiness to remove any actual irritants in West Berlin, but the freedom of that city is not negotiable. We cannot negotiate with those who say, "What's mine is mine and what's yours is negotiable." But we are willing to consider any arrangement or treaty in Germany consistent with the maintenance of peace and freedom, and with the legitimate security interests of all nations.

We recognize the Soviet Union's historical concern about their security in Central and Eastern Europe, after a series of ravaging invasions, and we believe arrangements can be worked out which will help to meet those concerns, and make it possible for both security and freedom to exist in this troubled area.

For it is not the freedom of West Berlin which is "abnormal" in Germany today, but the situation in that entire divided country. If anyone doubts the legality of our rights in Berlin, we are ready to have it submitted to international adjudication. If anyone doubts the extent to which our presence is desired by the people of West Berlin, compared to East German feelings about their regime, we are ready to have that question submitted to a free vote in Berlin and, if possible, among all the German people. And let us hear at that time from the two and one-half million refugees who have fled the Communist regime in East Germany—voting for Western-type freedom with their feet.

The world is not deceived by the Communist attempt to label Berlin as a hotbed of war. There is peace in Berlin today. The source of world trouble and tension is Moscow, not Berlin. And if war begins, it will have begun in Moscow and not Berlin.

For the choice of peace or war is largely theirs, not ours. It is the Soviets who have stirred up this crisis. It is they who are trying to force a change. It is they who have opposed free elections. It is they who have rejected an all-German peace treaty, and the rulings of international law. And as Americans know from our history on our own old frontier, gun battles are caused by outlaws, and not by officers of the peace.

In short, while we are ready to defend our interests, we shall also be ready to search for peace—in quiet exploratory talks—in formal or informal meetings. We do not want military considerations to dominate the thinking of either East or West. And Mr. Khrushchev may find that his invitation to other nations to join in a meaningless treaty may lead to their inviting him to join in the community of peaceful men, in abandoning the use of force, and in respecting the sanctity of agreements.

While all of these efforts go on, we must not be diverted from our total responsibilities, from other dangers, from other tasks. If new threats in Berlin or elsewhere should cause us to weaken our program of assistance to the developing nations who are also under heavy pressure from the same source, or to halt our efforts for realistic disarmament, or to disrupt or slow down our economy, or to neglect the education of our children, then those threats will surely be the most successful and least costly maneuver in Communist history. For we can afford all these efforts, and more—but we cannot afford not to meet this challenge.

And the challenge is not to us alone. It is a challenge to every nation which asserts its sovereignty under a system of liberty. It is a challenge to all those who want a world of free choice. It is a special challenge to the Atlantic Community—the heartland of human freedom.

We in the West must move together in building military strength. We must consult one another more closely than ever before. We must together design our proposals for peace, and labor together as they are pressed at the conference table. And together we must share the burdens and the risks of this effort.

The Atlantic Community, as we know it, has been built in response to challenge: the challenge of European chaos in 1947, of the Berlin blockade in 1948, the challenge of Communist aggression in Korea in 1950. Now, standing strong and prosperous, after an unprecedented decade of progress, the Atlantic Community will not forget either its history or the principles which gave it meaning.

The solemn vow each of us gave to West Berlin in time of peace will not be broken in time of danger. If we do not meet our commitments to Berlin, where will we later stand? If we are not true to our word there, all that we have achieved in collective security, which relies on these words, will mean nothing. And if there is one path above all others to war, it is the path of weakness and disunity.

Today, the endangered frontier of freedom runs through divided Berlin. We want it to remain a frontier of peace. This is the hope of every citizen of the Atlantic Community; every citizen of Eastern Europe; and, I am confident, every citizen of the Soviet Union. For I cannot believe that the Russian people—who bravely suffered enormous losses in the Second World War—would now wish to see the peace upset once more in Germany. The Soviet government alone can convert Berlin's frontier of peace into a pretext for war.

The steps I have indicated tonight are aimed at avoiding that war. To sum it all up: we seek peace—but we shall not surrender. That is the central meaning of this crisis, and the meaning of your government's policy.

With your help, and the help of other free men, this crisis can be surmounted. Freedom can prevail—and peace can endure.

I would like to close with a personal word. When I ran for the Presidency of the United States, I knew that this country faced serious challenges, but I could not realize—nor could any man realize who does not bear the burdens of this office—how heavy and constant would be those burdens.

Three times in my lifetime our country and Europe have been involved in major wars. In each case serious misjudgments were made on both sides of the intentions of others, which brought about great devastation.

Now, in the thermonuclear age, any misjudgment on either side about the intentions of the other could rain more devastation in several hours than has been wrought in all the wars of human history.

Therefore I, as President and Commander-in-Chief, and all of us as Americans, are moving through serious days. I shall bear this responsibility under our Constitution for the next three and one-half years, but I am sure that we all, regardless of our occupations, will do our very best for our country, and for our cause. For all of us want to see our children grow up in a country at peace, and in a world where freedom endures. . . .

In meeting my responsibilities in these coming months as President, I need your goodwill, and your support—and above all, your prayers.

Televised Address on the Berlin Crisis
Washington, D.C., July 25, 1961

The Berlin Wall

. . . Sealing off the eastern sector of the city is . . . a direct violation of the Soviet government's commitment to "the economic and political unity of Germany" and the pledged word of the Soviet government to cooperate with the allied governments "to mitigate the effects of the administrative division of Germany and Berlin" by "facilitation of the movement of persons and goods and the exchange of information" throughout Germany, including Berlin. . . .

The United States must serve a solemn warning to the Soviet Union that any interference by the Soviet government or its East German regime with free [allied] access to West Berlin would be an aggressive act for the consequences of which the Soviet government would bear full responsibility.

Statement on Berlin Wall
Washington, D.C., August 24, 1961

NOTE: Several months later the President related to the press his deeper concerns at the time of the construction of the wall.

Q: Mr. President, criticism that we did not tear down the Berlin Wall seems to be increasing rather than declining. Just about a week ago the chairman of the Republican National Committee criticized your administration very strenuously. I don't recall that

The Continuing Dialogue

MR. ADZHUBEI: Mr. President, I am happy to get this interview from you, and I would like to tell you quite frankly that your election to the high post of President of the United States was met with great hope by public opinion in our country. In connection with this, I would like to ask you the following question—

THE PRESIDENT: May I just say that I appreciate very much your coming to the United States. I also appreciate the opportunity to talk, through you and through your newspaper, to the people of the Soviet Union. I think that communication, an exchange of views, an honest report of what our countries are like and what they want and what the people wish, is in the interests of both our countries and in the interests of peace. So we are delighted to have this opportunity.

MR. ADZHUBEI: . . . Mr. President, what do you think about the present state of Soviet–American relations, and what in your opinion must be done by the American as well as the Soviet government to improve the relations between our two countries?

THE PRESIDENT: Well, I would say that the relations today are not as satisfactory as I had hoped they would be when I first took office. In fact, one of the first things that I did on becoming President was to commit the United States to an earnest effort to achieve a satisfactory agree-

---

you've ever publicly discussed this particular phase of the question. Do you think it would be helpful for you to do so now?

THE PRESIDENT: Well, I have discussed it. I stated that no one at that time in any position of responsibility—and I would use that term—either in the West Berlin–American contingent, in West Germany, France, or Great Britain, suggested that the United States or the other countries go in and tear down the wall.

The Soviet Union has had a *de facto* control for many years, really stretching back to the late forties, in East Berlin. It had been turned over as a capital for East Germany a long time ago. And the United States has a very limited force surrounded by a great many divisions. We are going to find ourselves severely challenged to maintain what we have considered to be our basic rights—which is our presence in West Berlin, and the right of access to West Berlin, and the freedom of the people of West Berlin.

But in my judgment, I think that [such an action] could have had a very violent reaction, which might have taken us down a very rocky road. I think it was for that reason—because it was recognized by those people in positions of responsibility—that no recommendation was made along the lines you've suggested at that time.

President's News Conference
Washington, D.C., January 15, 1962

ment with the Soviet Union on the cessation of nuclear tests. As a result of that effort, at the end of March, we sent our representatives, along with Great Britain's, to Geneva for the first time with a complete treaty which we tabled for discussion. I had hoped that this would be one area where we could make real progress. It would lessen the contamination of the air, it would be a first step toward disarmament, and I felt that if we could achieve an agreement in this area, we could then move on to the other areas of disarmament which required action.

We were not successful. And, as you know, we were in fact still at the table in Geneva in August when, still negotiating, the Soviet Union resumed its tests which must have been in preparation for many months, at the very time that the conversations were going on. So that has been a disappointment.

In addition, Berlin and Germany have become, I think, areas of heightened crisis since the Vienna meeting, and I think extremely dangerous to the peace which I am sure—I know—both of our people want. . . . If we can keep the peace for twenty years, the life of the people of the Soviet Union and the life of the people of the United States will be far richer and will be far happier as the standard of living steadily rises. . . .

We want the people of the Soviet Union to live in peace—we want the same for our own people. It is this effort to push outward the Communist system, on to country after country, that represents, I think, the great threat to peace. If the Soviet Union looked only to its national interest and to providing a better life for its people under conditions of peace, I think there would be nothing that would disturb the relations between the Soviet Union and the United States.

MR. ADZHUBEI: . . . Mr. President, what is your attitude toward the idea of concluding a pact of peace between the United States and the Soviet Union? That would be a great step forward.

THE PRESIDENT: I think we should have not only an agreement between our countries, but take those steps which make peace possible. I don't think that paper, and words on paper, are as significant as looking at those areas which provide tension between our two systems and seeing if we can dispel that tension. . . .

I stated that if we had been able to get an agreement on the nuclear tests cessation, that would lead to other agreements on disarmament. . . . If we can conclude our efforts in Laos and insure a government and a country which are neutral and independent, as Chairman Khrushchev and I agreed at Vienna, then we would be able to move into other areas of tension. If we can now make an agreement on a satisfactory basis on Berlin and Germany, which is the most critical area—because it represents a matter of great interest to both our countries, and great concern to our peoples—then we could take other steps. . . .

I know that the Soviet Union suffered more from World War II than any country. It represented a terrible blow, and the casualties affected every family, including many of the families of those now in government.

I will say that the United States also suffered, though not so heavily as the Soviet Union, quite obviously. My brother was killed in Europe. My sister's husband was killed in Europe.

The point is that that war is now over. We want to prevent another war arising out of Germany. I think the important thing between the United States and the U.S.S.R. is not to create the kind of tension and pressure which in the name of settling World War II increase the chances of a conflict. . . .

I do not say that the Soviet Union is responsible for all the changes that are coming in the world. . . . People want to live in different ways. That is what we want, also. If they have a fair opportunity to make a choice, if they choose to support communism, we accept that. What we object to is the attempt to impose communism by force, or a situation where once a people may have fallen under communism the Communists do not give them a fair opportunity to make another choice. . . .

We believe that if the Soviet Union—without attempting to impose the Communist system—will permit the people of the world to live as they wish to live, relations between the Soviet Union and the United States will then be very satisfactory, and our two peoples, which now live in danger, will be able to live in peace and with a greatly increased standard of living. And I believe we have such vast economic opportunities now in both of our countries that we should consider how we can get along, and not attempt to impose our views, one on the other or on anyone else. . . .

MR. ADZHUBEI: Mr. President, since I'm talking to you in a very frank and friendly manner, I would like to ask you to imagine, at least for a moment, the following impossible thing. Imagine that you were an officer, a veteran of the Soviet Navy, who fought in World War II. You won the war, and then the very events occurred which are now taking place. One of the parts of Germany—the Federal Republic of Germany—does not recognize the borders which have been established after the war. It is again building up its armed forces. The Chancellor of that country goes to the United States to talk to the President of the United States and they have secret talks. The spirit of revanchism is very high in that part of Germany. What would your attitude be toward this, if you were a veteran of the Soviet Navy?

THE PRESIDENT: If I were a Soviet veteran, I would see that West Germany now has only nine divisions, which is a fraction of the Soviet forces. Nine divisions. It has no nuclear weapons of its own. It has a very small air force—almost no navy, I think perhaps two or three submarines. So it is not a military threat. Its nine divisions are under the international control of NATO, and subject to the command of the NATO organization, which is made up of fifteen countries of Europe which altogether have, in West Germany now, about twenty-two or twenty-three divisions—about the same number as the Soviet divisions in East Germany. So that I do not see that this country represents a military threat now to the Soviet Union, even though I recognize how bitter was the struggle in World War II—in the same way that Japan today represents no threat to the United States, even though twenty years ago there were four years of war in the Pacific against the Japanese. The power of countries changes—weapons change—science changes—without missiles, without nuclear capability, with very few divisions today, I don't believe West Germany is a military threat.

Then I would look at the power of the United States, and I would look at the power of the Soviet Union, and I would say that the important thing is for the Soviet Union and the United States not to get into a war, which would destroy both of our systems. So as a Soviet veteran, I would want the Soviet Union to reach an agreement with the United States which recognizes the interests and the commitments of the United States, as well as our own, and not attempt to enforce single-handedly a new situation upon the United States which would be against previous commitments we had made. The Soviet Union made a commitment in regard to Berlin in 1945. Germany today is divided. Germany today is not a threat to the Soviet Union militarily.

The important thing is to attempt to reach an accord which recognizes the interests of all; and I believe that can be done with respect to Germany. I recognize that there are going to be two Germanys as long as the Soviet Union believes that that is in her interest. The problem now is to make sure that, in any treaty which the Soviet Union reaches with East Germany, the rights of the other powers are recognized in Berlin. That's all we're talking about. We are not talking about encouraging revanchism, building a great German military machine, or anything else you mention. In any peace treaty which is signed with East Germany, there must be a recognition of the rights of the United States and the other powers. . . .

So, if I were a Soviet officer and wanted peace, I would think peace can be won and my country's security can be assured. The Soviet Union is a strong military power. It has great nuclear capacity. It has missiles, planes—it has a great number of divisions—it has countries associated with it. No one is ever going to invade the Soviet Union again. There is no military power that can do that. The problem is to make an agreement which will permit us to have our interests recognized, as well as yours. That should not be beyond the capacity of us both.

Chairman Khrushchev did not, nor did I, make the arrangements in 1945 in regard to Berlin. Our responsibility, given the situation, which is a difficult one, is to bring about peace, and I believe it can be done.

In short, if I were a Soviet naval officer, I would feel that the security of the Soviet Union was well protected, and that the important thing now is to reach an accord with the United States, our ally during that second war.

Interview with Aleksei Adzhubei, Editor of **Izvestia**
and son-in-law of Soviet Chairman Nikita Khrushchev
Hyannis Port, Massachusetts, November 25, 1961

The Wave of the Future

I sometimes think that we are too much impressed by the clamor of daily events. The newspaper headlines and the television screens give us a short view. They so flood us with the stop-press details of daily stories that we lose sight of the great movements of history. Yet it is the profound tendencies of history and not the passing excitements that will shape our future.

The short view gives us the impression as a nation of being shoved and harried, everywhere on the defensive. But this impression is surely an optical illusion. From the perspective of Moscow, the world today may seem even more troublesome, more intractable, more frustrating than it does to us. The leaders of the Communist world are confronted not only by acute internal problems in each Communist country—the failure of agriculture, the rising discontent of the youth and the intellectuals, the demands of technical and managerial groups for status and security. They are confronted in addition by profound divisions within the Communist world itself—divisions which have already shattered the image of communism as a universal system guaranteed to abolish all social and international conflicts—the most valuable asset the Communists had for many years.

Wisdom requires the long view. And the long view shows us that the revolution of national independence is a fundamental fact of our era. This revolution will not be stopped. As new nations emerge from the oblivion of centuries, their first aspiration is to affirm their national identity. Their deepest hope is for a world where, within a framework of international cooperation, every country can solve its own problems according to its own traditions and ideals.

It is in the interests of the pursuit of knowledge—and it is in our own national interest—that this revolution of national independence succeed. For the Communists rest everything on the idea of a monolithic world—a world where all knowledge has a single pattern, all societies move toward a single model, and all problems and roads have a single solution and a single destination. The pursuit of knowledge, on the other hand, rests everything on the opposite idea—on the idea of a world based on diversity, self-determination, freedom. And that is the kind of world to which we Americans, as a nation, are committed by the principles upon which the great Republic was founded.

As men conduct the pursuit of knowledge, they create a world which freely unites national diversity and international partnership. This emerging world is incompatible with the Communist world order. It will irresistibly burst the bonds of the Communist organization and the Communist ideology. And diversity and independence, far from being opposed to the American conception of world order, represent the very essence of our view of the future of the world.

Wisdom requires the long view. And the long view shows us that the revolution of national independence is a fundamental fact of our era. . . . The deepest hope [of new nations] is for a world where, within a framework of international co-operation, every country can solve its own problems according to its own traditions and ideals.

There used to be so much talk a few years ago about the inevitable triumph of communism. We hear such talk much less now. No one who examines the modern world can doubt that the great currents of history are carrying the world away from the monolithic idea toward the pluralistic idea—away from communism and toward national independence and freedom. No one can doubt that the wave of the future is not the conquest of the world by a single dogmatic creed but the liberation of the diverse energies of free nations and free men. No one can doubt that cooperation in the pursuit of knowledge must lead to freedom of the mind and freedom of the soul.

Beyond the drumfire of daily crisis, therefore, there is arising the outline of a robust and vital world community, founded on nations secure in their own independence, and united by allegiance to world peace. It would be foolish to say that this world will be won tomorrow, or the day after. The processes of history are fitful and uncertain and aggravating. There will be frustrations and setbacks. There will be times of anxiety and gloom. The specter of thermonuclear war will continue to hang over mankind; and we must heed the advice of Oliver Wendell Holmes of "freedom leaning on her spear" until all nations are wise enough to disarm safely and effectively.

Yet we can have a new confidence today in the direction in which history is moving. . . . We must reject oversimplified theories of international life—the theory that American power is unlimited, or that the American mission is to remake the world in the American image. We must seize the vision of a free and diverse world—and shape our policies to speed progress toward a more flexible world order.

This is the unifying spirit of our policies in the world today. The purpose of our aid programs must be to help developing countries move forward as rapidly as possible on the road to genuine national independence. Our military policies must assist nations to protect the processes of democratic reform and development against disruption and intervention. Our diplomatic policies must strengthen our relations with the whole world, with our several alliances, and within the United Nations. . . .

I am reminded of the story of the great French marshal Lyautey, who once asked his gardener to plant a tree. The gardener objected that the tree was slow-growing and would not reach maturity for a hundred years. The marshal replied, "In that case, there is no time to lose, plant it this afternoon."

Today a world of knowledge—a world of cooperation—a just and lasting peace—may be years away. But we have no time to lose. Let us plant our trees this afternoon.

University of California
Berkeley, California, March 23, 1962

The Cuban Missile Crisis

This government, as promised, has maintained the closest surveillance of the Soviet military buildup on the island of Cuba. Within the past week, unmistakable evidence has established the fact that a series of offensive missile sites is now in preparation on that imprisoned island. The purpose of these bases can be none other than to provide a nuclear strike capability against the Western Hemisphere.

Upon receiving the first preliminary hard information of this nature last Tuesday morning at 9 a.m., I directed that our surveillance be stepped up. And having now confirmed and completed our evaluation of the evidence and our decision on a course of action, this government feels obliged to report this new crisis to you in fullest detail.

The characteristics of these new missile sites indicate two distinct types of installations. Several of them include medium-range ballistic missiles, capable of carrying a nuclear warhead for a distance of more than a thousand nautical miles. Each of these missiles, in short, is capable of striking Washington, D.C., the Panama Canal, Cape Canaveral, Mexico City, or any other city in the southeastern part of the United States, in Central America, or in the Caribbean area.

Additional sites not yet completed appear to be designed for intermediate-range ballistic missiles—capable of traveling more than twice as far—and thus capable of striking most of the major cities in the Western Hemisphere, ranging as far north as Hudson Bay, Canada, and as far south as Lima, Peru. In addition, jet bombers, capable of carrying nuclear weapons, are now being uncrated and assembled in Cuba, while the necessary air bases are being prepared.

This urgent transformation of Cuba into an important strategic base —by the presence of these large, long-range, and clearly offensive weapons of sudden mass destruction—constitutes an explicit threat to the peace and security of all the Americas, in flagrant and deliberate defiance of the Rio Pact of 1947, the traditions of this nation and hemisphere, the joint resolution of the 87th Congress, the Charter of the United Nations, and my own public warnings to the Soviets on September 4 and 13. This action also contradicts the repeated assurances of Soviet spokesmen, both publicly and privately delivered, that the arms buildup in Cuba would retain its original defensive character, and that the Soviet Union had no need or desire to station strategic missiles on the territory of any other nation.

The size of this undertaking makes clear that it has been planned for some months. Yet only last month, after I had made clear the distinction between any introduction of ground-to-ground missiles and the existence of defensive antiaircraft missiles, the Soviet government publicly stated on September 11 that, and I quote, "the armaments and military equipment sent to Cuba are designed exclusively for defensive purposes," that, and I quote the Soviet government, "there is no need for the Soviet government to shift its weapons for a retaliatory blow to any other country, for instance Cuba," and that, and I quote their government, "the Soviet Union has so powerful rockets to carry these nuclear warheads that there is no need to search for sites for them beyond the boundaries of the Soviet Union." That statement was false.

This urgent transformation of Cuba into an important strategic base—by the presence of these large, long-range, and clearly offensive weapons of sudden mass destruction—constitutes an explicit threat to the peace and security of all the Americas.

Only last Thursday, as evidence of this rapid offensive buildup was already in my hand, Soviet Foreign Minister Gromyko told me in my office that he was instructed to make it clear once again, as he said his government had already done, that Soviet assistance to Cuba, and I quote, "pursued solely the purpose of contributing to the defense capabilities of Cuba," that, and I quote him, "training by Soviet specialists of Cuban nationals in handling defensive armaments was by no means offensive, and if it were otherwise," Mr. Gromyko went on, "the Soviet government would never become involved in rendering such assistance." That statement also was false.

Neither the United States of America nor the world community of nations can tolerate deliberate deception and offensive threats on the part of any nation, large or small. We no longer live in a world where only the actual firing of weapons represents a sufficient challenge to a nation's security to constitute maximum peril. Nuclear weapons are so destructive, and ballistic missiles are so swift, that any substantially increased possibility of their use or any sudden change in their deployment may well be regarded as a definite threat to peace.

For many years, both the Soviet Union and the United States, recognizing this fact, have deployed strategic nuclear weapons with great care, never upsetting the precarious status quo which insured that these weapons would not be used in the absence of some vital challenge. Our own strategic missiles have never been transferred to the territory of any other nation under a cloak of secrecy and deception; and our history —unlike that of the Soviets since the end of World War II—demonstrates that we have no desire to dominate or conquer any other nation or impose our system upon its people. Nevertheless, American citizens have become adjusted to living daily on the bull's-eye of Soviet missiles located inside the U.S.S.R. or in submarines.

In that sense, missiles in Cuba add to an already clear and present danger—although it should be noted the nations of Latin America have never previously been subjected to a potential nuclear threat.

But this secret, swift, and extraordinary buildup of Communist missiles—in an area well known to have a special and historical relationship to the United States and the nations of the Western Hemisphere, in violation of Soviet assurances, and in defiance of American and hemispheric policy—this sudden, clandestine decision to station strategic weapons for the first time outside of Soviet soil—is a deliberately provocative and unjustified change in the status quo which cannot be accepted by this country, if our courage and our commitments are ever to be trusted again by either friend or foe.

The 1930s taught us a clear lesson: aggressive conduct, if allowed to go unchecked and unchallenged, ultimately leads to war. This nation is opposed to war. We are also true to our word. Our unswerving objective, therefore, must be to prevent the use of these missiles against this or any other country, and to secure their withdrawal or elimination from the Western Hemisphere.

Our policy has been one of patience and restraint, as befits a peaceful and powerful nation which leads a worldwide alliance. We have been determined not to be diverted from our central concerns by mere irritants and fanatics. But now further action is required—and it is under way; and these actions may only be the beginning. We will not prematurely or unnecessarily risk the costs of worldwide nuclear war in which even the fruits of victory would be ashes in our mouth—but neither will we shrink from that risk at any time it must be faced.

Acting, therefore, in the defense of our own security and of the entire Western Hemisphere, and under the authority entrusted to me by the Constitution as endorsed by the resolution of the Congress, I have directed that the following initial steps be taken immediately:

First: To halt this offensive buildup, a strict quarantine on all offensive military equipment under shipment to Cuba is being initiated. All ships of any kind bound for Cuba from whatever nation or port will, if found to contain cargoes of offensive weapons, be turned back. This quarantine will be extended, if needed, to other types of cargo and carriers. We are not at this time, however, denying the necessities of life as the Soviets attempted to do in their Berlin blockade of 1948.

Second: I have directed the continued and increased close surveillance of Cuba and its military buildup. The foreign ministers of the OAS, in their communiqué of October 6, rejected secrecy on such matters in this hemisphere. Should these offensive military preparations continue, thus increasing the threat to the hemisphere, further action will be justified. I have directed the Armed Forces to prepare for any eventualities; and I trust that in the interest of both the Cuban people and the Soviet technicians at the sites, the hazards to all concerned of continuing this threat will be recognized.

Third: It shall be the policy of this nation to regard any nuclear missile launched from Cuba against any nation in the Western Hemisphere as an attack by the Soviet Union on the United States, requiring a full retaliatory response upon the Soviet Union.

Fourth: As a necessary military precaution, I have reinforced our base at Guantánamo, evacuated today the dependents of our personnel there, and ordered additional military units to be on a standby alert basis.

Fifth: We are calling tonight for an immediate meeting of the Organ of Consultation under the Organization of American States, to consider this threat to hemispheric security and to invoke articles six and eight of the Rio Treaty in support of all necessary action. The United Nations Charter allows for regional security arrangements—and the nations of this hemisphere decided long ago against the military presence of outside powers. Our other allies around the world have also been alerted.

Sixth: Under the Charter of the United Nations, we are asking tonight that an emergency meeting of the Security Council be convoked without delay to take action against this latest Soviet threat to world peace. Our resolution will call for the prompt dismantling and withdrawal of all offensive weapons in Cuba, under the supervision of UN observers, before the quarantine can be lifted.

Seventh and finally: I call upon Chairman Khrushchev to halt and eliminate this clandestine, reckless, and provocative threat to world peace and to stable relations between our two nations. I call upon him further to abandon this course of world domination, and to join in an historic effort to end the perilous arms race and to transform the history of man. He has an opportunity now to move the world back from the abyss of destruction—by returning to his government's own words that it had no need to station missiles outside its own territory, and withdrawing these weapons from Cuba—by refraining from any action which will widen or deepen the present crisis—and then by participating in a search for peaceful and permanent solutions.

This nation is prepared to present its case against the Soviet threat to peace, and our own proposals for a peaceful world, at any time and in any forum—in the OAS, in the United Nations, or in any other meeting that could be useful—without limiting our freedom of action. We have in the past made strenuous efforts to limit the spread of nuclear weapons. We have proposed the elimination of all arms and military bases in a fair and effective disarmament treaty. We are prepared to discuss new proposals for the removal of tensions on both sides—including the possibilities of a genuinely independent Cuba, free to determine its own destiny. We have no wish to war with the Soviet Union—for we are a peaceful people who desire to live in peace with all other peoples.

I call upon Chairman Khrushchev to halt and eliminate this clandestine, reckless, and provocative threat to world peace and to stable relations between our two nations.

But it is difficult to settle or even discuss these problems in an atmosphere of intimidation. That is why this latest Soviet threat—or any other threat which is made either independently or in response to our actions this week—must and will be met with determination. Any hostile move anywhere in the world against the safety and freedom of peoples to whom we are committed—including in particular the brave people of West Berlin—will be met by whatever action is needed.

Finally, I want to say a few words to the captive people of Cuba, to whom this speech is being directly carried by special radio facilities. I speak to you as a friend, as one who knows of your deep attachment to your fatherland, as one who shares your aspirations for liberty and justice for all. And I have watched and the American people have watched with deep sorrow how your nationalist revolution was betrayed —and how your fatherland fell under foreign domination. Now your leaders are no longer Cuban leaders inspired by Cuban ideals. They are puppets and agents of an international conspiracy which has turned Cuba against your friends and neighbors in the Americas—and turned it into the first Latin American country to become a target for nuclear war—the first Latin American country to have these weapons on its soil.

These new weapons are not in your interest. They contribute nothing to your peace and well-being. They can only undermine it. But this country has no wish to cause you to suffer or to impose any system upon you. We know that your lives and land are being used as pawns by those who deny your freedom.

Many times in the past, the Cuban people have risen to throw out tyrants who destroyed their liberty. And I have no doubt that most Cubans today look forward to the time when they will be truly free—free from foreign domination, free to choose their own leaders, free to select their own system, free to own their own land, free to speak and write and worship without fear or degradation. And then shall Cuba be welcomed back to the society of free nations and to the associations of this hemisphere.

My fellow citizens: let no one doubt that this is a difficult and dangerous effort on which we have set out. No one can foresee precisely what course it will take or what costs or casualties will be incurred. Many months of sacrifice and self-discipline lie ahead—months in which both our patience and our will will be tested—months in which many threats and denunciations will keep us aware of our dangers. But the greatest danger of all would be to do nothing.

The path we have chosen for the present is full of hazards, as all paths are—but it is the one most consistent with our character and courage as a nation and our commitments around the world. The cost of freedom is always high—but Americans have always paid it. And one path we shall never choose, and that is the path of surrender or submission.

Our goal is not the victory of might, but the vindication of right—not peace at the expense of freedom, but both peace and freedom, here in this hemisphere, and, we hope, around the world. God willing, that goal will be achieved.

Televised Address on Cuban Missile Crisis
Washington, D.C., October 22, 1962

Dear Mr. Chairman,

I have read your letter of October 26th with great care and welcomed the statement of your desire to seek a prompt solution to the problem. The first thing that needs to be done, however, is for work to cease on offensive missile bases in Cuba and for all weapons systems in Cuba capable of offensive use to be rendered inoperable, under effective United Nations arrangements.

Assuming this is done promptly, I have given my representatives in New York instructions that will permit them to work out this weekend—in cooperation with the Acting Secretary-General and your representative—an arrangement for a permanent solution to the Cuban problem along the lines suggested in your letter of October 26th. As I read your letter, the key elements of your proposals—which seem generally acceptable as I understand them—are as follows:

1. You would agree to remove these weapons systems from Cuba under appropriate United Nations observation and supervision; and undertake, with suitable safeguards, to halt the further introduction of such weapons systems into Cuba.

2. We, on our part, would agree—upon the establishment of adequate arrangements through the United Nations to ensure the carrying out and continuation of these commitments—(a) to remove promptly the quarantine measures now in effect and (b) to give assurances against an invasion of Cuba. I am confident that other nations of the Western Hemisphere would be prepared to do likewise.

If you will give your representative similar instructions, there is no reason why we should not be able to complete these arrangements and announce them to the world within a couple of days. The effect of such a settlement on easing world tensions would enable us to work toward a more general arrangement regarding "other armaments," as proposed in your second letter which you made public. I would like to say again that the United States is very much interested in reducing tensions and halting the arms race; and if your letter signifies that you are prepared to discuss a détente affecting NATO and the Warsaw Pact, we are quite prepared to consider with our allies any useful proposals.

But the first ingredient, let me emphasize, is the cessation of work on missile sites in Cuba and measures to render such weapons inoperable, under effective international guarantees. The continuation of this threat, or a prolonging of this discussion concerning Cuba by linking these problems to the broader questions of European and world security, would surely lead to an intensification of the Cuban crisis and a grave risk to the peace of the world. For this reason I hope we can quickly agree along the lines outlined in this letter and in your letter of October 26th.

Letter to Soviet Chairman Nikita Khrushchev
Washington, D.C., October 27, 1962

I welcome Chairman Khrushchev's statesmanlike decision to stop building bases in Cuba, dismantling offensive weapons and returning them to the Soviet Union under United Nations verification.

I welcome Chairman Khrushchev's statesmanlike decision to stop building bases in Cuba, dismantling offensive weapons and returning them to the Soviet Union under United Nations verification. This is an important and constructive contribution to peace.

We shall be in touch with the Secretary-General of the United Nations with respect to reciprocal measures to assure peace in the Caribbean area.

It is my earnest hope that the governments of the world can, with a solution of the Cuban crisis, turn their urgent attention to the compelling necessity for ending the arms race and reducing world tensions. This applies to the military confrontation between the Warsaw Pact and NATO countries as well as to other situations in other parts of the world where tensions lead to the wasteful diversion of resources to weapons of war.

Statement on Soviet Withdrawal of Missiles from Cuba
Washington, D.C., October 28, 1962

I have today been informed by Chairman Khrushchev that all of the IL-28 bombers now in Cuba will be withdrawn in thirty days. He also agrees that these planes can be observed and counted as they leave. Inasmuch as this goes a long way toward reducing the danger which faced this hemisphere four weeks ago, I have this afternoon instructed the Secretary of Defense to lift our naval quarantine.

In view of this action, I want to take this opportunity to bring the American people up to date on the Cuban crisis and to review the progress made thus far in fulfilling the understandings between Soviet Chairman Khrushchev and myself as set forth in our letters of October 27 and 28. Chairman Khrushchev, it will be recalled, agreed to remove from Cuba all weapons systems capable of offensive use, to halt the further introduction of such weapons into Cuba, and to permit appropriate United Nations observation and supervision to insure the carrying out and continuation of these commitments. We on our part agreed that once these adequate arrangements for verification had been established we would remove our naval quarantine and give assurances against an invasion of Cuba.

The evidence to date indicates that all known offensive missile sites in Cuba have been dismantled. The missiles and their associated equipment have been loaded on Soviet ships. And our inspection at sea of these departing ships has confirmed that the number of missiles reported by the Soviet Union as having been brought into Cuba, which closely corresponded to our own information, has now been removed. In addition, the Soviet government has stated that all nuclear weapons have been withdrawn from Cuba and no offensive weapons will be reintroduced.

Nevertheless, important parts of the understanding of October 27 and 28 remain to be carried out. The Cuban government has not yet permitted the United Nations to verify whether all offensive weapons have been removed, and no lasting safeguards have yet been established against the future introduction of offensive weapons back into Cuba.

Consequently, if the Western Hemisphere is to continue to be protected against offensive weapons, this government has no choice but to pursue its own means of checking on military activities in Cuba. The importance of our continued vigilance is underlined by our identification in recent days of a number of Soviet ground combat units in Cuba, although we are informed that these and other Soviet units were associated with the protection of offensive weapons systems, and will also be withdrawn in due course.

I repeat, we would like nothing better than adequate international arrangements for the task of inspection and verification in Cuba, and we are prepared to continue our efforts to achieve such arrangements. Until that is done, difficult problems remain. As for our part, if all offensive weapons systems are removed from Cuba and kept out of the hemisphere in the future, under adequate verification and safeguards, and if Cuba is not used for the export of aggressive Communist purposes, there will be peace in the Caribbean. And as I said in September, "we shall neither initiate nor permit aggression in this hemisphere."

We will not, of course, abandon the political, economic, and other efforts of this hemisphere to halt subversion from Cuba nor our purpose and hope that the Cuban people shall someday be truly free. But these policies are very different from any intent to launch a military invasion of the island.

In short, the record of recent weeks shows real progress and we are hopeful that further progress can be made. The completion of the commitment on both sides and the achievement of a peaceful solution to the Cuban crisis might well open the door to the solution of other outstanding problems.

May I add this final thought in this week of Thanksgiving: There is much for which we can be grateful as we look back to where we stood only four weeks ago—the unity of this hemisphere, the support of our allies, and the calm determination of the American people. These qualities may be tested many more times in this decade, but we have increased reason to be confident that those qualities will continue to serve the cause of freedom with distinction in the years to come.

Opening Statement, President's News Conference
Washington, D.C., November 20, 1962

The Strategy of Peace

Professor Woodrow Wilson once said that every man sent out from a university should be a man of his nation as well as a man of his time, and I am confident that the men and women who carry the honor of graduating from this institution will continue to give from their lives, from their talents, a high measure of public service and public support.

"There are few earthly things more beautiful than a university," wrote John Masefield in his tribute to English universities—and his words are equally true today. He did not refer to spires and towers, to campus greens and ivied walls. He admired the splendid beauty of the university, he said, because it was "a place where those who hate ignorance may strive to know, where those who perceive truth may strive to make others see."

I have therefore chosen this time and this place to discuss a topic on which ignorance too often abounds and the truth is too rarely perceived—yet it is the most important topic on earth: world peace.

What kind of peace do I mean? What kind of peace do we seek? Not a Pax Americana enforced on the world by American weapons of war. Not the peace of the grave or the security of the slave. I am talking about genuine peace, the kind of peace that makes life on earth worth living, the kind that enables men and nations to grow and to hope and to build a better life for their children—not merely peace for Americans but peace for all men and women—not merely peace in our time but peace for all time.

I speak of peace because of the new face of war. Total war makes no sense in an age when great powers can maintain large and relatively invulnerable nuclear forces and refuse to surrender without resort to those forces. It makes no sense in an age when a single nuclear weapon contains almost ten times the explosive force delivered by all of the allied air forces in the Second World War. It makes no sense in an age when the deadly poisons produced by a nuclear exchange would be carried by wind and water and soil and seed to the far corners of the globe and to generations yet unborn.

Today the expenditure of billions of dollars every year on weapons acquired for the purpose of making sure we never need to use them is essential to keeping the peace. But surely the acquisition of such idle stockpiles—which can only destroy and never create—is not the only, much less the most efficient, means of assuring peace.

I speak of peace, therefore, as the necessary rational end of rational men. I realize that the pursuit of peace is not as dramatic as the pursuit of war—and frequently the words of the pursuer fall on deaf ears. But we have no more urgent task.

Some say that it is useless to speak of world peace or world law or world disarmament—and that it will be useless until the leaders of the Soviet Union adopt a more enlightened attitude. I hope they do. I believe we can help them do it. But I also believe that we must reexamine our own attitude—as individuals and as a nation—for our attitude is as essential as theirs. And every graduate of this school, every thoughtful citizen who despairs of war and wishes to bring peace, should begin by looking inward—by examining his own attitude toward the possibilities of peace, toward the Soviet Union, toward the course of the Cold War, and toward freedom and peace here at home.

First: Let us examine our attitude toward peace itself. Too many of us think it is impossible. Too many think it unreal. But that is a dangerous, defeatist belief. It leads to the conclusion that war is inevitable—that mankind is doomed—that we are gripped by forces we cannot control.

We need not accept that view. Our problems are man-made—therefore, they can be solved by man. And man can be as big as he wants. No problem of human destiny is beyond human beings. Man's reason and spirit have often solved the seemingly unsolvable—and we believe they can do it again.

I am not referring to the absolute, infinite concept of universal peace and goodwill of which some fantasies and fanatics dream. I do not deny the value of hopes and dreams but we merely invite discouragement and incredulity by making that our only and immediate goal.

Let us focus instead on a more practical, more attainable peace—based not on a sudden revolution in human nature but on a gradual evolution in human institutions—on a series of concrete actions and effective agreements which are in the interest of all concerned. There is no single, simple key to this peace—no grand or magic formula to be adopted by one or two powers. Genuine peace must be the product of many nations, the sum of many acts. It must be dynamic, not static, changing to meet the challenge of each new generation. For peace is a process—a way of solving problems.

With such a peace, there will still be quarrels and conflicting interests, as there are within families and nations. World peace, like community peace, does not require that each man love his neighbor—it requires only that they live together in mutual tolerance, submitting their disputes to a just and peaceful settlement. And history teaches us that enmities between nations, as between individuals, do not last forever. However fixed our likes and dislikes may seem, the tide of time and events will often bring surprising changes in the relations between nations and neighbors.

So let us persevere. Peace need not be impracticable, and war need not be inevitable. By defining our goal more clearly, by making it seem more manageable and less remote, we can help all peoples to see it, to draw hope from it, and to move irresistibly toward it.

Second: Let us reexamine our attitude toward the Soviet Union. It is discouraging to think that their leaders may actually believe what their propagandists write. It is discouraging to read a recent authoritative Soviet text on military strategy and find, on page after page, wholly baseless and incredible claims—such as the allegation that "American imperialist circles are preparing to unleash different types of wars . . . that there is a very real threat of a preventive war being unleashed by American imperialists against the Soviet Union [and that] the political aims of the American imperialists are to enslave economically and politically the European and other capitalist countries [and] to achieve world domination . . . by means of aggressive wars."

Truly, as it was written long ago: "The wicked flee when no man pursueth." Yet it is sad to read these Soviet statements—to realize the extent of the gulf between us. But it is also a warning—a warning to the American people not to fall into the same trap as the Soviets, not to see only a distorted and desperate view of the other side, not to see conflict as inevitable, accommodation as impossible, and communication as nothing more than an exchange of threats.

No government or social system is so evil that its people must be considered as lacking in virtue. As Americans, we find communism profoundly repugnant as a negation of personal freedom and dignity. But we can still hail the Russian people for their many achievements—in science and space, in economic and industrial growth, in culture and in acts of courage.

Today the expenditure of billions of dollars every year on weapons acquired for the purpose of making sure we never need to use them is essential to keeping the peace. But surely the acquisition of such idle stockpiles—which can only destroy and never create—is not the only, much less the most efficient, means of assuring peace.

Among the many traits the peoples of our two countries have in common, none is stronger than our mutual abhorrence of war. Almost unique among the major world powers, we have never been at war with each other. And no nation in the history of battle ever suffered more than the Soviet Union suffered in the course of the Second World War. At least twenty million lost their lives. Countless millions of homes and farms were burned or sacked. A third of the nation's territory, including nearly two thirds of its industrial base, was turned into a wasteland—a loss equivalent to the devastation of this country east of Chicago.

Today, should total war ever break out again—no matter how—our two countries would become the primary targets. It is an ironic but accurate fact that the two strongest powers are the two in the most danger of devastation. All we have built, all we have worked for, would be destroyed in the first twenty-four hours. And even in the Cold War, which brings burdens and dangers to so many countries, including this nation's closest allies—our two countries bear the heaviest burdens. For we are both devoting massive sums of money to weapons that could be better devoted to combating ignorance, poverty, and disease. We are both caught up in a vicious and dangerous cycle in which suspicion on one side breeds suspicion on the other, and new weapons beget counterweapons.

In short, both the United States and its allies, and the Soviet Union and its allies, have a mutually deep interest in a just and genuine peace and in halting the arms race. Agreements to this end are in the interests of the Soviet Union as well as ours—and even the most hostile nations can be relied upon to accept and keep those treaty obligations, and only those treaty obligations, which are in their own interest.

So, let us not be blind to our differences—but let us also direct attention to our common interests and to the means by which those differences can be resolved. And if we cannot end now our differences, at least we can help make the world safe for diversity. For, in the final analysis, our most basic common link is that we all inhabit this small planet. We all breathe the same air. We all cherish our children's future. And we are all mortal.

Third: Let us reexamine our attitude toward the Cold War, remembering that we are not engaged in a debate, seeking to pile up debating points. We are not here distributing blame or pointing the finger of judgment. We must deal with the world as it is, and not as it might have been had the history of the last eighteen years been different.

We must therefore persevere in the search for peace in the hope that constructive changes within the Communist bloc might bring within reach solutions which now seem beyond us. We must conduct our affairs in such a way that it becomes in the Communists' interest to agree on a genuine peace. Above all, while defending our own vital interests, nuclear powers must avert those confrontations which bring an adversary to a choice of either a humiliating retreat or a nuclear war. To adopt that kind of course in the nuclear age would be evidence only of the bankruptcy of our policy—or of a collective death-wish for the world.

To secure these ends, America's weapons are nonprovocative, carefully controlled, designed to deter, and capable of selective use. Our military forces are committed to peace and disciplined in self-restraint. Our diplomats are instructed to avoid unnecessary irritants and purely rhetorical hostility.

For we can seek a relaxation of tensions without relaxing our guard.

And, for our part, we do not need to use threats to prove that we are resolute. We do not need to jam foreign broadcasts out of fear our faith will be eroded. We are unwilling to impose our system on any unwilling people—but we are willing and able to engage in peaceful competition with any people on earth.

Meanwhile, we seek to strengthen the United Nations, to help solve its financial problems, to make it a more effective instrument for peace, to develop it into a genuine world security system—a system capable of resolving disputes on the basis of law, of insuring the security of the large and the small, and of creating conditions under which arms can finally be abolished.

At the same time we seek to keep peace inside the non-Communist world, where many nations, all of them our friends, are divided over issues which weaken Western unity, which invite Communist intervention or which threaten to erupt into war. Our efforts in West New Guinea, in the Congo, in the Middle East, and in the Indian subcontinent, have been persistent and patient, despite criticism from both sides. We have also tried to set an example for others—by seeking to adjust small but significant differences with our own closest neighbors in Mexico and in Canada.

Speaking of other nations, I wish to make one point clear. We are bound to many nations by alliances. Those alliances exist because our concern and theirs substantially overlap. Our commitment to defend Western Europe and West Berlin, for example, stands undiminished because of the identity of our vital interests. The United States will make no deal with the Soviet Union at the expense of other nations and other peoples, not merely because they are our partners, but also because their interests and ours converge.

Our interests converge, however, not only in defending the frontiers of freedom, but in pursuing the paths of peace. It is our hope—and the purpose of allied policies—to convince the Soviet Union that she, too, should let each nation choose its own future, so long as that choice does not interfere with the choices of others. The Communist drive to impose their political and economic system on others is the primary cause of world tension today. For there can be no doubt that, if all nations could refrain from interfering in the self-determination of others, the peace would be much more assured.

This will require a new effort to achieve world law—a new context for world discussions. It will require increased understanding between the Soviets and ourselves. And increased understanding will require increased contact and communication. One step in this direction is the proposed arrangement for a direct line between Moscow and Washington, to avoid on each side the dangerous delays, misunderstandings, and misreadings of the other's actions which might occur at a time of crisis.

We have also been talking in Geneva about other first-step measures of arms control, designed to limit the intensity of the arms race and to reduce the risks of accidental war. Our primary long-range interest in Geneva, however, is general and complete disarmament—designed to take place by stages, permitting parallel political developments to build the new institutions of peace which would take the place of arms. The pursuit of disarmament has been an effort of this government since the 1920s. It has been urgently sought by the past three administrations. And however dim the prospects may be today, we intend to continue this effort—to continue it in order that all countries, including our own, can better grasp what the problems and possibilities of disarmament are.

No government or social system is so evil that its people must be considered as lacking in virtue.

The one major area of these negotiations where the end is in sight, yet where a fresh start is badly needed, is in a treaty to outlaw nuclear tests. The conclusion of such a treaty, so near and yet so far, would check the spiraling arms race in one of its most dangerous areas. It would place the nuclear powers in a position to deal more effectively with one of the greatest hazards which man faces in 1963, the further spread of nuclear arms. It would increase our security—it would decrease the prospects of war. Surely this goal is sufficiently important to require our steady pursuit, yielding to neither the temptation to give up the whole effort nor the temptation to give up our insistence on vital and responsible safeguards.

I am taking this opportunity, therefore, to announce two important decisions in this regard.

First: Chairman Khrushchev, Prime Minister Macmillan, and I have agreed that high-level discussions will shortly begin in Moscow looking toward early agreement on a comprehensive test-ban treaty. Our hopes must be tempered with the caution of history—but with our hopes go the hopes of all mankind.

Second: To make clear our good faith and solemn convictions on the matter, I now declare that the United States does not propose to conduct nuclear tests in the atmosphere so long as other states do not do so. We will not be the first to resume. Such a declaration is no substitute for a formal binding treaty, but I hope it will help us achieve one. Nor would such a treaty be a substitute for disarmament, but I hope it will help us achieve it.

Finally, my fellow Americans, let us examine our attitude toward peace and freedom here at home. The quality and spirit of our own society must justify and support our efforts abroad. We must show it in the dedication of our own lives—and many of you who are graduating today will have a unique opportunity to do, by serving without pay in the Peace Corps abroad or in the proposed National Service Corps here at home.

But wherever we are, we must all, in our daily lives, live up to the age-old faith that peace and freedom walk together. In too many of our cities today, the peace is not secure because freedom is incomplete.

It is the responsibility of the executive branch at all levels of government—local, state, and national—to provide and protect that freedom for all of our citizens by all means within their authority. It is the responsibility of the legislative branch at all levels, wherever that authority is not now adequate, to make it adequate. And it is the responsibility of all citizens in all sections of this country to respect the rights of all others and to respect the law of the land.

All this is not unrelated to world peace. "When a man's ways please the Lord," the Scriptures tell us, "he maketh even his enemies to be at peace with him." And is not peace, in the last analysis, basically a matter of human rights—the right to live out our lives without fear of devastation—the right to breathe air as nature provided it—the right of future generations to a healthy existence?

While we proceed to safeguard our national interests, let us also safeguard human interests. And the elimination of war and arms is clearly in the interest of both. No treaty, however much it may be to the advantage of all, however tightly it may be worded, can provide absolute security against the risks of deception and evasion. But it can—if it is sufficiently effective in its enforcement and if it is sufficiently in the interests of its signers—offer far more security and far fewer risks than an unabated, uncontrolled, unpredictable arms race.

The United States, as the world knows, will never start a war. We do not want a war. We do not now expect a war. This generation of Americans has already had enough—more than enough—of war and hate and oppression. We shall be prepared if others wish it. We shall be alert to try to stop it. But we shall also do our part to build a world of peace where the weak are safe and the strong are just. We are not helpless before that task or hopeless of its success. Confident and unafraid, we labor on—not toward a strategy of annihilation but toward a strategy of peace.

American University
Washington, D.C., June 10, 1963

The Nuclear Test-Ban Treaty

I speak to you tonight in a spirit of hope. Eighteen years ago the advent of nuclear weapons changed the course of the world as well as the war. Since that time, all mankind has been struggling to escape from the darkening prospect of mass destruction on earth. In an age when both sides have come to possess enough nuclear power to destroy the human race several times over, the world of communism and the world of free choice have been caught up in a vicious circle of conflicting ideology and interest. Each increase of tension has produced an increase of arms; each increase of arms has produced an increase of tension.

In these years, the United States and the Soviet Union have frequently communicated suspicion and warnings to each other, but very rarely hope. Our representatives have met at the summit and at the brink; they have met in Washington and in Moscow; in Geneva and at the United Nations. But too often these meetings have produced only darkness, discord, or disillusion.

Yesterday a shaft of light cut into the darkness. Negotiations were concluded in Moscow on a treaty to ban all nuclear tests in the atmosphere, in outer space, and under water. For the first time, an agreement has been reached on bringing the forces of nuclear destruction under international control—a goal first sought in 1946 when Bernard Baruch presented a comprehensive control plan to the United Nations.

That plan, and many subsequent disarmament plans, large and small, have all been blocked by those opposed to international inspection. A ban on nuclear tests, however, requires on-the-spot inspection only for underground tests. This nation now possesses a variety of techniques to detect the nuclear tests of other nations which are conducted in the air or under water, for such tests produce unmistakable signs which our modern instruments can pick up.

The treaty initialed yesterday, therefore, is a limited treaty which permits continued underground testing and prohibits only those tests that we ourselves can police. It requires no control posts, no on-site inspection, no international body.

We should also understand that it has other limits as well. Any nation which signs the treaty will have an opportunity to withdraw if it finds that extraordinary events related to the subject matter of the treaty have jeopardized its supreme interests; and no nation's right of self-defense will in any way be impaired. Nor does this treaty mean an end to the threat of nuclear war. It will not reduce nuclear stockpiles; it will not halt the production of nuclear weapons; it will not restrict their use in time of war.

Nevertheless, this limited treaty will radically reduce the nuclear testing which would otherwise be conducted on both sides; it will prohibit the United States, the United Kingdom, the Soviet Union, and all others who sign it, from engaging in the atmospheric tests which have so alarmed mankind; and it offers to all the world a welcome sign of hope.

For this is not a unilateral moratorium, but a specific and solemn legal obligation. While it will not prevent this nation from testing underground, or from being ready to conduct atmospheric tests if the acts of others so require, it gives us a concrete opportunity to extend its coverage to other nations and later to other forms of nuclear tests.

This treaty is in part the product of Western patience and vigilance. We have made clear—most recently in Berlin and Cuba—our deep resolve to protect our security and our freedom against any form of aggression. We have also made clear our steadfast determination to limit the arms race. In three administrations, our soldiers and diplomats have worked together to this end, always supported by Great Britain. Prime Minister Macmillan joined with President Eisenhower in proposing a limited test ban in 1959, and again with me in 1961 and 1962.

But the achievement of this goal is not a victory for one side—it is a victory for mankind. It reflects no concessions either to or by the Soviet Union. It reflects simply our common recognition of the dangers in further testing.

This treaty is not the millennium. It will not resolve all conflicts, or cause the Communists to forgo their ambitions, or eliminate the dangers of war. It will not reduce our need for arms or allies or programs of assistance to others. But it is an important first step—a step toward peace—a step toward reason—a step away from war.

Here is what this step can mean to you and to your children and your neighbors:

First, this treaty can be a step toward reduced world tension and broader areas of agreement. The Moscow talks have reached no agreement on any other subject, nor is this treaty conditioned on any other matter. Under Secretary Harriman made it clear that any nonaggression arrangements about the division in Europe would require full consultation with our allies and full attention to their interests. He also made clear our strong preference for a more comprehensive treaty banning all tests everywhere, and our ultimate hope for general and complete disarmament. The Soviet government, however, is still unwilling to accept the inspection such goals require.

No one can predict with certainty, therefore, what further agreements, if any, can be built on the foundations of this one. They could include controls on preparations for surprise attack, or on numbers and type of armaments. There could be further limitations on the spread of nuclear weapons. The important point is that efforts to seek new agreements will go forward.

But the difficulty of predicting the next step is no reason to be reluctant about this step. Nuclear test-ban negotiations have long been a symbol of East-West disagreement. If this treaty can also be a symbol—if it can symbolize the end of one era and the beginning of another—if both sides can by this treaty gain confidence and experience in peaceful collaboration—then this short and simple treaty may well become an historic mark in man's age-old pursuit of peace.

Western policies have long been designed to persuade the Soviet Union to renounce aggression, direct or indirect, so that their people and all people may live and let live in peace. The unlimited testing of new weapons of war cannot lead toward that end—but this treaty, if it can be followed by further progress, can clearly move in that direction.

I do not say that a world without aggression or threats of war would be an easy world. It will bring new problems, new challenges from the Communists, new dangers of relaxing our vigilance or of mistaking their intent.

But those dangers pale in comparison to those of the spiraling arms race and a collision course toward war. Since the beginning of history, war has been mankind's constant companion. It has been the rule, not the exception. Even a nation as young and as peace-loving as our own has fought through eight wars. And three times in the last two years and a half I have been required to report to you as President that this nation and the Soviet Union stood on the verge of direct military confrontation—in Laos, in Berlin, and in Cuba.

A war today or tomorrow, if it led to nuclear war, would not be like any war in history. A full-scale nuclear exchange, lasting less than sixty minutes, with the weapons now in existence, could wipe out more than 300 million Americans, Europeans, and Russians, as well as untold numbers elsewhere. And the survivors, as Chairman Khrushchev warned the Communist Chinese, "the survivors would envy the dead." For they would inherit a world so devastated by explosions and poison and fire that today we cannot even conceive of its horrors. So let us try to turn the world away from war. Let us make the most of this opportunity, and every opportunity, to reduce tension, to slow down the perilous nuclear arms race, and to check the world's slide toward final annihilation.

Second, this treaty can be a step toward freeing the world from the fears and dangers of radioactive fallout. Our own atmospheric tests last year were conducted under conditions which restricted such fallout to an absolute minimum. But over the years the number and the yield of weapons tested have rapidly increased and so have the radioactive hazards from such testing. Continued unrestricted testing by the nuclear powers, joined in time by other nations which may be less adept in limiting pollution, will increasingly contaminate the air that all of us must breathe.

Even then, the number of children and grandchildren with cancer in their bones, with leukemia in their blood, or with poison in their lungs might seem statistically small to some, in comparison with natural health hazards. But this is not a natural health hazard—and it is not a statistical issue. The loss of even one human life, or the malformation of even one baby—who may be born long after we are gone—should be of concern to us all. Our children and grandchildren are not merely statistics toward which we can be indifferent.

Nor does this affect the nuclear powers alone. These tests befoul the air of all men and all nations, the committed and the uncommitted alike, without their knowledge and without their consent. That is why the continuation of atmospheric testing causes so many countries to regard all nuclear powers as equally evil; and we can hope that its prevention will enable those countries to see the world more clearly, while enabling all the world to breathe more easily.

Yesterday a shaft of light cut into the darkness. Negotiations were concluded in Moscow on a treaty to ban all nuclear tests in the atmosphere, in outer space, and under water.

Third, this treaty can be a step toward preventing the spread of nuclear weapons to nations not now possessing them. During the next several years, in addition to the four current nuclear powers, a small but significant number of nations will have the intellectual, physical, and financial resources to produce both nuclear weapons and the means of delivering them. In time, it is estimated, many other nations will have either this capacity or other ways of obtaining nuclear warheads, even as missiles can be commercially purchased today.

I ask you to stop and think for a moment what it would mean to have nuclear weapons in so many hands, in the hands of countries large and small, stable and unstable, responsible and irresponsible, scattered throughout the world. There would be no rest for anyone then, no stability, no real security, and no chance of effective disarmament. There would only be the increased chance of accidental war, and an increased necessity for the great powers to involve themselves in what otherwise would be local conflicts.

If only one thermonuclear bomb were to be dropped on any American, Russian, or any other city, whether it was launched by accident or design, by a madman or by an enemy, by a large nation or by a small, from any corner of the world, that one bomb could release more destructive power on the inhabitants of that one helpless city than all the bombs dropped in the Second World War.

Neither the United States nor the Soviet Union nor the United Kingdom nor France can look forward to that day with equanimity. We have a great obligation, all four nuclear powers have a great obligation, to use whatever time remains to prevent the spread of nuclear weapons, to persuade other countries not to test, transfer, acquire, possess, or produce such weapons.

This treaty can be the opening wedge in that campaign. It provides that none of the parties will assist other nations to test in the forbidden environments. It opens the door for further agreements on the control of nuclear weapons, and it is open for all nations to sign. For it is in the interest of all nations, and already we have heard from a number of countries who wish to join with us promptly.

Fourth and finally, this treaty can limit the nuclear arms race in ways which, on balance, will strengthen our nation's security far more than the continuation of unrestricted testing. For in today's world, a nation's security does not always increase as its arms increase, when its adversary is doing the same, and unlimited competition in the testing and development of new types of destructive nuclear weapons will not make the world safer for either side. Under this limited treaty, on the other hand, the testing of other nations could never be sufficient to offset the ability of our strategic forces to deter or survive a nuclear attack and to penetrate and destroy an aggressor's homeland.

We have, and under this treaty we will continue to have, the nuclear strength that we need. It is true that the Soviets have tested nuclear weapons of a yield higher than that which we thought to be necessary, but the hundred-megaton bomb of which they spoke two years ago does not and will not change the balance of strategic power. The United States has chosen, deliberately, to concentrate on more mobile and more efficient weapons, with lower but entirely sufficient yield, and our security is therefore not impaired by the treaty I am discussing.

It is also true, as Mr. Khrushchev would agree, that nations cannot afford in these matters to rely simply on the good faith of their adversaries. We have not, therefore, overlooked the risk of secret violations. There is at present a possibility that deep in outer space, hundreds and thousands and millions of miles away from the earth, illegal tests might go undetected. But we already have the capability to construct a system of observation that would make such tests almost impossible to conceal, and we can decide at any time whether such a system is needed in the light of the limited risk to us and the limited reward to others of violations attempted at that range. For any tests which might be conducted so far out in space, which cannot be conducted more easily and efficiently and legally underground, would necessarily be of such a magnitude that they would be extremely difficult to conceal. We can also employ new devices to check on the testing of smaller weapons in the lower atmosphere. Any violations, moreover, involves, along with the risk of detection, the end of the treaty and the worldwide consequences for the violator.

Secret violations are possible and secret preparations for a sudden withdrawal are possible, and thus our own vigilance and strength must be maintained, as we remain ready to withdraw and to resume all forms of testing, if we must. But it would be a mistake to assume that this treaty will be quickly broken. The gains of illegal testing are obviously slight compared to their cost and the hazard of discovery: and the nations which have initialed and will sign this treaty prefer it, in my judgment, to unrestricted testing as a matter of their own self-interest. For these nations, too, and all nations, have a stake in limiting the arms race, in holding the spread of nuclear weapons, and in breathing air that is not radioactive. While it may be theoretically possible to demonstrate the risks inherent in any treaty, and such risks in this treaty are small, the far greater risks to our security are the risks of unrestricted testing, the risk of a nuclear arms race, the risk of new nuclear powers, nuclear pollution, and nuclear war.

This limited test ban, in our most careful judgment, is safer by far for the United States than an unlimited nuclear arms race. For all these reasons, I am hopeful that this nation will promptly approve the limited test-ban treaty. There will, of course, be debate in the country and in the Senate. The Constitution wisely requires the advice and consent of the Senate to all treaties, and that consultation has already begun. All this is as it should be. A document which may mark an historic and constructive opportunity for the world deserves an historic and constructive debate.

It is my hope that all of you will take part in that debate, for this treaty is for all of us. It is particularly for our children and our grandchildren, and they have no lobby here in Washington. This debate will involve military, scientific, and political experts, but it must not be left to them alone. The right and the responsibility are yours.

If we are to open new doorways to peace, if we are to seize this rare opportunity for progress, if we are to be as bold and farsighted in our control of weapons as we have been in their invention, then let us now show all the world on this side of the wall and the other that a strong America also stands for peace. There is no cause for complacency.

We have learned in times past that the spirit of one moment or place can be gone in the next. We have been disappointed more than once, and we have no illusions now that there are shortcuts on the road to peace. At many points around the globe the Communists are continuing their efforts to exploit weakness and poverty. Their concentration of nuclear and conventional arms must still be deterred.

The familiar contest between choice and coercion, the familiar places of danger and conflict, are all still there, in Cuba, in Southeast Asia, in Berlin, and all around the globe, still requiring all the strength and the vigilance that we can muster. Nothing could more greatly damage our cause than if we and our allies were to believe that peace has already been achieved, and that our strength and unity were no longer required.

But now, for the first time in many years, the path of peace may be open. No one can be certain what the future will bring. No one can say whether the time has come for an easing of the struggle. But history and our own conscience will judge us harsher if we do not now make every effort to test our hopes by action; and this is the place to begin. According to the ancient Chinese proverb, "A journey of a thousand miles must begin with a single step."

My fellow Americans, let us take that first step. Let us, if we can, step back from the shadows of war and seek out the way of peace. And if that journey is a thousand miles, or even more, let history record that we, in this land, at this time, took the first step.

Televised Address on Limited Nuclear Test-Ban Treaty
Washington, D.C., July 26, 1963

In its first two decades the age of nuclear energy has been full of fear, yet never empty of hope. Today the fear is a little less and the hope a little greater. For the first time we have been able to reach an agreement which can limit the dangers of this age.

The agreement itself is limited, but its message of hope has been heard and understood not only by the peoples of the three originating nations, but by the peoples and governments of the hundred other countries that have signed. This treaty is the first fruit of labor in which multitudes have shared—citizens, legislators, statesmen, diplomats, and soldiers, too.

Soberly and unremittingly this nation—but never this nation alone—has sought the doorway to effective disarmament into a world where peace is secure. Today we have a beginning and it is right for us to acknowledge all whose work across the years has helped make this beginning possible.

What the future will bring, no one of us can know. This first fruit of hope may or may not be followed by larger harvests. Even this limited treaty, great as it is with promise, can survive only if it has from others the determined support in letter and in spirit which I hereby pledge in behalf of the United States.

If this treaty fails, it will not be our doing, and even if it fails, we shall not regret that we have made this clear and honorable national commitment to the cause of man's survival. For under this treaty we can and must still keep our vigil in defense of freedom.

But this treaty need not fail. This small step toward safety can be followed by others longer and less limited, if also harder in the taking.

With our courage and understanding enlarged by this achievement, let us press onward in quest of man's essential desire for peace.

As President of the United States and with the advice and consent of the Senate, I now sign the instruments of ratification of this treaty.

Remarks upon signing the Nuclear Test-Ban Treaty
Washington, D.C., October 7, 1963

The Quest for Peace

We meet again in the quest for peace.

Twenty-four months ago, when I last had the honor of addressing this body, the shadow of fear lay darkly across the world. The freedom of West Berlin was in immediate peril. Agreement on a neutral Laos seemed remote. The mandate of the United Nations in the Congo was under fire. The financial outlook for this organization was in doubt. Dag Hammarskjöld was dead. The doctrine of troika was being pressed in his place, and atmospheric nuclear tests had been resumed by the Soviet Union.

Those were anxious days for mankind—and some men wondered aloud whether this organization could survive. But the sixteenth and seventeenth General Assemblies achieved not only survival but progress. Rising to its responsibility, the United Nations helped reduce the tensions and helped to hold back the darkness.

Today the clouds have lifted a little so that new rays of hope can break through. The pressures on West Berlin appear to be temporarily eased. Political unity in the Congo has been largely restored. A neutral coalition in Laos, while still in difficulty, is at least in being. The integrity of the United Nations Secretariat has been reaffirmed. A United Nations Decade of Development is under way. And, for the first time in seventeen years of effort, a specific step has been taken to limit the nuclear arms race.

I refer, of course, to the treaty to ban nuclear tests in the atmosphere, outer space, and under water concluded by the Soviet Union, the United Kingdom, and the United States—and already signed by nearly one hundred countries. It has been hailed by people the world over who are thankful to be free from the fears of nuclear fallout. . . .

The world has not escaped from the darkness. The long shadows of conflict and crisis envelop us still. But we meet today in an atmosphere of rising hope, and at a moment of comparative calm. My presence here today is not a sign of crisis, but of confidence. I am not here to report on a new threat to the peace or new signs of war. I have come to salute the United Nations and to show the support of the American people for your daily deliberations.

For the value of this body's work is not dependent on the existence of emergencies, nor can the winning of peace consist only of dramatic victories. Peace is a daily, a weekly, a monthly process, gradually changing opinions, slowly eroding old barriers, quietly building new structures. And however undramatic the pursuit of peace, that pursuit must go on.

Today we may have reached a pause in the Cold War—but that is not a lasting peace. A test-ban treaty is a milestone—but it is not the millennium. We have not been released from our obligations—we have been given an opportunity. And if we fail to make the most of this moment and this momentum—if we convert our newfound hopes and understandings into new walls and weapons of hostility—if this pause in the Cold War merely leads to its renewal and not to its end—then the indictment of posterity will rightly point its finger at us all. But if we can stretch this pause into a period of cooperation—if both sides can now gain new confidence and experience in concrete collaborations for peace—if we can now be as bold and farsighted in the control of deadly weapons as we have been in their creation—then surely this first small step can be the start of a long and fruitful journey.

The task of building the peace lies with the leaders of every nation, large and small. For the great powers have no monopoly on conflict or ambition. The Cold War is not the only expression of tension in this world—and the nuclear race is not the only arms race. Even little wars are dangerous in a nuclear world. The long labor of peace is an undertaking for every nation—and in this effort none of us can remain unaligned. To this goal none can be uncommitted.

The reduction of global tension must not be an excuse for the narrow pursuit of self-interest. If the Soviet Union and the United States, with all of their global interests and clashing commitments of ideology, and with nuclear weapons still aimed at each other today, can find areas of common interest and agreement, then surely other nations can do the same—nations caught in regional conflicts, in racial issues, or in the death throes of old colonialism. Chronic disputes which divert precious resources from the needs of the people or drain the energies of both sides serve the interests of no one—and the badge of responsibility in the modern world is a willingness to seek peaceful solutions.

It is never too early to try; and it's never too late to talk; and it's high time that many disputes on the agenda of this Assembly were taken off the debating schedule and placed on the negotiating table.

The fact remains that the United States, as a major nuclear power, does have a special responsibility in the world. It is, in fact, a threefold responsibility—a responsibility to our own citizens; a responsibility to the people of the whole world who are affected by our decisions; and a responsibility to the next generation of humanity. We believe the Soviet Union also has these special responsibilities—and that those responsibilities require our two nations to concentrate less on our differences and more on the means of resolving them peacefully. For too long both of us have increased our military budgets, our nuclear stockpiles, and our capacity to destroy all life in this hemisphere—human, animal, vegetable—without any corresponding increase in our security.

I have come to salute the United Nations and to show the support of the American people for your daily deliberations . . . The great powers have no monopoly on conflict or ambition. . . . Even little wars are dangerous in a nuclear world.

Our conflicts, to be sure, are real. Our concepts of the world are different. No service is performed by failing to make clear our disagreements. A central difference is the belief of the American people in self-determination for all people.

We believe that the people of Germany and Berlin must be free to reunite their capital and their country.

We believe that the people of Cuba must be free to secure the fruits of the revolution that have been betrayed from within and exploited from without.

In short, we believe that in all the world—in Eastern Europe as well as Western, in southern Africa as well as northern, in old nations as well as new—people must be free to choose their own future, without discrimination or dictation, without coercion or subversion.

These are the basic differences between the Soviet Union and the United States, and they cannot be concealed. So long as they exist, they set limits to agreement, and they forbid the relaxation of our vigilance. Our defense around the world will be maintained for the protection of freedom—and our determination to safeguard that freedom will measure up to any threat or challenge.

But I would say to the leaders of the Soviet Union, and to their people, that if either of our countries is to be fully secure, we need a much better weapon than the H-bomb—a weapon better than ballistic missiles or nuclear submarines—and that better weapon is peaceful cooperation.

We have, in recent years, agreed on a limited test-ban treaty, on an emergency communications link between our capitals, on a statement of principles for disarmament, on an increase in cultural exchange, on cooperation in outer space, on the peaceful exploration of the Antarctic, and on tempering last year's crisis over Cuba.

I believe, therefore, that the Soviet Union and the United States, together with their allies, can achieve further agreements—agreements which spring from our mutual interest in avoiding mutual destruction.

There can be no doubt about the agenda of further steps. We must continue to seek agreements on measures which prevent war by accident or miscalculation. We must continue to seek agreement on safeguards against surprise attack, including observation posts at key points. We must continue to seek agreement on further measures to curb the nuclear arms race, by controlling the transfer of nuclear weapons, converting fissionable materials to peaceful purposes, and banning underground testing, with adequate inspection and enforcement. We must continue to seek agreement on a freer flow of information and people from East to West and West to East.

We must continue to seek agreement, encouraged by yesterday's affirmative response to this proposal by the Soviet Foreign Minister, on an arrangement to keep weapons of mass destruction out of outer space. Let us get our negotiators back to the negotiating table to work out a practicable arrangement to this end.

In these and other ways, let us move up the steep and difficult path toward comprehensive disarmament, securing mutual confidence through mutual verification, and building the institutions of peace as we dismantle the engines of war. We must not let failure to agree on all points delay agreements where agreement is possible. And we must not put forward proposals for propaganda purposes.

Finally, in a field where the United States and the Soviet Union have a special capacity—in the field of space—there is room for new cooperation, for further joint efforts in the regulation and exploration of space. I include among these possibilities a joint expedition to the moon. Space offers no problems of sovereignty; by resolution of this Assembly, the members of the United Nations have forsworn any claim to territorial rights in outer space or on celestial bodies, and declared that international law and the United Nations Charter will apply. Why, therefore, should man's first flight to the moon be a matter of national competition? Why should the United States and the Soviet Union, in preparing for such expeditions, become involved in immense duplications of research, construction, and expenditure? Surely we should explore whether the scientists and astronauts of our two countries—indeed of all the world—cannot work together in the conquest of space, sending someday in this decade to the moon not the representatives of a single nation, but the representatives of all of our countries.

All these and other new steps toward peaceful cooperation may be possible. Most of them will require on our part full consultation with our allies—for their interests are as much involved as our own, and we will not make an agreement at their expense. Most of them will require long and careful negotiation. And most of them will require a new approach to the Cold War—a desire not to "bury" one's adversary, but to compete in a host of peaceful arenas, in ideas, in production, and ultimately in service to all mankind.

The contest will continue—the contest between those who see a monolithic world and those who believe in diversity—but it should be a contest in leadership and responsibility instead of destruction, a contest in achievement instead of intimidation. Speaking for the United States of America, I welcome such a contest. For we believe that truth is stronger than error—and that freedom is more enduring than coercion. And in the contest for a better life, all the world can be a winner.

The effort to improve the conditions of man, however, is not a task for the few. It is the task of all nations—acting alone, acting in groups, acting in the United Nations. For plague and pestilence and plunder and pollution, the hazards of nature and the hunger of children, are the foes of every nation. The earth, the sea, and the air are the concern of every nation. And science, technology, and education can be the ally of every nation.

We have the power to make this the best generation of mankind in the history of the world—or to make it the last.

Never before has man had such capacity to control his own environment, to end thirst and hunger, to conquer poverty and disease, to banish illiteracy and massive human misery. We have the power to make this the best generation of mankind in the history of the world—or to make it the last. . . .

But man does not live by bread alone. The members of this organization are committed by the Charter to promote and respect human rights. Those rights are not respected when a Buddhist priest is driven from his pagoda, when a synagogue is shut down, when a Protestant church cannot open a mission, when a cardinal is forced into hiding, or when a crowded church service is bombed. The United States of America is opposed to discrimination and persecution on grounds of race and religion anywhere in the world, including our own nation. We are working to right the wrongs of our own country. . . .

The United Nations cannot survive as a static organization. Its obligations are increasing as well as its size. Its Charter must be changed as well as its customs. The authors of that Charter did not intend that it be frozen in perpetuity. The science of weapons and war has made us all, far more than eighteen years ago in San Francisco, one world and one human race, with one common destiny. In such a world, absolute sovereignty no longer assures us of absolute security. The conventions of peace must pull abreast and then ahead of the inventions of war. The

United Nations, building on its successes and learning from its failures, must be developed into a genuine world security system.

But peace does not rest in charters and covenants alone. It lies in the hearts and minds of all people. And if it is cast out there, then no act, no pact, no treaty, no organization can hope to preserve it without the support and the wholehearted commitment of all people. So let us not rest all our hopes on parchment and on paper; let us strive to build peace, a desire for peace, a willingness to work for peace, in the hearts and minds of all of our people. I believe that we can. I believe the problems of human destiny are not beyond the reach of human beings.

Two years ago I told this body that the United States had proposed, and was willing to sign, a limited test-ban treaty. Today that treaty has been signed. It will not put an end to war. It will not remove basic conflicts. It will not secure freedom for all. But it can be a lever; and Archimedes, in explaining the principles of the lever, was said to have declared to his friends: "Give me a place where I can stand—and I shall move the world."

My fellow inhabitants of this planet: Let us take our stand here in this Assembly of nations. And let us see if we, in our own time, can move the world to a just and lasting peace.

United Nations General Assembly
New York, New York, September 20, 1963

The Sale of American Wheat

The Soviet Union and various Eastern European countries have expressed a willingness to buy from our private grain dealers at the regular world price several million tons of surplus American wheat or wheat flour for shipment during the next several months. They may also wish to purchase from us surplus feed grains and other agricultural commodities.

After consultation with the National Security Council, and informing the appropriate leaders of the Congress, I have concluded that such sales by private dealers for American dollars or gold, either cash on delivery or normal commercial terms, should not be prohibited by the government. . . .

The Russian people will know they are receiving American wheat. The United States has never had a policy against selling consumer goods, including agricultural commodities, to the Soviet Union and Eastern Europe. On the contrary, we have been doing exactly that for a number of years, and to the extent that their limited supplies of gold, dollars, and foreign exchange must be used for food, they cannot be used to purchase military or other equipment.

Our allies have long been engaged in extensive sales of wheat and other farm products to the Communist bloc, and, in fact, it would be foolish to halt the sales of our wheat when other countries can buy wheat from us today and then sell this flour to the Communists. In recent weeks Australia and NATO allies have agreed to sell ten million to fifteen million tons of wheat and wheat flour to the Communist bloc.

This transaction advertises to the world as nothing else could the success of free American agriculture. It demonstrates our willingness to relieve food shortages, to reduce tensions, and to improve relations with all countries. And it shows that peaceful agreements with the United States which serve the interests of both sides are a far more worthwhile course than a course of isolation and hostility.

For this government to tell our grain traders that they cannot accept these offers, on the other hand, would accomplish little or nothing. The Soviets would continue to buy wheat and flour elsewhere, including wheat flour from those nations which buy our wheat. Moreover, having for many years sold them farm products which are not in surplus, it would make no sense to refuse to sell those products on which we must otherwise pay the cost of storage. In short, this particular decision with respect to sales to the Soviet Union, which is not inconsistent with many smaller transactions over a long period of time, does not represent a new Soviet-American trade policy. That must await the settlement of many matters. But it does represent one more hopeful sign that a more peaceful world is both possible and beneficial to us all.

Opening Statement, President's News Conference
Washington, D.C., October 9, 1963

CHAPTER 14

The Western Alliance

Kennedy welcomed the political and economic integration of Western Europe as a means both of preventing any recurrence of the bitter rivalries that had produced two world wars in his lifetime and of strengthening the alliance for a rapidly changing world. Western diplomacy and trade policy, he knew, could not stand still in the face of those changes, including a resurgent Moscow and an emergent Third World. By 1963, determined to prevent any outbreak of war and any erosion of Western liberty, he sought still closer relations with his allies in a balanced use of both defense and diplomacy. His commitment to peace and security was memorably hailed in his visit to beleaguered West Berlin.

The Political-Military Link

NATO is remarkable among the alliances of history in its combination of political, military, economic, and even psychological components. What NATO is, at any time, depends not only upon its forces in being, but upon the resolution of its leaders, the state of mind of its people, and the view of all these elements which is held by those who do not always wish us well.

In this situation, it is clearly necessary that there should be close understanding between political leaders and the senior military officers. In our countries, of course, final responsibility always rests with political authorities. . . . But in NATO, from the very beginning, it has been essential that neither class of men should accept any arbitrary division of our problems into "the political" and "the military" spheres. The crucial problems have always been mixed. Political leaders have had a duty to share with their senior officers a full understanding of the political purposes of the alliance, and military leaders for their part have had to recognize that in NATO all the important military problems are political problems also.

This recognition of the interconnection between policy and force is an even more compelling necessity today, especially in all the questions which relate to the command, the deployment, and the possible use of nuclear weapons.

In the months ahead, as we share in the framing of NATO's policy and in new decisions which must guide us safely toward the future, we shall need to have the closest and most understanding communication not only from country to country, but from soldier to civilian. Political planning must be aware of military realities, and military plans in turn must be responsive to political considerations—among them such varied and important matters as resource capabilities, national attitudes, and other alliance objectives. . . . Military and political problems are not separable, and military and political men must work ever more closely together.

I hold an office which by our very Constitution unites political and military responsibility, and therefore it is no more than my duty to pledge my own best effort to keep these two kinds of problems together on my mind. I ask the same of you.

Remarks to NATO Military Committee
Washington, D.C., April 10, 1961

The Change in World Power

I do not think it altogether inappropriate to introduce myself to this audience. I am the man who accompanied Jacqueline Kennedy to Paris, and I have enjoyed it. . . .

I come on the same mission which occupied many of my predecessors, stretching all the way back to President Wilson at the conclusion of the First World War, and that is how . . . to bind more intimately for the common interest France and the United States, Europe and the United States. . . . But . . . all of the power relationships in the world have changed in the last fifteen years, and therefore our policies must take these changes into account. First is the change in Europe itself . . . its economic growth rate higher than that of the new world . . . the most outstanding example of strength through unity. . . .

I am the man who accompanied Jacqueline Kennedy to Paris, and I have enjoyed it.

The second great change is the change in weaponry. The United States no longer has a nuclear monopoly. . . . The intercontinental ballistic missile has made my own country vulnerable to attack and . . .

reinforced our view that your defense and ours are indivisible. In terms of potential destruction, Washington today is closer to Moscow than this city was to any other city in any other country before the outbreak of World War II. . . .

Third and most important is the change in the location and nature of the threat. The cause of freedom is under pressure all over the world. But because of the extraordinary rebirth of Western European strength, the struggle has been switched . . . to the whole southern half of the globe where the attack potentially comes not from massive land armies but from subversion, insurrection, and despair. Europe has conquered her own internal problems. Those that remain are on the way to solution. The time has now come for us to associate more closely together than ever in the past in a massive and concerted attack on the poverty, injustice, and oppression which overshadow so much of the globe.

Press Luncheon
Paris, France, June 2, 1961

The Trade Expansion Act

In May of 1962, we stand at a great dividing point. We must either trade or fade. We must either go backward or go forward. For more than a quarter of a century the reciprocal trade legislation fathered by Cordell Hull of Tennessee and sponsored by Franklin Roosevelt has served this country well. On eleven different occasions it has been renewed by Congresses of both parties. But that act is no longer adequate to carry us through the channels and the locks of world trade today.

For the whole pattern of trade is changing and we must change with it. The Common Market uniting the countries of Western Europe together in one great trading group indicates both a promise, and a threat, to our economy. Our international balance of payments is in deficit, requiring an increase in our exports. Japan has regained force as a trading nation; nearly fifty new nations of Asia and Africa are seeking new markets; our friends in Latin America need to trade to develop their capital; and the Communist bloc has developed a vast new arsenal of trading weapons which can be used against us. . . .

I believe that American trade leadership must be maintained and . . . furthered—and I have therefore submitted to the Congress the Trade Expansion Act of 1962.

It is not a partisan measure—its provisions have been endorsed by leaders of both parties. It is not a radical measure—its newest features merely add force to traditional American concepts. And it is not a measure favoring one section of our country over another—farm, labor, business and consumer groups, from every part of the nation, support this legislation. I am convinced that the passage of this bill is of vital importance to you and to every other American—not only to those vast numbers of people who are engaged in trade, but to every citizen: as a consumer who is concerned about the prices you must pay, as a patriot concerned about national security, as an American concerned about freedom. The basic economic facts make it essential that we pass this legislation this year.

Our businessmen, workers, and farmers are in need of new markets—and the fastest growing market in the world is the European Common Market. Its consumers will soon be nearly 250 million people. Its sales possibilities have scarcely begun to be tapped. Its demand for American goods is without precedent—if only we can obtain the tools necessary to open the door.

Our own markets here at home expand as our economy and population expand. But think of the tremendous demand in the Common Market countries, where most consumers have never had the goods which we take so much for granted. Think of the opportunities in a market where, compared to the ratio of ownership in this country, only one fourth as many consumers have radios, one seventh television sets, one fifth automobiles, washing machines, refrigerators!

Our businessmen, workers, and farmers are in need of new markets—and the fastest growing market in the world is the European Common Market. . . . Its demand for American goods is without precedent—if only we can obtain the tools necessary to open the door.

If our American producers can share in this market, it will mean more investment and more plants and more jobs and a faster rate of growth. To share in that market we must strike a bargain—we must have something to offer the Europeans—we must be willing to give them increased access to our markets. Let us not avoid the fact: we cannot sell unless we buy. And there will be those who will be opposed to this competition. But, let those who believe in competition—those who welcome the challenge of world trade, as our predecessors have done—let them recognize the value that will come from this exchange of goods. It will enrich the choice of consumers. It will make possible a higher standard of living. It will help hold the lid on the cost of living. It will stimulate our producers to modernize their products. A few—a very few—may be adversely affected, but for the benefit of those few we have expanded and refined the safeguards of the act. . . .

But let us not miss the main point: the new jobs opened through trade will be far greater than any jobs which will be adversely affected. And these new jobs will come in those enterprises that are today leading the economy of the country—our growth industries, those that pay the highest wages, those that are among the most efficiently organized, those that are most active in research and in the innovation of new products. The experience of the European Common Market, where tariffs were gradually cut down, has shown that increased trade brings employment. They have full employment in the Common Market and an economic growth rate twice that of the United States. In short, trade expansion will emphasize the modern instead of the obsolete, the strong instead of the weak, the new frontiers of trade instead of the ancient strongholds of protection.

We cannot continue to bear the burden that we must bear of helping freedom defend itself, all the way from the American soldier guarding the Brandenburg Gate to the Americans now in Vietnam, or the Peace Corps men in Colombia, unless we have the resources to finance those great expenditures which in the last year totaled over three billion dollars. Unless we are able to increase our surplus of balance of payments, the United States will be faced with a hard choice of either lessening those commitments or beginning to withdraw this great national effort.

One answer to this problem is the negative answer: raise our tariffs, restrict our capital, pull back from the world—and our adversaries would be only too glad to fill any gap that we should leave. This administration was not elected to preside over the liquidation of American responsibility. . . .

There is a much better answer—and that is to increase our exports, to meet our commitments, and to maintain our defense of freedom. I have every confidence that once this bill is passed, the ability of American initiative and know-how will increase our exports and our export surplus by competing successfully in every market of the world.

Third and last, the new trade act can strengthen our foreign policy. . . . The Alliance for Progress seeks to help these Latin American neighbors of ours. That effort must, and will, continue. But foreign aid cannot do the job alone. In the long run, our sister republics must develop the means themselves to finance their development. They must sell more of their goods on the world market, and earn the exchange necessary to buy the machinery and the technology that they need to raise their standard of living. The Trade Expansion Act is designed to keep this great market as a part of the world community, because the security of the United States is tied up with the well-being of our sister republics. . . .

For we are moving toward a full partnership of all the free nations of the world, a partnership which will have within its area ninety percent of the industrial productive power of the Free World, which will have in it the greatest market that the world has ever known, a productive power far greater than that of the Communist bloc, a trillion-dollar economy where goods can move freely back and forth. That is the prospect that lies before us, as citizens of this country, in the year 1962.

Those who preach the doctrine of the inevitability of the class struggle and Communist success should realize that . . . the great effort . . . to unify economically the countries of the Free World offers far greater promise than the sterile and broken promises of the Communist system. Against the Communist system of iron discipline, the Atlantic partnership will present a world of free choice. Against their predictions of our collapse, it will present a challenge of free nations working in harmony. . . .

In the life of every nation, as in the life of every man, there comes a time when a nation stands at the crossroads; when it can either shrink from the future and retire into its shell, or move ahead, asserting its will and its faith in an uncertain sea. I believe that we stand at such a juncture in our foreign economic policy. And I come to this city because I believe New Orleans and Louisiana and the United States choose to move ahead in 1962.

Port of New Orleans
New Orleans, Louisiana, May 4, 1962

The Atlantic Partnership

As this effort for independence, inspired by the American Declaration of Independence, now approaches a successful close, a great new effort for interdependence is transforming the world about us. And the spirit of that new effort is the same spirit which gave birth to the American Constitution.

That spirit is today most clearly seen across the Atlantic Ocean. The nations of Western Europe, long divided by feuds far more bitter than any which existed among the thirteen colonies, are today joining together, seeking, as our forefathers sought, to find freedom in diversity and in unity, strength.

The United States looks on this vast new enterprise with hope and admiration. We do not regard a strong and united Europe as a rival but as a partner. To aid its progress has been the basic object of our foreign policy for seventeen years. We believe that a united Europe will be capable of playing a greater role in the common defense, of responding more generously to the needs of poorer nations, of joining with the United States and others in lowering trade barriers, resolving problems of commerce, commodities, and currency, and developing coordinated policies in all economic, political, and diplomatic areas. We see in such a Europe a partner with whom we can deal on a basis of full equality in all the great and burdensome tasks of building and defending a community of free nations.

It would be premature at this time to do more than indicate the high regard with which we view the formation of this partnership. The first order of business is for our European friends to go forward in forming the more perfect union which will someday make this partnership possible.

A great new edifice is not built overnight. It was eleven years from the Declaration of Independence to the writing of the Constitution. The construction of workable federal institutions required still another generation. The greatest works of our nation's founders lay not in documents and in declarations, but in creative, determined action. The building of the new house of Europe has followed the same practical, purposeful course. Building the Atlantic partnership now will not be easily or cheaply finished.

But I will say here and now, on this Day of Independence, that the

United States will be ready for a Declaration of Interdependence, that we will be prepared to discuss with a united Europe the ways and means of forming a concrete Atlantic partnership, a mutually beneficial partnership between the new union now emerging in Europe and the old American Union founded here 175 years ago.

All this will not be completed in a year, but let the world know it is our goal.

In urging the adoption of the United States Constitution, Alexander Hamilton told his fellow New Yorkers "to think continentally." Today Americans must learn to think intercontinentally.

Acting on our own, by ourselves, we cannot establish justice throughout the world; we cannot insure its domestic tranquillity, or provide for its common defense, or promote its general welfare, or secure the blessings of liberty to ourselves and our posterity. But joined with other free nations, we can do all this and more. We can assist the developing nations to throw off the yoke of poverty. We can balance our worldwide trade and payments at the highest possible level of growth. We can mount a deterrent powerful enough to deter any aggression. And ultimately we can help to achieve a world of law and free choice, banishing the world of war and coercion.

For the Atlantic partnership of which I speak would not look inward only, preoccupied with its own welfare and advancement. It must look outward, to cooperate with all nations in meeting their common concern. It would serve as a nucleus for the eventual union of all free men—those who are now free and those who are vowing that someday they will be free.

On Washington's birthday in 1861 . . . President-elect Abraham Lincoln spoke in this hall on his way to the nation's capital. And he paid a brief but eloquent tribute to the men who wrote, who fought for, and who died for the Declaration of Independence. Its essence, he said, was its promise not only of liberty "to the people of this country, but hope to the world, [hope] that in due time the weights should be lifted from the shoulders of all men, and that all should have an equal chance."

On this fourth day of July 1962, we who are gathered at this same hall, entrusted with the fate and future of our states and nation, declare now our vow to do our part to lift the weights from the shoulders of all, to join other men and nations in preserving both peace and freedom, and to regard any threat to the peace or freedom of one as a threat to the peace and freedom of all. "And for the support of this Declaration, with a firm reliance on the protection of Divine Providence, we mutually pledge to each other our Lives, our Fortunes, and our sacred Honor."

Independence Hall
Philadelphia, Pennsylvania, July 4, 1962

The Exemplar of Service

Dear Mr. Monnet:

I am delighted to join my friends at Freedom House in doing honor to your great achievements. You come at a moment of high importance—and you come as the exemplar of disinterested service to Europe and to the Atlantic world.

For centuries, emperors, kings, and dictators have sought to impose unity on Europe by force. For better or worse, they have failed. But under your inspiration, Europe has moved closer to unity in less than twenty years than it had done before in a thousand. You and your associates have built with the mortar of reason and the brick of economic and political interest. You are transforming Europe by the power of a constructive idea.

Ever since the war, the reconstruction and the knitting together of Europe have been objectives of United States policy, for we have recognized with you that in unity lies strength. And we have also recognized with you that a strong Europe would be good not only for Europeans but for the world. America and a united Europe, working in full and effective partnership, can find solutions to those urgent problems that confront all mankind in this crucial time.

I have been happy, therefore, to read your statement of January 16th in which you call attention to the responsibility of Europe to share with the United States in the common defense of the West. I believe, with you, that "Americans and Europeans must recognize that neither one nor the other is defending a particular country, but that the ensemble is defending a common civilization." The United States will be true to this conviction, and we trust that it will have the support of Europeans too.

Your practical wisdom, your energy in persuasion, your tested courage, and your earned eminence in Europe are the reasons for this celebration in your honor. They are also a great resource for freedom, and I wish you many years of continued strength in your service to our cause.

Sincerely,
John F. Kennedy

Letter to Jean Monnet
Washington, D.C., January 22, 1963

The Champion of Liberty

We gather today at a moment unique in the history of the United States.

This is the first time that the United States Congress has solemnly resolved that the President of the United States shall proclaim an honorary citizenship for the citizen of another country. In enjoining me to perform this happy duty, the Congress gives Sir Winston Churchill a distinction shared only with the Marquis de Lafayette.

In proclaiming him an honorary citizen, I only propose a formal recognition of the place he has long since won in the history of freedom and in the affections of my—and now his—fellow countrymen.

Whenever and wherever tyranny threatened, he has always championed liberty. Facing firmly toward the future, he has never forgotten the past. Serving six monarchs of his native Great Britain, he has served all men's freedom and dignity.

In the dark days and darker nights when England stood alone—and most men save Englishmen despaired of England's life—he mobilized the English language and sent it into battle. The incandescent quality of his words illuminated the courage of his countrymen.

Indifferent himself to danger, he wept over the sorrows of others. A child of the House of Commons, he became its father. Accustomed to the hardships of battle, he has no distaste for pleasure.

Now his stately ship of life, having weathered the severest storms of a troubled century, is anchored in tranquil waters, proof that courage and faith and zest for freedom are truly indestructible. The record of his triumphant passage will inspire free hearts all over the globe.

By adding his name to our rolls, we mean to honor him—but his acceptance honors us far more. For no statement or proclamation can enrich his name now—the name Sir Winston Churchill is already legend.

Remarks upon signing proclamation conferring honorary citizenship on Sir Winston Churchill Washington, D.C., April 9, 1963

The Only War We Seek

I am grateful for your invitation and I am happy to be here. I have crossed the Atlantic, some 3,500 miles, at a crucial time in the life of the Grand Alliance. Our unity was forged in a time of danger; it must be maintained in a time of peace. Our Alliance was founded to deter a new war; it must now find the way to a new peace. Our strategy was born in a divided Europe, but it must look to the goal of European unity and an end to the divisions of people and countries.

Our Alliance is in a period of transition, and that is as it should be. For Western Europe is no longer weakened by conflict, but is fast becoming a full partner in prosperity and security. Western Europe is no longer the seedbed of world war, but an instrument of unity and an example of reconciliation. And Western Europe, finally, is no longer an area in need of assistance, but can now be a source of strength to all the forces of freedom all around the globe.

I have also come to this country, the most populous in Western Europe, to express the respect of the people of the United States for the

German people's industry and their initiative, for their culture and their courage.

Here in Western Germany you have achieved a solid framework of freedom, a miracle of economic recovery, and an opportunity to express your political ideals through action in Europe and through the world.

The people of West Germany have freed themselves from the forces of tyranny and aggression. The people of the United States have now freed themselves from the long process of isolation. Together we look forward to a new future. Former foes have become faithful friends. Nations bitterly arrayed against each other have now become closely allied, sharing common values and common sentiments, as well as common interests, working within a growing partnership of equals, for peace and the common defense, on problems of trade and monetary policy, and on helping the less developed countries, and on building Western unity.

Above all, we recognize a duty to defend and to develop the long Western tradition which we share, resting as it does on a common heritage. Economically, militarily, politically, our two nations and all the other nations of the Alliance are now dependent upon one another. We are allies in the only war we seek—the war against poverty, hunger, disease, and ignorance in our own countries, and around the world.

We all know the meaning of freedom and our people are determined upon its peaceful survival and success.

My stay in this country will be all too brief, but in a larger sense the United States is here on this continent to stay. So long as our presence is desired and required, our forces and commitments will remain. For your safety is our safety, your liberty is our liberty, and any attack on your soil is an attack upon our own. Out of necessity, as well as sentiment, in our approach to peace as well as war, our fortunes are one.

Finally, I have also come to Germany to pay tribute to a great European statesman, an architect of unity, a champion of liberty, a friend of the American people—Chancellor Konrad Adenauer. Already he lives in the history he helped to make. I look forward to this visit of Chancellor Adenauer with me, with the warmth of your greeting already in my memory.

Remarks upon arrival in Germany
at Bonn-Cologne Airport, Federal Republic of Germany
June 23, 1963

The Age of Interdependence

One hundred and fifteen years ago a most learned Parliament was convened in this historic hall. Its goal was a united German Federation. Its members were poets and professors, lawyers and philosophers, doctors and clergymen, freely elected in all parts of the land. No nation applauded its endeavors as warmly as my own. No assembly ever strove more ardently to put perfection into practice. And though in the end it failed, no other building in Germany deserves more the title of "cradle of German democracy."

But can there be such a title? In my own home city of Boston, Faneuil Hall—once the meeting place of the authors of the American Revolution—has long been known as the "cradle of American liberty." But when, in 1852, the Hungarian patriot Kossuth addressed an audience there, he criticized its name. "It is," he said, "a great name—but there is something in it which saddens my heart. You should not say 'American liberty.' You should say 'liberty in America.' Liberty should not be either American or European—it should just be 'liberty.' "

Kossuth was right. For unless liberty flourishes in all lands, it cannot flourish in one. Conceived in one hall, it must be carried out in many. Thus, the seeds of the American Revolution had been brought earlier from Europe, and they later took root around the world. The German Revolution of 1848 transmitted ideas and idealists to America and to other lands. Today, in 1963, democracy and liberty are more international than ever before. And the spirit of the Frankfurt Assembly, like the spirit of Faneuil Hall, must live in many hearts and nations if it is to live at all.

For we live in an age of interdependence as well as independence—an age of internationalism as well as nationalism. In 1848 many countries were indifferent to the goals of the Frankfurt Assembly. It was, they said, a German problem. Today there are no exclusively German problems, or American problems, or even European problems. There are world problems—and our two countries and continents are inextricably bound together in the tasks of peace as well as war.

We are partners for peace—not in a narrow bilateral context but in a framework of Atlantic partnership. The ocean divides us less than the Mediterranean divided the ancient world of Greece and Rome. Our Constitution is old and yours is young, and our culture is young and yours is old, but in our commitment we can and must speak and act with but one voice. Our roles are distinct but complementary—and our goals are the same: peace and freedom for all men, for all time, in a world of abundance, in a world of justice.

I would not diminish the miracle of West Germany's economic achievements. But the true German miracle has been your rejection of the past for the future—your reconciliation with France, your participation in the building of Europe, your leading role in NATO, and your growing support for constructive undertakings throughout the world.

But Goethe tells us in his greatest poem that Faust lost the liberty of his soul when he said to the passing moment: "Stay, thou art so fair." And our liberty, too, is endangered if we pause for the passing moment, if we rest on our achievements, if we resist the pace of progress. For time and the world do not stand still. Change is the law of life. And those who look only to the past or the present are certain to miss the future.

The future of the West lies in Atlantic partnership—a system of cooperation, interdependence, and harmony whose peoples can jointly meet their burdens and opportunities throughout the world. Some say this is only a dream, but I do not agree. A generation of achievement—the Marshall Plan, NATO, the Schuman Plan, and the Common Market—urges us up the path to greater unity.

Some say that the United States will neither hold to these purposes nor abide by its pledge—that we will revert to a narrow nationalism. But such doubts fly in the face of history. For eighteen years the United States has stood its watch for freedom all around the globe. The firmness of American will, and the effectiveness of American strength, have been shown, in support of free men and free government, in Asia, in Africa, in the Americas, and, above all, here in Europe. Our commitment to Europe is indispensable—in our interest as well as yours.

For war in Europe, as we learned twice in forty years, destroys peace in America. A threat to the freedom of Europe is a threat to the freedom of America. And that is why we look forward to a united Europe in an Atlantic partnership, an entity of interdependent parts sharing equally both burdens and decisions, and linked together in the tasks of defense as well as the arts of peace.

The first task of the Atlantic Community was to assure its common defense. That defense was and still is indivisible. The United States will risk its cities to defend yours because we need your freedom to protect ours. Hundreds of thousands of our soldiers serve with yours on this continent, as tangible evidence of that pledge. Those who would doubt our pledge or deny this indivisibility—those who would separate Europe from America or split one ally from another—would only give aid and comfort to the men who make themselves our adversaries and welcome any Western disarray.

The purpose of our common military effort is not war but peace—not the destruction of nations but the protection of freedom. . . .

Second: Our partnership is not military alone. Economic unity is also imperative—not only among the nations of Europe, but across the wide Atlantic.

Indeed, economic cooperation is needed throughout the entire free world. By opening our markets to the developing countries of Africa, Asia, and Latin America, by contributing our capital and our skills, by stabilizing basic prices, we can help assure them of a favorable climate for freedom and growth. This is an Atlantic responsibility. For the Atlantic nations themselves helped to awaken these people. Our merchants and our traders plowed up their soils—and their societies as well—in search of minerals and oil and rubber and coffee. Now we must help them gain full membership in the twentieth century, closing the gap between rich and poor.

For time and the world do not stand still. Change is the law of life. And those who look only to the past or the present are certain to miss the future.

We must not return to the 1930s when we exported to each other our own stagnation. We must not return to the discredited view that trade favors some nations at the expense of others. . . . As they say on my own Cape Cod, a rising tide lifts all the boats. And a partnership, by definition, serves both partners, without domination or unfair advantage. Together we have been partners in adversity—let us also be partners in prosperity. . . .

Third and finally: Our partnership depends on common political purpose. . . . History tells us that disunity and relaxation are the great internal dangers of an alliance. Thucydides reported that the Peloponnesians and their allies were mighty in battle but handicapped by their policy-making body—in which, he related, "each presses its own ends . . . which generally results in no action at all. . . ."

Is this also to be the story of the Grand Alliance? Welded in a moment of imminent danger, will it disintegrate into complacency, with each member pressing its own ends to the neglect of the common cause? This must not be the case. Our old dangers are not gone beyond return, and any division among us would bring them back in doubled strength.

Together we must work to strengthen the spirit of those Europeans who are now not free, to reestablish their old ties to freedom and the West, so that their desire for liberty and their sense of nationhood and their sense of belonging to the Western community over hundreds of years will survive for future expression. We ask those who would be our adversaries to understand that in our relations with them we will not bargain one nation's interest against another's and that the commitment to the cause of freedom is common to us all.

All of us in the West must be faithful to our conviction that peace in Europe can never be complete until everywhere in Europe, and that includes Germany, men can choose, in peace and freedom, how their countries shall be governed, and choose—without threat to any neighbor—reunification with their countrymen.

I preach no easy liberation and I make no empty promises; but my countrymen, since our country was founded, have believed strongly in the proposition that all men shall be free and all free men shall have this right of choice.

In short, the words of Thucydides are a warning, not a prediction. We have it in us, as eighteen years have shown, to build our defenses, to strengthen our economies, and to tighten our political bonds, both in good weather and in bad. We can move forward with the confidence that is born of success and the skill that is born of experience. And as we move, let us take heart from the certainty that we are united not only by danger and necessity, but by hope and purpose as well.

For we know now that freedom is more than the rejection of tyranny—that prosperity is more than an escape from want—that partnership is more than a sharing of power. These are, above all, great human adventures. They must have meaning and conviction and purpose—and because they do, in your country now and in mine, in all the nations of the Alliance, we are called to a great new mission.

It is not a mission of self-defense alone, for that is a means, not an end. It is not a mission of arbitrary power—for we reject the idea of one nation dominating another. The mission is to create a new social order, founded on liberty and justice, in which men are the masters of their fate, in which states are the servants of their citizens, and in which all men and women can share a better life for themselves and their children. That is the object of our common policy.

To realize this vision, we must seek a world of peace—a world in which peoples dwell together in mutual respect and work together in mutual regard—a world where peace is not a mere interlude between wars, but an incentive to the creative energies of humanity. We will not find such a peace today, or even tomorrow. The obstacles to hope are large and menacing. Yet the goal of a peaceful world—today and tomorrow—must shape our decisions and inspire our purposes.

So we are all idealists. We are all visionaries. Let it not be said of this Atlantic generation that we left ideals and visions to the past, nor purpose and determination to our adversaries. We have come too far, we have sacrificed too much, to disdain the future now. And we shall ever remember what Goethe told us—that the "highest wisdom, the best that mankind ever knew," was the realization that "he only earns his freedom and existence who daily conquers them anew."

Paulskirche Assembly Hall
Frankfurt, Federal Republic of Germany
June 25, 1963

The Proudest Boast

I am proud to come to this city as the guest of your distinguished Mayor, who has symbolized throughout the world the fighting spirit of West Berlin. And I am proud to visit the Federal Republic with your distinguished Chancellor, who for so many years has committed Germany to democracy and freedom and progress, and to come here in the company of my fellow American, General Clay, who has been in this city during its great moments of crisis and will come again if ever needed.

Two thousand years ago the proudest boast was "civis Romanus sum." Today, in the world of freedom, the proudest boast is "Ich bin ein Berliner."

I appreciate my interpreter translating my German!

There are many people in the world who really don't understand, or say they don't, what is the great issue between the Free World and the Communist world. Let them come to Berlin. There are some who say that communism is the wave of the future. Let them come to Berlin. And there are some who say in Europe and elsewhere we can work with the Communists. Let them come to Berlin. And there are even a few who say that it is true that communism is an evil system, but it permits us to make economic progress. "Lass' sie nach Berlin kommen." Let them come to Berlin!

Today, in the world of freedom, the proudest boast is "Ich bin ein Berliner."

Freedom has many difficulties and democracy is not perfect, but we have never had to put a wall up to keep our people in, to prevent them from leaving us. I want to say, on behalf of my countrymen, who live many miles away on the other side of the Atlantic, who are far distant from you, that they take the greatest pride that they have been able to share with you, even from a distance, the story of the last eighteen years. I know of no town, no city, that has been besieged for eighteen years that still lives with the vitality and the force and the hope and the determination of the city of West Berlin.

While the wall is the most obvious and vivid demonstration of the failures of the Communist system, for all the world to see, we take no satisfaction in it. For it is, as your Mayor has said, an offense not only against history but an offense against humanity, separating families, dividing husbands and wives and brothers and sisters, and dividing a people who wish to be joined together.

What is true of this city is true of Germany—real, lasting peace in Europe can never be assured as long as one German out of four is denied the elementary right of free men, and that is to make a free choice. In eighteen years of peace and good faith, this generation of Germans has earned the right to be free, including the right to unite their families and their nation in lasting peace, with goodwill to all people. You live in a defended island of freedom, but your life is part of the main. So let me ask you, as I close, to lift your eyes beyond the dangers of today to the hopes of tomorrow, beyond the freedom merely of this city of Berlin, or your country of Germany, to the advance of freedom everywhere, beyond the wall to the day of peace with justice, beyond yourselves and ourselves to all mankind.

Freedom is indivisible, and when one man is enslaved, all are not free. When all are free, then we can look forward to that day when this city will be joined as one, and this country, and this great Continent of Europe, in a peaceful and hopeful globe. When that day finally comes, as it will, the people of West Berlin can take sober satisfaction in the fact that they were in the front lines for almost two decades.

All free men, wherever they may live, are citizens of Berlin, and, therefore, as a free man, I take pride in the words "Ich bin ein Berliner."

City Hall
West Berlin, Federal Republic of Germany
June 26, 1963

CHAPTER 15

The Third World

No president before or after Kennedy has matched the depth of his empathy for the struggling peoples of Latin America, Africa, and Asia, or the strength of his vow to facilitate their political and economic independence. No subsequent president fought so hard so often for development assistance, or offered so much encouragement to the United Nations. No other president welcomed so many foreign students to the White House. Kennedy's concern for the Third World's plight began during his congressional travels and developed still further in a series of scholarly Senate speeches. While, as President, he failed to make clear a realistically successful position on Vietnam, he nevertheless remained remarkably clear in not accepting the repeated recommendation that he send combat divisions and bombers to make war on behalf of a government in the south that had increasingly lost the support of its own constituents.

The Concerned Young Congressman

MR. KENNEDY: Last year when this bill was before the House, I offered a motion to cut technical assistance. But, this fall, I had an opportunity to visit . . . Southeast Asia and I think we would be making a tremendous mistake to cut this money out of the bill.

Many of us feel that the United States has concentrated its attention too much on Western Europe. We will spend several billions for Western Europe in this bill. Yet, here is an area, Asia, where the Communists are attempting to seize control, where the money is to be spent among several hundred million people, and where the tide of events has been moving against us.

The Communists are now the second largest party in India. . . . The life expectancy of people in India is twenty-six or twenty-seven years, and they are increasing at the rate of five million a year—at a rate much faster than the available food supply.

The Communists have a chance of seizing all of Asia in the next five or six years. What weapons do we have that will stop them? The most effective is technical assistance. The amount of money involved here is not sufficient to prevent their being attracted to the Communists. But it gives them some hope, at least, that their problems can be solved without turning to the Communists. We are planning to spend a very large amount of money in this area for military assistance, which is of secondary importance compared to this program. To cut technical assistance when the Communists are concentrating their efforts in this vital area seems to me a costly and great mistake.

Debate, Technical Assistance Appropriations Bill
House of Representatives
Washington, D.C., June 28, 1952

The Challenge of Imperialism: Algeria

Mr. President, the most powerful single force in the world today is neither communism nor capitalism, neither the H-bomb nor the guided missile—it is man's eternal desire to be free and independent. The great enemy of that tremendous force of freedom is called, for want of a more precise term, imperialism—and today that means Soviet imperialism and, whether we like it or not, and though they are not to be equated, Western imperialism.

Thus the single most important test of American foreign policy today is how we meet the challenge of imperialism, what we do to further man's desire to be free. On this test more than any other, this nation shall be critically judged by the uncommitted millions in Asia and Africa, and anxiously watched by the still-hopeful lovers of freedom behind the Iron Curtain. If we fail to meet the challenge of either Soviet or Western imperialism, then no amount of foreign aid, no aggrandizement of armaments, no new pacts or doctrines or high-level conferences, can prevent further setbacks to our course and to our security. . . .

There are many cases of the clash between independence and imperialism in the Western world that demand our attention. But again, one, above all the rest, is critically outstanding today—Algeria. . . .

Mr. President, the war in Algeria confronts the United States with its most critical diplomatic impasse since the crisis in Indochina—and yet we have not only failed to meet the problem forthrightly and effectively, we have refused to even recognize that it is our problem at all. No issue poses a more difficult challenge to our foreign-policy makers—and no issue has been more woefully neglected. Though I am somewhat reluctant to undertake the kind of public review of this case which I had hoped—when I first began an intensive study of the problem fifteen months ago—that the State Department might provide to the Congress and people, the Senate is, in my opinion, entitled to receive the answers to the basic questions involved in this crisis.

I am even more reluctant to appear critical of our oldest and first ally, whose assistance in our own war for independence will never be forgotten and whose role in the course of world events has traditionally been one of constructive leadership and cooperation. I do not want our policy to be anti-French any more than I want it to be antinationalist—and I am convinced that growing numbers of the French people, whose patience and endurance we must all salute, are coming to realize that the views expressed in this speech are, in the long run, in their own best interest.

I say nothing today that has not been said by responsible leaders of French opinion and by a growing number of the French people themselves.

Algeria is no longer a problem for the French alone—nor will it ever be again. . . . We have deceived ourselves into believing that we have thus pleased both sides and displeased no one with this head-in-the-sands policy.

American and French diplomats, it must be noted at the outset, have joined in saying for several years that Algeria is not even a proper subject for American foreign policy debates or world consideration—that it is wholly a matter of internal French concern, a provincial uprising, a crisis which will respond satisfactorily to local anesthesia. But whatever the original truth of these clichés may have been, the blunt facts of the matter today are that the changing face of African nationalism, and the ever-widening by-products of the growing crisis, have made Algeria a matter of international, and consequently American, concern.

The war in Algeria, engaging more than 400,000 French soldiers, has stripped the continental forces of NATO to the bone. It has dimmed Western hopes for a European common market, and seriously compromised the liberalizing reforms of OEEC, by causing France to impose new import restrictions under a wartime economy. It has repeatedly been appealed for discussion to the United Nations, where our equivocal remarks and opposition to its consideration have damaged our leadership and prestige in that body. It has undermined our relations with Tunisia and Morocco, who naturally have a sense of common cause with the aims of Algerian leaders, and who have felt proper grievance that our economic and military base settlements have heretofore required clearance with a French government now taking economic reprisal for their assistance to Algerian nationalism.

It has diluted the effective strength of the Eisenhower doctrine for the Middle East, and our foreign aid and information programs. It has endangered the continuation of some of our most strategic airbases, and threatened our geographical advantages over the Communist orbit. It has affected our standing in the eyes of the free world, our leadership in the fight to keep that world free, our prestige, and our security; as well as our moral leadership in the fight against Soviet imperialism in the countries behind the Iron Curtain. It has furnished powerful ammunition to anti-Western propagandists throughout Asia and the Middle East—and will be the most troublesome item facing the October conference in Accra of the free nations of Africa, who hope, by easing the transition to independence of other African colonies, to seek common paths by which that great continent can remain aligned with the West.

Finally, the war in Algeria has steadily drained the manpower, the resources, and the spirit of one of our oldest and most important allies —a nation whose strength is absolutely vital to the free world, but who has been forced by this exhausting conflict to postpone new reforms and social services at home, to choke important new plans for economic and political development in French West Africa, the Sahara, and in a united Europe, to face a consolidated domestic Communist movement at a time when communism is in retreat elsewhere in Europe, to stifle free journalism and criticism, and to release the anger and frustrations of its people in perpetual governmental instability and in a precipitous attack on Suez.

No, Algeria is no longer a problem for the French alone—nor will it ever be again. And though their sensitivity to its consideration by this nation or the UN is understandable, a full and frank discussion of an issue so critical to our interests as well as theirs ought to be valued on both sides of an Atlantic alliance that has any real meaning and solidarity.

This is not to say that there is any value in the kind of discussion which has characterized earlier U.S. consideration of this and similar problems—tepid encouragement and moralizations to both sides, cautious neutrality on all real issues, and a restatement of our obvious dependence upon our European friends, our obvious dedication nevertheless to the principles of self-determination, and our obvious desire not to become involved. We have deceived ourselves into believing that we have thus pleased both sides and displeased no one with this head-in-the-sands policy—when, in truth, we have earned the suspicion of all.

It is time, therefore, that we came to grips with the real issues which confront us in Algeria—the issues which can no longer be avoided in the UN or in NATO—issues which become more and more difficult of solution, as a bitter war seemingly without end destroys, one by one, the ever fewer bridgeheads of reasonable settlement that remain. With each month the situation becomes more taut, the extremists gain more and more power on both the French and Algerian sides. . . .

Instead of recognizing France's refusal to bargain in good faith with nationalist leaders or to grant the reforms earlier promised, our ambassador to the UN, Mr. Lodge, in his statement this year as previously, and our former ambassador to Paris, Mr. Dillon, in his statement last year apparently representing the highest administration policy, both expressed firm faith in the French government's handling of the entire matter. . . .

This is not a record to view with pride as Independence Day approaches. No matter how complex the problems posed by the Algerian issue may be, the record of the United States in this case is, as elsewhere, a retreat from the principles of independence and anticolonialism, regardless of what diplomatic niceties, legal technicalities, or even strategic considerations are offered in its defense. . . .

Terrorism must be combated, not condoned, it is said; it is not right to "negotiate with murderers." Yet once again this is a problem which neither postponement nor attempted conquest can solve. The fever chart of every successful revolution—including, of course, the French—reveals a rising temperature of terrorism and counterterrorism; but this does not of itself invalidate the legitimate goals that fired the original revolution. Most political revolutions—including our own—have been buoyed by outside aid in men, weapons, and ideas. Instead of abandoning African nationalism to the anti-Western agitators and Soviet agents who hope to capture its leadership, the United States, a product of political revolution, must redouble its efforts to earn the respect and friendship of nationalist leaders. . . .

The most important reason we have sided with the French in Algeria and North Africa is our reluctance to antagonize a traditional friend and important ally in her hour of crisis. . . .

The United States and other Western allies poured money and material into Indochina in a hopeless attempt to save for the French a land that did not want to be saved, in a war in which the enemy was both everywhere and nowhere at the same time.

Yet, did we not learn in Indochina, where we delayed action as the result of similar warnings, that we might have served both the French and our own causes infinitely better, had we taken a more firm stand much earlier than we did? Did that tragic episode not teach us that, whether France likes it or not, admits it or not, or has our support or not, their oversea territories are sooner or later, one by one, inevitably going to break free and look with suspicion on the Western nations who impeded their steps to independence? In the words of Turgot: "Colonies are like fruit which cling to the tree only till they ripen."

I want to emphasize that I do not fail to appreciate the difficulties of our hard-pressed French allies. It staggers the imagination to realize that France is one nation that has been in a continuous state of war since 1939—against the Axis, then in Syria, in Indochina, in Morocco, in Tunisia, in Algeria. It has naturally not been easy for most Frenchmen to watch the successive withdrawals from Damascus, Hanoi, Saigon, Pondicherry, Tunis, and Rabat. With each departure a grand myth has been more and more deflated. But the problem is no longer to save a myth of French empire. The problem is to save the French nation, as well as free Africa. . . .

Not only the French, however, needed to be convinced of the ultimate futility and cost of an Algerian-type struggle. The United States and other Western allies poured money and material into Indochina in a hopeless attempt to save for the French a land that did not want to be saved, in a war in which the enemy was both everywhere and nowhere at the same time, as I pointed out to the Congress on several occasions. We accepted for years the predictions that victory was just around the corner, the promises that Indochina would soon be set free, the arguments that this was a question for the French alone.

And even after we had witnessed the tragic consequences of our vacillation, in terms of not only Communist gains but the decimation of French military strength and political effectiveness, we still listened to the same predictions, the same promises, and the same arguments in Tunisia and Morocco. The strong pro-Western bent in each of these countries today, despite beguiling offers from the Communist East, is a tribute to the leadership of such men as Prime Minister Bourguiba, whose years in French confinement never dimmed his appreciation of Western democratic values. . . .

The time has come when our government must recognize that this is no longer a French problem alone; and that the time has passed, where a series of piecemeal adjustments, or even a last attempt to incorporate Algeria fully within France, can succeed. The time has come for the United States to face the harsh realities of the situation and to fulfill its responsibilities as leader of the free world—in the UN, in NATO, in the administration of our aid programs and in the exercise of our diplomacy—in shaping a course toward political independence for Algeria.

It should not be the purpose of our government to impose a solution on either side, but to make a contribution toward breaking the vicious circle in which the Algerian controversy whirls. . . .

The United States must be prepared to lend all efforts to such a settlement, and to assist in the economic problems which will flow from it. This is not a burden which we lightly or gladly assume. But our efforts in no other endeavor are more important in terms of once again seizing the initiative in foreign affairs, demonstrating our adherence to the principles of national independence, and winning the respect of those long suspicious of our negative and vacillating record on colonial issues.

It is particularly important, inasmuch as Hungary will be a primary issue at the United Nations meeting this fall, that the United States clear the air and take a clear position on this issue, on which we have been vulnerable in the past. And we must make it abundantly clear to the French as well as the North Africans that we seek no economic advantages for ourselves in that area, no opportunities to replace French economic ties or exploit African resources.

If we are to secure the friendship of the Arab, the African, and the Asian—and we must, despite what Mr. Dulles says about our not being in a popularity contest—we cannot hope to accomplish it solely by means of billion-dollar foreign-aid programs. We cannot win their hearts by making them dependent upon our handouts. Nor can we keep them free by selling them free enterprise, by describing the perils of communism or the prosperity of the United States, or limiting our dealings to military pacts. No, the strength of our appeal to these key populations—and it is rightfully our appeal, and not that of the Communists—lies in our traditional and deeply felt philosophy of freedom and independence for all peoples everywhere.

Perhaps it is already too late for the United States to save the West from total catastrophe in Algeria. Perhaps it is too late to abandon our negative policies on these issues, to repudiate the decades of anti-Western suspicion, to press firmly but boldly for a new generation of friendship among equal and independent states. But we dare not fail to make the effort.

"Men's hearts wait upon us," said Woodrow Wilson in 1913. "Men's lives hang in the balance; men's hopes call upon us to say what we will do. Who shall live up to the great trust? Who dares fail to try?"

United States Senate
Washington, D.C., July 2, 1957

The New Nationalism: India

Mr. President, at no time since the war has American and Western policy been so gripped by a sense of paralysis, by a waning of hope, by the loss of its compass points. More and more the thoughts of those abroad—and of Americans themselves—have been riveted on Russia's capabilities, on Russia's educational system and educational achievements, on Russia's new diplomatic and economic initiatives, on Russia's seemingly greater flexibility and power of maneuver. Less and less have we and our allies been concerned with our own capacities, our own positive objectives. . . . The uneasiness which has stirred even our closest friends is directed not against a President or secretary of state or party. In very large measure it attaches to the whole tone and thrust of our national effort in foreign policy. Indeed, we have come increasingly to doubt ourselves, to question the impact of a policy whose substance seems so very largely military, to scrutinize actions whose origins very often were in reflex to Soviet moves and transitory crises rather than rooted in a settled policy of our own.

Our sense of drift, our gnawing dissatisfaction, our seemingly hopeless predicament in reaching but the fringes of a great crisis is nowhere more evident than in our search for policies adopted effectively and concretely to the new and generally uncommitted nations which run from Casablanca to the Celebes. Over the past few years we have begun to appreciate that the tested formulas we have applied to events in Western Europe and NATO have only limited application to the broad medley of changes occurring in the uncommitted world. Though we have learned that we must come to terms with the new nationalisms, we have tended to interpret their meanings too much against the backdrop of our own historic experience on this continent and in Europe.

We have certainly begun to learn that a purely military response to the tides in the Middle East and Asia is an illusory breakwater. For military pacts and arms shipments, though sometimes a necessary instrument of national policy, are themselves new divisive forces in those areas shot through with national and regional rivalries and often lacking historic boundaries and allegiances. . . .

No thoughtful citizen can fail to see our stake in the survival of free government in India. India stands as the only effective competitor to China for the faith and following of the millions of uncommitted and restless peoples. Should India fall prey to internal disorder or disillusionment among either its masses or [its] leaders and become absorbed in the Communist system, the free world would suffer an incalculable blow. . . .

Let us not be confused by talk of Indian neutrality. Let us remember that our nation also during the period of its formative growth adopted a policy of noninvolvement in the great international controversies of the nineteenth century. Nothing serves the ultimate interests of all of the West better than the opportunity for the emergent uncommitted nations of the world to absorb the primary energies now in programs of real economic improvement.

This is the only basis on which Asian and African nations can find the political balance and social stability which provide the true defense against Communist penetration. Our friendships should not be equated with military alliances or "voting the Western ticket." To do so only drives these countries closer to totalitarianism or polarizes the world in such a way as to increase rather than diminish the chances for local war. . . .

India, for better or worse, is a world power with a world audience. Its democratic future is delicately and dangerously poised; it would be catastrophic if its leadership were now humiliated in its quest for Western assistance when its cause is good.

There is no visible political glory for either party in coming to the aid of India, particularly at a time of high taxes and pressing defense needs. The task of selling such a program to the American people is far more difficult than that of a decade ago, for we were more familiar with the people and problems of Europe, our ties were closer, their economies were more directly aligned with our own and held more certain promise of success. But the need—and the danger—are as great now as then. India today represents as great a hope, as commanding a challenge as Western Europe did in 1947—and our people are still, I am confident, equal to the effort.

I realize that it is difficult to give resonance to such words and proposals in the mood which has governed the approach to foreign aid and economic policy in both parties during the past sessions of Congress. But this mood has, in part, been induced by the persistent counsels of caution, by the lack of vision and purposefulness with which we have approached the problems of the underdeveloped world. If we are to break the aimless drifts and deadlocks in policy, if we are to regain the initiative in world affairs, if we are to arouse the decent emotions of Americans, it is time again that we seek projects with the power of stirring and rallying our hopes and energies. Once again our national interest and creative magnanimity can merge in the service of freedom.

United States Senate
Washington, D.C., March 25, 1958

The Fight for Foreign Aid

In recent years, the scale of our effort in foreign economic policy has been based upon what the administration considered to be the requirements of the domestic budgetary and political situation.

It is time now for that effort to be based upon the requirements of the international economic situation—and our own national security. Let us see exactly what is needed, when it is needed, how much of it must come from this country, and how much it will cost.

And then let us enact the program that will do the job. To do less than is needed is just as wasteful as to do more than is needed. To put it off is just as dangerous as refusing to do it at all. . . .

Congress should, of course, base its aid programs on sound criteria and productive investment. But let us remember economies need time to mature. Our own nation, in the days of its youth, sold railroad bonds to the British and other Europeans—and these were long forty- or fifty-year debentures. With the growth of our productive capacity, we gradually became a creditor nation with the ability to repay these foreign investments. . . .

I am confident that this nation can recover the initiative, that we can give to a doubting world the realization that we, and not Russia and China, can help them achieve stability and growth. We cannot be content merely to oppose what the Kremlin may propose, nor can we pretend that the East-West conflict is the only basis for our policy.

Above all, we must not resolve these difficult issues of foreign aid by perpetual postponement and compromise. There are times when it is far better to do the right thing as a result of debate and sacrifice than the wrong thing as a testimonial to national unity.

In short, it is our job to prove that we can devote as much energy, intelligence, idealism, and sacrifice to the survival and triumph of the open society as the Russian despots can extort by compulsion in defense of their closed system of tyranny. We can give a convincing demonstration that we have not a propaganda or crisis interest but an enduring long-term interest in the productive economic growth of the less developed nations. We can finally make it clear to ourselves that international economic development is not, somehow, a nagging responsibility, to be faced each year in the context of giveaways and taxes —but a vast international effort, an enterprise of positive association, which lies close to the heart of our relations with the whole free world and which requires active American leadership.

There are times when it is far better to do the right thing as a result of debate and sacrifice than the wrong thing as a testimonial to national unity.

As a nation, we think not of war but of peace; not of crusades of conflict but of covenants of cooperation; not of the pageantry of imperialism but of the pride of new states freshly risen to independence. We like to look, with Mr. Justice Holmes, beyond the vision of battling races and an impoverished earth to catch a dreaming glimpse of peace. In the words of Edmund Burke, we sit on a "conspicuous stage," and the whole world marks our demeanor. In this year and in this Congress we have an opportunity to be worthy of that role.

United States Senate
Washington, D.C., February 19, 1959

The Frontiers of Freedom

. . . No amount of arms and armies can help stabilize those governments which are unable or unwilling to achieve social and economic reform and development. Military pacts cannot help nations whose social injustice and economic chaos invite insurgency and penetration and subversion. The most skillful counterguerrilla efforts cannot succeed where the local population is too caught up in its own misery to be concerned about the advance of communism.

But for those who share this view, we stand ready now, as we have in the past, to provide generously of our skills, and our capital, and our food to assist the peoples of the less developed nations to reach their goals in freedom—to help them before they are engulfed in crisis.

This is also our great opportunity in 1961. If we grasp it, then subversion to prevent its success is exposed as an unjustifiable attempt to keep these nations from being either free or equal. But if we do not pursue it, and if they do not pursue it, the bankruptcy of unstable governments . . . and of unfilled hopes will surely lead to a series of totalitarian receiverships. . . .

I do not see how anyone who is concerned—as we all are—about the growing threats to freedom around the globe—and who is asking what more we can do as a people—can weaken or oppose the single most important program available for building the frontiers of freedom. . . .

The main burden of local defense against local attack, subversion, insurrection, or guerrilla warfare must of necessity rest with local forces. Where these forces have the necessary will and capacity to cope with such threats, our intervention is rarely necessary or helpful. Where the will is present and only capacity is lacking, our Military Assistance Program can be of help.

But this program, like economic assistance, needs a new emphasis. It cannot be extended without regard to the social, political, and military reforms essential to internal respect and stability. The equipment and training provided must be tailored to legitimate local needs and to our own foreign and military policies, not to our supply of military stocks or a local leader's desire for military display.

Special Address to Congress
The Capitol, Washington, D.C.
May 25, 1961

The Uncommitted and Underdeveloped

It is always encouraging when responsible world leaders join together to consider the problems that beset mankind. We recognize that most of the countries at Belgrade do not consider themselves committed on certain of the issues which confront us today, but we do know that they are committed to the United Nations Charter. The people of the United States share this commitment.

We know that those gathering in Belgrade are committed to finding a way to halt the waste of the earth's resources in the building of the implements of death and destruction, and the people of the United States have constantly pledged themselves to this goal.

We believe that the peoples represented at this conference are committed to a world society in which men have the right and the freedom to determine their own destiny, a world in which one people is not enslaved by the other, in which the powerful do not devour the weak. The American people share that commitment, and we have pledged the influence of this nation to the abolition of exploitation in all of its forms.

The peoples represented at Belgrade are committed to achieving a world at peace in which nations have the freedom to choose their own political and economic systems and to live their own way of life, and since our earliest beginnings this nation has shared that commitment.

All this and much more the leaders at Belgrade have in common. This and much more the people of the United States have in common with them. So for myself, and I'm sure for the American people, I express the hope that their deliberations there will bring us all nearer these goals.

Message to Belgrade Conference on Nonaligned States
Washington, D.C., August 30, 1961

Today, many Americans tend to think of developing underdeveloped countries in terms only of faraway nations. But in 1863, even measured by 1963 dollars, our own per capita income—and this should be a source of encouragement to many who are laboring with the problem of underdevelopment in far-off countries—our own per capita income was less than one dollar a day, approximately the same as Chile's. Nearly sixty percent of our labor force was engaged in agriculture, the same percentage as is today engaged in the Philippines. An estimated twenty percent of our population was illiterate, the same percentage of the population of Ceylon. Only one fifth of our 34 million people lived in towns or cities of over 5,000 in population, as is roughly true now of Turkey. In 1863, this nation had fewer railroad tracks laid than India has today, and its children had a shorter life expectancy than a child born this year in Thailand or Zanzibar.

American Bankers Association
Symposium on Economic Growth
Washington, D.C., February 25, 1963

The Future Prime Ministers

I want to welcome all of you to the White House and also to the United States. We appreciate very much your coming to this country and I am sure that you will teach us a good deal more than you can possibly learn here. . . . I am not sure it is possible to transfer the experience of any country to another country, particularly a country with inadequate resources and with inadequate skilled manpower. . . .

But . . . whatever differences there may be, what we are interested in, what I am most interested in, is the commitment to individual freedom which our country and your country permit, and the commitment to national independence. . . . I believe it is worthwhile for us to have the most intimate exchange of ideas and thoughts and hopes for the future.

So, we are very glad to have you here. I am confident I am talking to a number of future prime ministers, presidents, and others, and I just want you to know that, when you visit in that role a decade hence and the Kennedys are long gone, I am sure you will be equally welcome.

Remarks to foreign students visiting the White House
Washington, D.C., April 10, 1963

The Family of Man

I want to speak tonight very briefly . . . about the Family of Man beyond the United States. Just as the Family of Man is not limited to a single race or religion, neither can it be limited to a single city or country. The Family of Man is more than three billion strong. It lives in more than one hundred nations. Most of its members are not white. Most of them are not Christians. Most of them know nothing about free enterprise or due process of law or the Australian ballot.

If our society is to promote the Family of Man, let us realize the magnitude of our task. This is a sobering assignment. For the Family of Man in the world of today is not faring very well.

The members of a family should be at peace with one another, but they are not. And the hostilities are not confined to the great powers of the East and the West. On the contrary, the United States and the Soviet Union, each fully aware of [its] mutually destructive powers and [its] worldwide responsibilities and obligations, have on occasion sought to introduce a greater note of caution in their approach to areas of conflict.

Yet lasting peace between East and West would not bring peace to the Family of Man. Within the last month, the last four weeks, the world has witnessed active or threatened hostilities in a dozen or more disputes independent of the struggle between communism and the free world—disputes between Africans and Europeans in Angola, between North African neighbors in the Maghreb, between two Arab states over Yemen, between India and Pakistan, between Indonesia and Malaysia, Cambodia and Vietnam, Ethiopia and Somalia, and a long list of others.

In each of these cases of conflict, neither party can afford to divert to these needless hostilities the precious resources that their people require. In almost every case, the parties to these disputes have more in common ethnically and ideologically than do the Soviet Union and the United States, yet they often seem less able and less willing to get together and negotiate. In almost every case, their continuing conflict invites outside intervention and threatens worldwide escalation—yet the major powers are hard put to limit events in these areas.

As I said recently at the United Nations, even little wars are dangerous in this nuclear world. The long labor of peace is an undertaking for every nation, large and small, for every member of the Family of Man. In this effort none of us can remain unaligned. To this goal none can be uncommitted. If the Family of Man cannot achieve greater unity and harmony, the very planet which serves as its home may find its future in peril.

But there are other troubles besetting the human family. Many of its members live in poverty and misery and despair. More than one out of three, according to the FAO [Food and Agriculture Organization], suffers from malnutrition or undernutrition or both—while more than one in ten live "below the breadline." Two out of every five adults on this planet are, according to UNESCO, illiterate. One out of eight suffers from trachoma or lives in an area where malaria is still a clear and present danger. Ten million—nearly as many men, women, and children as inhabit this city and Los Angeles combined—still suffer from leprosy; and countless others suffer from yaws or tuberculosis or intestinal parasites.

If our society is to promote the Family of Man, let us realize the magnitude of our task. . . . For the Family of Man in the world of today is not faring very well.

For the blessings of life have not been distributed evenly to the Family of Man. Life expectancy in this most fortunate of nations has reached the biblical three score years and ten; but in the less developed nations of Africa, Asia, and Latin America, the overwhelming majority of infants cannot expect to live even two score years and five. In those vast continents, more than half of the children of primary school age are not in school. More than half the families live in substandard dwellings. More than half the people live on less than a thousand dollars a year. Two out of every three adults are illiterate.

The Family of Man can survive differences of race and religion. Contrary to the assertions of Mr. Khrushchev, it can accept differences of ideology, politics, and economics. But it cannot survive, in the form in which we know it, a nuclear war—and neither can it long endure the growing gulf between the rich and the poor.

The rich must help the poor. The industrialized nations must help the developing nations. And the United States, along with its allies, must do better—not worse—by its foreign-aid program, which is now being subjected to such intense debate in the Senate of the United States.

Too often we advance the need of foreign aid only in terms of our economic self-interest. To be sure, foreign aid is in our economic self-interest. It provides more than a half a million jobs for workers in every state. It finances a rising share of our exports and builds new and growing export markets. It generates the purchase of military and civilian equipment by other governments in this country. It makes possible the stationing of three and a half million troops along the Communist periphery at a price one tenth the cost of maintaining a comparable number of American soldiers. And it helps to stave off the kind of chaos or Communist takeover or Communist attack that would surely demand our critical and costly attention. The Korean conflict alone, forgetting for a moment the thousands of Americans who lost their lives, cost four times as much as our total worldwide aid budget for the current year. . . .

This is not a partisan matter. For seventeen years, through three administrations, this program has been supported by presidents and leaders of both parties. It is being supported today in the Congress by those in leadership on both sides of the aisle who recognize the urgency of this program in the achievement of peace and freedom. Yet there are still those who are unable or unwilling to accept these simple facts—who find it politically convenient to denounce foreign aid on the one hand, and in the same sentence to denounce the Communist menace. I do not say that there have been no mistakes in aid administration. I do not say it has purchased for us lasting popularity or servile satellites. I do say it is one essential instrument in the creation of a better, more peaceful world. I do say that it has substituted strength for weakness all over the globe, encouraging nations struggling to be free to stand on their own two feet. And I do not say that, merely because others may not bear their share of the burden, that is any excuse for the United States not to meet its responsibility.

To those who say foreign aid has been a failure, how can we measure success—by the economic viability of fourteen nations in Western Europe, Japan, Spain, Lebanon, where our economic aid, after having completed its task, has ended; by the refusal of a single one of the more than fifty new members of the United Nations to go the Communist route; by the reduction of malaria in India, for example, from 75 million cases to 2,000; by the 18,000 classrooms and 4 million textbooks bringing learning to Latin America under the infant Alliance for Progress?

Nearly two years ago my wife and I visited Bogotá, Colombia, where a vast new Alliance for Progress housing project was just getting under way. Earlier this year I received a letter from the first resident of this twelve hundred new home development. "Now," he wrote, "we have dignity and liberty."

Dignity and liberty—these words are the foundation, as they have been since '47, of the mutual security program. . . .

I think we can meet those obligations. I think we can afford to fulfill these commitments around the world when ninety percent of them are used to purchase goods and services here in the United States, including, for example, one third of this nation's total fertilizer exports, one fourth of our iron and steel exports around the world, one third of our locomotive exports. A cut of $1 billion in our total foreign aid program may save $100 million in our balance of payments—but it costs us $900 million in exports.

I think the American people are willing to shoulder this burden. Contrary to repeated warnings . . . I know of no single officeholder who was ever defeated because he supported this program. The burden is less today than ever before. . . .

Many members of Congress today complain that four percent of our federal budget is too much to devote to foreign aid—yet in 1951 that program amounted to nearly twenty percent of our budget—twenty percent in 1951, and four percent today. They refuse today to vote more than $4 billion to this effort—yet in 1951, when this country was not nearly as well off, the Congress voted $8 billion to the same cause. They are fearful today of the effects of sending to other people seven tenths of one percent of our gross national product—but in 1951 we devoted nearly four times that proportion to this purpose. . . .

This Congress has already reduced this year's aid budget $600 million below the amount recommended by the Clay committee. Is this nation stating it cannot afford to spend an additional $600 million to help the developing nations of the world become strong and free and independent—an amount less than this country's annual outlay for lipstick, face cream, and chewing gum? Are we saying that we cannot help nineteen needy neighbors in Latin America and do as much for the nineteen as the Communist bloc is doing for the island of Cuba alone?

Some say that they are tiring of this task or tired of world problems and their complexities, or tired of hearing those who receive our aid disagree with us. But are we tired of living in a free world? Do we expect that world overnight to be like the United States? Are we going to stop now merely because we have not produced complete success?

I do not believe our adversaries are tired and I cannot believe that the United States of America in 1963 is fatigued.

Surely the Americans of the 1960s can do half as well as the Americans of the 1950s. Surely we are not going to throw away our hopes and means for peaceful progress in an outburst of irritation and frustration. I do not want it said of us what T. S. Eliot said of others some years ago: "These were a decent people. Their only monument: the asphalt road and a thousand lost golf balls."

I think we can do better than that. . . .

It is essential, in short, that the word go forth from the United States to all who are concerned about the future of the Family of Man; that we are not weary in well-doing. And we shall, I am confident, if we maintain the pace, in due season reap the kind of world we deserve and deserve the kind of world we will have.

Remarks upon receiving Annual Family of Man Award
New York Protestant Council
New York, New York, November 8, 1963

The Alliance for Progress

One hundred and thirty-nine years ago this week the United States, stirred by the heroic struggle of its fellow Americans, urged the independence and recognition of the new Latin American republics. It was then, at the dawn of freedom throughout this hemisphere, that Bolívar spoke of his desire to see the Americas fashioned into the greatest region in the world, "greatest," he said, "not so much by virtue of her area and her wealth, as by her freedom and her glory."

Never in the long history of our hemisphere has this dream been nearer to fulfillment, and never has it been in greater danger.

The genius of our scientists has given us the tools to bring abundance to our land, strength to our industry, and knowledge to our people. For the first time we have the capacity to strike off the remaining bonds of poverty and ignorance—to free our people for the spiritual and intellectual fulfillment which has always been the goal of our civilization.

Yet at this very moment of maximum opportunity, we confront the same forces which have imperiled America throughout its history. . . .

We meet together as firm and ancient friends, united by history and experience and by our determination to advance the values of American civilization. For this New World of ours is not a mere accident of geography. Our continents are bound together by a common history, the endless exploration of new frontiers. Our nations are the product of a common struggle, the revolt from colonial rule. And our people share a common heritage, the quest for the dignity and the freedom of man.

The revolutions which gave us birth ignited, in the words of Thomas Paine, "a spark never to be extinguished." And across vast, turbulent continents these American ideals still stir man's struggle for national independence and individual freedom. But as we welcome the spread of the American revolution to other lands, we must also remember that our own struggle—the revolution which began in Philadelphia in 1776, and in Caracas in 1811—is not yet finished. Our hemisphere's mission is not yet completed. For our unfulfilled task is to demonstrate to the entire world that man's unsatisfied aspiration for economic progress and social justice can best be achieved by free men working within a framework of democratic institutions. If we can do this in our own hemisphere, and for our own people, we may yet realize the prophecy of the great Mexican patriot, Benito Juárez, that "democracy is the destiny of future humanity."

As a citizen of the United States let me be the first to admit that we North Americans have not always grasped the significance of this common mission, just as it is also true that many in your own countries have not fully understood the urgency of the need to lift people from poverty and ignorance and despair. But we must turn from these mistakes—from the failures and the misunderstandings of the past to a future full of peril but bright with hope.

Throughout Latin America, a continent rich in resources and in the spiritual and cultural achievements of its people, millions of men and women suffer the daily degradations of poverty and hunger. They lack decent shelter or protection from disease. Their children are deprived of the education or the jobs which are the gateway to a better life. Each day the problems grow more urgent. Population growth is outpacing economic growth—low living standards are further endangered—and discontent, the discontent of a people who know that abundance and the tools of progress are at last within their reach, is growing. In the words of José Figueres, "once dormant peoples are struggling upward toward the sun, toward a better life."

If we are to meet a problem so staggering in its dimensions, our approach must itself be equally bold—an approach consistent with the majestic concept of Operation Pan America. Therefore I have called on all people of the hemisphere to join in a new Alliance for Progress—*Alianza para el Progreso*—a vast cooperative effort, unparalleled in magnitude and nobility of purpose, to satisfy the basic needs of the American people for homes, work and land, health and schools—*techo, trabajo y tierra, salud y escuela.*

First, I propose that the American republics begin on a vast new Ten Year Plan for the Americas, a plan to transform the 1960s into a historic decade of democratic progress.

These ten years will be the years of maximum progress, maximum effort, the years when the greatest obstacles must be overcome, the years when the need for assistance will be the greatest.

If we are successful, if our effort is bold enough and determined enough, then the close of this decade will mark the beginning of a new era in the American experience. The living standards of every American family will be on the rise, basic education will be available to all, hunger will be a forgotten experience, the need for massive outside help will have passed, most nations will have entered a period of self-sustaining growth, and though there will be still much to do, every American republic will be the master of its own revolution and its own hope and progress.

Let me stress that only the most determined efforts of the American nations themselves can bring success to this effort. They, and they alone, can mobilize their resources, enlist the energies of their people, and modify their social patterns so that all, and not just a privileged few, share in the fruits of growth. If this effort is made, then outside assistance will give vital impetus to progress; without it, no amount of help will advance the welfare of the people.

Thus if the countries of Latin America are ready to do their part, and I am sure they are, then I believe the United States, for its part, should help provide resources of a scope and magnitude sufficient to make this bold development plan a success—just as we helped to provide, against equal odds nearly, the resources adequate to help rebuild the economies of Western Europe. For only an effort of towering dimensions can insure fulfillment of our plan for a decade of progress.

Therefore I have called on all people of the hemisphere to join in a new Alliance for Progress*—Alianza para el Progreso *—a vast cooperative effort, unparalleled in magnitude and nobility of purpose.

Secondly, I will shortly request a ministerial meeting of the Inter-American Economic and Social Council, a meeting at which we can begin the massive planning effort which will be at the heart of the Alliance for Progress.

For if our Alliance is to succeed, each Latin nation must formulate long-range plans for its own development, plans which establish targets and priorities, insure monetary stability, establish the machinery for vital social change, stimulate private activity and initiative, and provide for a maximum national effort. These plans will be the foundation of our development effort, and the basis for the allocation of outside resources.

A greatly strengthened IA-ECOSOC, working with the Economic Commission for Latin America and the Inter-American Development Bank, can assemble the leading economists and experts of the hemisphere to help each country develop its own development plan—and provide a continuing review of economic progress in this hemisphere.

Third, I have this evening signed a request to the Congress for $500 million as a first step in fulfilling the Act of Bogotá. This is the first large-scale inter-American effort, instituted by my predecessor President Eisenhower, to attack the social barriers which block economic progress. The money will be used to combat illiteracy, improve the productivity and use of their land, wipe out disease, attack archaic tax and land tenure structures, provide educational opportunities, and offer a broad range of projects designed to make the benefits of increasing abundance available to all. We will begin to commit these funds as soon as they are appropriated.

Fourth, we must support all economic integration which is a genuine step toward larger markets and greater competitive opportunity. The fragmentation of Latin American economies is a serious barrier to industrial growth. Projects such as the Central American common market and free trade areas in South America can help to remove these obstacles.

Fifth, the United States is ready to cooperate in serious, case-by-case examinations of commodity market problems. Frequent violent change in commodity prices seriously injure the economies of many Latin American countries, draining their resources and stultifying their growth. Together we must find practical methods of bringing an end to this pattern.

Sixth, we will immediately step up our Food for Peace emergency program, help establish food reserves in areas of recurrent drought, help provide school lunches for children, and offer feed grains for use in rural development. For hungry men and women cannot wait for economic discussions or diplomatic meetings—their need is urgent and their hunger rests heavily on the conscience of their fellow men.

Seventh, all the people of the hemisphere must be allowed to share in the expanding wonders of science—wonders which have captured man's imagination, challenged the powers of his mind, and given him the tools for rapid progress. I invite Latin American scientists to work with us in new projects in fields such as medicine and agriculture, physics and astronomy, and desalinization, to help plan for regional research laboratories in these and other fields, and to strengthen cooperation between American universities and laboratories.

We also intend to expand our science-teacher training programs to include Latin American instructors, to assist in establishing such programs in other American countries, and translate and make available revolutionary new teaching materials in physics, chemistry, biology, and mathematics, so that the young of all nations may contribute their skills to the advance of science.

Eighth, we must rapidly expand the training of those needed to man the economies of rapidly developing countries. This means expanded technical training programs, for which the Peace Corps, for example, will be available when needed. It also means assistance to Latin American universities, graduate schools, and research institutes.

We welcome proposals in Central America for intimate cooperation in higher education—cooperation which can achieve a regional effort of increased effectiveness and excellence. We are ready to help fill the gap in trained manpower, realizing that our ultimate goal must be a basic education for all who wish to learn.

Ninth, we reaffirm our pledge to come to the defense of any American nation whose independence is endangered. As its confidence in the collective security system of the OAS spreads, it will be possible to devote to constructive use a major share of those resources now spent on the instruments of war. Even now, as the government of Chile has said, the time has come to take the first steps toward sensible limitations of arms. And the new generation of military leaders has shown an increasing awareness that armies cannot only defend their countries—they can, as we have learned through our own Corps of Engineers, they can help to build them.

Tenth, we invite our friends in Latin America to contribute to the enrichment of life and culture in the United States. We need teachers of your literature and history and tradition, opportunities for our young people to study in your universities, access to your music, your art, and the thought of your great philosophers. For we know we have much to learn.

In this way you can help bring a fuller spiritual and intellectual life to the people of the United States—and contribute to understanding and mutual respect among the nations of the hemisphere.

With steps such as these, we propose to complete the revolution of the Americas, to build a hemisphere where all men can hope for a suitable standard of living, and all can live out their lives in dignity and in freedom.

To achieve this goal political freedom must accompany material progress. Our Alliance for Progress is an alliance of free governments, and it must work to eliminate tyranny from a hemisphere in which it has no rightful place. Therefore let us express our special friendship to the people of Cuba and the Dominican Republic—and the hope they will soon rejoin the society of free men, uniting with us in common effort.

This political freedom must be accompanied by social change. For unless necessary social reforms, including land and tax reform, are freely made—unless we broaden the opportunity for all of our people—unless the great mass of Americans share in increasing prosperity—then our alliance, our revolution, our dream, and our freedom will fail. But we call for social change by free men—change in the spirit of Washington and Jefferson, of Bolívar and San Martín and Martí—not change which seeks to impose on men tyrannies which we cast out a century and a half ago. Our motto is what it has always been—progress yes, tyranny no—*progreso sí, tiranía no!*

But our greatest challenge comes from within—the task of creating an American civilization where spiritual and cultural values are strengthened by an ever-broadening base of material advance—where, within the rich diversity of its own traditions, each nation is free to follow its own path toward progress.

The completion of our task will, of course, require the efforts of all governments of our hemisphere. But the efforts of governments alone will never be enough. In the end, the people must choose and the people must help themselves.

And so I say to the men and women of the Americas—to the *campesino* in the fields, to the *obrero* in the cities, to the *estudiante* in the schools—prepare your mind and heart for the task ahead—call forth your strength and let each devote his energies to the betterment of all, so that your children and our children in this hemisphere can find an ever richer and a freer life.

Let us once again transform the American continent into a vast crucible of revolutionary ideas and efforts—a tribute to the power of the creative energies of free men and women—an example to all the world that liberty and progress walk hand in hand. Let us once again awaken our American revolution until it guides the struggle of people everywhere—not with an imperialism of force or fear, but with the rule of courage and freedom and hope for the future of man.

Address to Latin American Diplomatic Corps
White House, Washington, D.C.
March 13, 1961

In 1934, one of the greatest of my predecessors, President Franklin Roosevelt, was the first President of the United States to visit this country. He came in pursuit of a new policy—the policy of the Good Neighbor. This policy based on the ideas of Bolívar and San Martín and Santander recognized the common interests of the American states. denied that any nation in this hemisphere had the right to impose its will on any other nation; and called for a great cooperative effort to strengthen the spirit of human liberty here in the Americas.

I am here today—the second American President to visit Colombia—in that same spirit. For our generation also has a new policy—*la Alianza para el Progreso.* Today again, that policy calls for a joint effort to protect and extend the values of our civilization—going beyond the Good Neighbor policy to a great unified attack on the problems of our age. Today again, we deny the right of any state to impose its will upon any other. And today again, these new policies are based upon the vision and the imagination of the great statesmen of Latin America. . . .

Bolívar, in a letter written when he was in exile, and the cause of liberty seemed dim, wrote: "The veil has been torn asunder. We have already seen the light and it is not our desire to be thrust back into the darkness." In our time the veil again has been torn asunder. The millions of our people who have lived in hopeless poverty—patiently suffering hunger, social injustice, and ignorance—have now glimpsed the hope of a better and more abundant life for themselves and their children. And they do not intend to be thrust back into darkness.

La Alianza para el Progreso is designed to transform this hope into a reality. It calls for a vast and immediate effort on the part of all the Americas to satisfy the basic needs of our people for work and land, and homes and schools. It expects within the next ten years—the Decade of Development—to be well on the way toward satisfying these basic needs.

Much has already been done since *la Alianza para el Progreso* was announced on March 13. And today at Techo I saw some of the results of this effort.

There President Lleras and I—in the presence of the families of hundreds of workers—dedicated a housing project in which more than 80,000 people will, for the first time, know what it will be like to live in a home in which they would want to raise their children. We also dedicated one of eighteen schools—in which 30,000 children, the most valuable asset of this hemisphere—will be given their opportunity to study and to learn, and to build their lives. . . .

Thus *la Alianza para el Progreso* is a program which is revolutionary in its dimensions. It calls for staggering efforts by us all and unprecedented changes by us all. It raises far-reaching aspirations and demands difficult sacrifices. And although we have already done much in a short time, we must do much more and act much more swiftly in the months to come. For on the success of the Alliance—on our success in this hemisphere—depends the future of that human dignity and national independence for which our forebears in every country of the hemisphere struggled.

After the American wars of independence, the President of Colombia, Santander, said: "Arms have given us independence; laws will give us freedom." These prophetic words indicate the history of our hemisphere. For our real progress has not come about through violence or tyranny, but under the guidance of democratic leaders who realized the great capacity of free society for peaceful change—men such as Franklin Roosevelt in my own country and your distinguished President in your country.

It is this knowledge and experience which is the great contribution of our nations to the other nations of the world. There are those who tell us that the only road to economic progress is by violent Communist revolution, followed by the complete subjection of man to the will of the state.

They come with banners proclaiming that they have new doctrines; that history is on their side. But, in reality, they bring a doctrine which is as old as the pharaohs of Egypt, and like the pharaohs of Egypt, doomed by history.

They promise free elections, and free speech, and freedom of religion. But once power is achieved, elections are eliminated, speech is stifled, and the worship of God is prohibited.

They pledge economic progress and increased human welfare. But they have been unable to fulfill these pledges and their failure is etched in the dramatic contrast between a free and powerful and prosperous Western Europe and the grim, drab poverty of Communist Eastern Europe, or the hunger of China, or the wall which separates West Berlin from East Berlin. The fact is that the wall and the rifle squads of the last twelve months have shown us again—if we did not need to be shown—that when such doctrines have had to face the united will of free men, they have been defeated.

We are a young and strong people. Our doctrines—the doctrines lit by the leaders of your country and mine—now burn brightly in Africa and Asia and wherever men struggle to be free. And here in our own hemisphere we have successfully resisted efforts to impose the despotisms of the Old World on the nations of the New.

Today we face the greatest challenge to the vitality of our American revolution. Millions of our people—scattered across a vast and rich continent—endure lives of misery. We must prove to them that free institutions can best answer their implacable demand for social justice, for food, for material welfare, and above all, for a new hope—for themselves and for their children. And in so proving the blessings of freedom in Latin America, we will be teaching the same lesson to a watchful and impatient world.

We in the United States have made many mistakes in our relations with Latin America. We have not always understood the magnitude of your problems, or accepted our share of responsibility for the welfare of the hemisphere. But we are committed in the United States—our will and our energy—to an untiring pursuit of that welfare and I have come to this country to reaffirm that dedication.

The leaders of Latin America, the industrialists and the landowners, are, I am sure, also ready to admit past mistakes and accept new responsibilities. For unless all of us are willing to contribute our resources to national development, unless all of us are prepared not merely to accept but initiate basic land and tax reforms, unless all of us take the lead in improving the welfare of our people, that leadership will be taken from us and the heritage of centuries of Western civilization will be consumed in a few months of violence.

This is the message I bring to those of us who are here tonight—and I am grateful that I have had an opportunity to be with you.

But I also want to talk to those beyond this dinner table, and beyond this room, and this old house. And that message is for the millions of people in a thousand cities and villages throughout the mountains and lands of our hemisphere. To all of them—to the workers, to the *campesi-*

nos on the farms, to the women who toil each day for the welfare of their children—to all we bring a message of hope. Every day, every hour, in my country and in this country, and in all the countries of this hemisphere, dedicated men and women are struggling to bring nearer the day when all have more to eat, and a decent roof over their heads, and schools for their children—when all will have a better and more abundant life to accompany that human dignity to which all men are entitled, and that love of freedom to which all of us are committed by our inheritance and our desire. And tonight, here in this old city, I pledge to you the commitment of the United States of America to that great cause.

State Dinner
Bogotá, Colombia, December 17, 1961

I want to tell you how welcome you are to the White House. I think this is the most extraordinary collection of talent, of human knowledge, that has ever been gathered together at the White House, with the possible exception of when Thomas Jefferson dined alone. . . .

I know that the Nobel prize does not have any geographic or national implications. Mr. Nobel in his will, in fact, made it very clear . . . that no attention would be paid to nationality. . . .

But I think we can take some satisfaction that this hemisphere . . . has permitted the happy pursuit of knowledge and of peace; and that over forty percent of the Nobel prizes in the last thirty years have gone to men and women in this hemisphere.

And of particular pleasure today is the fact that thirteen Nobel prizes for peace have gone to those who live in this hemisphere. . . .

So I hope that you will join me in drinking to the Nobel prize winners of this year and other years—and, perhaps more widely, to all those people everywhere whom they serve.

White House Dinner
Honoring Western Hemisphere Nobel Prize Winners
Washington, D.C., April 29, 1962

In 1825 a son of El Salvador and citizen of Central America—Antonio José Canas—the first minister accredited by the United Provinces of Central America to the United States, delivered an invitation to Secretary of State Henry Clay. He asked him to send representatives to the first Inter-American Congress at Panama, a meeting at which, he said, the struggling new nations of the hemisphere "might consider upon and adopt the best plan for defending the states of the New World from foreign aggression, and . . . raise them to that elevation of wealth and power, which, from their resources, they may attain."

Today, 138 years later, we are gathered in this theater in pursuit of those same goals: the preservation of our independence, the extension of freedom, and the elevation of the welfare of our citizens to a level as high as "from our resources" we can attain. And today I have come from the United States at the invitation of a Central America which, with Panama, is rapidly attaining a unity of purpose, effort and achievement which has been unknown since the dissolution of that earliest federation.

That early conference did not achieve all its goals. But from it flowed the dream and creation of Bolívar, Canas, and José Cecilio de Valle of Costa Rica—the dream which became the inter-American system . . . the most successful, the most fruitful, and the most enduring international order in the history of the world.

Every effort to reimpose the despotisms of the Old World on the people of the New has ultimately been beaten back. . . . This system has maintained an unmatched record of peaceful relations among its members. There have been occasional conflicts to mar this record. But nowhere else have nations lived as neighbors with so little hostility and warfare. And today the principles of nonintervention and the peaceful resolution of disputes have been so firmly imbedded in our tradition that the heroic democracy in which we meet today can pursue its national goals without an armed force to guard its frontiers. In few other spots in the world could this be said today.

We have not attained this strength by merely trying to protect what was already won, to preserve the gains of the past, to maintain the status quo. If these were our system's goals, it would inevitably have crumbled as old orders crumbled. Instead it has survived, prospered, and grown despite wars and revolutions, despite changing ideologies and changing technologies, despite shifts in power and shifts in wealth—because it has been itself an instrument of change, profound revolutionary change, which has molded the history of this hemisphere and shaped the thinking of men seeking freedom and dignity in all lands. . . .

In the two-year period beginning July 1, 1961, under programs supported by the United States as part of its contribution to the Alliance, almost 3,000 new classrooms will have been built in the nations represented here today; . . . 2 million more books to children hungry for learning.

In the fifty years following its creation, the inter-American system worked to establish the political equality and national dignity of all its members, to extend political democracy and to strengthen the principle that no nation should forcibly impose its will upon another. These goals have been largely met. The equality of sovereign states is accepted by all. Intervention and force have been renounced. Machinery of peaceful settlement has been strengthened. Democracy rules in most of our lands. It will ultimately prevail over the last vestiges of tyranny in every land in this hemisphere. . . .

Today we are faced not merely with the protection of new nations, but with the remolding of ancient societies—not only with the destruction of political enemies, but with the destruction of poverty, hunger, ignorance, and disease—not alone with the creation of national dignity but with the preservation of human dignity.

To meet this enormous challenge, the peoples of the Americas have fashioned an *Alianza para el Progreso,* an alliance in which all the American states have mobilized their resources and energies to secure land for the landless, education for those without schools, and a faster rate of economic growth within a society where all can share in the fruits of progress. Here in Central America we have already begun to move toward the goals of the *Alianza*. . . .

In the two-year period beginning July 1, 1961, under programs supported by the United States as part of its contribution to the Alliance, almost 3,000 new classrooms will have been built in the nations represented here today; almost a million new books have been distributed; and tomorrow we will begin to distribute more than *2 million more books to children hungry for learning*. But much more remains to be done.

Some 7,600 new homes will have been built during this two-year period under *Alianza* programs in these nations—but much more remains to be done.

Three quarters of a million children will have been fed, but many are still hungry.

Six thousand new teachers have been trained, as well as many thousands of agricultural workers, public health and other public administrators. Still more are needed.

Yet we cannot be, and I know none of us are, satisfied with the progress we have made. Peoples who have waited centuries for opportunity and dignity cannot wait much longer. And unless those of us now making an effort are willing to redouble our efforts, unless the rich are willing to use some of their riches more wisely, unless the privileged are willing to yield up their privileges to a common good, unless the young and the educated are given opportunities to use their education, and unless governments are willing to dedicate themselves tirelessly to the tasks of governing efficiently and developing swiftly, then, let us realize, our *Alianza* will fail, and with it will fail the society of free nations which our forefathers labored to build. . . .

At the very time that newly independent nations rise in the Caribbean, the people of Cuba have been forcibly compelled to submit to a new imperialism, more ruthless, more powerful, and more deadly in its pursuit of power than any that this hemisphere has ever known. Just when it was hoped that Cuba was about to enter upon a new era of democracy and social justice, the Soviet Union, through its Cuban puppets, absorbed the Cuban nation into its empire. . . .

I am hopeful that at this meeting we will again increase our capacity to prevent the infiltration of Cuban agents, money, and propaganda. We will build a wall around Cuba—not a wall of mortar or brick or barbed wire, but a wall of dedicated men determined to protect their freedom and their sovereignty. And in this effort, as in all the other necessary efforts, I can assure you the United States will play its full part and bear its full burden.

In 1822, Bolívar, the father of the inter-American system, said this: "United in heart, in spirit and in aims, this Continent . . . must raise its eyes . . . to peer into the centuries which lie ahead. It can then contemplate with pride those future generations of men, happy and free, enjoying to the full the blessings that heaven bestows on this earth, and recalling in their hearts the protectors and liberators of our day."

My friends and colleagues; today we meet, representing seven of the great republics of America, united in spirit and in aims. We are confident of our ultimate success in protecting our freedom, in raising the living standards of our citizens, in beginning a new era of hope in American history. Secure in that confidence, we, too, can look forward to other centuries knowing that our descendants may also gratefully recall in their hearts the "protectors and liberators" of our day.

Conference of Central American Republics
San José, Costa Rica, March 18, 1963

The New Nations of Africa

For almost a century the course of the European empire had moved southward—along the coast of Africa, and around the Cape of Good Hope to the east. With the discovery of America, the kings, the generals, and the traders turned westward, leaving Africa to become the neglected and undeveloped province of a few European nations.

Today, more than four centuries later, the work of Columbus is being reversed. The nations of the West once more look toward Africa. And Africa itself is struggling for the freedom and the economic progress which centuries of neglect have denied it.

But if the voyages of Columbus led to history's retreat from Africa, they also were the first step toward the emergence of modern Africa.

For it was in the new world of Columbus that man began his first rebellion against control by ancient empires. In 1776, the year of the American Revolution, Tom Paine wrote that "A flame has arisen not to be extinguished."

Today that same flame of freedom burns brightly across the once "dark continent," creating new nations—driving old powers from the scene—and kindling in the African people the desire to shape their own destinies as free men. In 1953, three nations of Africa south of the Sahara were independent; today there are nineteen free nations. And freedom soon will cover the whole continent.

Each of these newly emerging African nations has, in varying degree, the same basic problems, the same needs, and the same dangers. And in each of them wait the same tireless and implacable agents of communism—watching for the opportunity to transform hunger, or poverty, or ignorance into revolt and Communist domination.

The new nations of Africa are determined to emerge from the poverty and hunger which now blanket much of that vast continent.

They are determined to build a modern and growing economy with a constantly rising standard of living. They are determined to educate their people—maintain their independence—and receive the respect of all the world.

There can be no question about this determination. The only real question is whether these new nations will look West or East—to Moscow or Washington—for sympathy, help, and guidance in their great effort to recapitulate, in a few decades, the entire history of modern Europe and America.

I believe that if we meet our responsibilities—if we extend the hand of friendship—if we live up to the ideals of our own revolution—then the course of the African revolution in the next decade will be toward democracy and freedom, rather than toward communism and slavery.

For it was the American Revolution—not the Russian—which began man's struggle for national independence and individual liberty. When the African National Congress in Northern Rhodesia called for reform and justice, it threatened a "Boston Tea Party," not a Bolshevik bomb plot. African leader Tom Mboya invokes the "American Dream"—not the Communist Manifesto. And in the most remote bushlands of central Africa there are children named Thomas Jefferson and George Washington—but there are none named Lenin or Stalin or Trotsky.

And our ties with Africa are not merely the ties of history and spirit. For our goals for today's Africa are the goals of the Africans themselves.

We want an Africa where the abysmally low standard of living is constantly rising—where industry and business are growing—where malnutrition and ignorance are disappearing.

And this is what Africa wants.

We want an Africa which is made up of a community of stable and independent governments—where the human rights of Negroes and white men alike are valued and protected—where men are given the opportunity to choose their own national course, free from the dictates or coercion of any other country.

We want an Africa which is not a pawn in the Cold War—or a battleground between East and West.

And this, too, is what the African people want.

And none of these goals is a goal of the Communists—who wish only to perpetuate the want and chaos on which Communist domination can be built.

Under such circumstances we would suppose that there was no place for communism in Africa—and that the new nations of Africa would increasingly look to the West and to America for help.

But the harsh facts of the matter are that the cause of freedom has been steadily losing ground in Africa—and communism has been gaining. . . .

We have lost ground in Africa because we have neglected and ignored the needs and the aspirations of the African people—because we failed to foresee the emergence of Africa and ally ourselves with the cause of independence—and because we failed to help the Africans develop the stable economy and the educated population on which their growth and freedom depend. And today we are still making the same mistakes and experiencing the same failures.

Although Africa's single greatest need is for educated men—men to man the factories, staff the government, and form the core of the educated electorate on which the success of democracy depends, we have done almost nothing to help educate the African people. There are only a handful of college graduates in the entire continent and less than one percent of all Africans who enter primary grades ever finish high school. Yet today we are aiding [fewer] than two hundred African students to study in this country—we are supplying virtually no books or teachers to Africa—and [fewer] than five percent of all our foreign technical assistance goes to Africa south of the Sahara. . . .

Although Africa is the poorest and least productive area on earth, we have done little to provide the development capital which is essential to a growing economy. Through the end of 1957 we had granted Africa less than two tenths of one percent of all our foreign assistance. And in 1959 Africa received only two percent of all the money spent by the Development Loan Fund, a fund specifically created to help underdeveloped countries.

The only real question is whether these new nations [of Africa] will look West or East—to Moscow or Washington—for sympathy, help, and guidance in their great effort to recapitulate, in a few decades, the entire history of modern Europe and America.

Although by 1952 it was obvious that the new African nations would be a growing force on the world scene, we ignored these nations until events forced them upon us. Our State Department did not even establish a Bureau of African Affairs until 1957—and that same year we sent more Foreign Service officers to West Germany than [to] all of Africa. Even today, barely five percent of our Foreign Service personnel is stationed in Africa—and five newly independent countries have no representation at all. . . .

These failures, and many more like them, this record of neglect and indifference, of failure and retreat, has created a steady decline of American prestige in Africa—and a steady growth of Soviet influence.

If we are to create an atmosphere in Africa where freedom can flourish, where long-enduring people hope for a better life for themselves and their children, where men are winning the fight against ignorance and hunger and disease, then we must embark on a bold and imaginative new program for the development of Africa.

First, to meet the need for education we must greatly increase the number of African students—future African leaders—brought to this country for university training. But training new leaders is not enough. We must help the African nations mount a large-scale attack on mass ignorance and illiteracy through the establishment of a multination African educational development fund [and] send an increasing stream of experts and educators—engineers and technicians—to train Africa in the tools of modern production and science, and in the skills and knowledge essential to the conduct of government.

Second, we must use our surpluses and our technology to meet the critical African need for food. Three quarters of the African people struggle to survive on subsistence farms, and malnutrition is Africa's greatest health problem. Our agricultural experts must train African farmers to use modern methods to increase food production—freeing labor and capital for industry, and putting an end to hunger. . . .

Third, we must provide the development capital which alone can transform limited resources into a higher standard of living for the African people . . . long-term capital loans essential to develop the roads, the power, the water, the hospitals, and . . . stimulate private investment. . . .

Fourth, we must make the United Nations the central instrument of our effort in Africa . . . to build a strong and free Africa, rather than use African nations as pawns in the Cold War. . . .

Fifth, we must ally ourselves with the rising tide of nationalism in Africa . . . the most powerful force in the modern world . . . because these are our historic principles. . . .

Sixth, we must wipe out all traces of discrimination and prejudice against Negroes at home. . . . Every instance of racial intolerance, every act of hatred or bigotry, which takes place in America, finds its way to the front pages of African newspapers. . . . More than six hundred African and Asian students cannot find decent housing—here in New York—because of their color. And African diplomats have similar difficulties finding homes in Washington. What picture of America will these leaders and future leaders bring back to their own land? . . .

In a recent film, *The Defiant Ones,* two men—a white man and a Negro —chained together, fall into a deep pit. The only way out is for one to stand on the shoulders of the other. But, since they were chained, after the first had climbed over the top of the pit, he had to pull the other out after him, if either one was to be free.

Today, Africa and America, black men and white men, new nations and old, are bound together. Our challenges rush to meet us. If we are to achieve our goals—if we are to fulfill man's eternal quest for peace and freedom—we must do it together.

National Council of Women
New York, New York, October 12, 1960

Q: Mr. President, your roving ambassador to Africa has been widely criticized for some of the statements he has made, that is, Mr. Williams, including the one of "Africa for the Africans," and the like. Do you find any validity in this criticism, and would you consider that his tour of Africa has been a plus for United States policy?

THE PRESIDENT: I think Governor Williams has done very well. I am wholly satisfied with his mission. It's a very difficult one. . . .

The statement "Africa for the Africans" does not seem to me to be a very unreasonable statement. He made it clear that he was talking about all those who felt that they were Africans, whatever their color might be, whatever their race might be. I do not know who else Africa should be for.

President's News Conference
Washington, D.C., March 1, 1961

The War in Indochina

Mr. President, the time has come for the American people to be told the blunt truth about Indochina.

I am reluctant to make any statement which may be misinterpreted as unappreciative of the gallant French struggle at Dien Bien Phu and elsewhere; or as partisan criticism of our Secretary of State just prior to his participation in the delicate deliberations in Geneva. Nor, as one who is not a member of those committees of the Congress which have been briefed—if not consulted—on this matter, do I wish to appear impetuous or alarmist in my evaluation of the situation.

But to pour money, material, and men into the jungles of Indochina without at least a remote prospect of victory would be dangerously futile and self-destructive. Of course, all discussion of "united action" assumes the inevitability of such victory; but such assumptions are not unlike similar predictions of confidence which have lulled the American people for many years and which, if continued, would present an improper basis for determining the extent of American participation.

Despite this series of optimistic reports about eventual victory, every member of the Senate knows that such victory today appears to be desperately remote, to say the least, despite tremendous amounts of economic and materiel aid from the United States, and despite a deplorable loss of French Union manpower. The call for either negotiations or additional participation by other nations underscores the remoteness of such a final victory today, regardless of the outcome at Dien Bien Phu. It is, of course, for these reasons that many French are reluctant to continue the struggle without greater assistance; for to record the sapping effect which time and the enemy have had on their will and strength in that area is not to disparage their valor. If "united action" can achieve the necessary victory over the forces of communism, and thus preserve the security and freedom of all Southeast Asia, then such united action is clearly called for. But if, on the other hand, the increase in our aid and the utilization of our troops would only result in further statements of confidence without ultimate victory over aggression, then now is the time when we must evaluate the conditions under which that pledge is made.

I am frankly of the belief that no amount of American military assistance in Indochina can conquer an enemy which is everywhere and at the same time nowhere, "an enemy of the people" which has the sympathy and covert support of the people.

Moreover, without political independence for the Associated States, the other Asiatic nations have made it clear that they regard this as a war of colonialism; and the "united action" which is said to be so desperately needed for victory in that area is likely to end up as unilateral action by our own country. Such intervention, without participation by the armed forces of the other nations of Asia, without the support of the great masses of the people of the Associated States, with increasing reluctance and discouragement on the part of the French—and, I might add, with hordes of Chinese Communist troops poised just across the border in anticipation of our unilateral entry into their kind of battleground—such intervention, Mr. President, would be virtually impossible in the type of military situation which prevails in Indochina.

This is not a new point, of course. In November of 1951, I reported upon my return from the Far East as follows:

> In Indochina we have allied ourselves to the desperate effort of a French regime to hang on to the remnants of empire. There is no broad, general support of the native Vietnam government among the people of that area. To check the southern drive of communism makes sense but not only through reliance on the force of arms. The task is rather to build strong native non-Communist sentiment within these areas and rely on that as a spearhead of defense rather than upon the legions of General de Lattre. To do this apart from and in defiance of innately nationalistic aims spells foredoomed failure.

In June of last year, I sought an amendment to the Mutual Security Act which would have provided for the distribution of American aid, to the extent feasible, in such a way as to encourage the freedom and independence desired by the people of the Associated States. My amendment was soundly defeated on the grounds that we should not pressure France into taking action on this delicate situation; and that the new French government could be expected to make "a decision which would obviate the necessity of this kind of amendment or resolution." The distinguished majority leader [Mr. Knowland] assured us that "We will all work, in conjunction with our great ally, France, toward the freedom of the people of those states."

Every year we are given three sets of assurances: First, that the independence of the Associated States is now complete; second, that the independence of the Associated States will soon be completed under steps "now" being undertaken; and, third, that military victory for the French Union forces in Indochina is assured, or is just around the corner, or lies two years off. But the stringent limitations upon the status of the Associated States as sovereign states remain; and the fact that military victory has not yet been achieved is largely the result of these limitations. Repeated failure of these prophecies has, however, in no way diminished the frequency of their reiteration, and they have caused this nation to delay definitive action until now the opportunity for any desirable solution may well be past.

To pour money, material, and men into the jungles of Indochina without at least a remote prospect of victory would be dangerously futile and self-destructive.

It is time, therefore, for us to face the stark reality of the difficult situation before us without the false hopes which predictions of military victory and assurances of complete independence have given us in the past. The hard truth of the matter is, first, that without the wholehearted support of the peoples of the Associated States, without a reliable and crusading native army with a dependable officer corps, a military victory, even with American support, in that area is difficult if not impossible, of achievement; and, second, that the support of the people of that area cannot be obtained without a change in the contractual relationships which presently exist between the Associated States and the French Union.

If the French persist in their refusal to grant the legitimate independence and freedom desired by the peoples of the Associated States; and if those peoples and the other peoples of Asia remain aloof from the conflict, as they have in the past, then it is my hope that Secretary Dulles, before pledging our assistance at Geneva, will recognize the futility of channeling American men and machines into that hopeless internecine struggle.

The facts and alternatives before us are unpleasant, Mr. President. But in a nation such as ours, it is only through the fullest and frankest appreciation of such facts and alternatives that any foreign policy can be effectively maintained. In an era of supersonic attack and atomic retaliation, extended public debate and education are of no avail, once such a policy must be implemented. The time to study, to doubt, to review, and revise is now, for upon our decisions now may well rest the peace and security of the world, and, indeed, the very continued existence of mankind. And if we cannot entrust this decision to the people, then, as Thomas Jefferson once said: "If we think them not enlightened enough to exercise their control with a wholesome discretion, the remedy is not to take it from them but to inform their discretion by education."

United States Senate
Washington, D.C., April 6, 1954

I want to make a brief statement about Laos. It is, I think, important for all Americans to understand this difficult and potentially dangerous problem. In my last conversation with General Eisenhower, the day before the inauguration, on January 19, we spent more time on this hard matter than on any other thing. And since then it has been steadily before the administration as the most immediate of the problems that we found upon taking office.

Our special concern with the problem in Laos goes back to 1954. That year at Geneva a large group of powers agreed to a settlement of the struggle for Indochina. Laos was one of the new states which had recently emerged from the French Union and it was the clear premise of the 1954 settlement that this new country would be neutral—free of external domination by anyone. The new country contained contending factions, but in its first years real progress was made toward a unified and neutral status. But the efforts of a Communist-dominated group to destroy this neutrality never ceased.

In the last half of 1960 a series of sudden maneuvers occurred and the Communists and their supporters turned to a new and greatly intensified military effort to take over. . . .

In this military advance the local Communist forces, known as the Pathet Lao, have had increasing support and direction from outside. Soviet planes, I regret to say, have been conspicuous in a large-scale airlift into the battle area—over one thousand sorties since last December 13, plus a whole supporting set of combat specialists, mainly from Communist North Vietnam, and heavier weapons have been provided from outside, all with the clear object of destroying by military action the agreed neutrality of Laos.

It is this new dimension of externally supported warfare that creates the present grave problem. The position of this administration has been carefully considered and we have sought to make it just as clear as we know how to the governments concerned.

Laos is far away from America, but the world is small.

First, we strongly and unreservedly support the goal of a neutral and independent Laos, tied to no outside power or group of powers, threatening no one, and free from any domination. Our support for the present duly constituted government is aimed entirely and exclusively at that result. And if in the past there has been any possible ground for misunderstanding of our desire for a truly neutral Laos, there should be none now.

Secondly, if there is to be a peaceful solution, there must be a cessation of the present armed attacks by externally supported Communists. If these attacks do not stop, those who support a truly neutral Laos will have to consider their response. The shape of this necessary response will, of course, be carefully considered, not only here in Washington, but in the SEATO conference with our allies which begins next Monday.

SEATO—the Southeast Asia Treaty Organization—was organized in 1954, with strong leadership from our last administration, and all members of SEATO have undertaken special treaty responsibilities toward an aggression in Laos.

No one should doubt our resolution on this point. We are faced with a clear and one-sided threat of a change in the internationally agreed position of Laos. This threat runs counter to the will of the Laotian people, who wish only to be independent and neutral. It is posed rather by the military operations of internal dissident elements directed from outside the country. This is what must end if peace is to be achieved in Southeast Asia.

Thirdly, we are earnestly in favor of constructive negotiation among the nations concerned and among the leaders of Laos which can help Laos back to the pathway of independence and genuine neutrality. We strongly support the present British proposal of a prompt end of hostilities and prompt negotiation. We are always conscious of the obligation which rests upon all members of the United Nations to seek peaceful solutions to problems of this sort. We hope that others may be equally aware of this responsibility.

My fellow Americans, Laos is far away from America, but the world is small. Its two million people live in a country three times the size of Austria. The security of all Southeast Asia will be endangered if Laos loses its neutral independence. Its own safety runs with the safety of us all—in a real neutrality observed by all.

I want to make it clear to the American people and to all of the world that all we want in Laos is peace, not war; a truly neutral government, not a Cold War pawn; a settlement concluded at the conference table and not on the battlefield.

Our response will be made in close cooperation with our allies and the wishes of the Laotian government. We will not be provoked, trapped, or drawn into this or any other situation; but I know that every American will want his country to honor its obligations.

Opening Statement, President's News Conference
Washington, D.C., March 23, 1961

MR. CRONKITE: Mr. President, the only hot war we've got running at the moment is of course the one in Vietnam, and we have our difficulties there, quite obviously. . . .

THE PRESIDENT: I don't think that unless a greater effort is made by the government to win popular support that the war can be won out there. In the final analysis, it is their war. They are the ones who have to win it or lose it. We can help them, we can give them equipment, we can send our men out there as advisers, but they have to win it, the people of Vietnam, against the Communists.

We are prepared to continue to assist them, but I don't think that the war can be won unless the people support the effort and, in my opinion, in the last two months, the government has gotten out of touch with the people.

The repressions against the Buddhists, we felt, were very unwise. Now all we can do is to make it very clear that we don't think this is the way to win. It is my hope that this will become increasingly obvious to the government, that they will take steps to try to bring back popular support for this very essential struggle.

MR. CRONKITE: Do you think this government still has time to regain the support of the people?

THE PRESIDENT: I do. With changes in policy, and perhaps with personnel, I think it can. If it doesn't make those changes, I would think that the chances of winning it would not be very good.

Interview, Walter Cronkite
CBS Television News
Washington, D.C., September 2, 1963

We would expect to withdraw a thousand men from South Vietnam before the end of the year . . . as the training intensifies and is carried on in South Vietnam.

President's News Conference
Washington, D.C., October 31, 1963

The United Nations

We must increase our support of the United Nations as an instrument to end the Cold War instead of an arena in which to fight it. In recognition of its increasing importance and the doubling of its membership

—we are enlarging and strengthening our own mission to the U.N.;

—we shall help insure that it is properly financed;

—we shall work to see that the integrity of the office of the Secretary-General is maintained.

And I would address a special plea to the smaller nations of the world —to join with us in strengthening this organization, which is far more essential to their security than it is to ours—the only body in the world where no nation need be powerful to be secure, where every nation has an equal voice, and where any nation can exert influence not according to the strength of its armies but according to the strength of its ideas. It deserves the support of all.

State of the Union Address
The Capitol, Washington, D.C.
January 30, 1961

We meet in an hour of grief and challenge. Dag Hammarskjöld is dead. But the United Nations lives. His tragedy is deep in our hearts, but the task for which he died is at the top of our agenda. A noble servant of peace is gone. But the quest for peace lies before us.

The problem is not the death of one man—the problem is the life of this organization. It will either grow to meet the challenges of our age, or it will be gone with the wind, without influence, without force, without respect. Were we to let it die, to enfeeble its vigor, to cripple its powers, we would condemn our future.

For in the development of this organization rests the only true alternative to war—and war appeals no longer as a rational alternative. Unconditional war can no longer lead to unconditional victory. It can no longer serve to settle disputes. It can no longer concern the great powers alone. For a nuclear disaster, spread by wind and water and fear, could well engulf the great and the small, the rich and the poor, the committed and the uncommitted alike. Mankind must put an end to war —or war will put an end to mankind.

So let us here resolve that Dag Hammarskjöld did not live, or die, in vain. Let us call a truce to terror. Let us invoke the blessings of peace. And, as we build an international capacity to keep peace, let us join in dismantling the national capacity to wage war.

This will require new strength and new roles for the United Nations. For disarmament without checks is but a shadow—and a community without law is but a shell. Already the United Nations has become both the measure and the vehicle of man's most generous impulses. Already it has provided—in the Middle East, in Asia, in Africa this year in the Congo—means of holding man's violence within bounds.

Every man, woman, and child lives under a nuclear sword of Damocles, hanging by the slenderest of threads, capable of being cut at any moment by accident or miscalculation or madness.

But the great question which confronted this body in 1945 is still before us: whether man's cherished hopes for progress and peace are to be destroyed by terror and disruption, whether the "foul winds of war" can be tamed in time to free the cooling winds of reason, and whether the pledges of our Charter are to be fulfilled or defied—pledges to secure peace, progress, human rights, and world law.

In this hall, there are not three forces, but two. One is composed of those who are trying to build the kind of world described in Articles I and II of the Charter. The other, seeking a far different world, would undermine this organization in the process. . . .

However difficult it may be to fill Mr. Hammarskjöld's place, it can better be filled by one man rather than by three. Even the three horses of the troika did not have three drivers, all going in different directions. They had only one—and so must the United Nations executive. To install a triumvirate, or any panel, or any rotating authority, in the

United Nations administrative offices would replace order with anarchy, action with paralysis, confidence with confusion. . . .

To give this organization three drivers—to permit each great power to decide its own case, would entrench the Cold War in the headquarters of peace. Whatever advantages such a plan may hold out to my own country, as one of the great powers, we reject it. For we far prefer world law in the age of self-determination, to world war, in the age of mass extermination.

Today, every inhabitant of this planet must contemplate the day when this planet may no longer be habitable. Every man, woman, and child lives under a nuclear sword of Damocles, hanging by the slenderest of threads, capable of being cut at any moment by accident or miscalculation or madness. The weapons of war must be abolished before they abolish us.

Men no longer debate whether armaments are a symptom or a cause of tension. The mere existence of modern weapons—ten million times more powerful than any that the world has ever seen, and only minutes away from any target on earth—is a source of horror and discord and distrust. Men no longer maintain that disarmament must await the settlement of all disputes—for disarmament must be a part of any permanent settlement. And men no longer pretend that the quest for disarmament is a sign of weakness—for in a spiraling arms race, a nation's security may well be shrinking even as its arms increase.

For fifteen years this organization has sought the reduction and destruction of arms. Now that goal is no longer a dream—it is a practical matter of life or death. The risks inherent in disarmament pale in comparison to the risks inherent in an unlimited arms race. . . .

In short, general and complete disarmament must no longer be a slogan, used to resist the first steps. It is no longer to be a goal without means of achieving it, without means of verifying its progress, without means of keeping the peace. It is now a realistic plan, and a test—a test of those only willing to talk and a test of those willing to act.

Such a plan would not bring a world free from conflict and greed—but it would bring a world free from the terrors of mass destruction. It would not usher in the era of the superstate—but it would usher in an era in which no state could annihilate or be annihilated by another. . . .

I therefore propose . . . that disarmament negotiations resume promptly, and continue without interruption until an entire program for general and complete disarmament has not only been agreed but has been actually achieved.

The logical place to begin is a treaty assuring the end of nuclear tests of all kinds, in every environment, under workable controls. The United States and the United Kingdom have proposed such a treaty that is reasonable, effective, and ready for signature. We are still prepared to sign that treaty today.

We also proposed a mutual ban on atmospheric testing, without inspection or controls, in order to save the human race from the poison of radioactive fallout. We regret that that offer has not been accepted. . . .

To destroy arms, however, is not enough. We must create even as we destroy—creating worldwide law and law enforcement as we outlaw worldwide war and weapons. . . .

For peace is not solely a matter of military or technical problems—it is primarily a problem of politics and people. And unless man can match his strides in weaponry and technology with equal strides in social and political development, our great strength, like that of the dinosaur, will become incapable of proper control—and like the dinosaur, vanish from the earth.

As we extend the rule of law on earth, so must we also extend it to man's new domain—outer space.

All of us salute the brave cosmonauts of the Soviet Union. The new horizons of outer space must not be driven by the old bitter concepts of imperialism and sovereign claims. The cold reaches of the universe must not become the new arena of an even colder war.

To this end, we shall urge proposals extending the United Nations Charter to the limits of man's exploration in the universe, reserving outer space for peaceful use, prohibiting weapons of mass destruction in space or on celestial bodies, and opening the mysteries and benefits of space to every nation. . . .

But the mysteries of outer space must not divert our eyes or our energies from the harsh realities that face our fellow men. Political sovereignty is but a mockery without the means of meeting poverty and illiteracy and disease. Self-determination is but a slogan if the future holds no hope. . . .

The first threat on which I wish to report is widely misunderstood: the smoldering coals of war in Southeast Asia. South Vietnam is already under attack—sometimes by a single assassin, sometimes by a band of guerrillas, recently by full battalions. The peaceful borders of Burma, Cambodia, and India have been repeatedly violated. And the peaceful people of Laos are in danger of losing the independence they gained not so long ago.

No one can call these "wars of liberation." For these are free countries living under their own governments. Nor are these aggressions any less real because men are knifed in their homes and not shot in the fields of battle.

The very simple question confronting the world community is whether measures can be devised to protect the small and the weak from such tactics. For if they are successful in Laos and South Vietnam, the gates will be opened wide.

The United States seeks for itself no base, no territory, no special position in this area of any kind. We support a truly neutral and independent Laos, its people free from outside interference, living at peace with themselves and with their neighbors, assured that their territory will not be used for attacks on others, and under a government comparable (as Mr. Khrushchev and I agreed at Vienna) to Cambodia and Burma.

But now the negotiations over Laos are reaching a crucial stage. The cease-fire is at best precarious. The rainy season is coming to an end. Laotian territory is being used to infiltrate South Vietnam. The world community—and all those who are involved—must recognize that this potent threat to Laotian peace and freedom is indivisible from all other threats to their own.

To this end, we shall urge proposals extending the United Nations Charter to the limits of man's exploration in the universe, reserving outer space for peaceful use, prohibiting weapons of mass destruction in space or on celestial bodies.

Secondly, I wish to report to you on the crisis over Germany and Berlin. This is not the time or the place for immoderate tones, but the world community is entitled to know the very simple issues as we see them. If there is a crisis it is because an existing peace is under threat, because an existing island of free people is under pressure, because solemn agreements are being treated with indifference. Established international rights are being threatened with unilateral usurpation. Peaceful circulation has been interrupted by barbed wire and concrete blocks.

One recalls the order of the Czar in Pushkin's *Boris Godunov:* "Take steps at this very hour that our frontiers be fenced in by barriers. . . . That not a single soul pass o'er the border, that not a hare be able to run or a crow to fly."

It is absurd to allege that we are threatening a war merely to prevent the Soviet Union and East Germany from signing a so-called treaty of peace. The Western Allies are not concerned with any paper arrangement the Soviets may wish to make with a regime of their own creation, on territory occupied by their own troops and governed by their own agents. No such action can affect either our rights or our responsibilities.

If there is a dangerous crisis in Berlin—and there is—it is because of threats against the vital interests and the deep commitment of the Western powers, and the freedom of West Berlin. We cannot yield these interests. We cannot fail these commitments. We cannot surrender the freedom of these people for whom we are responsible. A "peace treaty" which carried with it provisions which destroy the peace would be a fraud. A "free city" which was not genuinely free would suffocate freedom and would be an infamy.

For a city or a people to be truly free, they must have the secure right, without economic, political, or police pressure, to make their own choice and to live their own lives. And as I have said before, if anyone doubts the extent to which our presence is desired by the people of West Berlin, we are ready to have that question submitted to a free vote in all Berlin and, if possible, among all the German people.

The elementary fact about this crisis is that it is unnecessary. The elementary tools for a peaceful settlement are to be found in the Charter. Under its law, agreements are to be kept, unless changed by all those who made them. Established rights are to be respected. The political disposition of peoples should rest upon their own wishes, freely expressed in plebiscites or free elections. If there are legal problems, they can be solved by legal means. If there is a threat of force, it must be rejected. If there is desire for change, it must be a subject for negotiation and if there is negotiation, it must be rooted in mutual respect and concern for the rights of others.

The Western powers have calmly resolved to defend, by whatever means are forced upon them, their obligations and their access to the free citizens of West Berlin and the self-determination of those citizens. This generation learned from bitter experience that either brandishing or yielding to threats can only lead to war. But firmness and reason can lead to the kind of peaceful solution in which my country profoundly believes.

We are committed to no rigid formula. We see no perfect solution. We recognize that troops and tanks can, for a time, keep a nation divided against its will, however unwise that policy may seem to us. But we believe a peaceful agreement is possible which protects the freedom of West Berlin and allied presence and access, while recognizing the historic and legitimate interests of others in assuring European security. . . .

The events and decisions of the next ten months may well decide the fate of man for the next ten thousand years. There will be no avoiding those events. There will be no appeal from these decisions. And we in this hall shall be remembered either as part of the generation that turned this planet into a flaming funeral pyre or the generation that met its vow "to save succeeding generations from the scourge of war."

In the endeavor to meet that vow, I pledge you every effort this nation possesses. I pledge you that we shall neither commit nor provoke aggression, that we shall neither flee nor invoke the threat of force, that we shall never negotiate out of fear, we shall never fear to negotiate.

Terror is not a new weapon. Throughout history it has been used by those who could not prevail, either by persuasion or example. But inevitably they fail, either because men are not afraid to die for a life worth living, or because the terrorists themselves came to realize that free men cannot be frightened by threats, and that aggression would meet its own response. And it is in the light of that history that every nation today should know, be he friend or foe, that the United States has both the will and the weapons to join free men in standing up to their responsibilities.

But I come here today to look across this world of threats to a world of peace. In that search we cannot expect any final triumph—for new problems will always arise. We cannot expect that all nations will adopt like systems—for conformity is the jailor of freedom, and the enemy of growth. Nor can we expect to reach our goal by contrivance, by fiat, or even by the wishes of all.

But however close we sometimes seem to that dark and final abyss, let no man of peace and freedom despair. For he does not stand alone. If we all can persevere, if we can in every land and office look beyond our own shores and ambitions, then surely the age will dawn in which the strong are just and the weak secure and the peace preserved.

Ladies and gentlemen of this Assembly, the decision is ours. Never have the nations of the world had so much to lose, or so much to gain. Together we shall save our planet, or together we shall perish in its flames. Save it we can—and save it we must—and then shall we earn the eternal thanks of mankind and, as peacemakers, the eternal blessing of God.

United Nations General Assembly
New York, New York, September 25, 1961

I see little merit in the impatience of those who would abandon this imperfect world instrument because they dislike our imperfect world. For the troubles of a world organization merely reflect the troubles of the world itself. And if the organization is weakened, these troubles can only increase. We may not always agree with every detailed action taken by every officer of the United Nations, or with every voting majority. But as an institution, it should have in the future, as it has had in the past since its inception, no stronger or more faithful member than the United States of America. . . .

No policeman is universally popular—particularly when he uses his stick to restore law and order on his beat. Those members who are willing to contribute their votes and their views—but very little else—have created a serious deficit by refusing to pay their share of special UN assessments. Yet they do pay their annual assessments to retain their votes—and a new UN bond issue, financing special operations for the next eighteen months, is to be repaid with interest from these regular assessments. This is clearly in our interest.

State of the Union Address
The Capitol, Washington, D.C.
January 11, 1962

Q: Mr. President, Senator Jackson says that this administration and the last have been putting too much stock in the United Nations and that a strong Atlantic Community offers the best avenue to peace. What is your view on this?

THE PRESIDENT: I see nothing contradictory in a strong Atlantic Community and the United Nations. Nor is there anything contradictory in a strong Organization of American States and the United Nations. In fact, the United Nations, when it was written in 1945, gave room for these regional organizations, of which there are a great many and of which the United States is a member. I support the United Nations very strongly, and I think the American people do, not because its power is unlimited [but] because we believe that it serves the interests of the United States. . . .

Now, I would be very unhappy if the United Nations were weakened or eliminated. You would have a great increase in the chances of a direct confrontation in someplace like the Congo between the great powers. It might involve the United States directly and perhaps the Soviet Union on the other side. The United Nations serves as a means of channeling these matters, on which we disagree so basically, in a peaceful way. But that doesn't suggest that we have to choose between the Atlantic Community and the United Nations. We believe in the Atlantic Community; we are committed to strengthening it. . . . And we also support the United Nations.

President's News Conference
Washington, D.C., March 21, 1962

The Little Nations

. . . I am deeply honored to be your guest in the free Parliament of a free Ireland. If this nation had achieved its present political and economic stature a century or so ago, my great grandfather might never have left New Ross, and I might, if fortunate, be sitting down there with you. Of course, if your own President had never left Brooklyn, he might be standing up here instead of me! . . .

The White House was designed by James Hoban, a noted Irish-American architect, and I have no doubt that he believed by incorporating several features of the Dublin style he would make it more homelike for any President of Irish descent. It was a long wait, but I appreciate his efforts. . . .

I am proud to be the first American President to visit Ireland during his term of office, proud to be addressing this distinguished assembly, and proud of the welcome you have given me. My presence and your welcome, however, only symbolize the many and enduring links which have bound the Irish and the Americans since the earliest days.

Benjamin Franklin—the envoy of the American Revolution who was also born in Boston—was received by the Irish Parliament in 1772. It was neither independent nor free from discrimination at the time, but Franklin reported its members "disposed to be friends of America. By joining our interest with theirs," he said, "a more equitable treatment . . . might be obtained for both nations."

Our interests have been joined ever since. Franklin sent leaflets to Irish freedom fighters. O'Connell was influenced by Washington, and Emmet influenced Lincoln. Irish volunteers played so predominant a role in the American army that Lord Mountjoy lamented in the British Parliament that "we have lost America through the Irish." John Barry, whose statue we honored yesterday and whose sword is in my office, was only one who fought for liberty in America to set an example for liberty in Ireland. Yesterday was the 117th anniversary of the birth of Charles Stewart Parnell—whose grandfather fought under Barry and whose mother was born in America—and who, at the age of thirty-four, was invited to address the American Congress on the cause of Irish freedom. "I have seen since I have been in this country," he said, "so many tokens of the good wishes of the American people toward Ireland." And today, eighty-three years later, I can say to you that I have seen in this country so many tokens of good wishes of the Irish people toward America.

And so it is that our two nations, divided by distance, have been united by history. No people ever believed more deeply in the cause of Irish freedom than the people of the United States. And no country contributed more to building my own than your sons and daughters. They came to our shores in a mixture of hope and agony, and I would not underrate the difficulties of their course once they arrived in the United States. They left behind hearts, fields, and a nation yearning to be free. It is no wonder that James Joyce described the Atlantic as a bowl of bitter tears, and that an earlier poet wrote, "They are going, going, going, and we cannot bid them stay." . . .

There are those who regard this history of past strife and exile as better forgotten. But, to use the phrase of Yeats, let us not casually reduce "that great past to a trouble of fools." For we need not feel the bitterness of the past to discover its meaning for the present and the future. And it is the present and the future of Ireland that today holds so much promise to my nation as well as to yours, and, indeed, to all mankind. . . .

George Bernard Shaw, speaking as an Irishman, summed up its approach to life: Other people, he said, "see things and say: 'Why?' . . . But I dream things that never were and I say: 'Why not?' "

Eighty-three years ago, Henry Grattan, demanding the more independent Irish Parliament that would always bear his name, denounced those who were satisfied merely by new grants of economic opportunity. "A country," he said, "enlightened as Ireland, chartered as Ireland, armed as Ireland and injured as Ireland will be satisfied with nothing less than liberty." And today, I am certain, free Ireland—a full-fledged member of the world community, where some are not yet free, and where some counsel an acceptance of tyranny—free Ireland will not be satisfied with anything less than liberty.

I am glad, therefore, that Ireland is moving in the mainstream of current world events. For I sincerely believe that your future is as promising as your past is proud, and that your destiny lies not as a peaceful island in a sea of troubles, but as a maker and shaper of world peace.

For self-determination can no longer mean isolation; and the achievement of national independence today means withdrawal from the old status only to return to the world scene with a new one. New nations can build with their former governing powers the same kind of fruitful relationship that Ireland has established with Great Britain—a relationship founded on equality and mutual interests. And no nation, large or small, can be indifferent to the fate of others, near or far. Modern economics, weaponry, and communications have made us realize more than ever that we are one human family and this one planet is our home.

Across the gulfs and barriers that now divide us, we must remember that there are no permanent enemies. Hostility today is a fact, but it is not a ruling law. The supreme reality of our time is our indivisibility as children of God and our common vulnerability on this planet.

Some may say that all this means little to Ireland. In an age when "history moves with the tramp of earthquake feet," in an age when a handful of men and nations have the power literally to devastate mankind, in an age when the needs of the developing nations are so staggering that even the richest lands often groan with the burden of assistance —in such an age, it may be asked, how can a nation as small as Ireland play much of a role on the world stage?

I would remind those who ask that question, including those in other small countries, of the words of one of the great orators of the English language:

> All the world owes much to the little "five feet high" nations. The greatest art of the world was the work of little nations. The most enduring literature of the world came from little nations. The heroic deeds that thrill humanity through generations were the deeds of little nations fighting for their freedom. And oh, yes, the salvation of mankind came through a little nation.

Ireland has already set an example and a standard for other small nations to follow.

This has never been a rich or powerful country, and yet, since earliest times, its influence on the world has been rich and powerful. No larger nation did more to keep Christianity and Western culture alive in their darkest centuries. No larger nation did more to spark the cause of independence in America, indeed, around the world. And no larger nation has ever provided the world with more literary and artistic genius.

This is an extraordinary country. George Bernard Shaw, speaking as an Irishman, summed up its approach to life: Other people, he said, "see things and say: 'Why?' . . . But I dream things that never were and I say: 'Why not?' "

It is that quality of the Irish—that remarkable combination of hope, confidence, and imagination—that is needed more than ever today. The problems of the world cannot possibly be solved by skeptics or cynics whose horizons are limited by the obvious realities. We need men who can dream of things that never were, and ask why not. It matters not how small a nation is that seeks world peace and freedom, for, to paraphrase a citizen of my country, the humblest nation of all the world, "when clad in the armor of a righteous cause, is stronger than all the hosts of Error."

Ireland is clad in the cause of national and human liberty with peace. To the extent that the peace is disturbed by conflict between the former colonial powers and the new and developing nations, Ireland's role is unique. For every new nation knows that Ireland was the first of the small nations in the twentieth century to win its struggle for independence, and that the Irish have traditionally sent their doctors and technicians and soldiers and priests to help other lands to keep their liberty alive.

At the same time, Ireland is part of Europe, associated with the Council of Europe, progressing in the context of Europe, and a prospective member of an expanded European Common Market. Thus Ireland has excellent relations with both the new and the old, the confidence of both sides, and an opportunity to act where the actions of greater powers might be looked upon with suspicion.

The central issue of freedom, however, is between those who believe in self-determination and those in the East who would impose on others the harsh and oppressive Communist system; and here your nation wisely rejects the role of a go-between or a mediator. Ireland pursues an independent course in foreign policy, but it is not neutral between liberty and tyranny and never will be.

For knowing the meaning of foreign domination, Ireland is the example and inspiration to those enduring endless years of oppression. It was fitting and appropriate that this nation played a leading role in censuring the suppression of the Hungarian revolution. For how many times was Ireland's quest for freedom suppressed only to have that quest renewed by the succeeding generation?

Those who suffer beyond that wall I saw on Wednesday in Berlin must not despair of their future. Let them remember the constancy, the faith, the endurance, and the final success of the Irish. And let them remember, as I heard sung by your sons and daughters yesterday in Wexford, "the boys of Wexford, who fought with heart and hand, to burst in twain the galling chain and free our native land."

The major forum for your nation's greater role in world affairs is that protector of the weak and voice of the small, the United Nations. From Cork to the Congo, from Galway to the Gaza Strip, from this legislative assembly to the United Nations, Ireland is sending its most talented men to do the world's most important work—the work of peace.

In a sense, this export of talent is in keeping with an historic Irish role—but you no longer go as exiles and emigrants but for the service of your country and, indeed, of all men. Like the Irish missionaries of medieval days, like the "wild geese" after the Battle of the Boyne, you are not content to sit by your fireside while others are in need of your help.

Nor are you content with the recollections of the past when you face the responsibilities of the present. Twenty-six sons of Ireland have died in the Congo; many others have been wounded. I pay tribute to them and to all of you for your commitment and dedication to world order. Their sacrifice reminds us all that we must not falter now. . . .

I speak of these matters today, not because Ireland is unaware of its role, but because I think it important that you know that we know what you have done. And I speak to remind the other small nations that they, too, can and must help build a world peace. They, too, as we all are, are dependent on the United Nations for security, for an equal chance to be heard, for progress toward a world made safe for diversity.

The peacekeeping machinery of the United Nations cannot work without the help of the smaller nations, nations whose forces threaten no one and whose forces can thus help create a world in which no nation is threatened. Great powers have their responsibilities and their burdens, but the smaller nations of the world must fulfill their obligations as well.

A great Irish poet once wrote: "I believe profoundly . . . in the future of Ireland . . . that this is an isle of destiny, that that destiny will be glorious . . . and that when our hour is come, we will have something to give to the world."

My friends: Ireland's hour has come. You have something to give to the world—and that is a future of peace with freedom.

Irish Parliament
Dublin, Ireland, June 28, 1963

CHAPTER 16

The Uses and Limits of Power

John Kennedy shied away from all attempts to fix an ideological label on him, but "principled pragmatist" or "idealist without illusions" would not have offended him. With the detached objectivity that enabled him to analyze his own country's and administration's strengths and weaknesses, he recognized that a new war, particularly a nuclear war, would represent not a noble cause but the failure of all his aspirations. He did not confuse strength with force or peace with weakness. He knew that the superpowers had to find a more rational means than armed conflict of settling their very real differences. In this, as in so many other ways, his wisdom deserves remembering today.

The Role of Negotiations

In 1961 the world relations of this country have become tangled and complex. One of our former allies has become our adversary—and he has his own adversaries who are not our allies. . . .

We increase our arms at a heavy cost, primarily to make certain that we will not have to use them. We must face up to the chance of war, if we are to maintain the peace. We must work with certain countries lacking in freedom in order to strengthen the cause of freedom. We find some who call themselves neutral who are our friends and sympathetic to us, and others who call themselves neutral who are unremittingly hostile to us. And as the most powerful defender of freedom on earth, we find ourselves unable to escape the responsibilities of freedom, and yet unable to exercise it without restraints imposed by the very freedoms we seek to protect.

We cannot, as a free nation, compete with our adversaries in tactics of terror, assassination, false promises, counterfeit mobs and crises.

We cannot, under the scrutiny of a free press and public, tell different stories to different audiences, foreign and domestic, friendly and hostile.

We cannot abandon the slow processes of consulting with our allies to match the swift expediencies of those who merely dictate to their satellites.

We can neither abandon nor control the international organization in which we now cast less than one percent of the vote in the General Assembly.

We possess weapons of tremendous power—but they are least effective in combating the weapons most often used by freedom's foes: subversion, infiltration, guerrilla warfare, civil disorder.

We send arms to other peoples—just as we send them the ideals of democracy in which we believe—but we cannot send them the will to use those arms or to abide by those ideals.

And while we believe not only in the force of arms but in the force of right and reason, we have learned that reason does not always appeal to unreasonable men, that it is not always true that "a soft answer turneth away wrath," and that right does not always make might.

In short, we must face problems which do not lend themselves to easy or quick or permanent solutions. And we must face the fact that the

United States is neither omnipotent nor omniscient—that we are only six percent of the world's population—that we cannot impose our will upon the other ninety-four percent of mankind—that we cannot right every wrong or reverse each adversity—and that therefore there cannot be an American solution to every world problem.

These burdens and frustrations are accepted by most Americans with maturity and understanding. They may long for the days when war meant charging up San Juan Hill—or when our isolation was guarded by two oceans—or when the atomic bomb was ours alone—or when much of the industrialized world depended upon our resources and our aid. But they now know that those days are gone—and that gone with them are the old policies and the old complacencies. And they know, too, that we must make the best of our new problems and our new opportunities, whatever the risk and the cost.

But there are others who cannot bear the burden of a long twilight struggle. They lack confidence in our long-run capacity to survive and succeed. Hating communism, yet they see communism in the long run, perhaps, as the wave of the future. And they want some quick and easy and final and cheap solution—now.

There are two groups of these frustrated citizens, far apart in their views yet very much alike in their approach. On the one hand are those who urge upon us what I regard to be the pathway of surrender—appeasing our enemies, compromising our commitments, purchasing peace at any price, disavowing our arms, our friends, our obligations. If their view had prevailed, the world of free choice would be smaller today.

On the other hand are those who urge upon us what I regard to be the pathway of war: equating negotiations with appeasement and substituting rigidity for firmness. If their view had prevailed, we would be at war today, and in more than one place.

It is a curious fact that each of these extreme opposites resembles the other. Each believes that we have only two choices: appeasement or war, suicide or surrender, humiliation or holocaust, to be either Red or dead. Each side sees only "hard" and "soft" nations, hard and soft policies, hard and soft men. Each believes that any departure from its own course inevitably leads to the other: one group believes that any peaceful solution means appeasement; the other believes that any arms buildup means war. One group regards everyone else as warmongers, the other regards everyone else as appeasers. Neither side admits that its path will lead to disaster—but neither can tell us how or where to draw the line once we descend the slippery slopes of appeasement or constant intervention.

In short, while both extremes profess to be the true realists of our time, neither could be more unrealistic. While both claim to be doing the nation a service, they could do it no greater disservice. This kind of talk of easy solutions to difficult problems, if believed, could inspire a lack of confidence among our people when they must all—above all else—be united in recognizing the long and difficult days that lie ahead. It could inspire uncertainty among our allies when above all else they must be confident in us. And even more dangerously, it could, if believed, inspire doubt among our adversaries when they must above all else be convinced that we will defend our vital interests.

We must face the fact that the United States is neither omnipotent nor omniscient—that we are only six percent of the world's population . . . and that therefore there cannot be an American solution to every world problem.

The essential fact that both of these groups fail to grasp is that diplomacy and defense are not substitutes for one another. Either alone would fail. A willingness to resist force, unaccompanied by a willingness to talk, could provoke belligerence—while a willingness to talk, unaccompanied by a willingness to resist force, could invite disaster.

But as long as we know what comprises our vital interests and our long-range goals, we have nothing to fear from negotiations at the appropriate time, and nothing to gain by refusing to take part in them. At a time when a single clash could escalate overnight into a holocaust of mushroom clouds, a great power does not prove its firmness by leaving the task of exploring the other's intentions to sentries or those without full responsibility. Nor can ultimate weapons rightfully be employed, or the ultimate sacrifice rightfully demanded of our citizens, until every reasonable solution has been explored. "How many wars,"

Winston Churchill has written, "have been averted by patience and persisting good will! . . . How many wars have been precipitated by firebrands!"

If vital interests under duress can be preserved by peaceful means, negotiations will find that out. If our adversary will accept nothing less than a concession of our rights, negotiations will find that out. And if negotiations are to take place, this nation cannot abdicate to its adversaries the task of choosing the forum and the framework and the time. . . .

No one should be under the illusion that negotiations for the sake of negotiations always advance the cause of peace. If for lack of preparation they break up in bitterness, the prospects of peace have been endangered. If they are made a forum for propaganda or a cover for aggression, the processes of peace have been abused.

But it is a test of our national maturity to accept the fact that negotiations are not a contest spelling victory or defeat. They may succeed—they may fail. They are likely to be successful only if both sides reach an agreement which both regard as preferable to the status quo—an agreement in which each side can consider its own situation to be improved. And this is most difficult to obtain.

But, while we shall negotiate freely, we shall not negotiate freedom. Our answer to the classic question of Patrick Henry is still no—life is not so dear, and peace is not so precious, "as to be purchased at the price of chains and slavery." And that is our answer even though, for the first time since the ancient battles between Greek city-states, war entails the threat of total annihilation, of everything we know, of society itself. For to save mankind's future freedom, we must face up to any risk that is necessary. We will always seek peace—but we will never surrender.

In short, we are neither "warmongers" nor "appeasers," neither "hard" nor "soft." We are Americans, determined to defend the frontiers of freedom, by an honorable peace if peace is possible, but by arms if arms are used against us. . . .

University of Washington
Seattle, Washington, November 16, 1961

The Voices of Extremism

In the most critical periods of our nation's history, there have always been those on the fringes of our society who have sought to escape their own responsibility by finding a simple solution, an appealing slogan or a convenient scapegoat.

Financial crises could be explained by the presence of too many immigrants or too few greenbacks. War could be attributed to munitions makers or international bankers. Peace conferences failed because we were duped by the British, or tricked by the French, or deceived by the Russians. It was not the presence of Soviet troops in Eastern Europe that drove it to communism, it was the sellout at Yalta. It was not a civil war that removed China from the Free World, it was treason in high places.

At times these fanatics have achieved a temporary success among those who lack the will or the wisdom to face unpleasant facts or unsolved problems. But in time the basic good sense and stability of the great American consensus has always prevailed.

Now we are face-to-face once again with a period of heightened peril. The risks are great, the burdens heavy, the problems incapable of swift or lasting solution. And under the strains and frustrations imposed by constant tension and harassment, the discordant voices of extremism are once again heard in the land. Men who are unwilling to face up to the danger from without are convinced that the real danger is from within.

They look suspiciously at their neighbors and their leaders. They call for "a man on horseback" because they do not trust the people. They find treason in our churches, in our highest court, in our treatment of water. They equate the Democratic Party with the welfare state, the welfare state with socialism, socialism with communism. They object quite rightly to politics intruding on the military—but they are very anxious for the military to engage in their kind of politics

But you and I—most Americans, soldiers and civilians—take a different view of our peril. We know it comes from without, not within. It must be met by quiet preparedness, not provocative speeches. And the steps taken this year to bolster our defenses—to increase our missile forces, to put more planes on alert, to provide more airlift and sealift and ready divisions, to make more certain than ever before that this nation has all the power that it will need to deter any attack of any kind —these steps constitute the most effective answer that can be made to those who would sow the seeds of doubt and of hate.

So let us not heed these counsels of fear and suspicion. Let us concentrate more on keeping enemy bombers and missiles away from our shores, and concentrate less on keeping neighbors away from our shelters. Let us devote more energy to organizing the free and friendly nations of the world, with common trade and strategic goals, and devote less energy to organizing armed bands of civilian guerrillas that are more likely to supply local vigilantes than national vigilance.

Let our patriotism be reflected in the creation of confidence in one another, rather than in crusades of suspicion. Let us prove we think our country great, by striving to make it greater. And, above all, let us remember, however serious the outlook, however harsh the task, the one great irreversible trend in the history of the world is on the side of liberty—and we, for all time to come, are on the same side.

California State Democratic Party Dinner
Los Angeles, California, November 18, 1961

Q: Mr. President, a number of your right-wing critics say that your foreign policy is based on a no-win policy in the Cold War. Would you address yourself to this charge?

THE PRESIDENT: Well, of course, every American . . . wants the United States to be secure and at peace, and wants the cause of freedom around the world to prevail. . . . And what we are anxious to do, of course, is . . . permit what Thomas Jefferson called the disease of liberty to be caught. . . . . We want to do that, of course, without having a nuclear war. Now, if someone thinks we should have a nuclear war in order to win, I can inform them that there will not be winners in the next nuclear war, if there is one, and this country and other countries will suffer very heavy blows. So that we have to proceed with responsibility and with care in an age where the human race can obliterate itself. The objective of this administration, and I think the objective of the country, is to protect our security, keep the peace, protect our vital interests, and make it possible for what we believe to be a system of government which is in accordance with the basic aspirations of people everywhere to ultimately prevail. That is our objective and that's the one that we shall continue.

President's News Conference
Washington, D.C., February 14, 1962

Those self-appointed generals and admirals who want to send someone else's son to war ought to be kept at home by the voters and replaced in Washington by someone who understands what the twentieth century is all about.

. . . This is no time, in 1962, for rash talk which strengthens the claims of our adversaries. This is no time for confused and intemperate remarks on the part of those who have neither the facts nor the ultimate responsibility.

This is the time for a man who talks softly, but who'll also carry a big stick. . . . Those self-appointed generals and admirals who want to send someone else's son to war and who consistently vote against the instruments of peace ought to be kept at home by the voters and replaced in Washington by someone who understands what the twentieth century is all about.

Indianapolis Airport
Indianapolis, Indiana, October 13, 1962

Q: Mr. President, in some of our major cities, John Birch or right-wing-type groups have been organizing boycotts against stores which carry imports from so-called Iron Curtain countries, and in some cases intimidating the stores. The State Department suggests that this is contrary to our policy of encouraging nonstrategic trade with those countries. I wonder if you share that view about those boycotts?

THE PRESIDENT: Yes. I think that it harasses merchants and I don't think it carries on much of an effective fight against the spread of communism. If they really want to do something about the spread of communism, they will assist the Alliance for Progress, for one thing, or they will encourage their children to join the Peace Corps, or they will do a good many other things which are very greatly needed. They will be generous to students who come to the United States to study, and show them something of America. Those are the things that really make a difference, not going down and, because some merchant happens to have Polish hams in his shop, saying he is unpatriotic. That doesn't seem to me to be a great contribution in the fight against communism.

President's News Conference
Washington, D.C., December 12, 1962

The Unfinished Agenda

Ignorance and misinformation can handicap the progress of a city or a company, but they can, if allowed to prevail in foreign policy, handicap this country's security. In a world of complex and continuing problems, in a world full of frustrations and irritations, America's leadership must be guided by the lights of learning and reason—or else those who confuse rhetoric with reality and the plausible with the possible will gain the popular ascendancy with their seemingly swift and simple solutions to every world problem.

There will always be dissident voices heard in the land, expressing opposition without alternatives, finding fault but never favor, perceiving gloom on every side and seeking influence without responsibility. Those voices are inevitable.

But today other voices are heard in the land—voices preaching doctrines wholly unrelated to reality, wholly unsuited to the sixties, doctrines which apparently assume that words will suffice without weapons, that vituperation is as good as victory and that peace is a sign of weakness. At a time when the national debt is steadily being reduced in terms of its burden on our economy, they see that debt as the greatest single threat to our security. At a time when we are steadily reducing the number of federal employees serving every thousand citizens, they fear those supposed hordes of civil servants far more than the actual hordes of opposing armies.

We cannot expect that everyone, to use the phrase of a decade ago, will "talk sense to the American people." But we can hope that fewer people will listen to nonsense. And the notion that this nation is headed for defeat through deficit, or that strength is but a matter of slogans, is nothing but just plain nonsense.

I want to discuss with you today the status of our strength and our security . . . strength and security are not easily or cheaply obtained, nor are they quickly and simply explained. There are many kinds of strength and no one kind will suffice. Overwhelming nuclear strength cannot stop a guerrilla war. Formal pacts of alliance cannot stop internal subversion. Displays of material wealth cannot stop the disillusionment of diplomats subjected to discrimination.

Above all, words alone are not enough. The United States is a peaceful nation. And where our strength and determination are clear, our words need merely to convey conviction, not belligerence. If we are strong, our strength will speak for itself. If we are weak, words will be of no help.

I realize that this nation often tends to identify turning points in world affairs with the major addresses which preceded them. But it was not the Monroe Doctrine that kept all Europe away from this hemisphere—it was the strength of the British fleet and the width of the Atlantic Ocean. It was not General Marshall's speech at Harvard which kept communism out of Western Europe—it was the strength and stability made possible by our military and economic assistance.

In this administration also it has been necessary at times to issue specific warnings—warnings that we could not stand by and watch the Communists conquer Laos by force, or intervene in the Congo, or swallow West Berlin, or maintain offensive missiles on Cuba. But while our goals were at least temporarily obtained in these and other instances, our successful defense of freedom was due not to the words we used, but to the strength we stood ready to use on behalf of the principles we stand ready to defend.

A nation can be no stronger abroad than she is at home. Only an America which practices what it preaches about equal rights and social justice will be respected by those whose choice affects our future.

This strength is composed of many different elements, ranging from the most massive deterrents to the most subtle influences. And all types of strength are needed—no one kind could do the job alone. Let us take a moment, therefore, to review this nation's progress in each major area of strength.

First . . . the strategic nuclear power of the United States has been so greatly modernized and expanded in the last one thousand days, by the rapid production and deployment of the most modern missile systems, that any and all potential aggressors are clearly confronted now with the impossibility of strategic victory—and the certainty of total destruction—if by reckless attack they should ever force upon us the necessity of a strategic reply. . . .

But the lessons of the last decade have taught us that freedom cannot be defended by strategic nuclear power alone. We have, therefore, in the last three years accelerated the development and deployment of tactical nuclear weapons . . . radically improved the readiness of our conventional force . . . and . . . moving beyond the traditional roles of our military forces . . . achieved an increase of nearly six hundred percent in our special forces—those forces that are prepared to work with our allies and friends against the guerrillas, saboteurs, insurgents, and assassins who threaten freedom in a less direct but equally dangerous manner.

But American military might should not and need not stand alone against the ambitions of international communism. Our security and strength, in the last analysis, directly depend on the security and strength of others, and that is why our military and economic assistance plays such a key role in enabling those who live on the periphery of the Communist world to maintain their independence of choice. Our assistance to these nations can be painful, risky and costly, as is true in Southeast Asia today. But we dare not weary of the task. For our assistance makes possible the stationing of 3.5 million allied troops along the Communist frontier at one tenth the cost of maintaining a comparable number of American soldiers. A successful Communist breakthrough in these areas, necessitating direct United States intervention, would cost us several times as much as our entire foreign-aid program, and might cost us heavily in American lives as well. . . .

And reducing the economic help needed to bolster these nations that undertake to help defend freedom can have the same disastrous result. . . .

I have spoken of strength largely in terms of the deterrence and resistance of aggression and attack. But, in today's world, freedom can be lost without a shot being fired, by ballots as well as bullets. The success of our leadership is dependent upon respect for our mission in the world as well as our missiles—on a clearer recognition of the virtues of freedom as well as the evils of tyranny.

That is why our Information Agency has doubled the shortwave broadcasting power of the Voice of America and . . . taken a host of other steps to carry our message of truth and freedom to all the far corners of the earth.

And that is also why we have regained the initiative in the exploration of outer space, making an annual effort greater than the combined total of all space activities undertaken during the fifties . . . and making it clear to all that the United States of America has no intention of finishing second in space. . . .

There is no longer any fear in the free world that a Communist lead in space will become a permanent assertion of supremacy and the basis of military superiority. There is no longer any doubt about the strength and skill of American science, American industry, American education, and the American free enterprise system. . . .

Finally, it should be clear by now that a nation can be no stronger abroad than she is at home. Only an America which practices what it preaches about equal rights and social justice will be respected by those whose choice affects our future. Only an America which has fully educated its citizens is fully capable of tackling the complex problems and perceiving the hidden dangers of the world in which we live. And only an America which is growing and prospering economically can sustain the worldwide defenses of freedom, while demonstrating to all concerned the opportunities of our system and society.

It is clear, therefore, that we are strengthening our security as well as our economy by our recent record increases in national income and output. . . .

My friends and fellow citizens: I cite these facts and figures to make it clear that America today is stronger than ever before. Our adversaries have not abandoned their ambitions, our dangers have not diminished, our vigilance cannot be relaxed. But now we have the military, the scientific, and the economic strength to do whatever must be done for the preservation and promotion of freedom.

That strength will never be used in pursuit of aggressive ambitions—it will always be used in pursuit of peace. It will never be used to promote provocations—it will always be used to promote the peaceful settlement of disputes.

We in this country, in this generation, are—by destiny rather than choice—the watchmen on the walls of world freedom. We ask, therefore, that we may be worthy of our power and responsibility, that we may exercise our strength with wisdom and restraint, and that we may achieve in our time and for all time the ancient vision of "peace on earth, goodwill toward men." That must always be our goal, and the righteousness of our cause must always underlie our strength. For as was written long ago, "except the Lord keep the city, the watchman waketh but in vain."

Remarks prepared for delivery at
Dallas Trade Mart Luncheon (undelivered)
November 22, 1963

Meeting the press.
PHOTO COURTESY CECIL W. STOUGHTON.

SOURCES

PART I THE PRESIDENCY

CHAPTER 1 *The Inaugural Address*

The Inaugural Address, Washington, D.C., January 20, 1961, "Public Papers of the Presidents: John F. Kennedy" (hereafter cited as Public Papers), 1961, pp. 1–3.

FOOTNOTE: Excerpt from remarks to a Democratic fund-raising dinner on the first anniversary of the Inaugural, Washington, D.C., January 20, 1962, ibid., 1962, pp. 40–41.

CHAPTER 2 *The Role of the President*

The Vital Center of Action:
National Press Club speech, Washington, D.C., January 14, 1960, "John Fitzgerald Kennedy, A Compilation of Statements and Speeches made During his Service in the United States Senate and House of Representatives," 88th Congress, 2d Session, Senate Document No. 79 (hereafter cited as Senate Document No. 79), pp. 1106–1109.

The Leader of the Free World:
California Democratic Clubs Convention, Fresno, California, February 12, 1960, from the John Fitzgerald Kennedy Library collection of various Kennedy speech files (hereafter cited as "Collection"), speech text, pp. 2–23.

The Champion of Freedom:
Labor Day campaign kickoff speech, Detroit, Michigan, September 5, 1960, "The Speeches, Remarks, Press Conferences, and Statements of Senator John F. Kennedy, August 1 through November 7, 1960," Report of the U.S.

Senate Committee on Commerce, Subcommittee on Freedom of Communications, 87th Congress, 1st Session, Report 994 (hereafter cited as Senate Report No. 994), p. 113.

Campaign remarks, Muskegon, Michigan, September 5, 1960, ibid., p. 120.

The Responsible Officer of Government:
The President's news conference, Washington, D.C., April 21, 1961, Public Papers, 1961, pp. 312–313.

The President's news conference, Washington, D.C., March 29, 1962, ibid., 1962, p. 276.

The President's news conference, Washington, D.C., May 9, 1962, ibid., p. 376.

The Ultimate Decision Maker:
Television and radio year-end conversation with the President, Washington, D.C., December 17, 1962, ibid., pp. 889–891, 903.

The Party Leader:
Remarks to members of National and State Democratic Committees, Washington, D.C., January 18, 1963, ibid., 1963, pp. 50–51.

The Happy President:
The President's news conference, Washington, D.C., October 31, 1963, ibid., p. 830.

CHAPTER 3 *The Call to Public Service*

The Politician and the Intellectual:
Harvard commencement address, Cambridge, Massachusetts, June 14, 1956, Senate Document No. 79, pp. 1035–1037.

The Senate's Distinguished Traditions:
Remarks to U.S. Senate on selection of portraits of outstanding senators, U.S. Senate, Washington, D.C., May 1, 1957, ibid., pp. 486–494.

The Best People We Can Get:
Campaign speech, Wittenberg College, Springfield, Ohio, October 17, 1960, Senate Report No. 994, pp. 634–638.

Campaign speech, Bangor, Maine, September 2, 1960, ibid., pp. 82–83.

The City Upon a Hill:
Farewell address to Massachusetts State Legislature, Boston, Massachusetts, January 9, 1961, Collection, Text, pp. 1–3.

The Pride of a Public Career:
State of the Union Address, the Capitol, Washington, D.C., January 30, 1961, Public Papers, p. 27.

The Peace Corps:
Statement upon the establishment of the Peace Corps, Washington, D.C., March 1, 1961, ibid., pp. 134–135.

The New Ethical Standard:
Special message to Congress on Ethics in Government, Washington, D.C., April 27, 1961, ibid., pp. 326–327, 330, 333–334.

The Obligations of Citizenship:
Letter to Mrs. Alicia Patterson, editor and publisher of *Newsday,* May 16, 1961, ibid., pp. 376–378.

The Front Line of Service:
Remarks to the American Foreign Service Association, Washington, D.C., May 31, 1962, ibid., 1962, pp. 532–534.

CHAPTER 4 *The President and Congress*

The Rules Committee Battle:
The President's news conference, Washington, D.C., January 25, 1961, Public Papers, 1961, p. 11.

The Separate Responsibilities of Each Branch:
State of the Union Address, the Capitol, Washington, D.C., January 30, 1961, ibid., p. 19.

State of the Union Address, the Capitol, Washington, D.C., January 11, 1962, ibid., 1962, p. 5.

The Inevitable Accord and Discord:
The President's news conference, Washington, D.C., March 21, 1962, ibid., p. 260.

The President's news conference, Washington, D.C., July 23, 1962, ibid., p. 573.

Television and radio year-end conversation with the President, Washington, D.C., December 17, 1962, ibid., pp. 892, 894.

The President's news conference, Washington, D.C., January 24, 1963, ibid., 1963, p. 95.

The President's news conference, Washington, D.C., May 8, 1963, ibid., p. 375.

PART II THE PRESIDENTIAL CAMPAIGN

CHAPTER 5 *The Road to the White House*

The "Parochial" Young Congressman of 1952:
Colloquy on House floor regarding Water Projects Appropriation Bill, House of Representatives, Washington, D.C., April 1, 1952, Senate Document No. 79, pp. 111–112.

The "National Interest" Senator of 1954:
Remarks during Senate debate on St. Lawrence Seaway, U.S. Senate, Washington, D.C., January 14, 1954, ibid., pp. 271–276.

The National Convention Speaker of 1956:
Nomination of Adlai E. Stevenson for Presdent of the United States, Democratic National Convention, Chicago, Illinois, August 16, 1956, Collection, Text, pp. 1–4.

The Defeated Vice-Presidential Contender of 1956:
Conceding the Vice-Presidential nomination, Democratic National Convention, Chicago, Illinois, August 17, 1956, Collection, Official Proceedings of the Democratic National Convention, 1956, p. 482.

The Presidential Prospect of 1958:
Remarks to the Gridiron Club, Washington, D.C., March 15, 1958, Collection, Text, pp. 1–2.

The Declaration of Candidacy in 1960:
Statement of Declaration for the Presidency, Washington, D.C., January 2, 1960, Collection, Text.

The Question of Age:
Nationally televised news conference, New York, New York, July 4, 1960, *The New York Times,* July 5, 1960, p. 1, col. 8.

The Final Appeal:
Remarks to Democratic National Committee Dinner on convention eve, Los Angeles, California, July 10, 1960, Collection, Text, pp. 1–2.

The Opening of the New Frontier:
Acceptance of presidential nomination, Democratic National Convention, Los Angeles, California, July 15, 1960, Collection, Text, pp. 1–7.

The First Debate:
Opening statement, first televised presidential candidates debate, Chicago, Illinois, September 26, 1960, Senate Report No. 994, Part 3.

The Definition of Liberal:
Acceptance of New York Liberal Party nomination, New York, New York, September 14, 1960, ibid., pp. 239–242.
The Issue of Latin America:
Campaign speech, Tampa, Florida, October 18, 1960, ibid., pp. 1159–1166.

The Issue of Peace:
Campaign speech, San Francisco, California, November 2, 1960, ibid., pp. 863–866.

The End of the Campaign:
Campaign remarks, street rally, Waterbury, Connecticut, November 6, 1960, ibid., p. 912.

Press conference, Hyannis Port, Massachusetts, November 9, 1960, Collection.

Democratic Dinner, Chicago, Illinois, April 28, 1961, Public Papers, 1961, p. 339.

National Association of Manufacturers, New York, New York, December 6, 1961, ibid., pp. 773–774.

Ohio Democratic Dinner, Columbus, Ohio, January 6, 1962, ibid., 1962, p. 1.

Wisconsin Democratic Dinner, Milwaukee, Wisconsin, May 12, 1962, ibid., p. 389.

CHAPTER **6** *The Religious Issue*

The Responsibility of the Press:
American Society of Newspaper Editors, Washington, D.C., April 21, 1960, Collection, Text, pp. 1–8.

Bronx County Democratic Dinner, New York, New York, April 1960, Collection.

The Refutation of Bigotry:
Greater Houston Ministerial Association, Houston, Texas, September 12, 1960, Senate Report No. 994, pp. 208–218.

The Differences From 1928:
Annual Al Smith Memorial Dinner, New York, New York, October 19, 1960, ibid., pp. 666–669.

The Responsibility of Parents:
The President's news conference, Washington, D.C., June 27, 1962, Public Papers, 1962, pp. 510–511.

PART III THE NEW FRONTIER

CHAPTER 7 *The Restoration of Economic Growth*

The Angry Young Congressman:
Statement on House floor, U.S. House of Representatives, Washington, D.C., July 24, 1947, Senate Document No. 79, pp. 9–11.

The Determined New President:
State of the Union Address, the Capitol, Washington, D.C., January 30, 1961, Public Papers, 1961, pp. 19–20, 22.

The Road to Recovery:
National Industrial Conference Board, Washington, D.C., February 13, 1961, ibid., pp. 87–89.

The Prudent Steward:
Special message to Congress on Budget and Fiscal Policy, Washington, D.C., March 24, 1961, ibid., p. 221.

The Expansion of Opportunity:
State of the Union Address, the Capitol, Washington, D.C., January 11, 1962, ibid., pp. 5–9.

The Preservation of Price Stability:
The President's news conference, Washington, D.C., April 11, 1962, ibid., pp. 315–319, 321.

The President's news conference, Washington, D.C., April 18, 1962, ibid., pp. 331, 335.

Footnote: Remarks at White House Correspondents and News Photographers Association Dinner, Washington, D.C., April 27, 1962, ibid., pp. 344–345.

The Myths of Economic Debate:
Commencement address, Yale University, New Haven, Connecticut, June 11, 1962, ibid., pp. 470–475.

The Politics of Confidence:
The President's news conference, Washington, D.C., June 14, 1962, ibid., pp. 491–492.

The Foundation for Freedom's Success:
State of the Union Address, the Capitol, Washington, D.C., January 14, 1963, ibid., 1963, pp. 12–15.

CHAPTER 8 *The Exploration of Space*

The Adventure of Space:
Special address to Congress on Urgent National Needs, the Capitol, Washington, D.C., May 25, 1961, Public Papers, 1961, pp. 403–405.

The President's news conference, Washington, D.C., November 29, 1961, ibid., p. 761.

The Universal Language of Space:
University of California, Berkeley, California, March 23, 1962, ibid., 1962, p. 264.

The New Ocean of Space:
Rice University, Houston, Texas, September 12, 1962, ibid., pp. 668–671.

The High Wall of Space:
Dedication of Aerospace Medical Health Center, San Antonio, Texas, November 21, 1963, ibid., 1963, p. 883.

CHAPTER 9 *The Fight for Civil Rights*

The American Vision:
NAACP rally, Los Angeles, California, July 10, 1960, Collection, Text, pp. 1–3.

The Standard of John C. Calhoun:
Campaign speech, Columbia, South Carolina, October 10, 1960, Senate Report No. 994, pp. 548–551.

The Enforcement of Court Orders:
Televised address to the nation, Washington, D.C., September 30, 1962, Public Papers, 1962, pp. 726–728.

The Right to Vote:
State of the Union Address, the Capitol, Washington, D.C., January 14, 1963, ibid., 1963, p. 14.

The Peaceful Revolution:
Televised address to the nation, Washington, D.C., June 11, 1963, ibid., pp. 468–471.

The Role of the Military:
Letter to the Secretary of Defense, Washington, D.C., June 22, 1963, ibid., p. 496.

The Civil Rights Act of 1963:
Special message to the Congress on Civil Rights and Job Opportunities, Washington, D.C., June 19, 1963, ibid., p. 483.

The March on Washington:
Statement on March on Washington for Jobs and Freedom, Washington, D.C., August 28, 1963, ibid., p. 645.

The Long View:
Excerpt, the President's news conference, Washington, D.C., September 12, 1963, ibid., p. 677.

The Final Word:
Remarks intended for delivery to Texas Democratic Dinner, Austin, Texas, November 22, 1963 (undelivered), ibid., pp. 896–897.

CHAPTER **10** *The Promotion of the Arts*

The Liberation of the Human Mind:
National Cultural Center Dinner, Washington, D.C., November 29, 1962, Public Papers, 1962, pp. 846–847.

The Central Purpose of Civilization:
National Gallery of Art, Opening of *Mona Lisa* Exhibition, Washington, D.C., January 8, 1963, ibid., 1963, p. 5.

The Fiber of Our National Life:
Amherst College, Amherst, Massachusetts, October 26, 1963, ibid., pp. 816–818.

PART **IV** THE PURSUIT OF PEACE AND SECURITY

CHAPTER **11** *The Tide Is Turned*

The Urgent Agenda:
Speech on Senate floor, the Capitol, Washington, D.C., June 14, 1960, Senate Document No. 79, pp. 926–934.

The Response to Multiple Crises:
State of the Union Address, the Capitol, Washington, D.C., January 30, 1961, Public Papers, 1961, pp. 19, 22–28.

The Freedom Doctrine:
Special address to Congress on Urgent National Needs, the Capitol, Washington, D.C., May 25, 1961, ibid., pp. 396–398, 405–406.

The Great Defender of Freedom:
State of the Union Address, the Capitol, Washington, D.C., January 11, 1962, ibid., 1962, pp. 9–12, 15.

The Tides of Human Freedom:
State of the Union Address, the Capitol, Washington, D.C., January 14, 1963, ibid., 1963, pp. 11–12, 15, 18–19.

CHAPTER **12** *The National Defense*

The Cautious Commander-in-Chief:
Special message to Congress on Defense Policies and Principles, Washington, D.C., March 28, 1961, Public Papers, 1961, pp. 229–233, 236–238, 240.

The Modern Military Officer:
United States Naval Academy Commencement, Annapolis, Maryland, June 7, 1961, ibid., pp. 447–448.

The Inequities of Service:
The President's news conference, Washington, D.C., March 21, 1962, ibid., 1962, pp. 259–260.

The Best Defense in the World:
State of the Union Address, the Capitol, Washington, D.C., January 14, 1963, ibid., 1963, p. 18.

CHAPTER **13** *The U.S.–Soviet Competition*

The Real Revolution:
Public message to Soviet Chairman Khrushchev after the invasion of the Bay of Pigs, Washington, D.C., April 18, 1961, Public Papers, 1961, p. 287.

The Summit Encounter:
Televised report to the American people on the U.S.–U.S.S.R. summit in Vienna, Washington, D.C., June 6, 1961, ibid., pp. 442–446.

The Running Tiger:
The President's news conference, Washington, D.C., June 28, 1961, ibid., p. 478.

The Berlin Crisis:
Statement on the Berlin crisis, Washington, D.C., July 19, 1961, ibid., pp. 521–523.

Televised address to the American people on the Berlin crisis, Washington, D.C., July 25, 1961, ibid., pp. 533–540.

The Berlin Wall:
White House statement on the Berlin Wall, Washington, D.C., August 24, 1961, ibid., pp. 568–569.

Footnote: Excerpt from the President's news conference, Washington, D.C., January 15, 1962, ibid., 1962, pp. 20–21.

The Continuing Dialogue:
Interview by Aleksei Adzhubei, editor of *Izvestia* and son-in-law of Soviet Chairman Khrushchev, Hyannis Port, Massachusetts, November 25, 1961, ibid., 1961, pp. 741–751.

The Wave of the Future:
University of California, Berkeley, California, March 23, 1962, ibid., 1962, pp. 265–266.

The Cuban Missile Crisis:
Televised address to the American people on the Cuban missile crisis, Washington, D.C., October 22, 1962, ibid., pp. 806–809.

Letter to Soviet Chairman Khrushchev, Washington, D.C., October 27, 1962, ibid., pp. 813–814.

Statement on Soviet withdrawal of missiles from Cuba, Washington, D.C., October 28, 1962, ibid., p. 815.

Opening statement, the President's news conference, Washington, D.C., November 20, 1962, ibid., pp. 830–831.

The Strategy of Peace:
Commencement address, American University, Washington, D.C., June 10, 1963, ibid., 1963, pp. 460–464.

The Nuclear Test-Ban Treaty:
Televised address to the American people on the Limited Nuclear Test-Ban Treaty, Washington, D.C., July 26, 1963, ibid., pp. 601–606.

Remarks upon signing the Nuclear Test-Ban Treaty, Washington, D.C., October 7, 1963, ibid., pp. 765–766.

The Quest for Peace:
General Assembly of the United Nations, New York, New York, September 20, 1963, ibid., pp. 693–698.

The Sale of American Wheat:
Opening statement, the President's news conference, Washington, D.C., October 9, 1963, ibid., pp. 767–768.

CHAPTER 14 *The Western Alliance*

The Political-Military Link:
NATO Military Committee, Washington, D.C., April 10, 1961, Public Papers, 1961, p. 255.

The Change in World Power:
Press luncheon, Paris, France, June 2, 1961, ibid., pp. 429–431.

The Trade Expansion Act:
Port of New Orleans, New Orleans, Louisiana, May 4, 1962, ibid., 1962, pp. 359–361.

The Atlantic Partnership:
Independence Hall, Philadelphia, Pennsylvania, July 4, 1962, ibid., pp. 538–539.

The Exemplar of Service:
Letter to Jean Monnet, Washington, D.C., January 22, 1963, ibid., 1963, p. 72.

The Champion of Liberty:
Remarks upon signing proclamation conferring honorary citizenship on Sir Winston Churchill, Washington, D.C., April 9, 1963, ibid., pp. 315–316.

The Only War We Seek:
Remarks upon arrival in Germany, Bonn-Cologne Airport, Federal Republic of Germany, June 23, 1963, ibid., pp. 497–498.

The Age of Interdependence:
Paulskirche Assembly Hall, Frankfurt, Federal Republic of Germany, June 25, 1963, ibid., pp. 516–521.

The Proudest Boast:
West Berlin City Hall, June 26, 1963, ibid., pp. 524–525.

CHAPTER 15 *The Third World*

The Concerned Young Congressman:
Debate on Technical Assistance Appropriation Bill, House of Representatives, Washington, D.C., June 28, 1952, Senate Document No. 79, p. 120.

The Challenge of Imperialism: Algeria:
Address to the Senate on imperialism and Algeria, U.S. Senate, Washington, D.C., July 2, 1957, ibid., pp. 511–514, 518–521, 523, 528, 530.

The New Nationalism: India:
U.S. Senate, Washington, D.C., March 25, 1958, ibid., pp. 591–608.

The Fight for Foreign Aid:
U.S. Senate, Washington, D.C., February 19, 1959, ibid., pp. 789–797.

The Frontiers of Freedom:
Special address to Congress on Urgent National Needs, the Capitol, Washington, D.C., May 25, 1961, Public Papers, 1961, pp. 399–400.

The Uncommitted and Underdeveloped:
Message to the Belgrade Conference of Nonaligned States, Washington, D.C., August 30, 1961, ibid., p. 573.

Remarks to American Bankers Association Symposium on Economic Growth, Washington, D.C., February 25, 1963, ibid., 1963, p. 210.

The Future Prime Ministers:
Remarks to a group of foreign students visiting the White House, Washington, D.C., April 10, 1963, ibid., p. 319.

The Family of Man:
Remarks upon receiving the annual Family of Man Award, New York Protestant Council, New York, New York, November 8, 1963, ibid., pp. 839–842.

The Alliance for Progress:
Address to Latin American Diplomatic Corps, White House, Washington, D.C., March 13, 1961, ibid., 1961, pp. 170–175.

State Dinner, Bogotá, Colombia, December 17, 1961, ibid., pp. 811–814.

Remarks at White House Dinner honoring Western Hemisphere Nobel prize winners, Washington, D.C., April 29, 1962, ibid., 1962, p. 347.

Conference of Central American Republics, San José, Costa Rica, March 18, 1963, ibid., 1963, pp. 264–267.

The New Nations of Africa:
National Council of Women, New York, New York, October 12, 1960, Senate Report No. 994, pp. 567–571.

The President's news conference, Washington, D.C., March 1, 1961, Public Papers, 1961, p. 139.

The War in Indochina:
Speech on Senate floor, U.S. Senate, Washington, D.C., April 6, 1954, Senate Document No. 79, pp. 284–292.

Opening statement, the President's news conference, Washington, D.C., March 23, 1961, Public Papers, 1961, pp. 213–215.

Interview by Walter Cronkite on CBS Television, September 2, 1963, ibid., 1963, pp. 651–652.

The President's news conference, Washington, D.C., October 31, 1963, ibid., p. 828.

The United Nations:
State of the Union Address, the Capitol, Washington, D.C., January 30, 1961, Public Papers, 1961, p. 26.

General Assembly of the United Nations, New York, New York, September 25, 1961, ibid., pp. 618–626.

State of the Union Address, the Capitol, Washington, D.C., January 11, 1962, ibid., 1962, pp. 10–11.

The President's news conference, Washington, D.C., March 21, 1962, ibid., pp. 254–255.

The Little Nations:
Irish Parliament, Dublin, Ireland, June 28, 1963, ibid., 1963, pp. 535–539.

CHAPTER 16 *The Uses and Limits of Power*

The Role of Negotiations:
University of Washington, Seattle, Washington, November 16, 1961, Public Papers, 1961, pp. 725–727.

The Voices of Extremism:
California State Democratic Party Dinner, Los Angeles, California, November 18, 1961, ibid., pp. 735–736.

The President's news conference, Washington, D.C., February 14, 1962, ibid., 1962, p. 141.

Campaign remarks, Indianapolis, Indiana, October 13, 1962, ibid., p. 772.

The President's news conference, Washington, D.C., December 12, 1962, ibid., pp. 872–873.

The Unfinished Agenda:
Remarks prepared for delivery at Dallas Trade Mart Luncheon (undelivered), November 22, 1963, ibid., 1963, pp. 891–894.

Defending his program, May 22,1963.
PHOTO BY ABBIE ROWE, COURTESY THE JOHN FITZGERALD KENNEDY LIBRARY.

INDEX

INDEX